Behind the Scenes!!

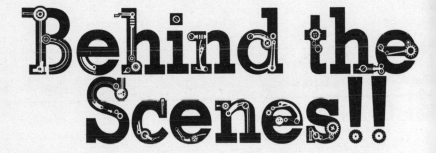

Behind the Scenes!!

06

STORY AND ART BY **BISCO HATORI**

Behind the Scenes!!

06

CONTENTS

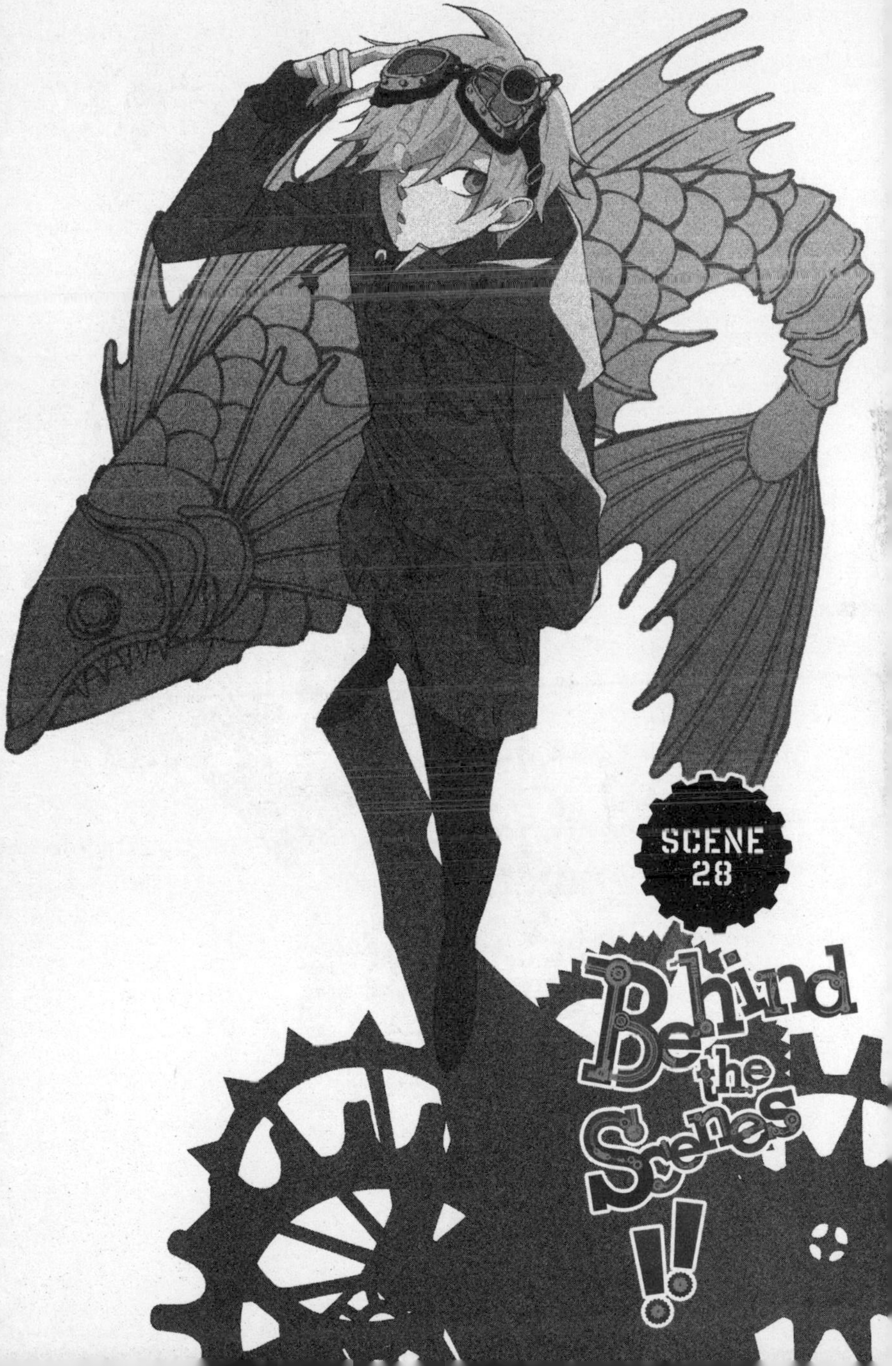
SCENE
28
Behind the Scenes!!

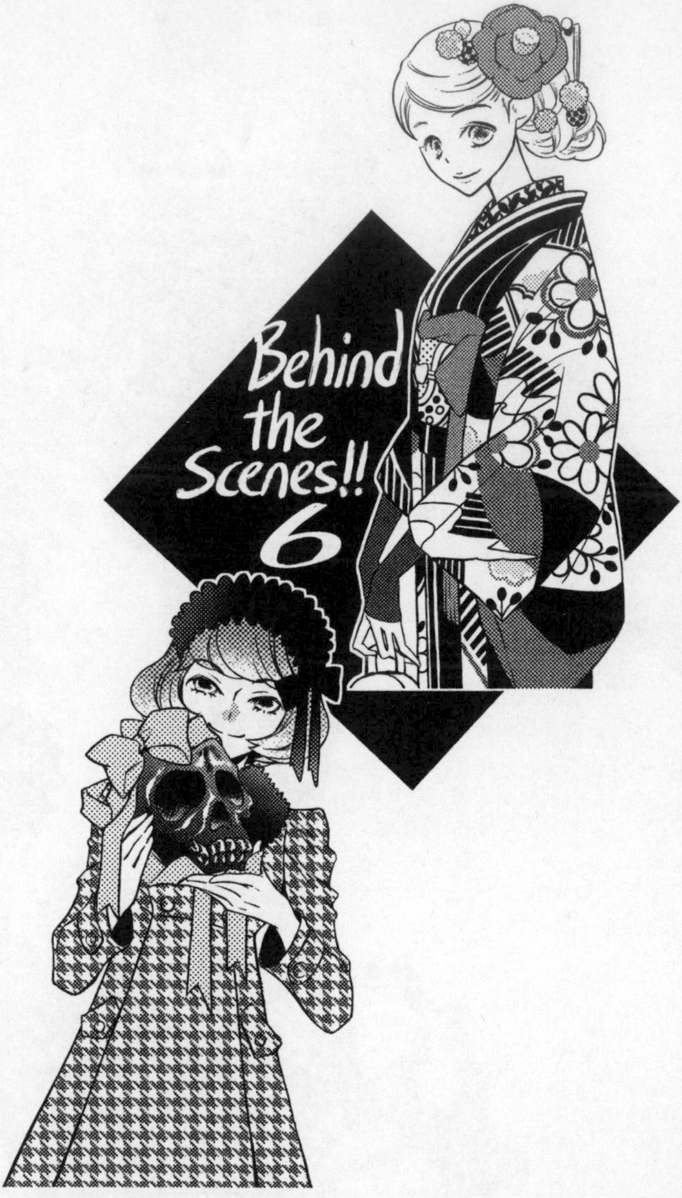
Behind the Scenes!!
6

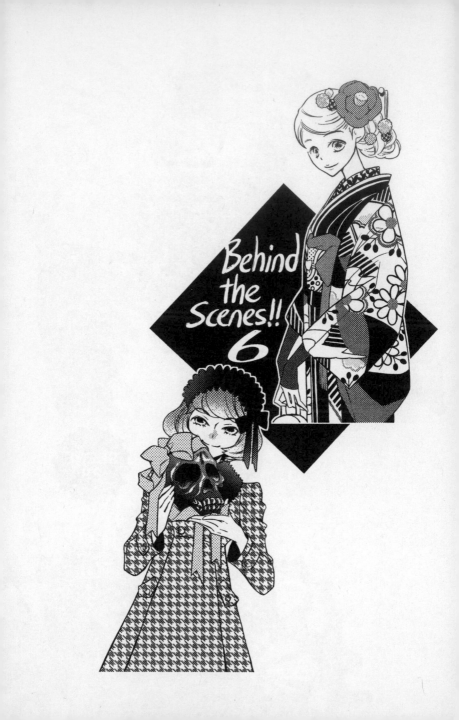

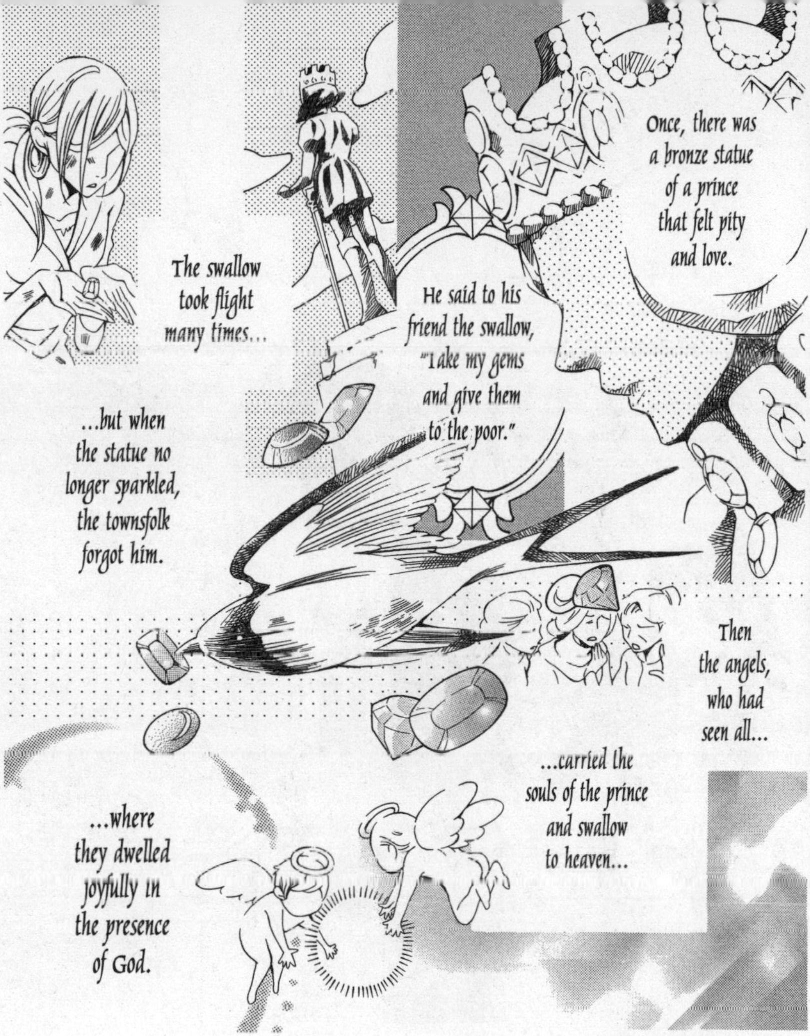
Once, there was a bronze statue of a prince that felt pity and love.
He said to his friend the swallow, "Take my gems and give them to the poor."
The swallow took flight many times...
...but when the statue no longer sparkled, the townsfolk forgot him.
Then the angels, who had seen all...
...carried the souls of the prince and swallow to heaven...
...where they dwelled joyfully in the presence of God.

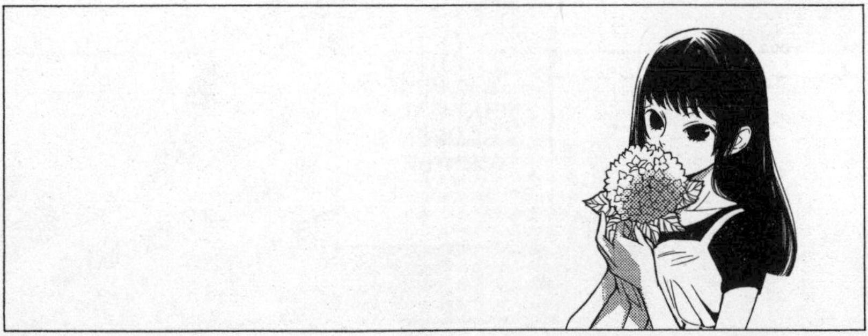

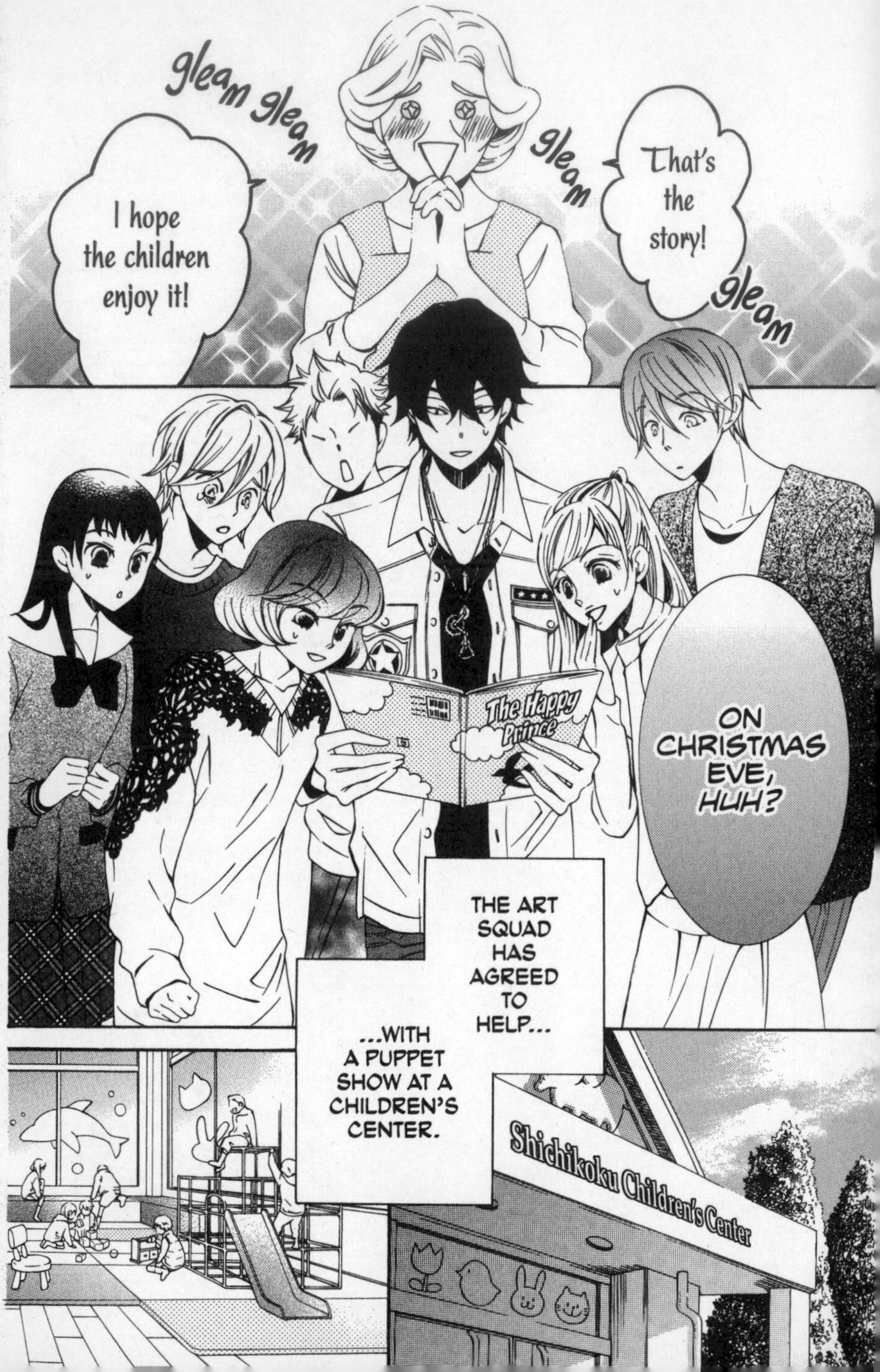
That's the story!
gleam
gleam
gleam gleam
I hope the children enjoy it!
ON CHRISTMAS EVE, HUH?
The Happy Prince
THE ART SQUAD HAS AGREED TO HELP...
...WITH A PUPPET SHOW AT A CHILDREN'S CENTER.
Shichikoku Children's Center

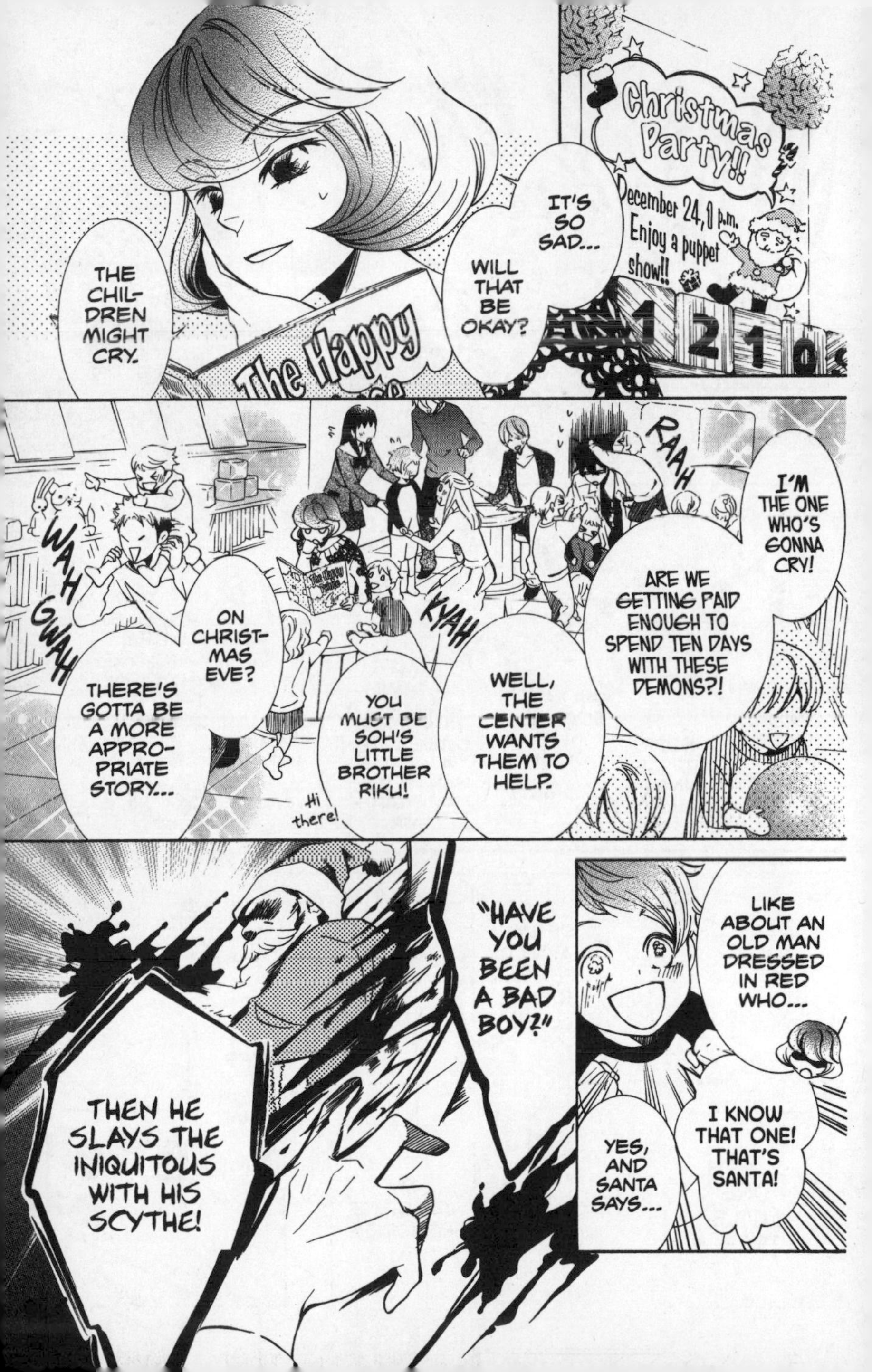
Christmas Party!!
December 24, 0 p.m.
Enjoy a puppet show!!
1 2 1 0
IT'S SO SAD...
WILL THAT BE OKAY?
THE CHILDREN MIGHT CRY.
The Happy
RAAH
I'M THE ONE WHO'S GONNA CRY!
ARE WE GETTING PAID ENOUGH TO SPEND TEN DAYS WITH THESE DEMONS?!
WELL, THE CENTER WANTS THEM TO HELP.
YOU MUST BE SOH'S LITTLE BROTHER RIKU!
Hi there!
KYAH
ON CHRISTMAS EVE?
THERE'S GOTTA BE A MORE APPROPRIATE STORY...
WAH
GWAH
LIKE ABOUT AN OLD MAN DRESSED IN RED WHO...
I KNOW THAT ONE! THAT'S SANTA!
YES, AND SANTA SAYS...
"HAVE YOU BEEN A BAD BOY?"
THEN HE SLAYS THE INIQUITOUS WITH HIS SCYTHE!

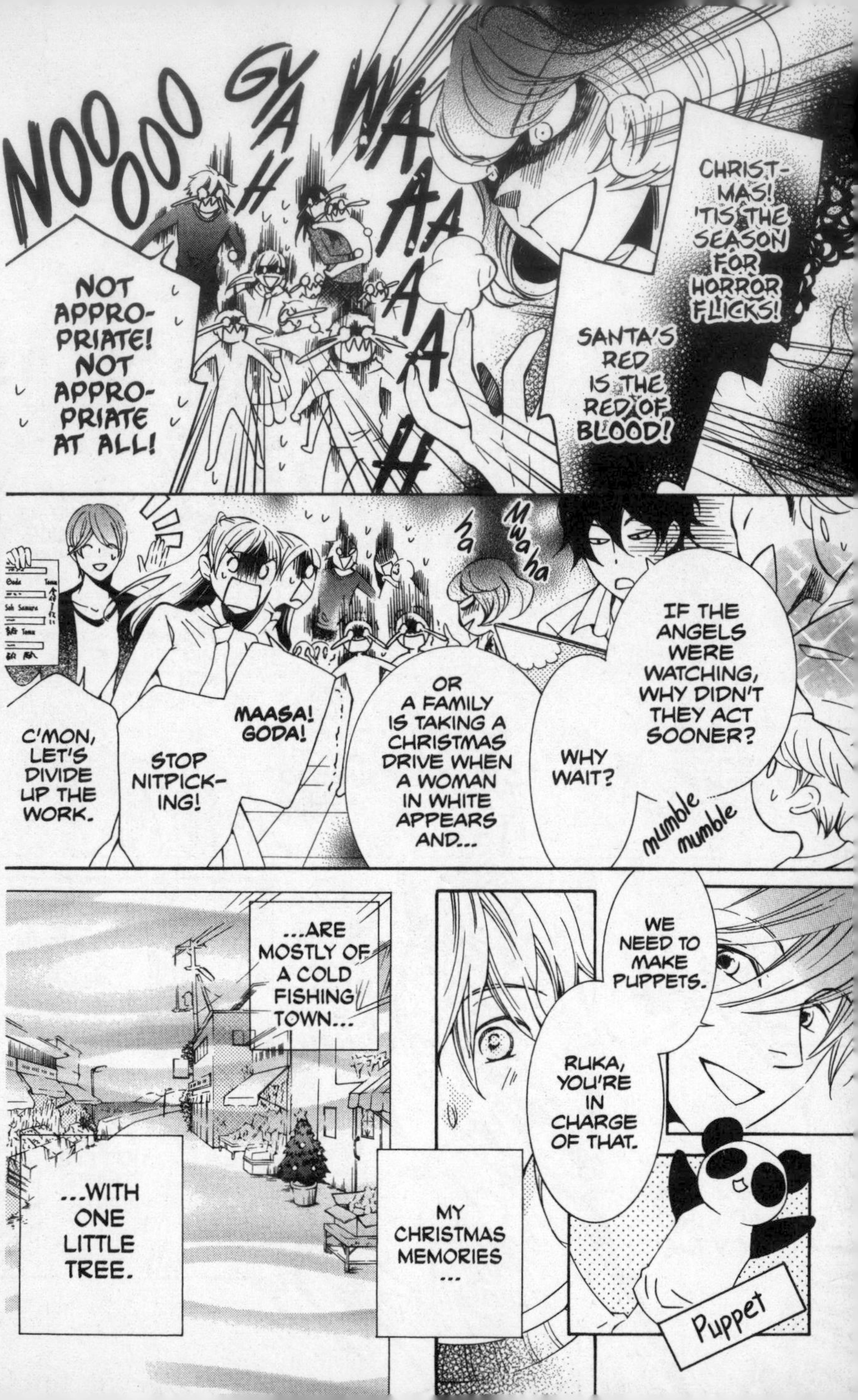
CHRIST-MAS! 'TIS THE SEASON FOR HORROR FLICKS!
SANTA'S RED IS THE RED OF BLOOD!
GYAWAAAAAAH
NOOOOOO
NOT APPRO-PRIATE! NOT APPRO-PRIATE AT ALL!
Mwahaha
IF THE ANGELS WERE WATCHING, WHY DIDN'T THEY ACT SOONER?
mumble mumble
WHY WAIT?
OR A FAMILY IS TAKING A CHRISTMAS DRIVE WHEN A WOMAN IN WHITE APPEARS AND...
MAASA! GODA!
STOP NITPICK-ING!
C'MON, LET'S DIVIDE UP THE WORK.
WE NEED TO MAKE PUPPETS.
RUKA, YOU'RE IN CHARGE OF THAT.
Puppet
MY CHRISTMAS MEMORIES ...
...ARE MOSTLY OF A COLD FISHING TOWN...
...WITH ONE LITTLE TREE.

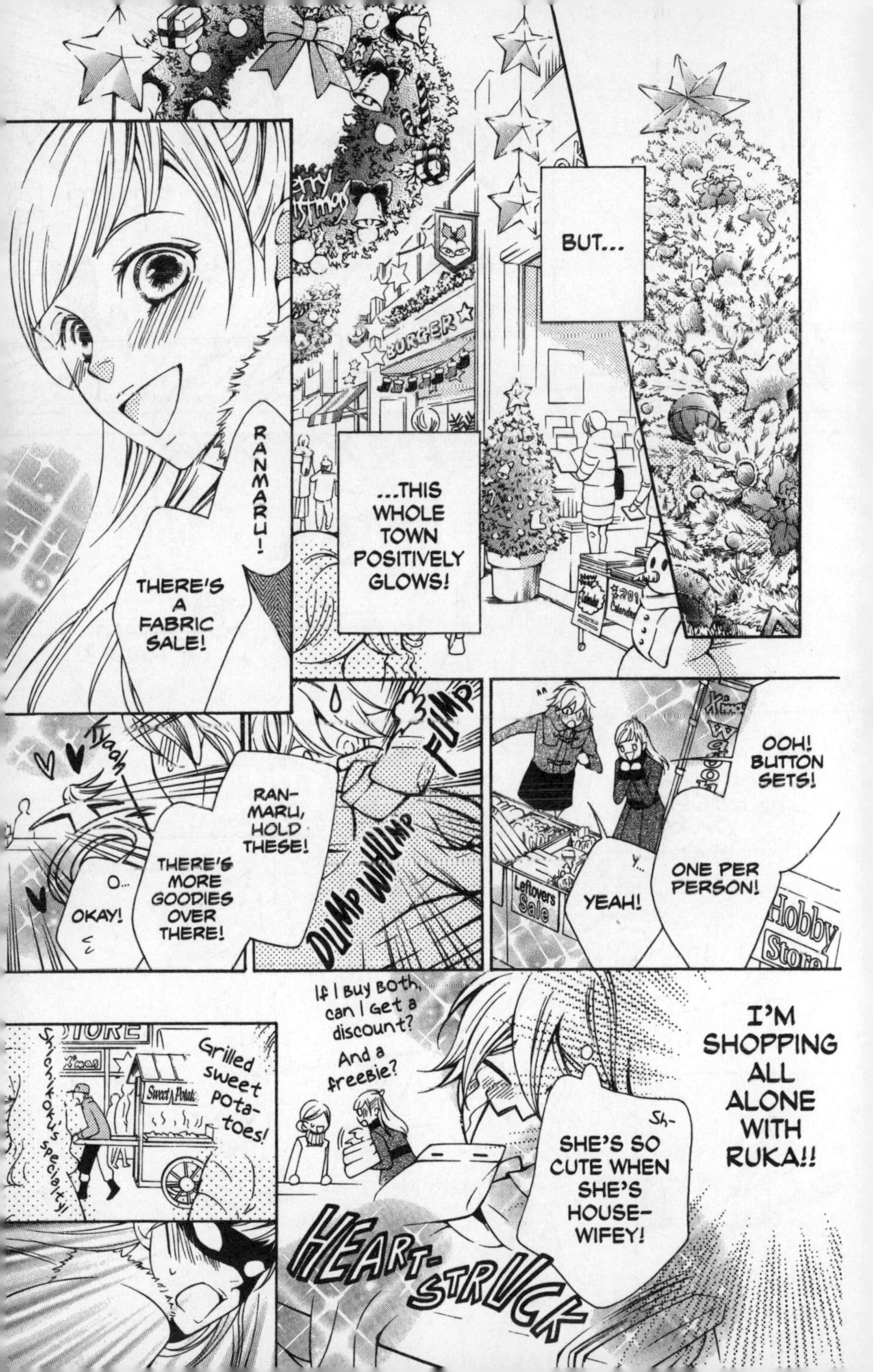
BUT...
...THIS WHOLE TOWN POSITIVELY GLOWS!
BURGER
RANMARU!
THERE'S A FABRIC SALE!
OOH! BUTTON SETS!
ONE PER PERSON!
Y...
YEAH!
Hobby Store
Leftovers Sale
RAN-MARU, HOLD THESE!
DUMP WHUMP FUMP
Kyaah
THERE'S MORE GOODIES OVER THERE!
O...
OKAY!
I'M SHOPPING ALL ALONE WITH RUKA!!
If I buy both, can I get a discount?
And a freebie?
Sh-
SHE'S SO CUTE WHEN SHE'S HOUSE-WIFEY!
HEART-STRUCK
Grilled sweet potatoes!
Shichikoku's specialty!

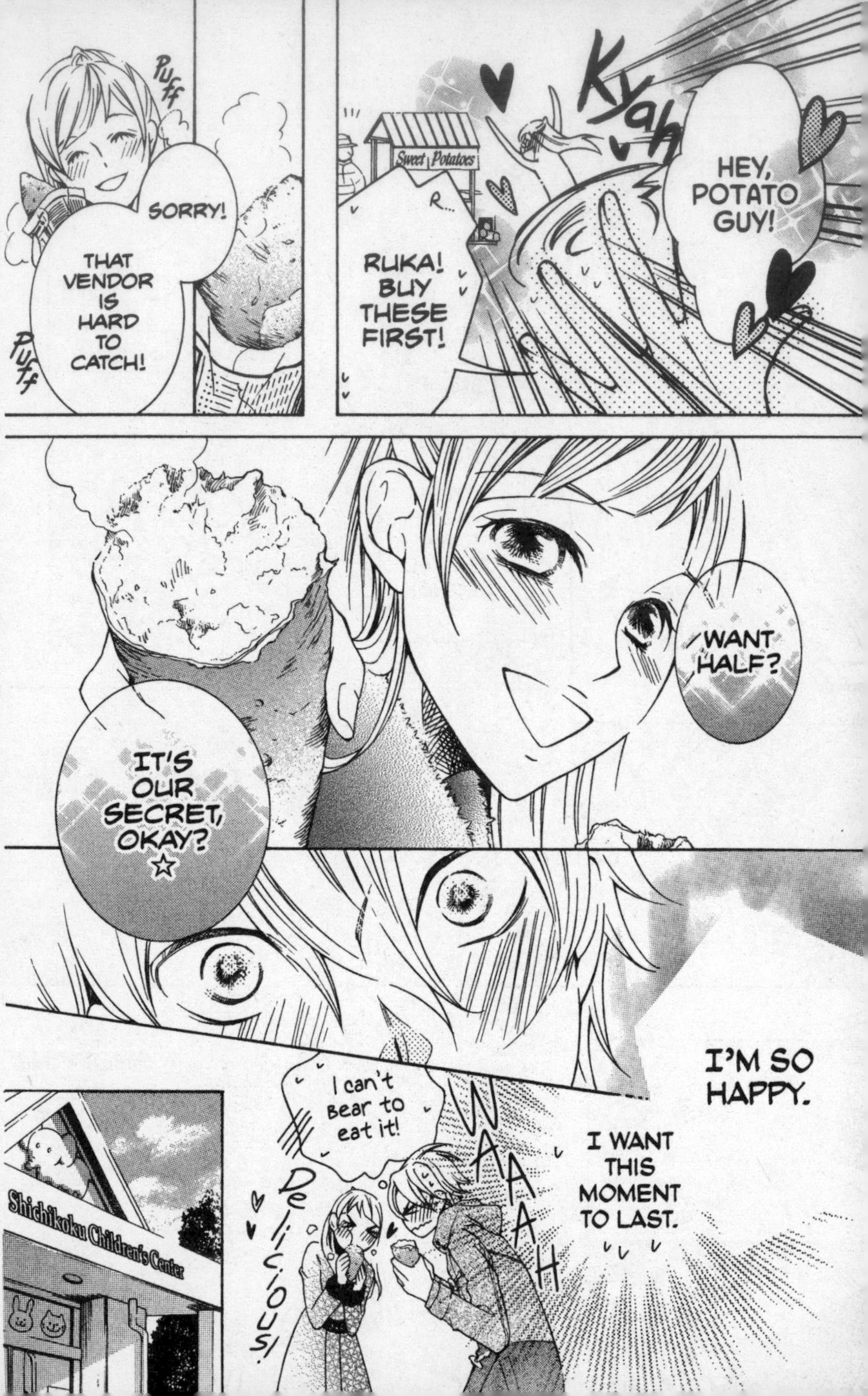
Kyah
HEY, POTATO GUY!
Sweet Potatoes
R...
RUKA! BUY THESE FIRST!
Puff
SORRY!
THAT VENDOR IS HARD TO CATCH!
Puff
WANT HALF?
IT'S OUR SECRET, OKAY? ☆
I'M SO HAPPY.
I WANT THIS MOMENT TO LAST.
WAAAH
I can't bear to eat it!
Delicious!
Shichikoku Children's Center

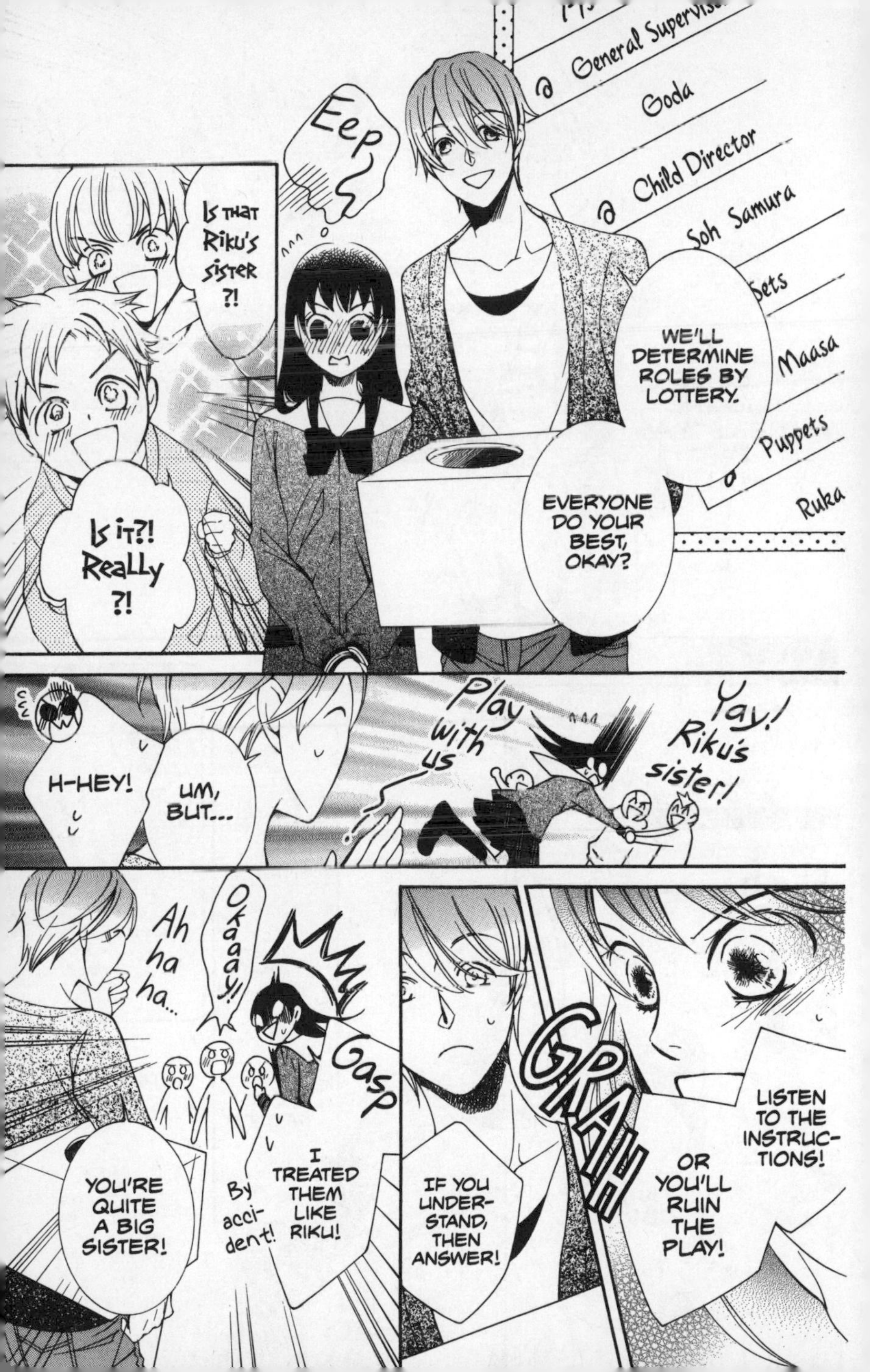
General Supervis
Goda
Child Director
Soh Samura
Sets
Maasa
Puppets
Ruka
Eep
WE'LL DETERMINE ROLES BY LOTTERY.
EVERYONE DO YOUR BEST, OKAY?
Is THAT Riku's sister ?!
Is it?! Really ?!
Yay! Riku's sister!
Play with us
UM, BUT...
H-HEY!
LISTEN TO THE INSTRUC-TIONS!
OR YOU'LL RUIN THE PLAY!
GRAH
IF YOU UNDER-STAND, THEN ANSWER!
Okaaay!
Gasp
Ah ha ha...
I TREATED THEM LIKE RIKU!
By acci-dent!
YOU'RE QUITE A BIG SISTER!

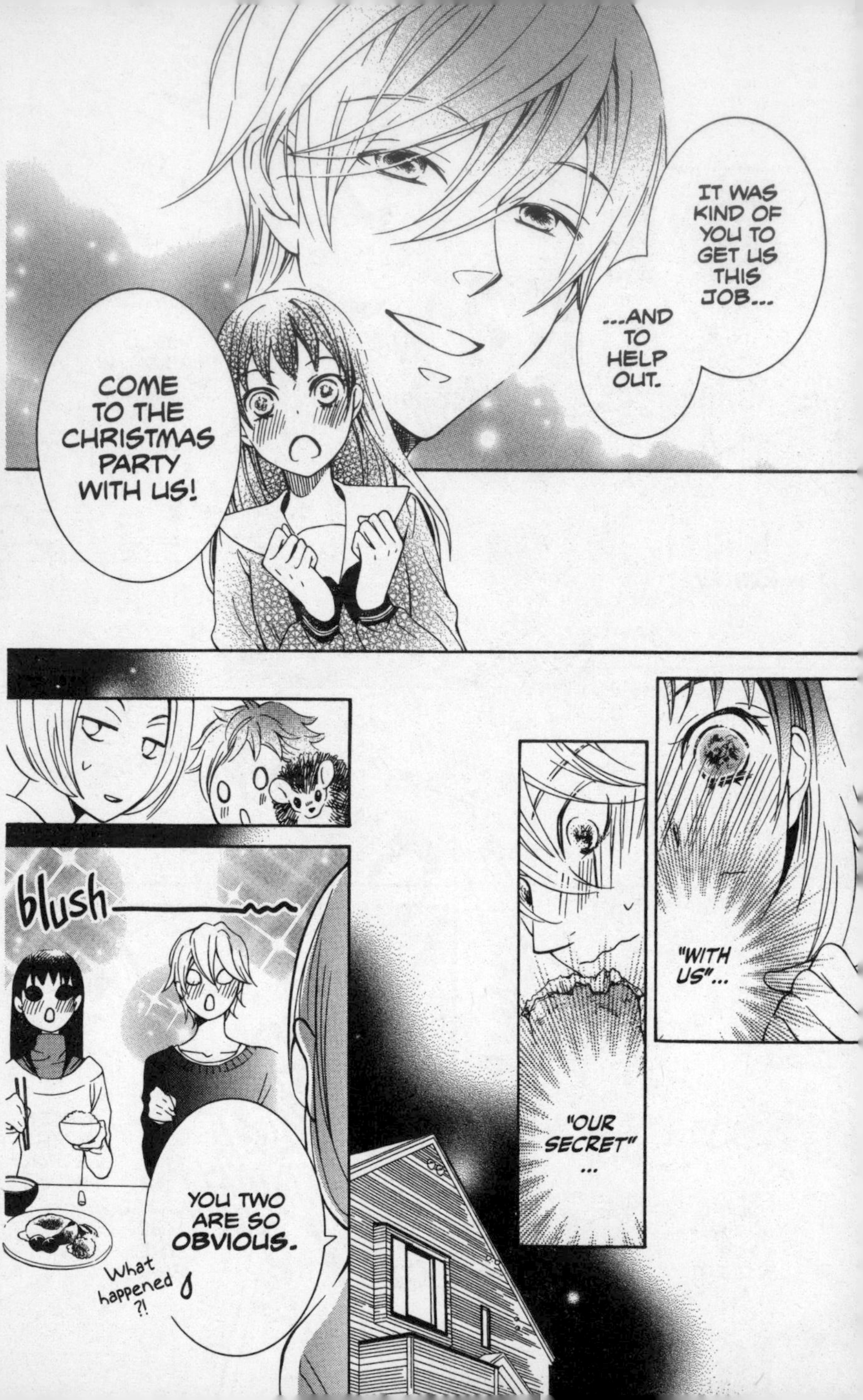
IT WAS KIND OF YOU TO GET US THIS JOB...
...AND TO HELP OUT.
COME TO THE CHRISTMAS PARTY WITH US!
"WITH US"...
"OUR SECRET" ...
blush
YOU TWO ARE SO OBVIOUS.
What happened ?!

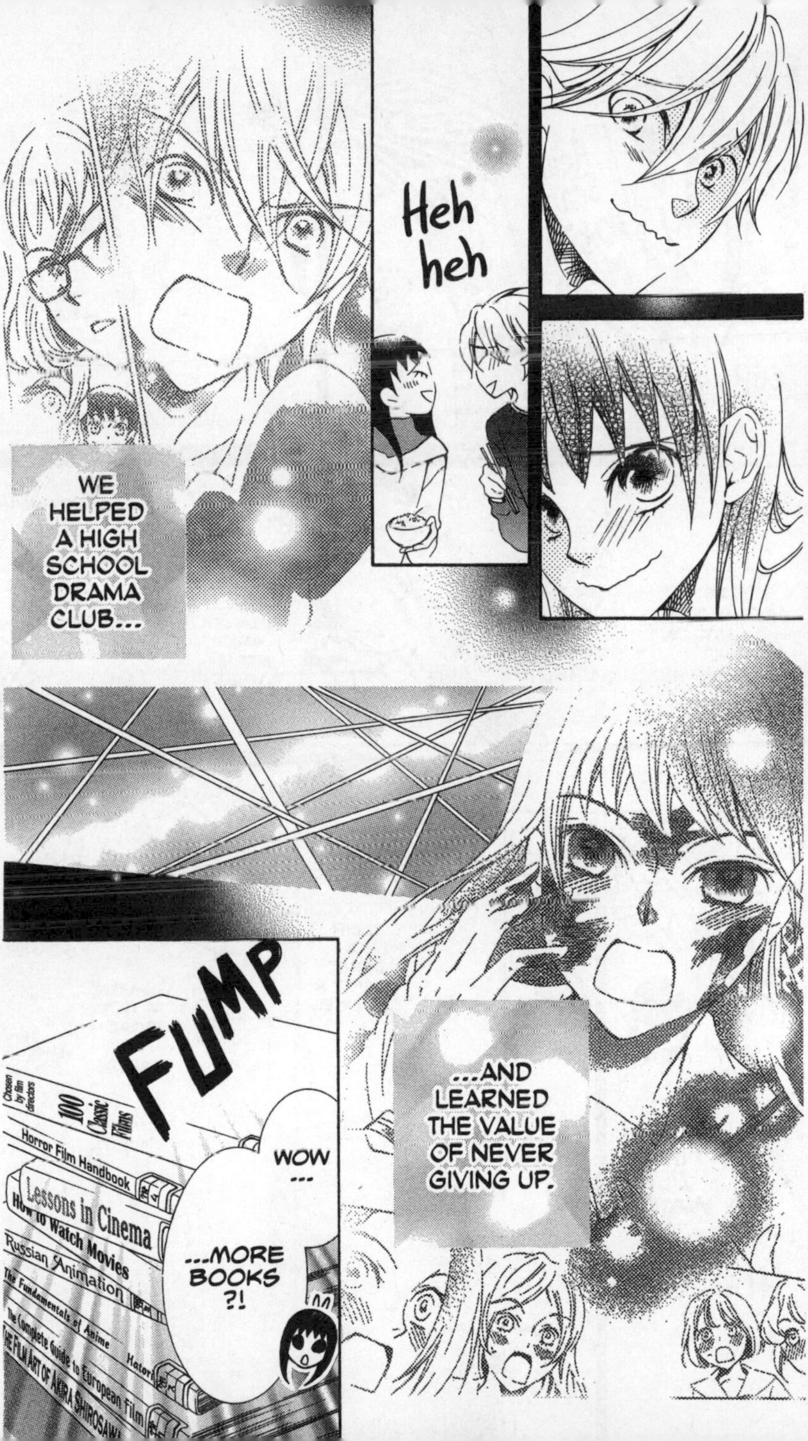
Heh heh
WE HELPED A HIGH SCHOOL DRAMA CLUB...
...AND LEARNED THE VALUE OF NEVER GIVING UP.
FUMP
Chosen by film directors 100 Classic Films
Horror Film Handbook
Lessons in Cinema
How to Watch Movies
Russian Animation
The Fundamentals of Anime
The Complete Guide to European Film
THE FILM ART OF AKIRA SHIROSAWA
WOW...
...MORE BOOKS?!

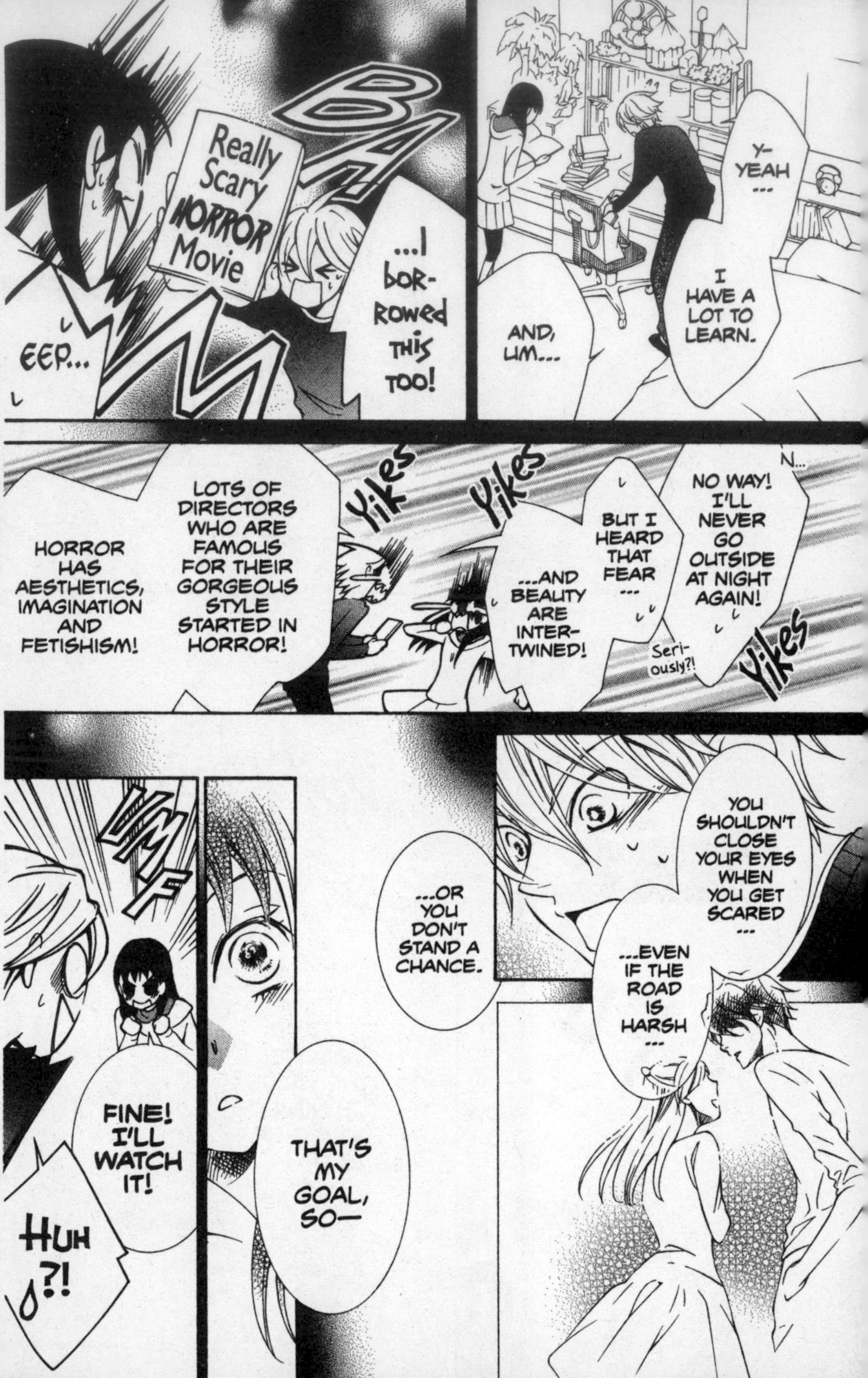
Y-YEAH ---
I HAVE A LOT TO LEARN.
AND, UM...
...I BORROWED THIS TOO!
BAM
Really Scary HORROR Movie
EEP...
N...
NO WAY! I'LL NEVER GO OUTSIDE AT NIGHT AGAIN!
Yikes
BUT I HEARD THAT FEAR ---
...AND BEAUTY ARE INTERTWINED!
Seriously?!
Yikes
Yikes
LOTS OF DIRECTORS WHO ARE FAMOUS FOR THEIR GORGEOUS STYLE STARTED IN HORROR!
HORROR HAS AESTHETICS, IMAGINATION AND FETISHISM!
YOU SHOULDN'T CLOSE YOUR EYES WHEN YOU GET SCARED ---
...EVEN IF THE ROAD IS HARSH ---
...OR YOU DON'T STAND A CHANCE.
THAT'S MY GOAL, SO—
WMF
FINE! I'LL WATCH IT!
HUH?!

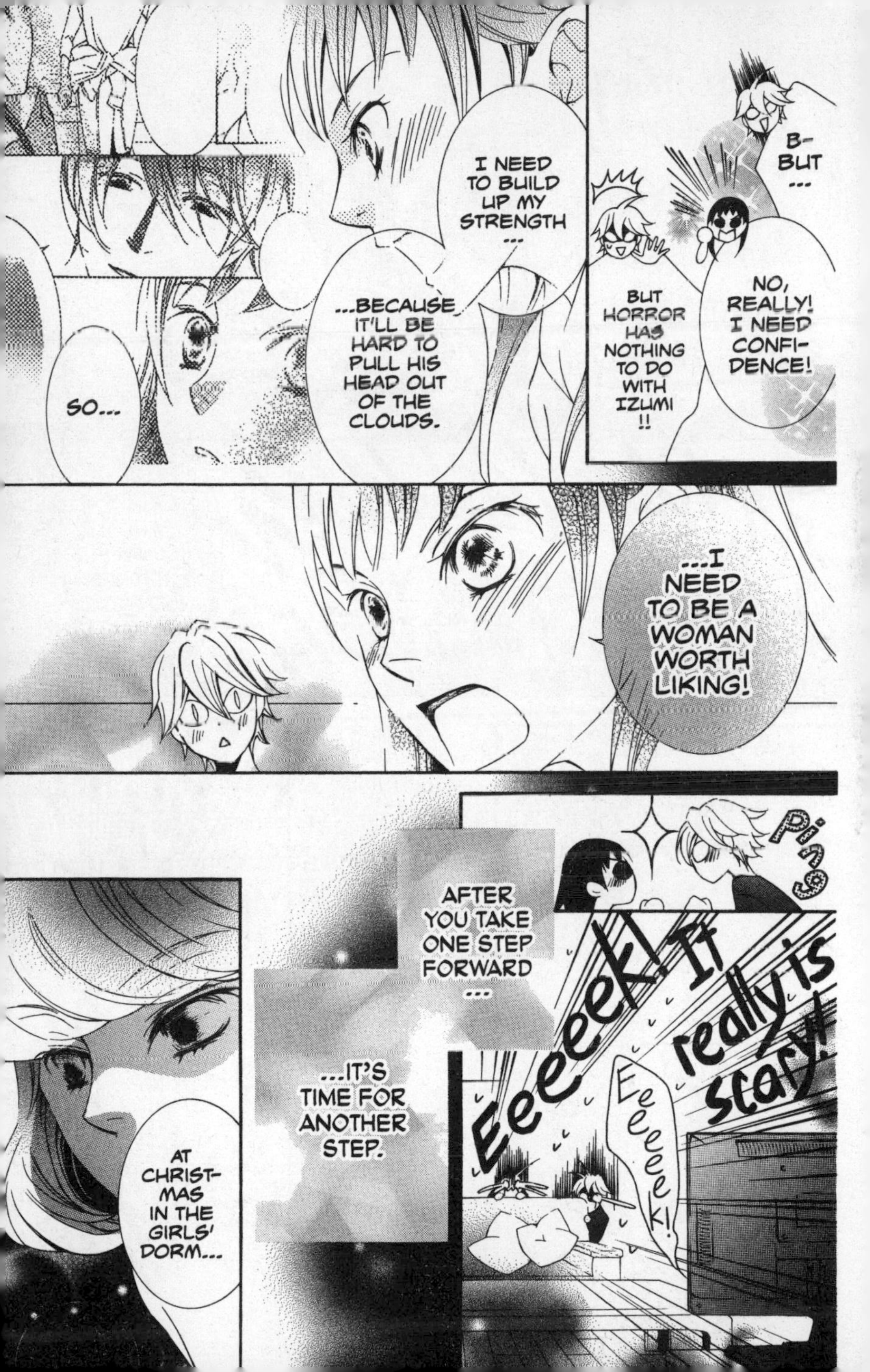
B-BUT...
NO, REALLY! I NEED CONFIDENCE!
BUT HORROR HAS NOTHING TO DO WITH IZUMI!!
I NEED TO BUILD UP MY STRENGTH...
...BECAUSE IT'LL BE HARD TO PULL HIS HEAD OUT OF THE CLOUDS.
SO...
...I NEED TO BE A WOMAN WORTH LIKING!
Ping
Eeeeek! It really is scary!
Eeeeeek!
AFTER YOU TAKE ONE STEP FORWARD...
...IT'S TIME FOR ANOTHER STEP.
AT CHRISTMAS IN THE GIRLS' DORM...

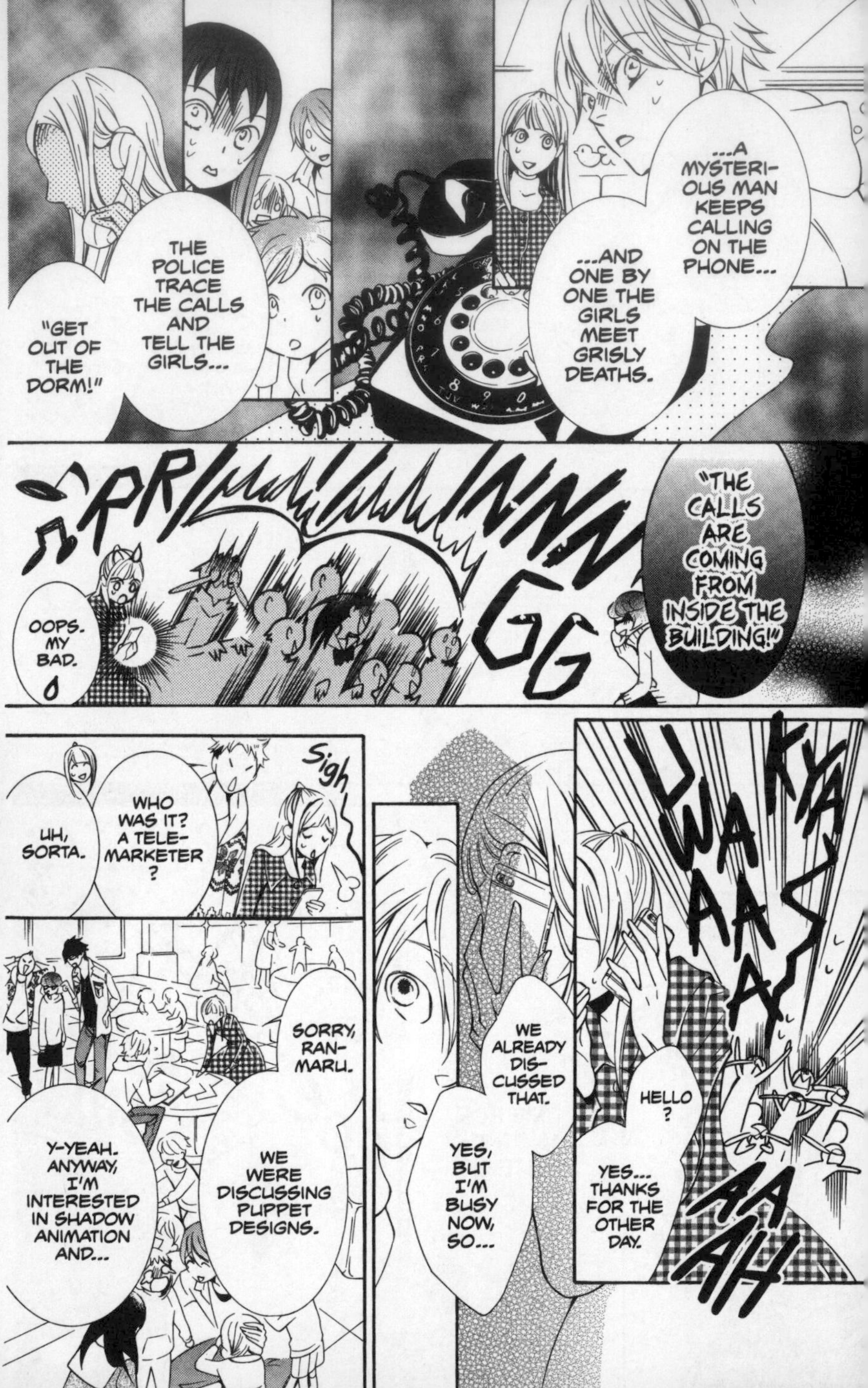
...A MYSTERIOUS MAN KEEPS CALLING ON THE PHONE...
...AND ONE BY ONE THE GIRLS MEET GRISLY DEATHS.
THE POLICE TRACE THE CALLS AND TELL THE GIRLS...
"GET OUT OF THE DORM!"
"THE CALLS ARE COMING FROM INSIDE THE BUILDING!"
RRIIIIIINNNGG
OOPS. MY BAD.
KYA
UWAAAAA
AAAH
HELLO?
YES... THANKS FOR THE OTHER DAY.
WE ALREADY DISCUSSED THAT.
YES, BUT I'M BUSY NOW, SO...
Sigh
WHO WAS IT? A TELEMARKETER?
UH, SORTA.
SORRY, RANMARU.
WE WERE DISCUSSING PUPPET DESIGNS.
Y-YEAH. ANYWAY, I'M INTERESTED IN SHADOW ANIMATION AND...

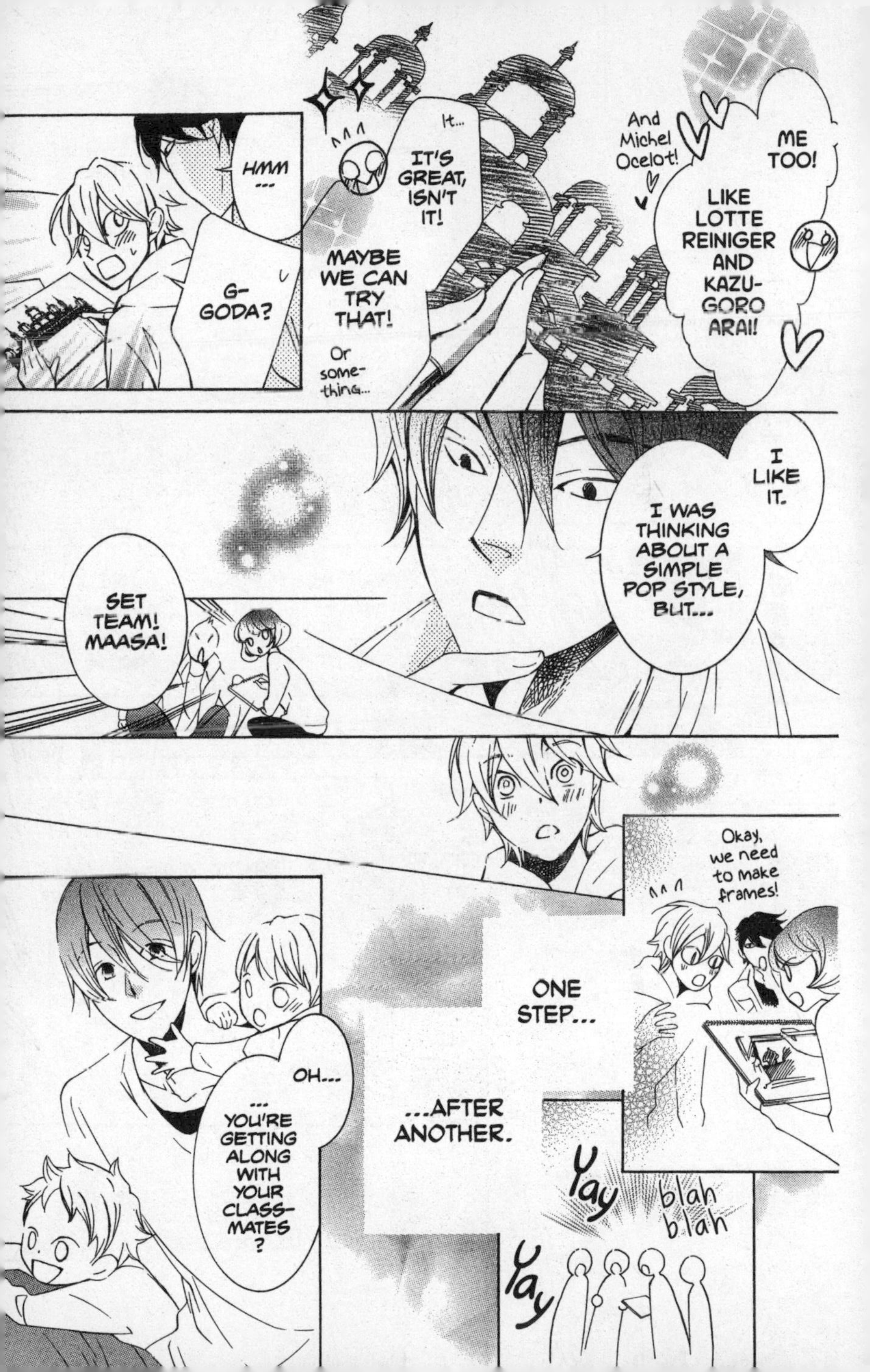
It...
IT'S GREAT, ISN'T IT!
MAYBE WE CAN TRY THAT!
Or something...
ME TOO!
LIKE LOTTE REINIGER AND KAZUGORO ARAI!
And Michel Ocelot!
HMM---
G-GODA?
I LIKE IT.
I WAS THINKING ABOUT A SIMPLE POP STYLE, BUT...
SET TEAM! MAASA!
Okay, we need to make frames!
Yay
blah blah
Yay
ONE STEP...
...AFTER ANOTHER.
OH...
...YOU'RE GETTING ALONG WITH YOUR CLASSMATES?

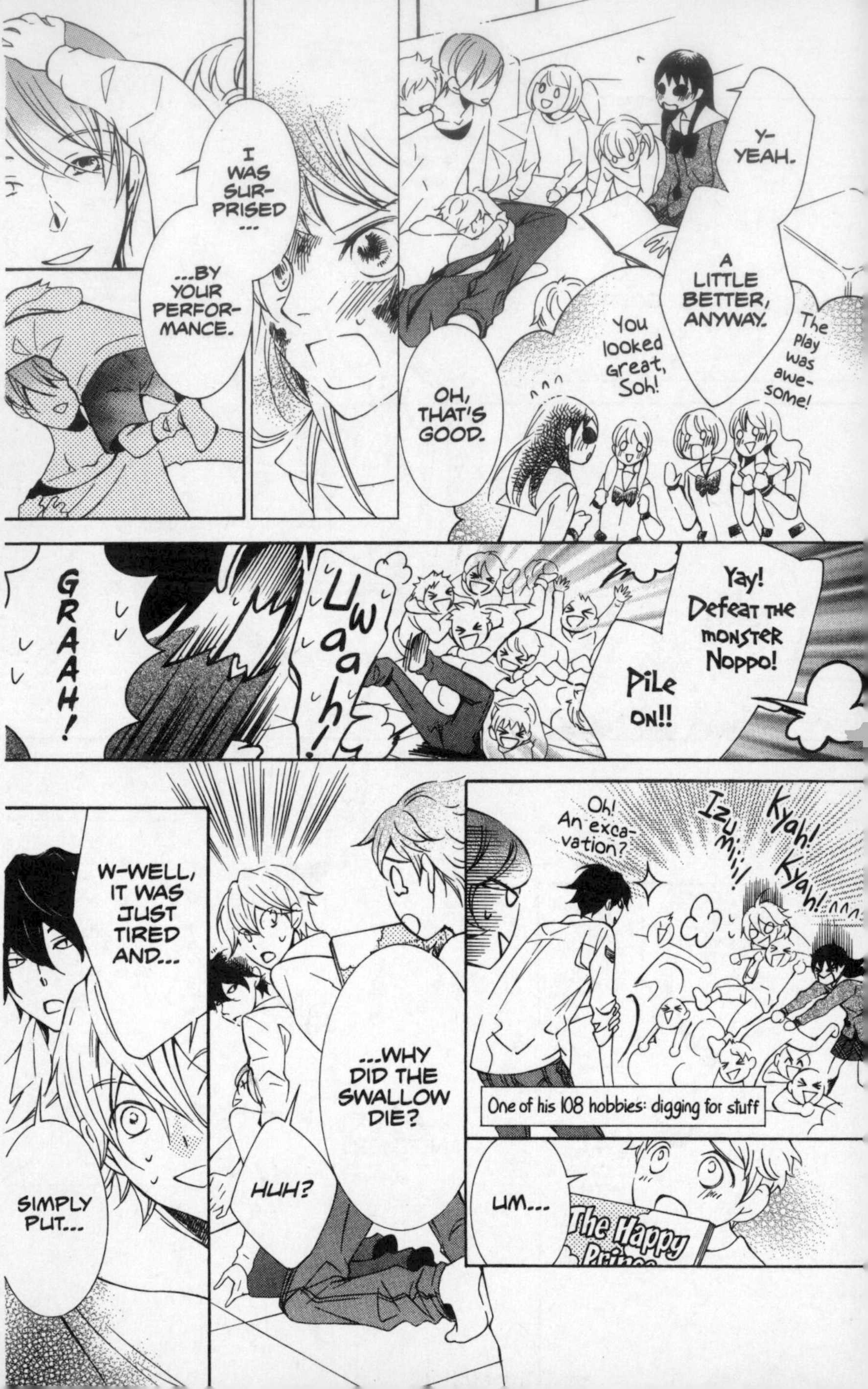
Y-YEAH.
A LITTLE BETTER, ANYWAY.
The play was awesome!
You looked great, Soh!
OH, THAT'S GOOD.
I WAS SURPRISED...
...BY YOUR PERFORMANCE.
Yay! Defeat the monster Noppo!
Pile on!!
Uwaah!
GRAAAH!
Kyah! Kyah!
Izumi!!
Oh! An excavation?
One of his 108 hobbies: digging for stuff
UM...
The Happy
...WHY DID THE SWALLOW DIE?
HUH?
W-WELL, IT WAS JUST TIRED AND...
SIMPLY PUT...

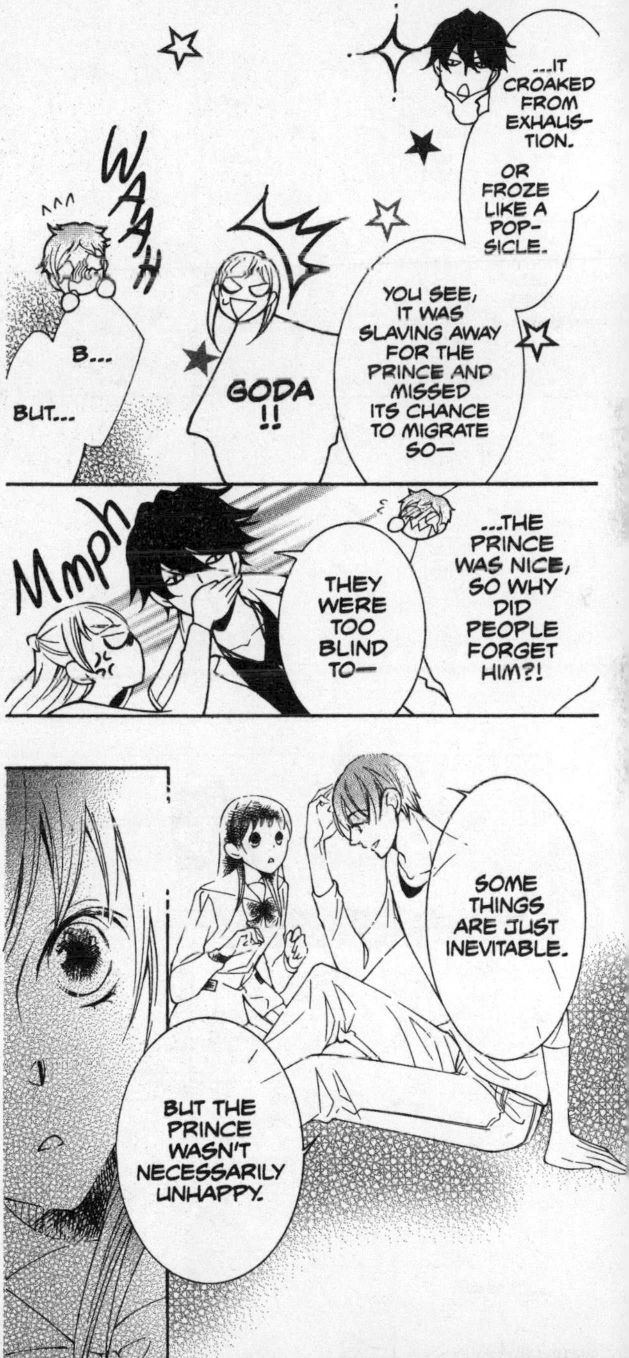
...IT CROAKED FROM EXHAUSTION.
OR FROZE LIKE A POPSICLE.
YOU SEE, IT WAS SLAVING AWAY FOR THE PRINCE AND MISSED ITS CHANCE TO MIGRATE SO—
GODA !!
WAAAH
B...
BUT...
...THE PRINCE WAS NICE, SO WHY DID PEOPLE FORGET HIM?!
THEY WERE TOO BLIND TO—
Mmph
SOME THINGS ARE JUST INEVITABLE.
BUT THE PRINCE WASN'T NECESSARILY UNHAPPY.

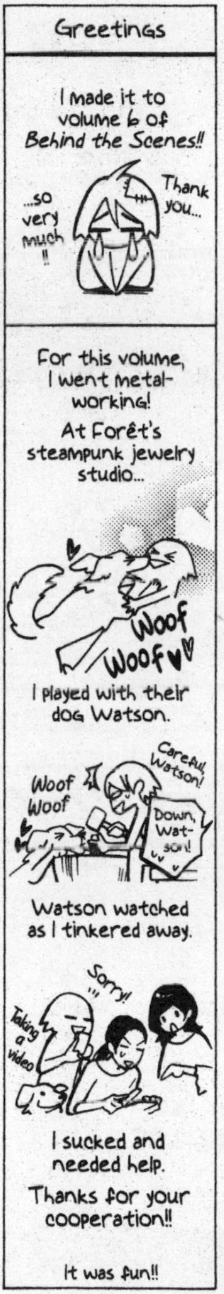
Greetings
I made it to volume 6 of Behind the Scenes!!
Thank you...
...so very much!!
For this volume, I went metal-working!
At Forêt's steampunk jewelry studio...
Woof Woof
I played with their dog Watson.
Careful, Watson!
Down, Watson!
Woof Woof
Watson watched as I tinkered away.
Sorry!
Taking a video
I sucked and needed help.
Thanks for your cooperation!!
It was fun!!

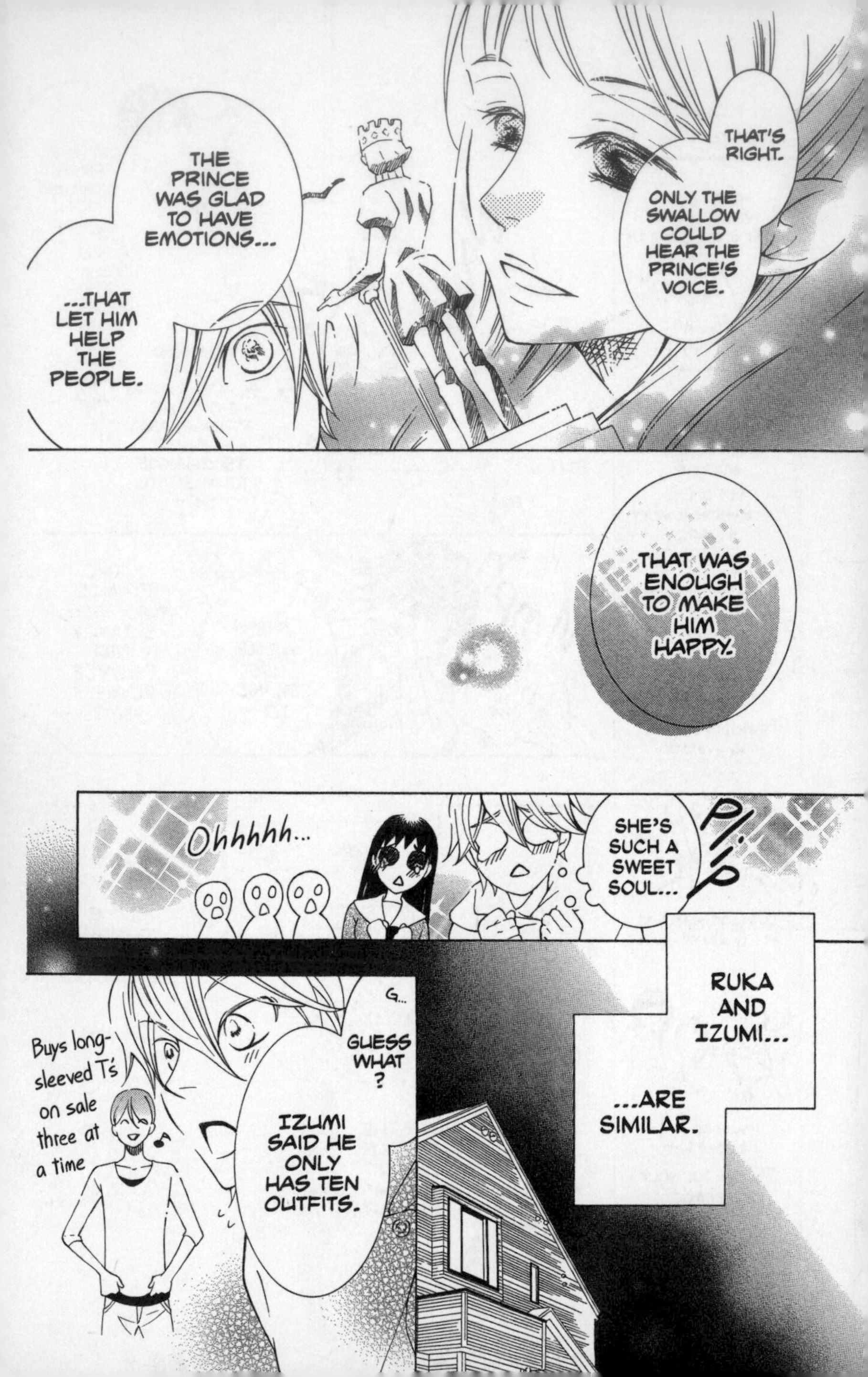
THAT'S RIGHT.
ONLY THE SWALLOW COULD HEAR THE PRINCE'S VOICE.
THE PRINCE WAS GLAD TO HAVE EMOTIONS...
...THAT LET HIM HELP THE PEOPLE.
THAT WAS ENOUGH TO MAKE HIM HAPPY.
SHE'S SUCH A SWEET SOUL...
Ohhhhh...
RUKA AND IZUMI...
...ARE SIMILAR.
G...
GUESS WHAT?
IZUMI SAID HE ONLY HAS TEN OUTFITS.
Buys long-sleeved T's on sale three at a time

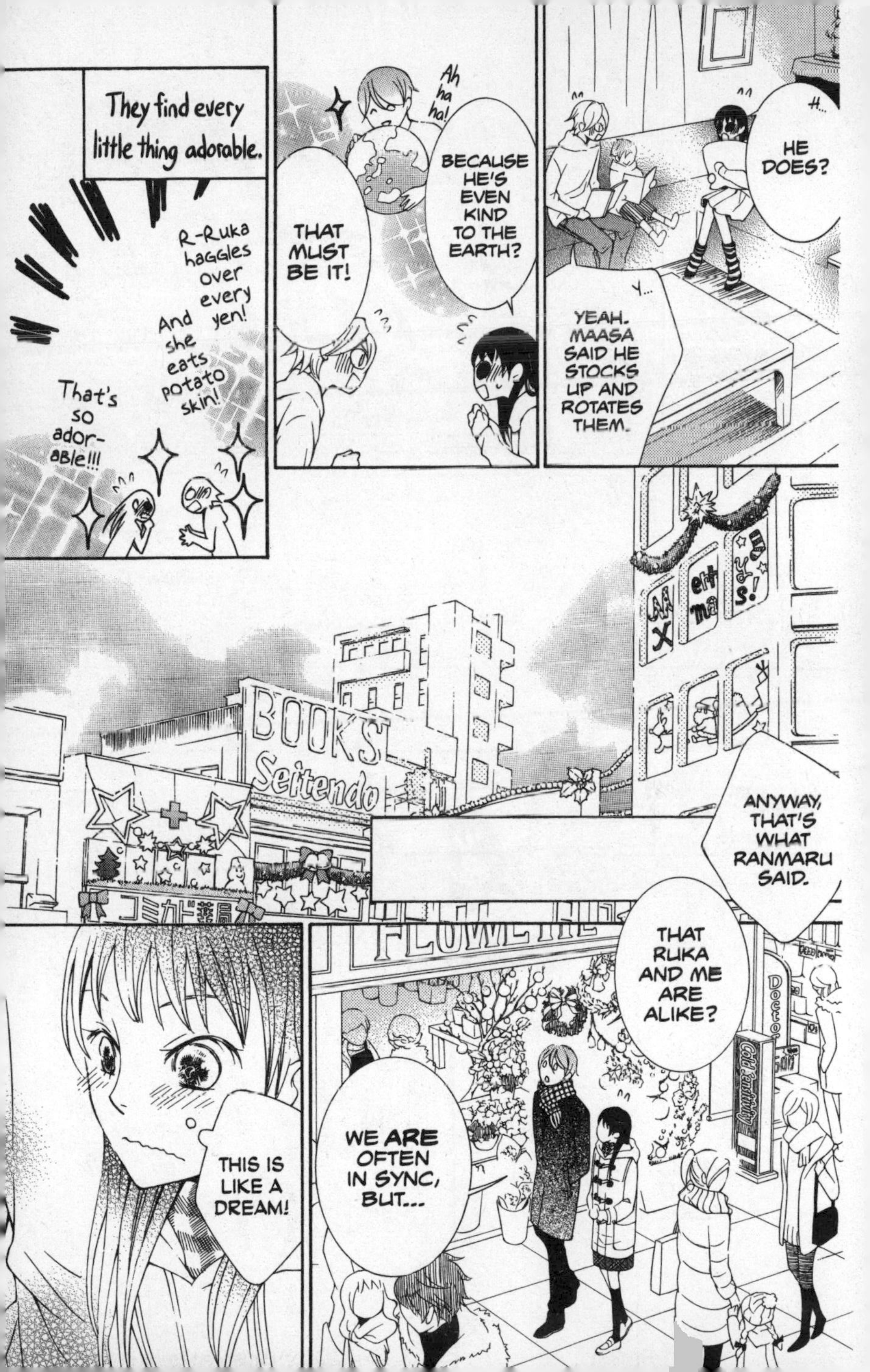
H...
HE DOES?
Y...
YEAH. MAASA SAID HE STOCKS UP AND ROTATES THEM.
Ah ha ha!
BECAUSE HE'S EVEN KIND TO THE EARTH?
THAT MUST BE IT!
They find every little thing adorable.
R-Ruka haggles over every yen!
And she eats potato skin!
That's so adorable!!!
BOOKS
Seitendo
ANYWAY, THAT'S WHAT RANMARU SAID.
THAT RUKA AND ME ARE ALIKE?
WE ARE OFTEN IN SYNC, BUT...
Cold Sensitivity
Doctor
THIS IS LIKE A DREAM!

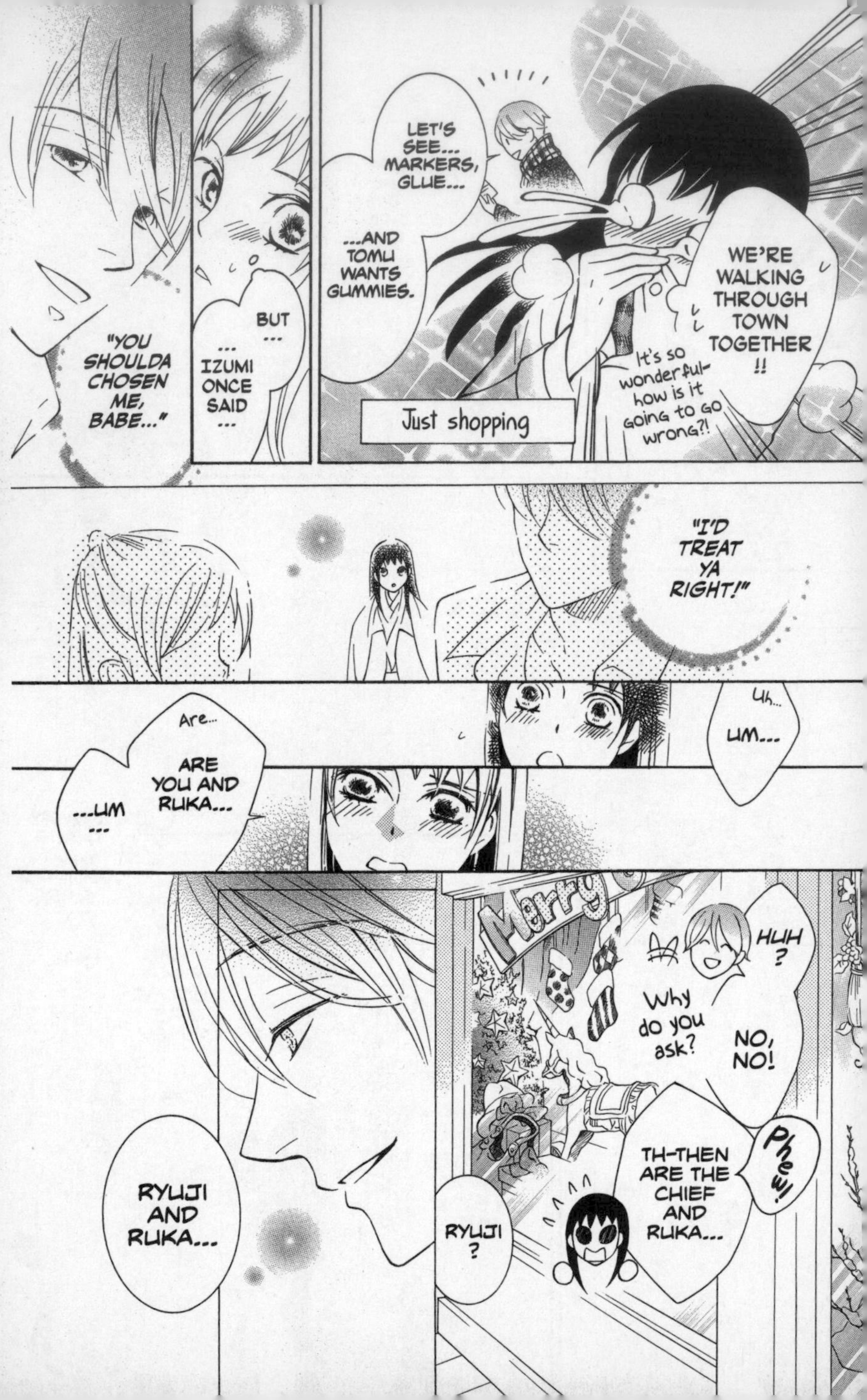
Just shopping
WE'RE WALKING THROUGH TOWN TOGETHER!!
It's so wonderful-how is it going to go wrong?!
LET'S SEE... MARKERS, GLUE...
...AND TOMU WANTS GUMMIES.
BUT... ...IZUMI ONCE SAID...
"YOU SHOULDA CHOSEN ME, BABE..."
"I'D TREAT YA RIGHT!"
Uh... UM...
Are... ARE YOU AND RUKA... ...UM...
Merry
HUH? Why do you ask?
NO, NO!
Phew!
TH-THEN ARE THE CHIEF AND RUKA...
RYUJI?
RYUJI AND RUKA...

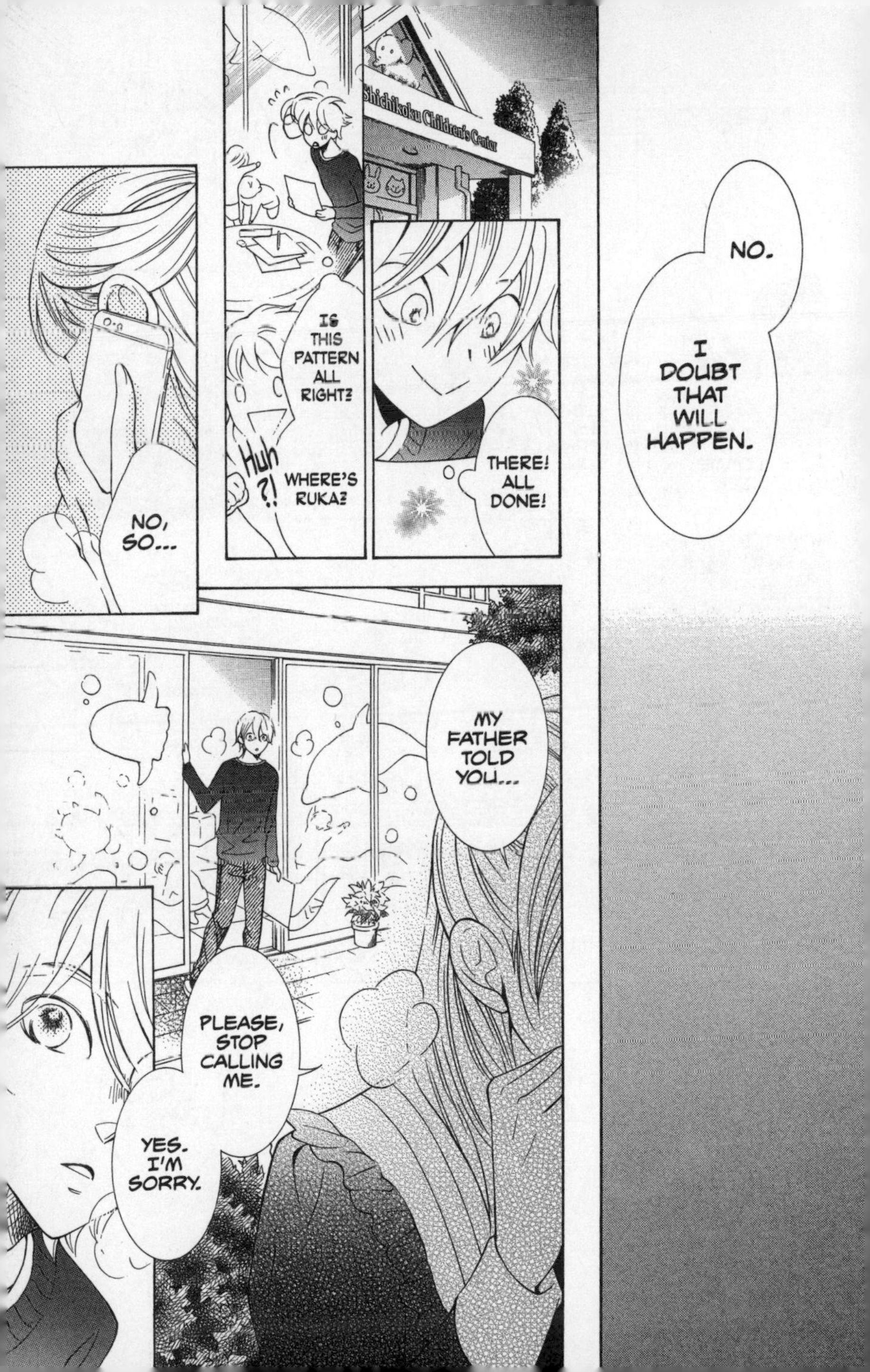
NO.
I DOUBT THAT WILL HAPPEN.
Shichikoku Children's Center
THERE! ALL DONE!
IS THIS PATTERN ALL RIGHT?
Huh ?!
WHERE'S RUKA?
NO, SO...
MY FATHER TOLD YOU...
PLEASE, STOP CALLING ME.
YES. I'M SORRY.

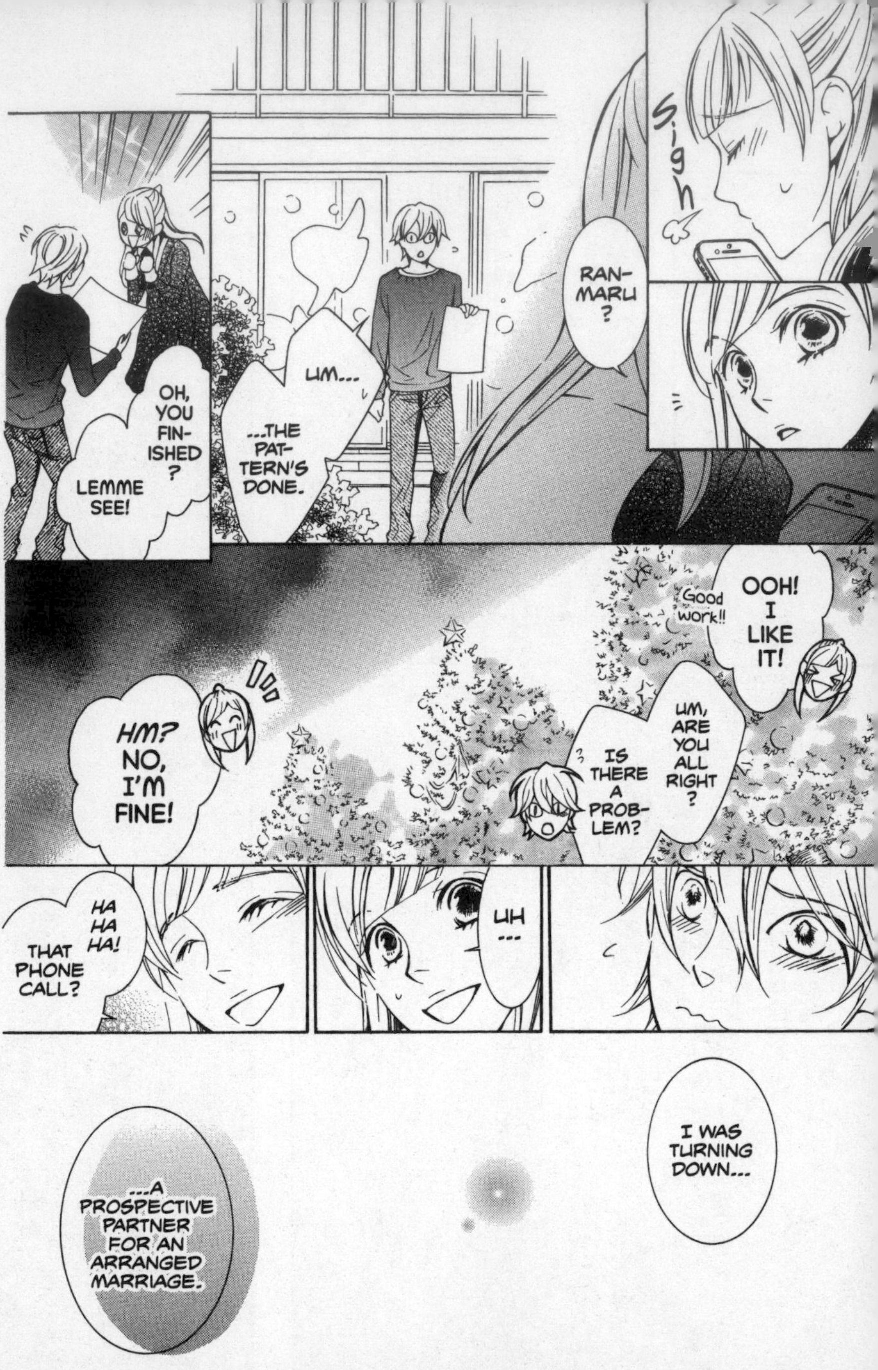
Sigh
RAN-MARU?
UM...
...THE PAT-TERN'S DONE.
OH, YOU FIN-ISHED?
LEMME SEE!
OOH! I LIKE IT!
Good work!!
UM, ARE YOU ALL RIGHT?
IS THERE A PROB-LEM?
HM? NO, I'M FINE!
UH...
HA HA HA!
THAT PHONE CALL?
I WAS TURNING DOWN...
...A PROSPECTIVE PARTNER FOR AN ARRANGED MARRIAGE.

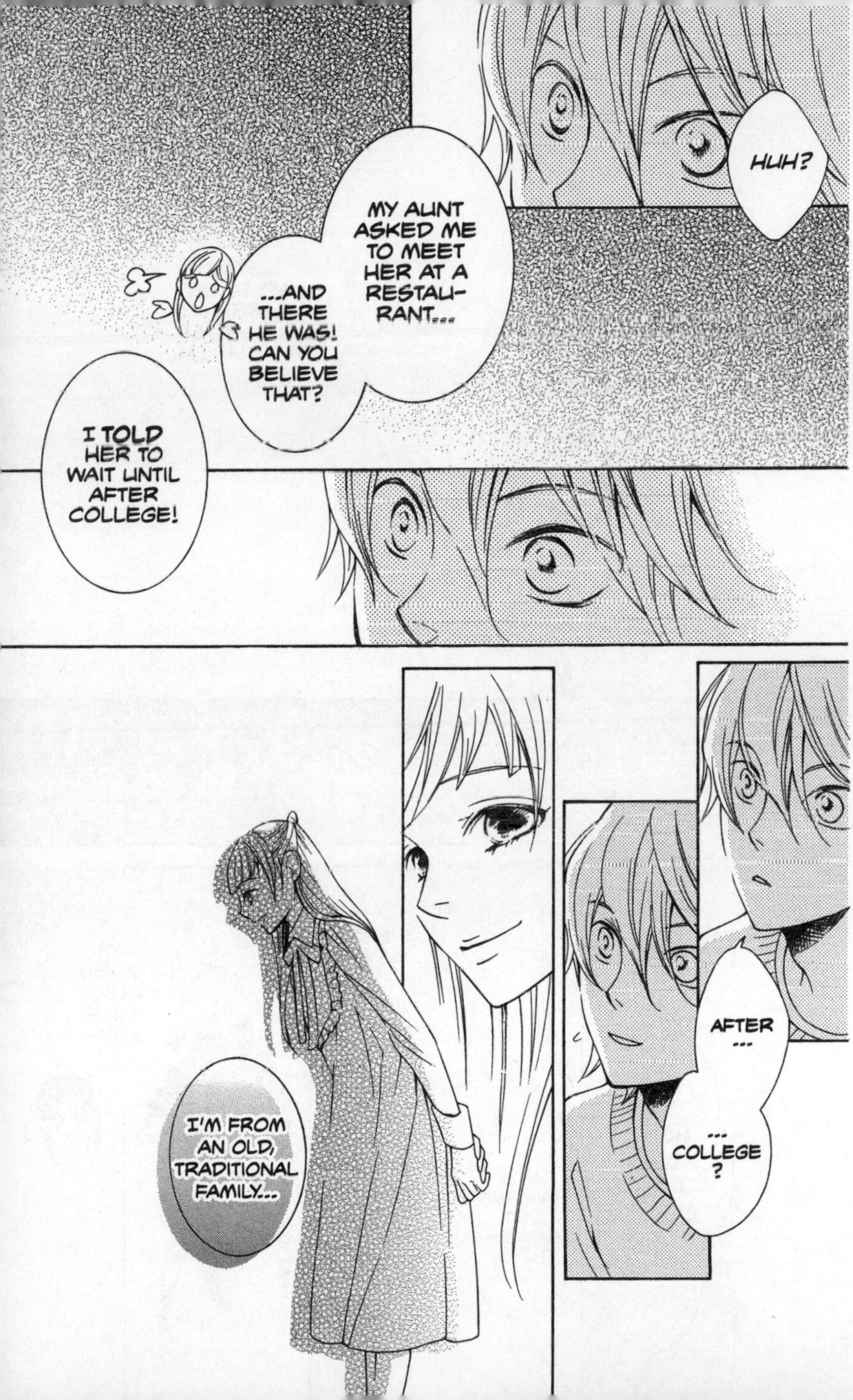
HUH?
MY AUNT ASKED ME TO MEET HER AT A RESTAU-RANT...
...AND THERE HE WAS! CAN YOU BELIEVE THAT?
I TOLD HER TO WAIT UNTIL AFTER COLLEGE!
AFTER...
...COLLEGE?
I'M FROM AN OLD, TRADITIONAL FAMILY...

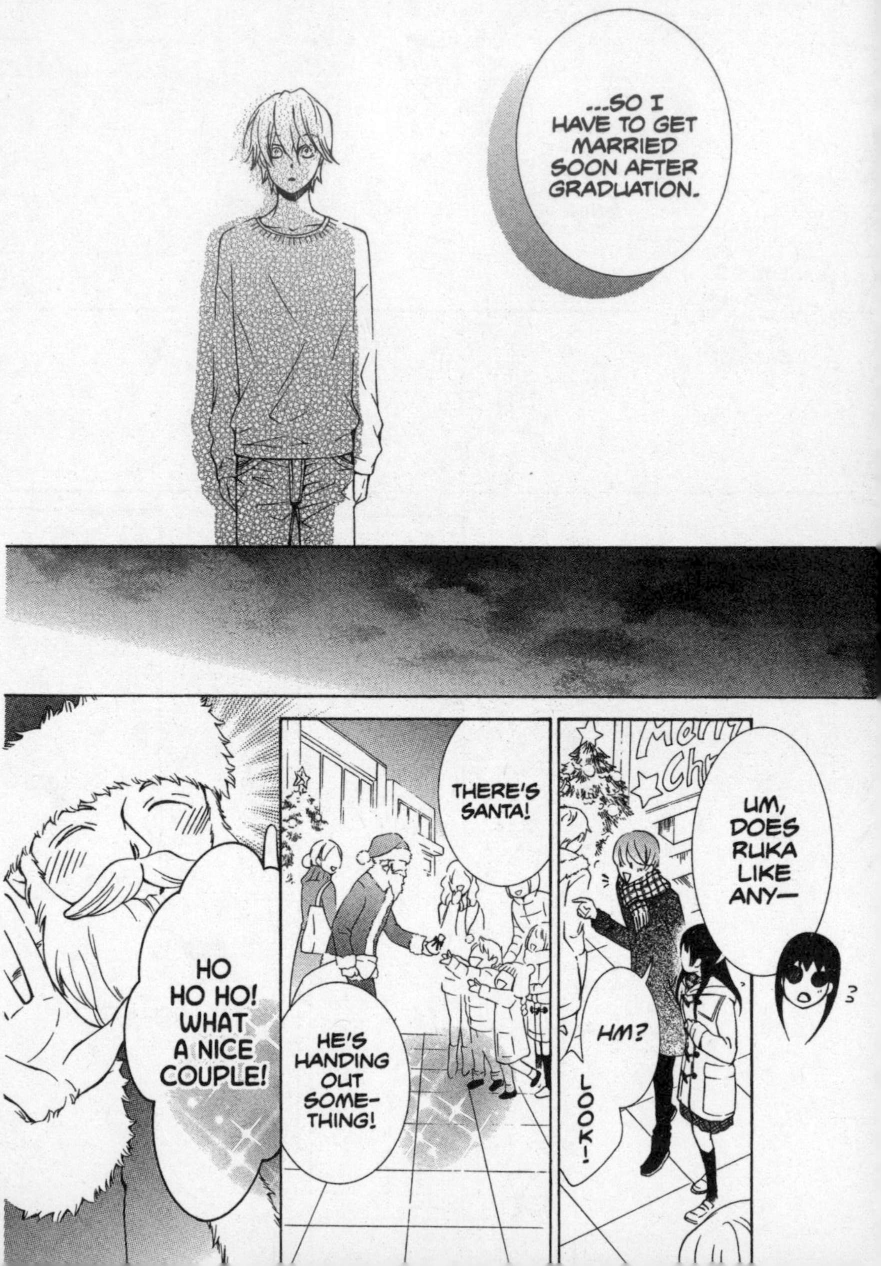
...SO I HAVE TO GET MARRIED SOON AFTER GRADUATION.
UM, DOES RUKA LIKE ANY—
HM?
LOOK!
THERE'S SANTA!
HE'S HANDING OUT SOME-THING!
HO HO HO! WHAT A NICE COUPLE!

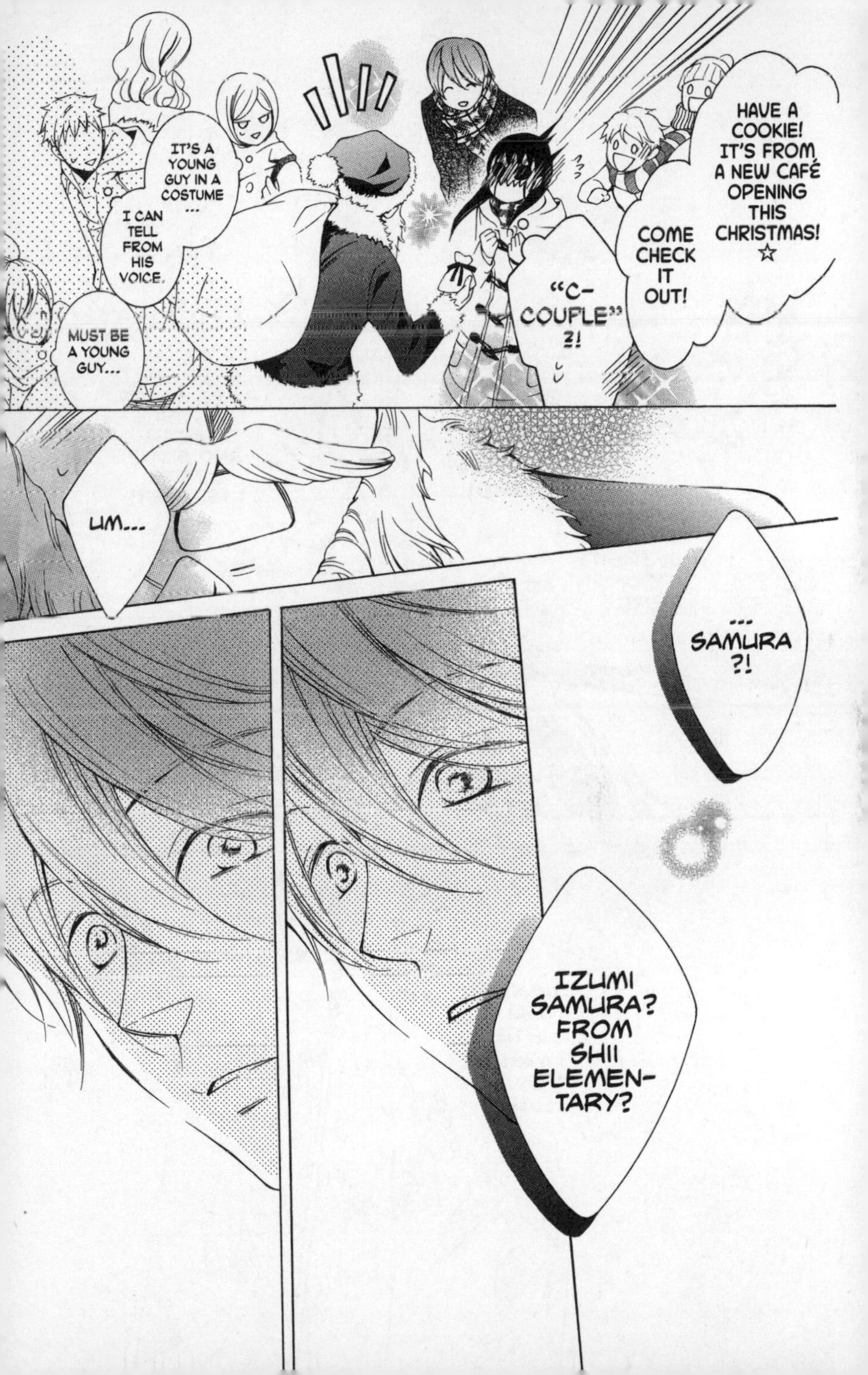
HAVE A COOKIE! IT'S FROM A NEW CAFÉ OPENING THIS CHRISTMAS! ☆
COME CHECK IT OUT!
“C-COUPLE” ?!
IT'S A YOUNG GUY IN A COSTUME...
I CAN TELL FROM HIS VOICE.
MUST BE A YOUNG GUY...
UM...
...SAMURA ?!
IZUMI SAMURA? FROM SHII ELEMENTARY?

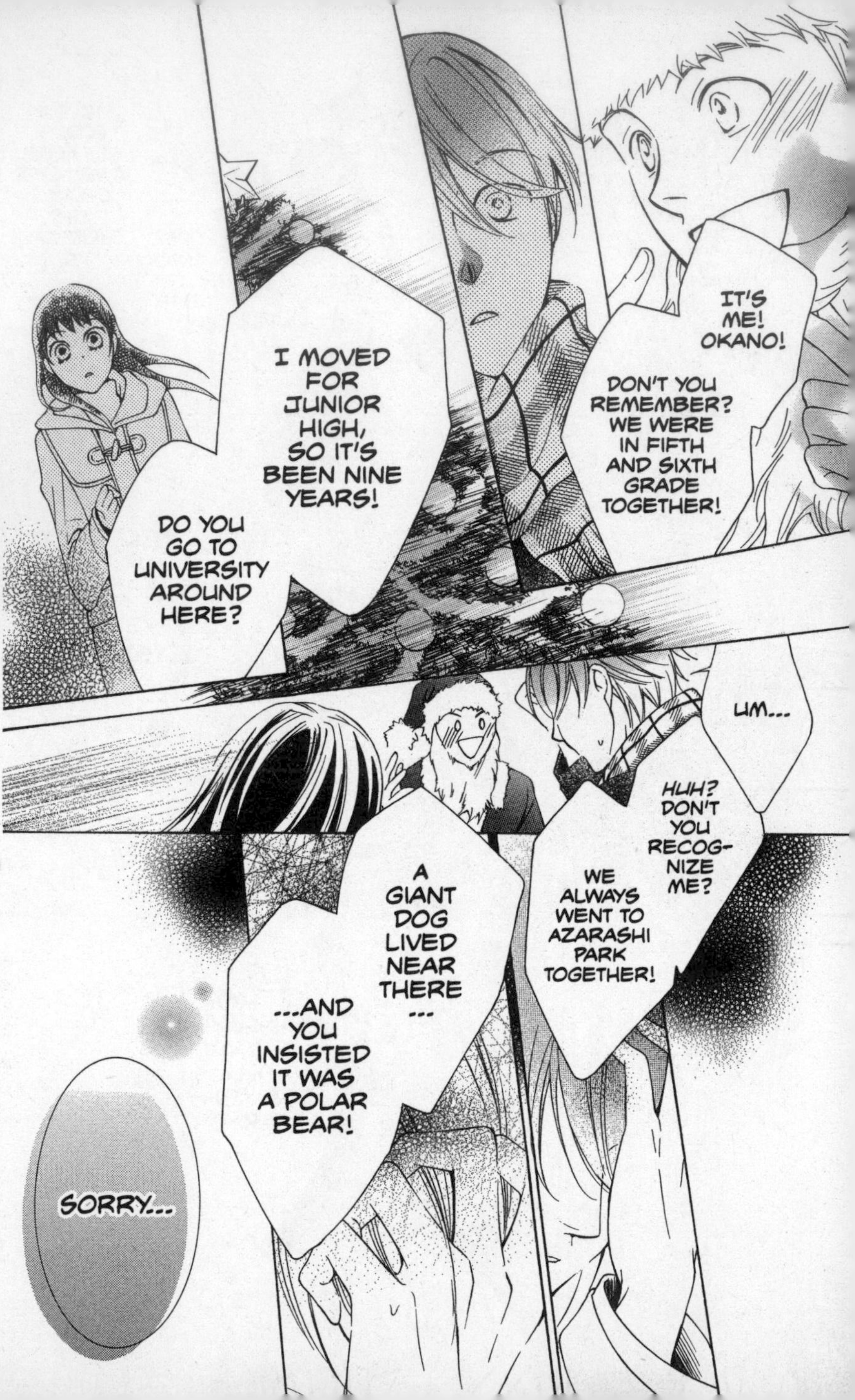
IT'S ME! OKANO!
DON'T YOU REMEMBER? WE WERE IN FIFTH AND SIXTH GRADE TOGETHER!
I MOVED FOR JUNIOR HIGH, SO IT'S BEEN NINE YEARS!
DO YOU GO TO UNIVERSITY AROUND HERE?
UM...
HUH? DON'T YOU RECOG-NIZE ME?
WE ALWAYS WENT TO AZARASHI PARK TOGETHER!
A GIANT DOG LIVED NEAR THERE...
...AND YOU INSISTED IT WAS A POLAR BEAR!
SORRY...

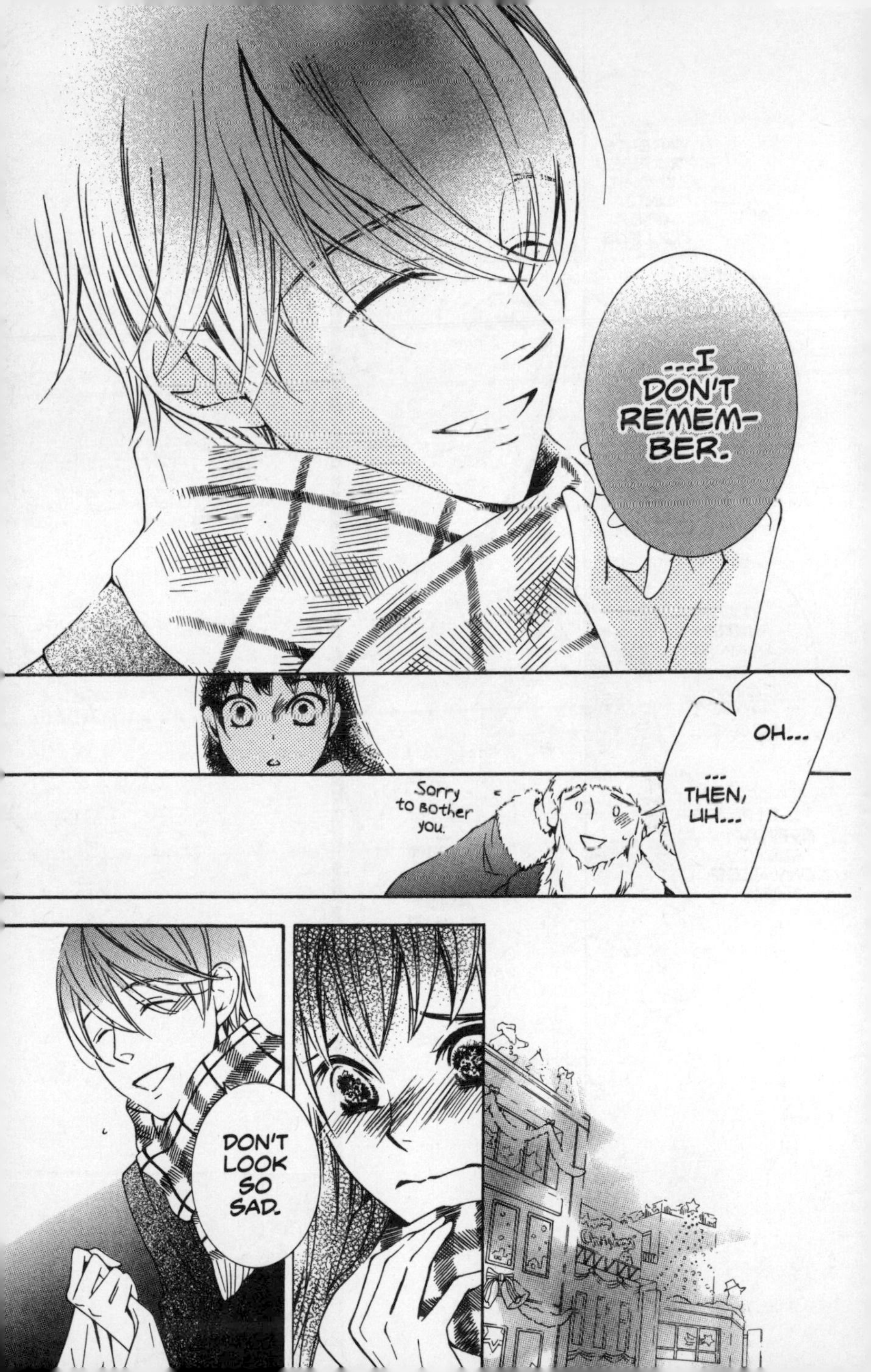
...I DON'T REMEMBER.
OH... ...THEN, UH...
Sorry to bother you.
DON'T LOOK SO SAD.

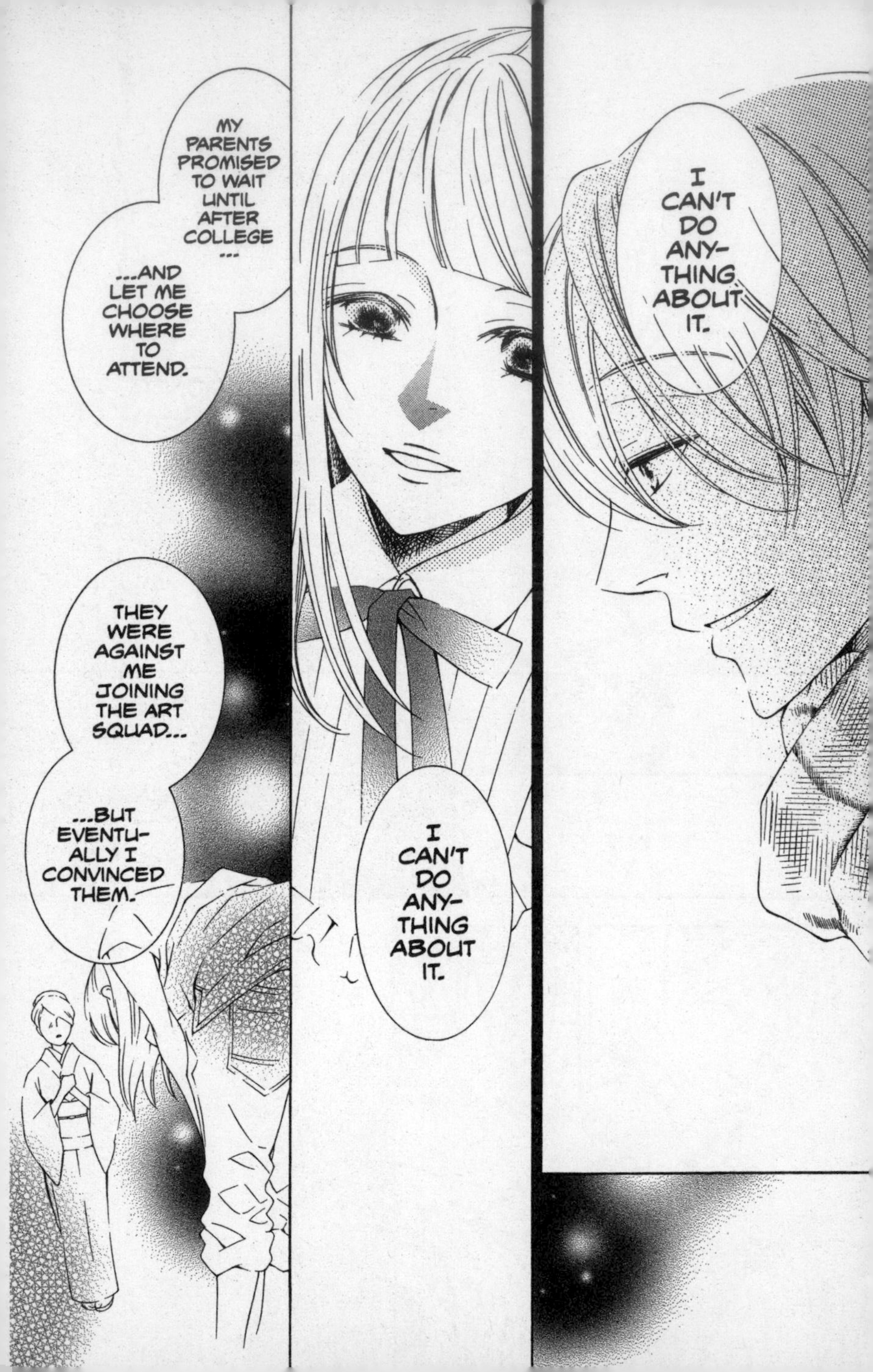
I CAN'T DO ANY-THING ABOUT IT.
I CAN'T DO ANY-THING ABOUT IT.
MY PARENTS PROMISED TO WAIT UNTIL AFTER COLLEGE...
...AND LET ME CHOOSE WHERE TO ATTEND.
THEY WERE AGAINST ME JOINING THE ART SQUAD...
...BUT EVENTU-ALLY I CONVINCED THEM.

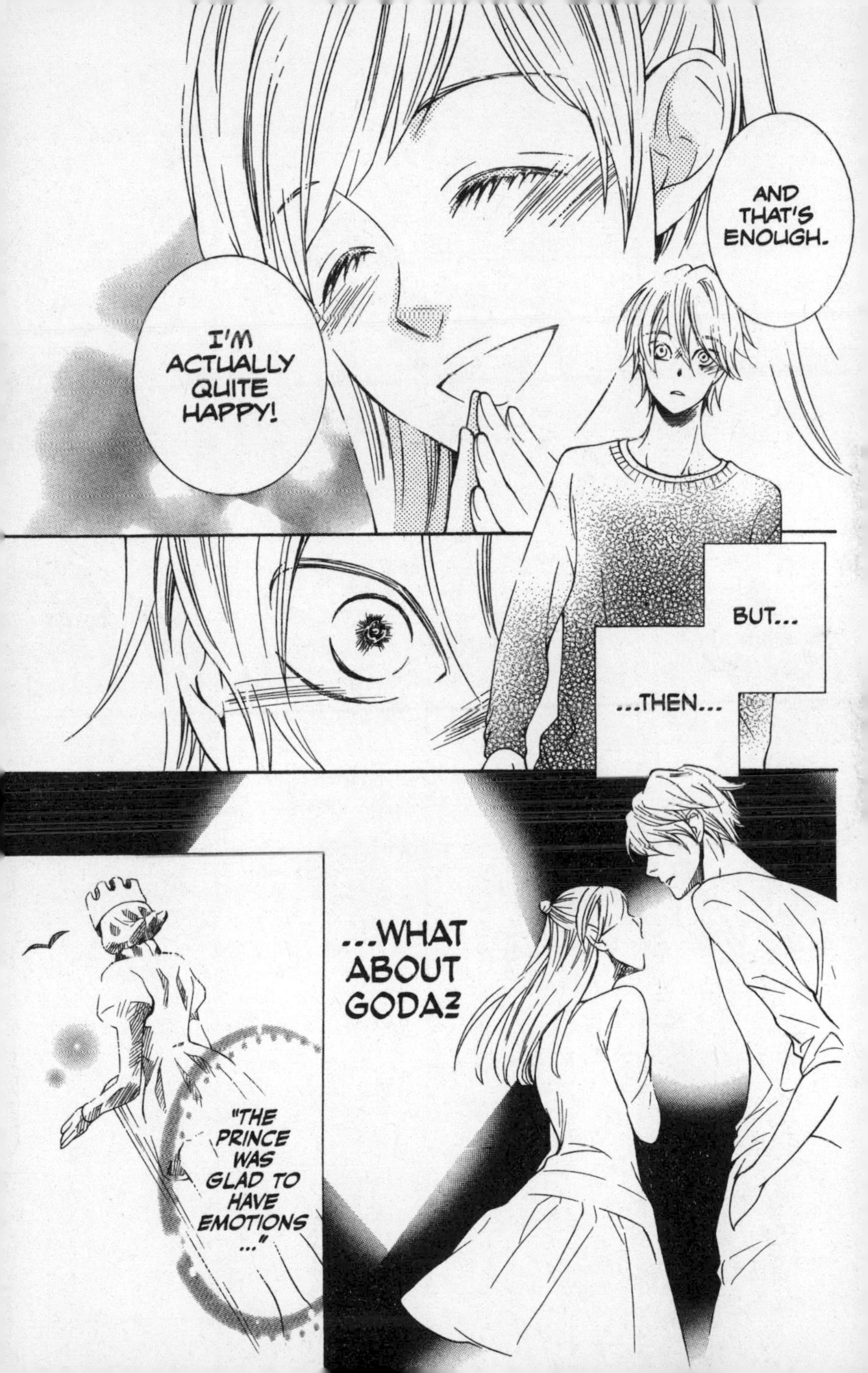
AND THAT'S ENOUGH.
I'M ACTUALLY QUITE HAPPY!
BUT...
...THEN...
...WHAT ABOUT GODA?
"THE PRINCE WAS GLAD TO HAVE EMOTIONS ..."

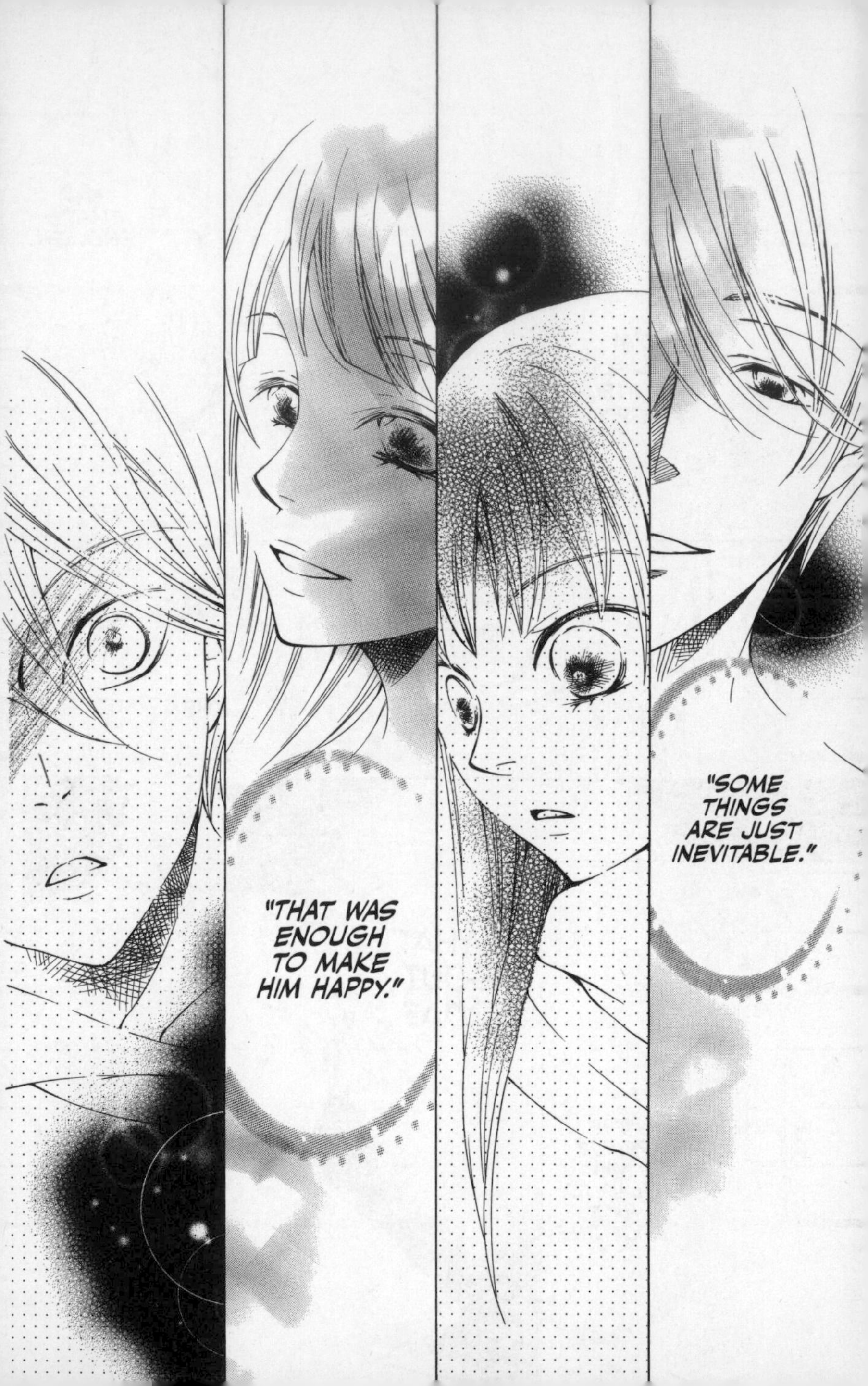
"SOME THINGS ARE JUST INEVITABLE."
"THAT WAS ENOUGH TO MAKE HIM HAPPY."

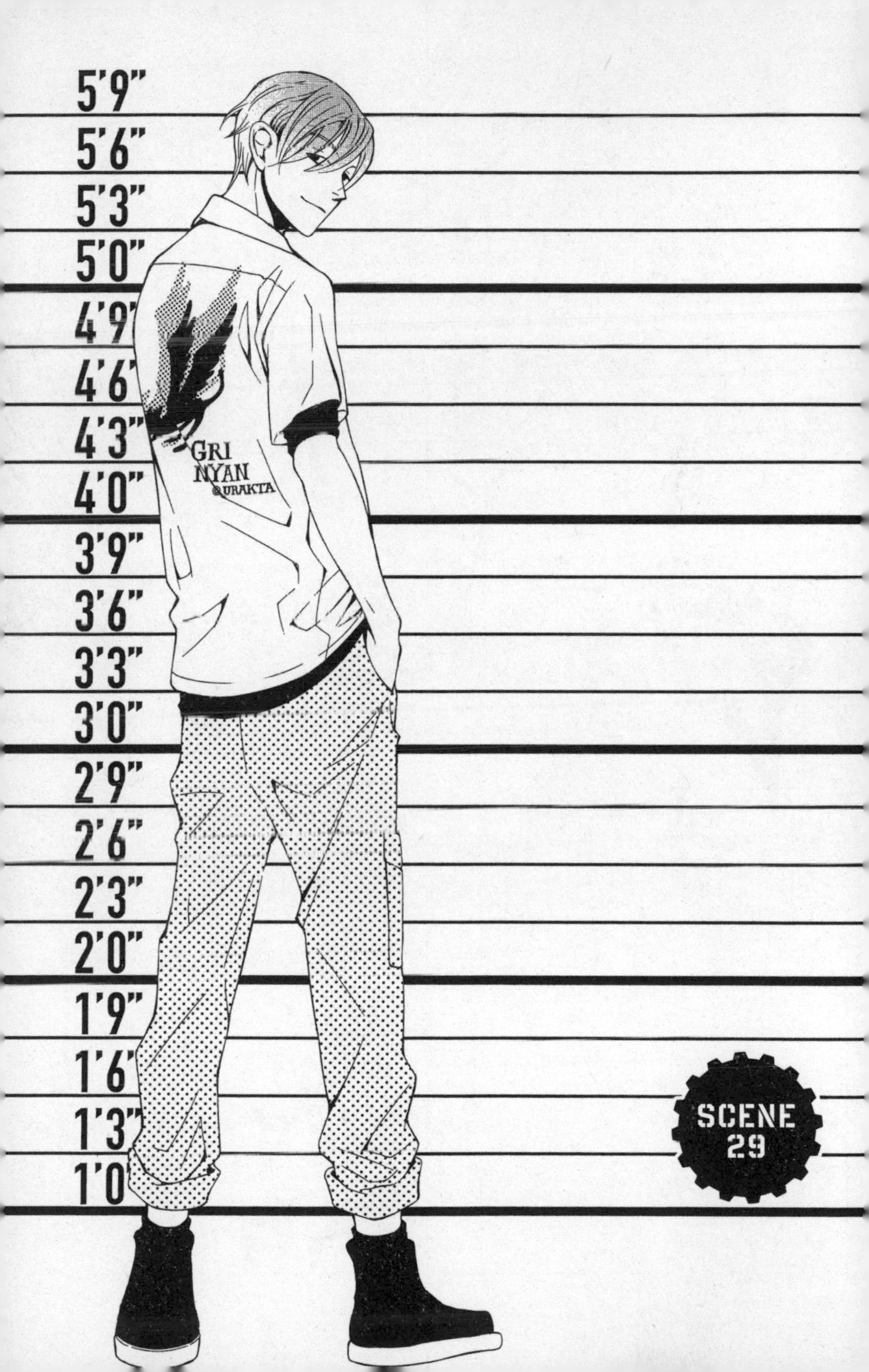
5'9"
5'6"
5'3"
5'0"
4'9"
4'6"
4'3"
4'0"
3'9"
3'6"
3'3"
3'0"
2'9"
2'6"
2'3"
2'0"
1'9"
1'6"
1'3"
1'0"
GRI
NYAN
SCENE
29

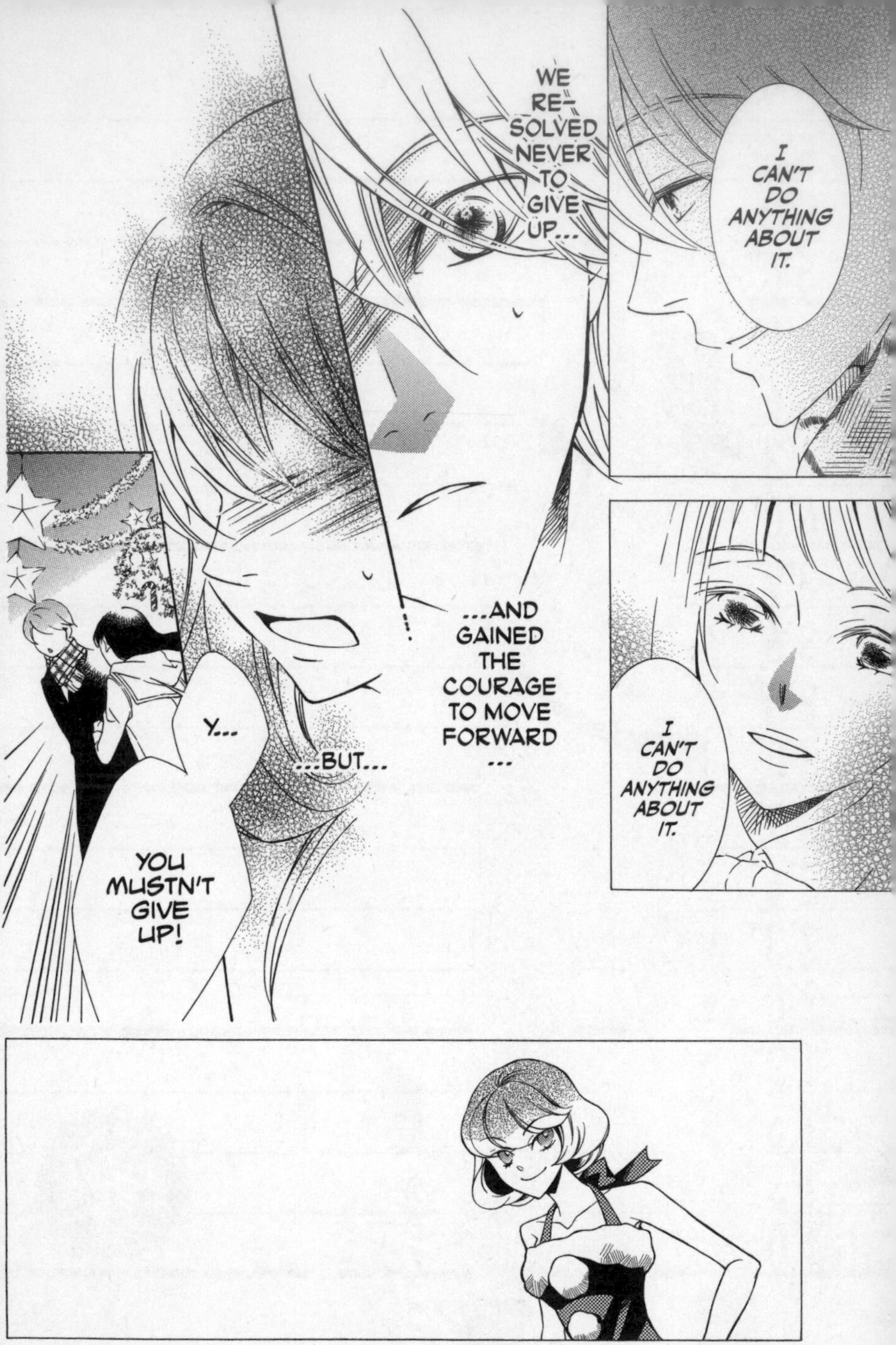
I CAN'T DO ANYTHING ABOUT IT.
I CAN'T DO ANYTHING ABOUT IT.
WE RE-SOLVED NEVER TO GIVE UP...
...AND GAINED THE COURAGE TO MOVE FORWARD...
...BUT...
Y...
YOU MUSTN'T GIVE UP!

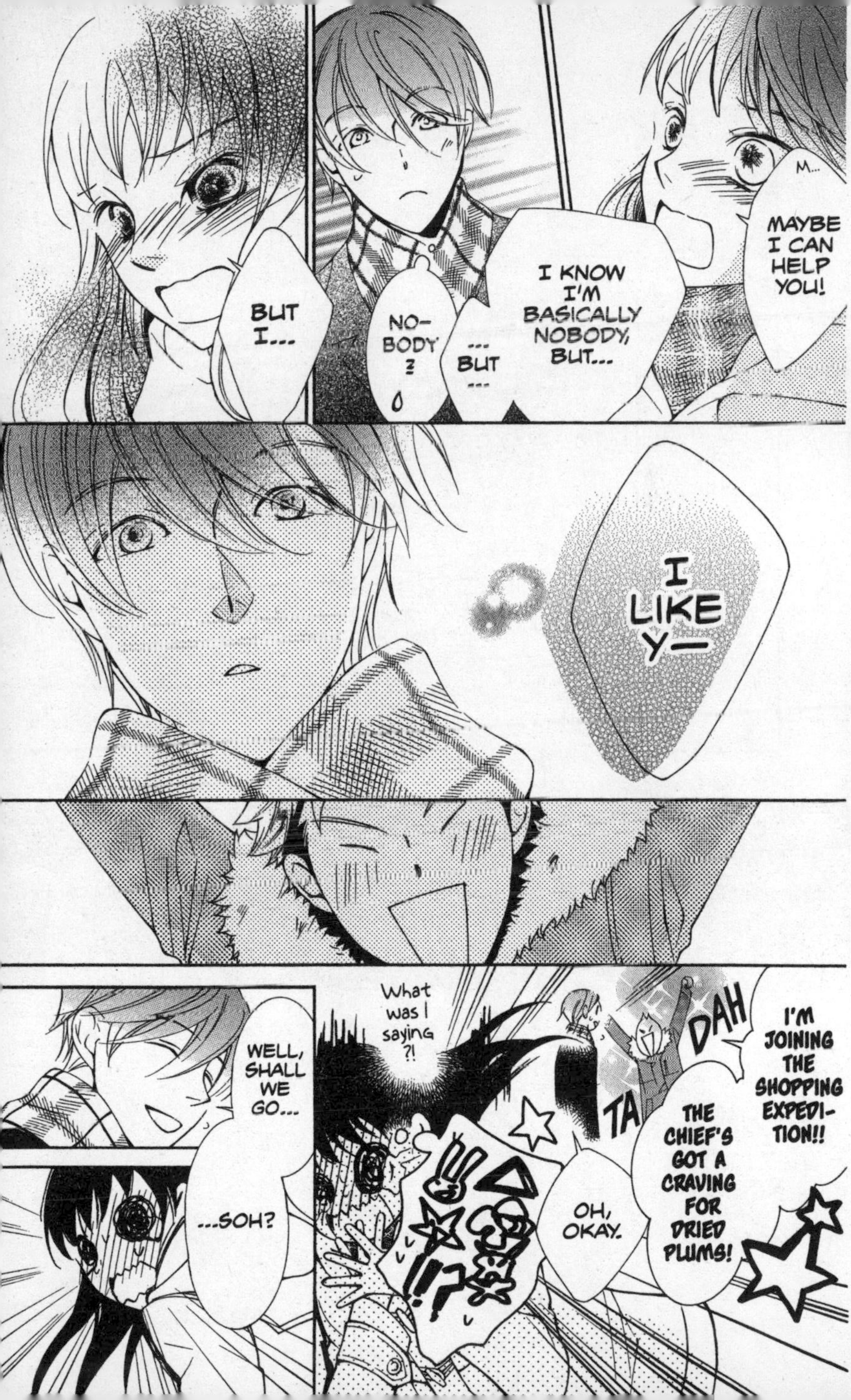
M...
MAYBE I CAN HELP YOU!
I KNOW I'M BASICALLY NOBODY, BUT...
...BUT...
NO-BODY?
BUT I...
I LIKE Y—
I'M JOINING THE SHOPPING EXPEDITION!!
TA DAH
THE CHIEF'S GOT A CRAVING FOR DRIED PLUMS!
OH, OKAY.
What was I saying?!
WELL, SHALL WE GO...
...SOH?

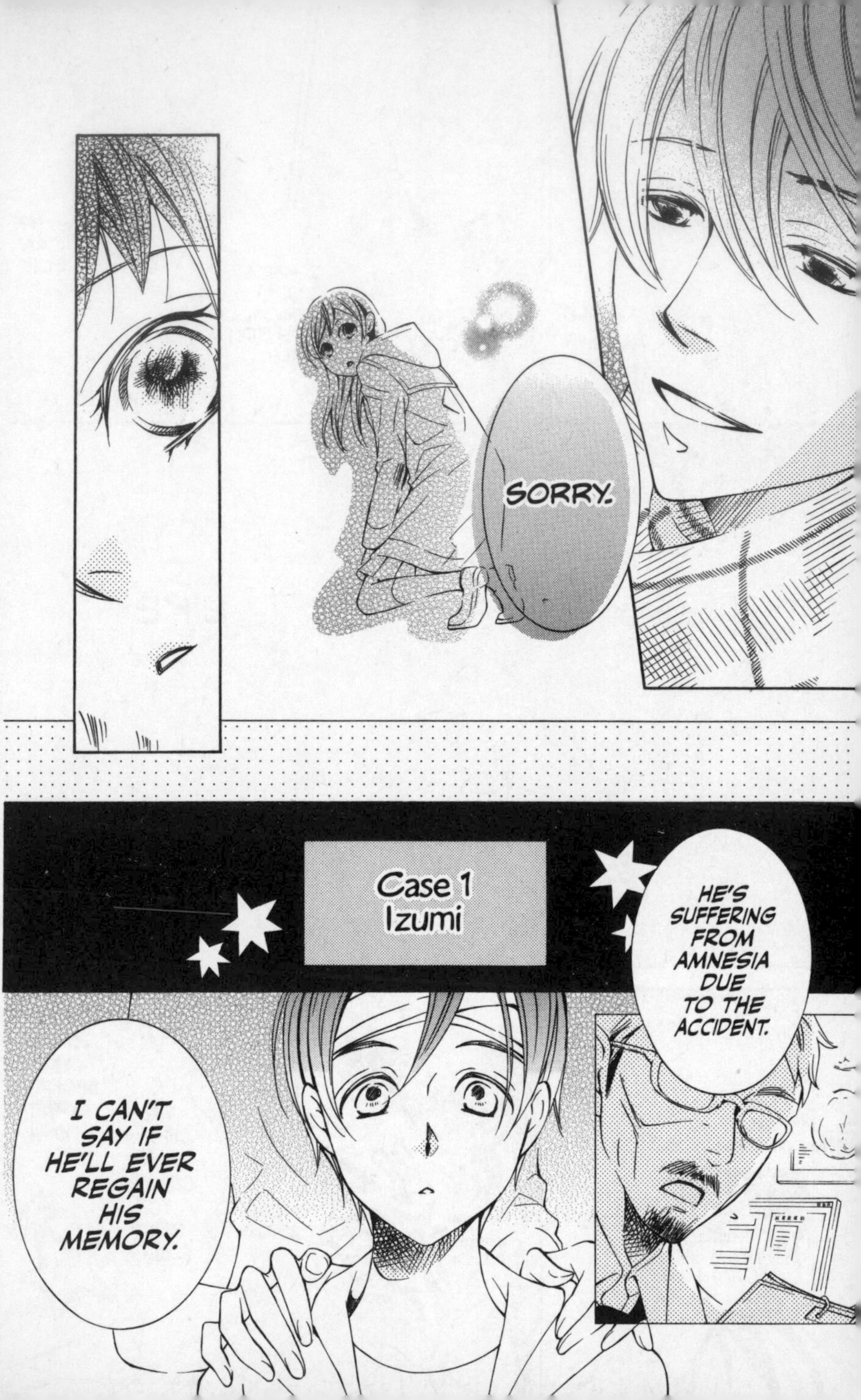
SORRY.
Case 1 Izumi
HE'S SUFFERING FROM AMNESIA DUE TO THE ACCIDENT.
I CAN'T SAY IF HE'LL EVER REGAIN HIS MEMORY.

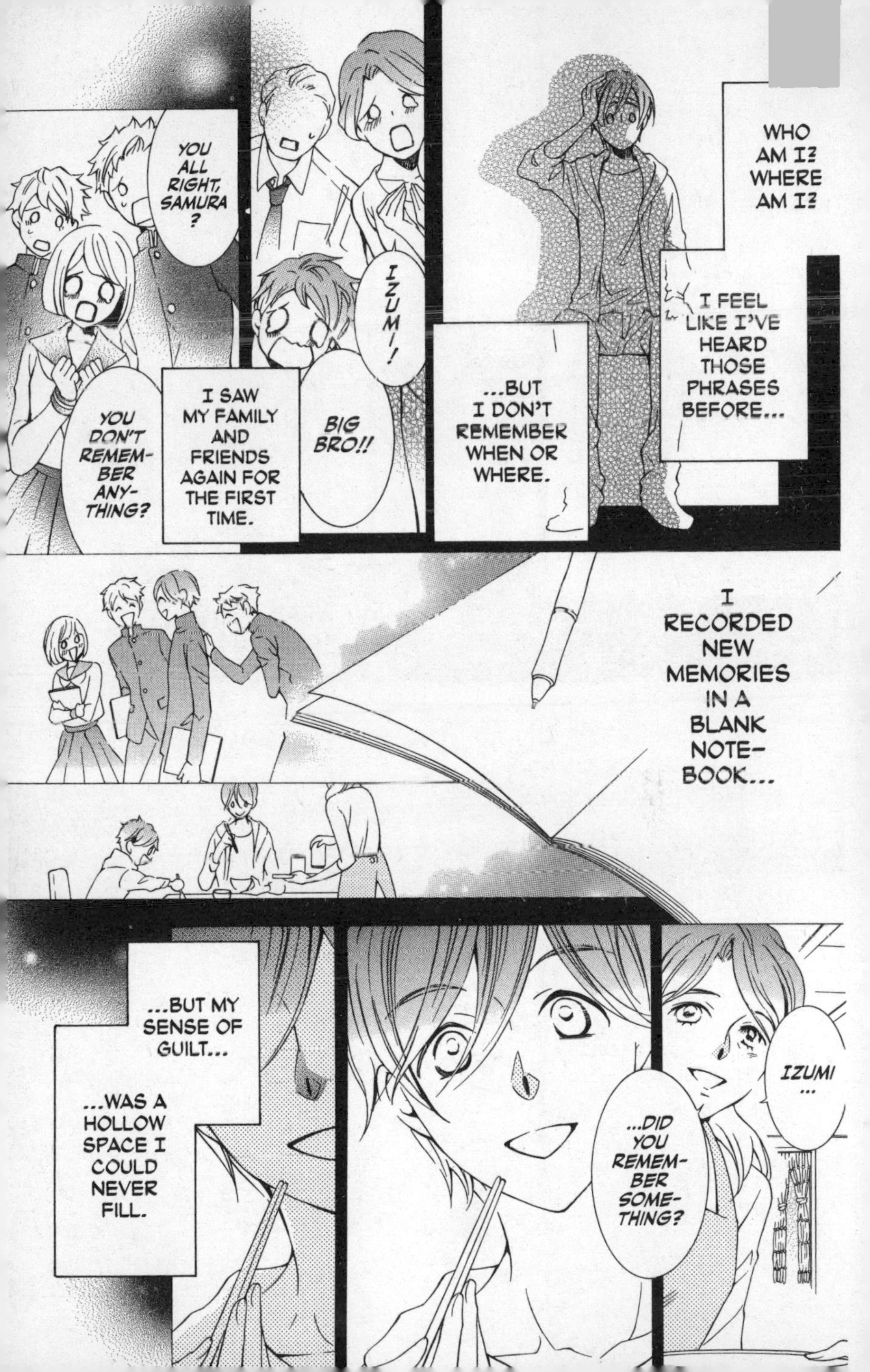
WHO AM I? WHERE AM I?
I FEEL LIKE I'VE HEARD THOSE PHRASES BEFORE...
...BUT I DON'T REMEMBER WHEN OR WHERE.
IZUMI!
BIG BRO!!
I SAW MY FAMILY AND FRIENDS AGAIN FOR THE FIRST TIME.
YOU ALL RIGHT, SAMURA?
YOU DON'T REMEMBER ANYTHING?
I RECORDED NEW MEMORIES IN A BLANK NOTEBOOK...
IZUMI...
...DID YOU REMEMBER SOMETHING?
...BUT MY SENSE OF GUILT...
...WAS A HOLLOW SPACE I COULD NEVER FILL.

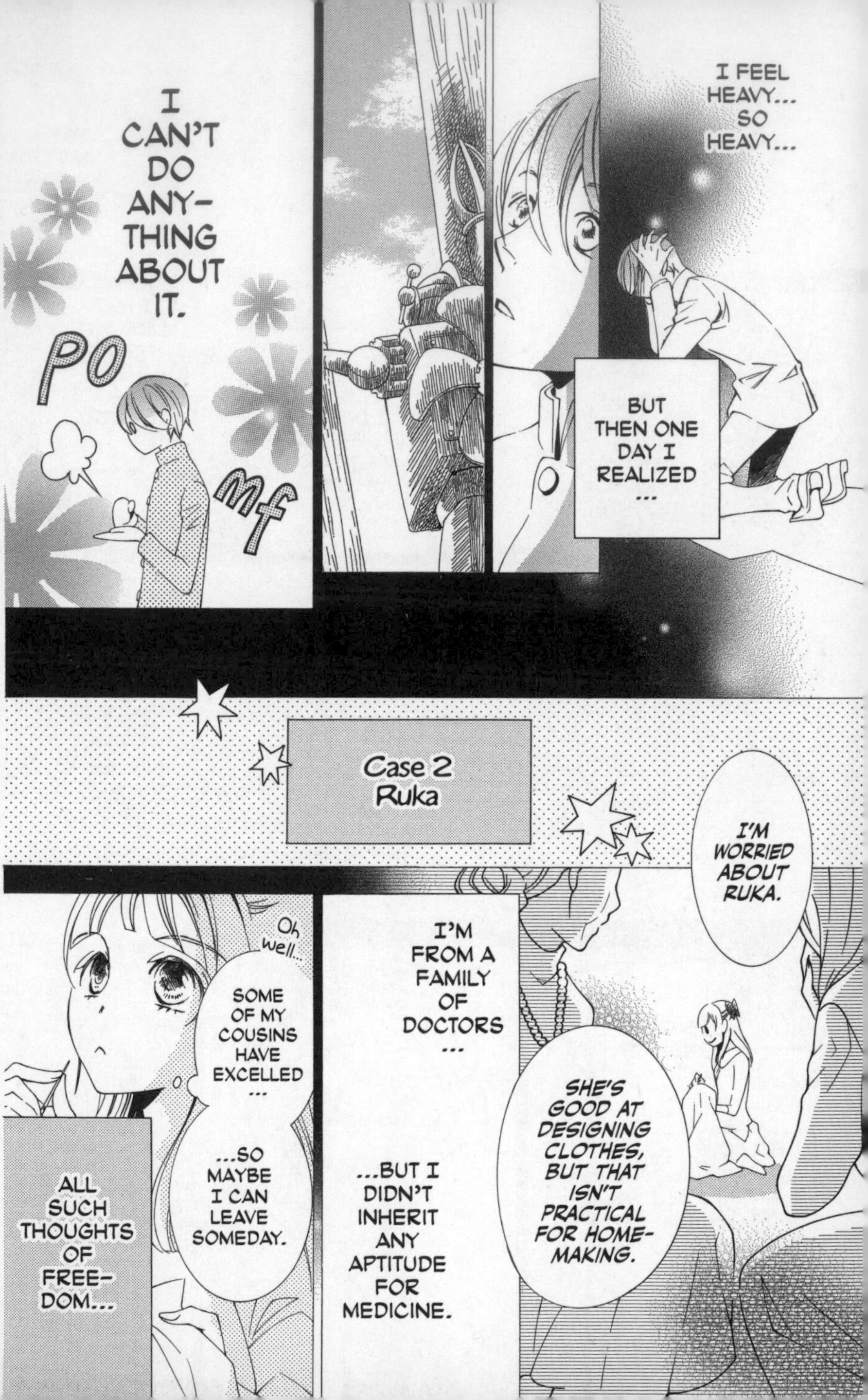
I FEEL HEAVY... SO HEAVY...
BUT THEN ONE DAY I REALIZED...
I CAN'T DO ANY-THING ABOUT IT.
PO
mf
Case 2
Ruka
I'M WORRIED ABOUT RUKA.
SHE'S GOOD AT DESIGNING CLOTHES, BUT THAT ISN'T PRACTICAL FOR HOME-MAKING.
I'M FROM A FAMILY OF DOCTORS...
...BUT I DIDN'T INHERIT ANY APTITUDE FOR MEDICINE.
Oh well...
SOME OF MY COUSINS HAVE EXCELLED...
...SO MAYBE I CAN LEAVE SOMEDAY.
ALL SUCH THOUGHTS OF FREE-DOM...

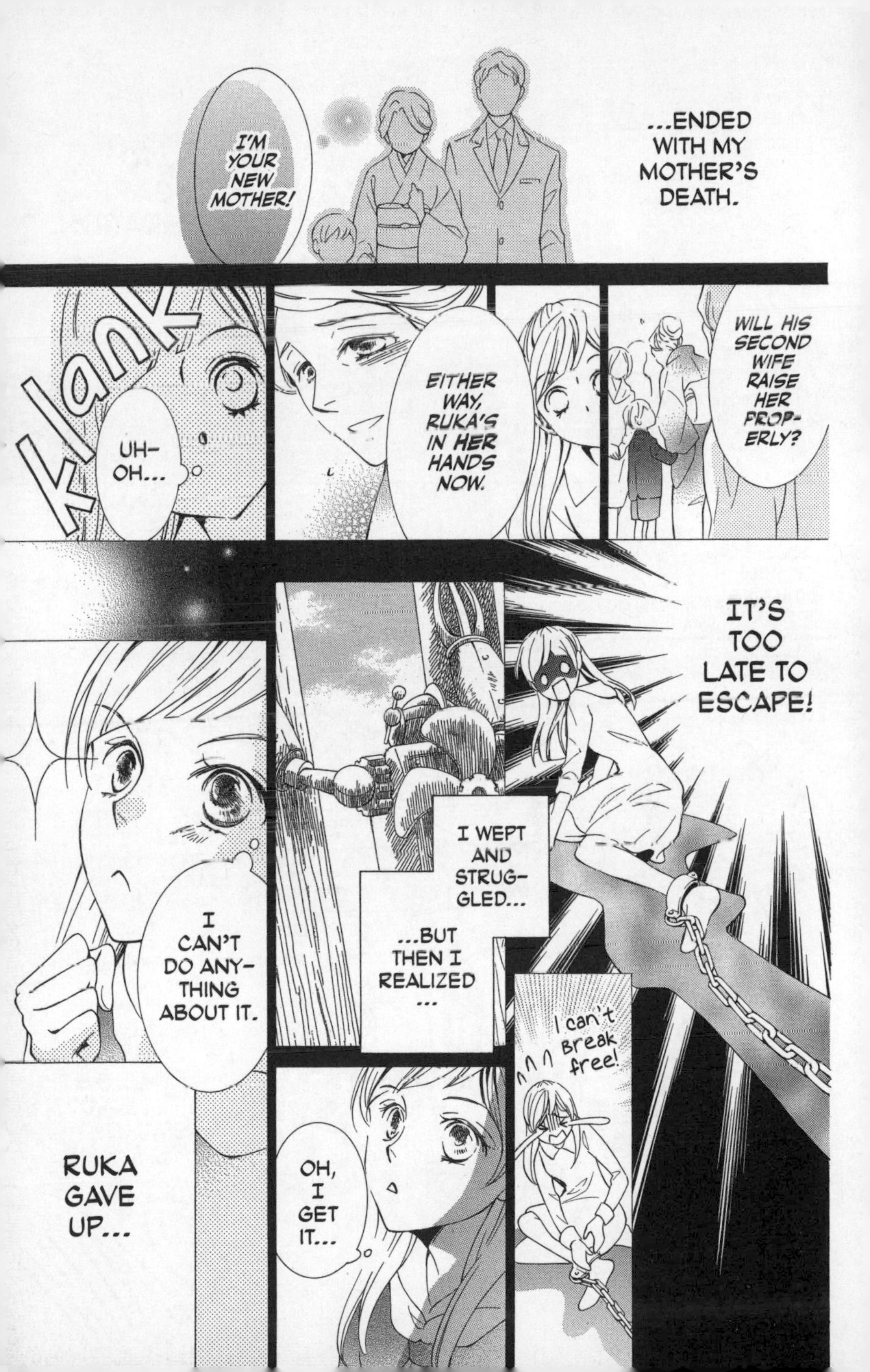
...ENDED WITH MY MOTHER'S DEATH.
I'M YOUR NEW MOTHER!
WILL HIS SECOND WIFE RAISE HER PROPERLY?
EITHER WAY, RUKA'S IN HER HANDS NOW.
Klank
UH-OH...
IT'S TOO LATE TO ESCAPE!
I can't break free!
I WEPT AND STRUGGLED...
...BUT THEN I REALIZED...
I CAN'T DO ANYTHING ABOUT IT.
OH, I GET IT...
RUKA GAVE UP...

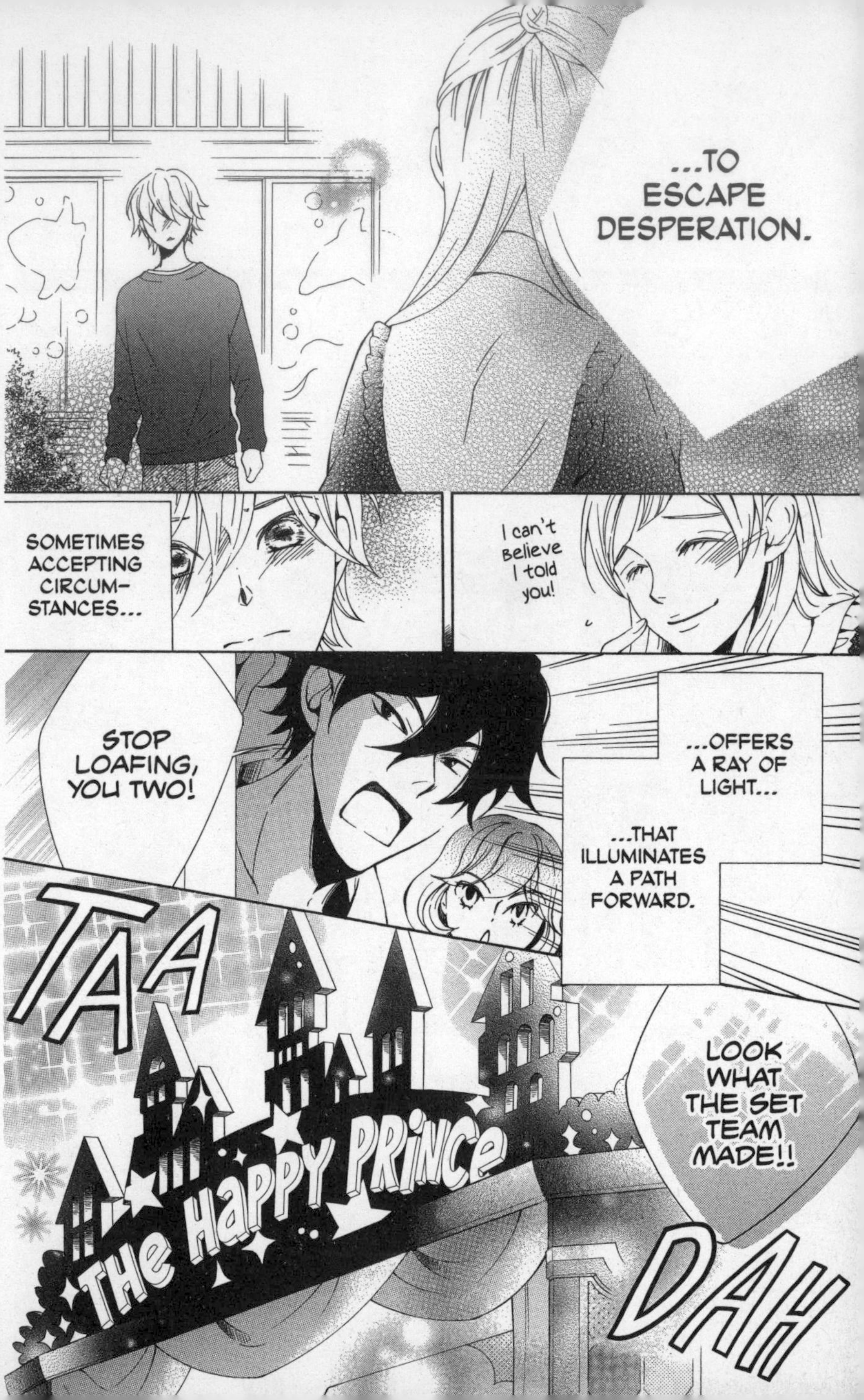
...TO ESCAPE DESPERATION.
I can't believe I told you!
SOMETIMES ACCEPTING CIRCUM-STANCES...
...OFFERS A RAY OF LIGHT...
...THAT ILLUMINATES A PATH FORWARD.
STOP LOAFING, YOU TWO!
LOOK WHAT THE SET TEAM MADE!!
TAA
The Happy Prince
DAH

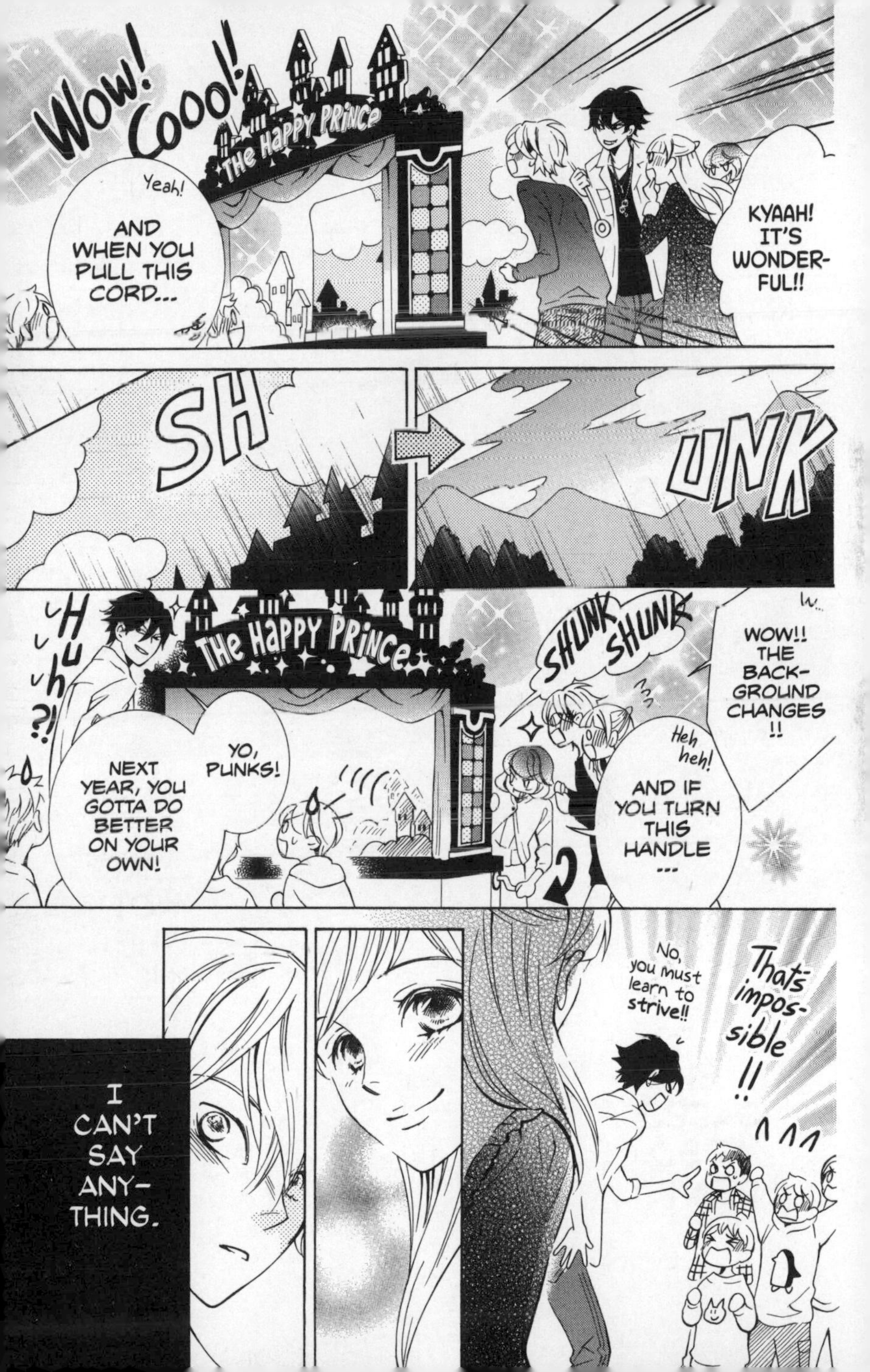
KYAAH! IT'S WONDERFUL!!
Wow! Coool!!
The Happy Prince
Yeah!
AND WHEN YOU PULL THIS CORD...
SH
UNK
w...
WOW!! THE BACKGROUND CHANGES !!
SHUNK SHUNK
Heh heh!
AND IF YOU TURN THIS HANDLE ...
The Happy Prince
Huh huh?!
YO, PUNKS!
NEXT YEAR, YOU GOTTA DO BETTER ON YOUR OWN!
That's impossible!!
No, you must learn to strive!!
I CAN'T SAY ANYTHING.

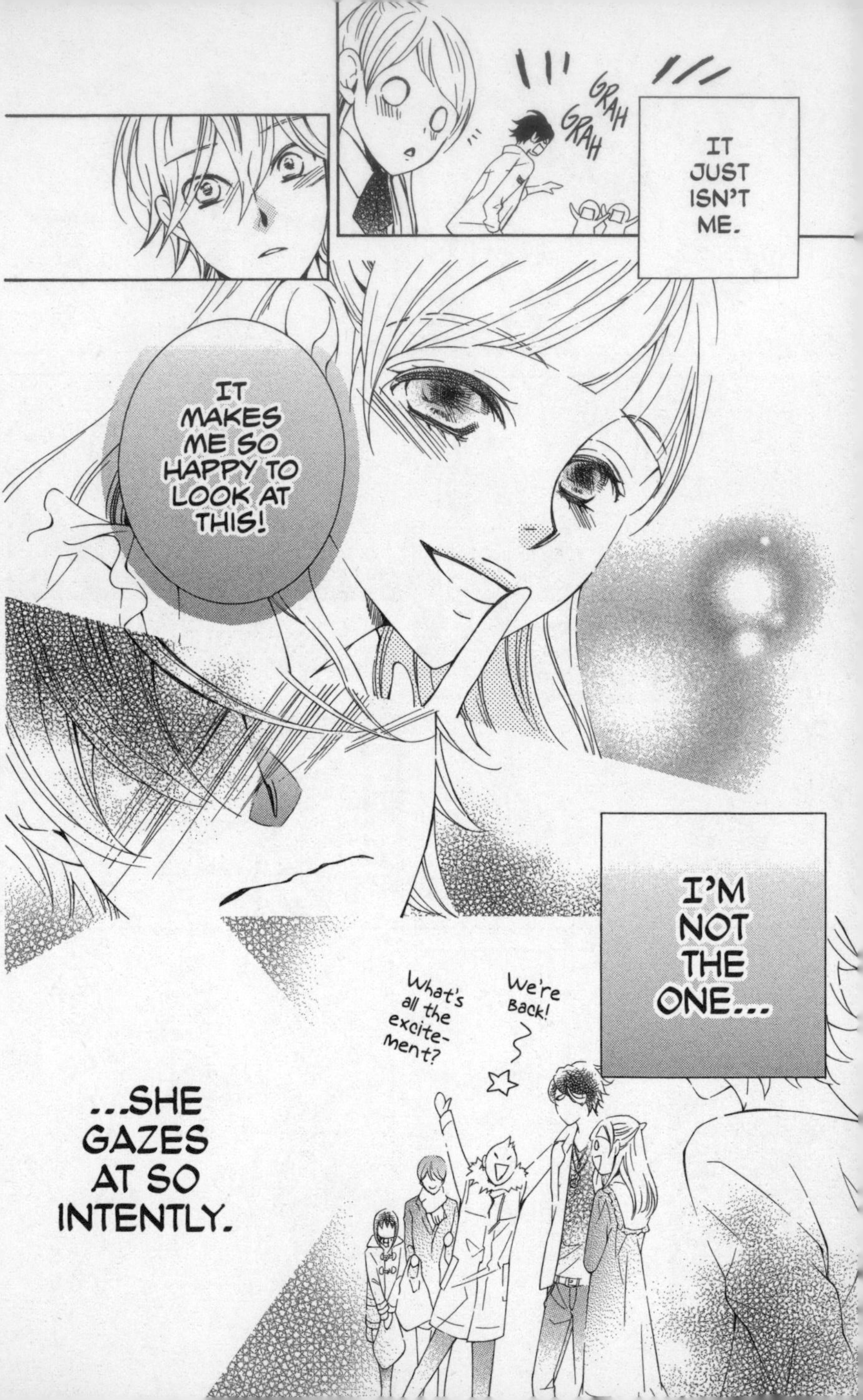
IT JUST ISN'T ME.
GRAH GRAH
IT MAKES ME SO HAPPY TO LOOK AT THIS!
I'M NOT THE ONE...
We're back!
What's all the excitement?
...SHE GAZES AT SO INTENTLY.

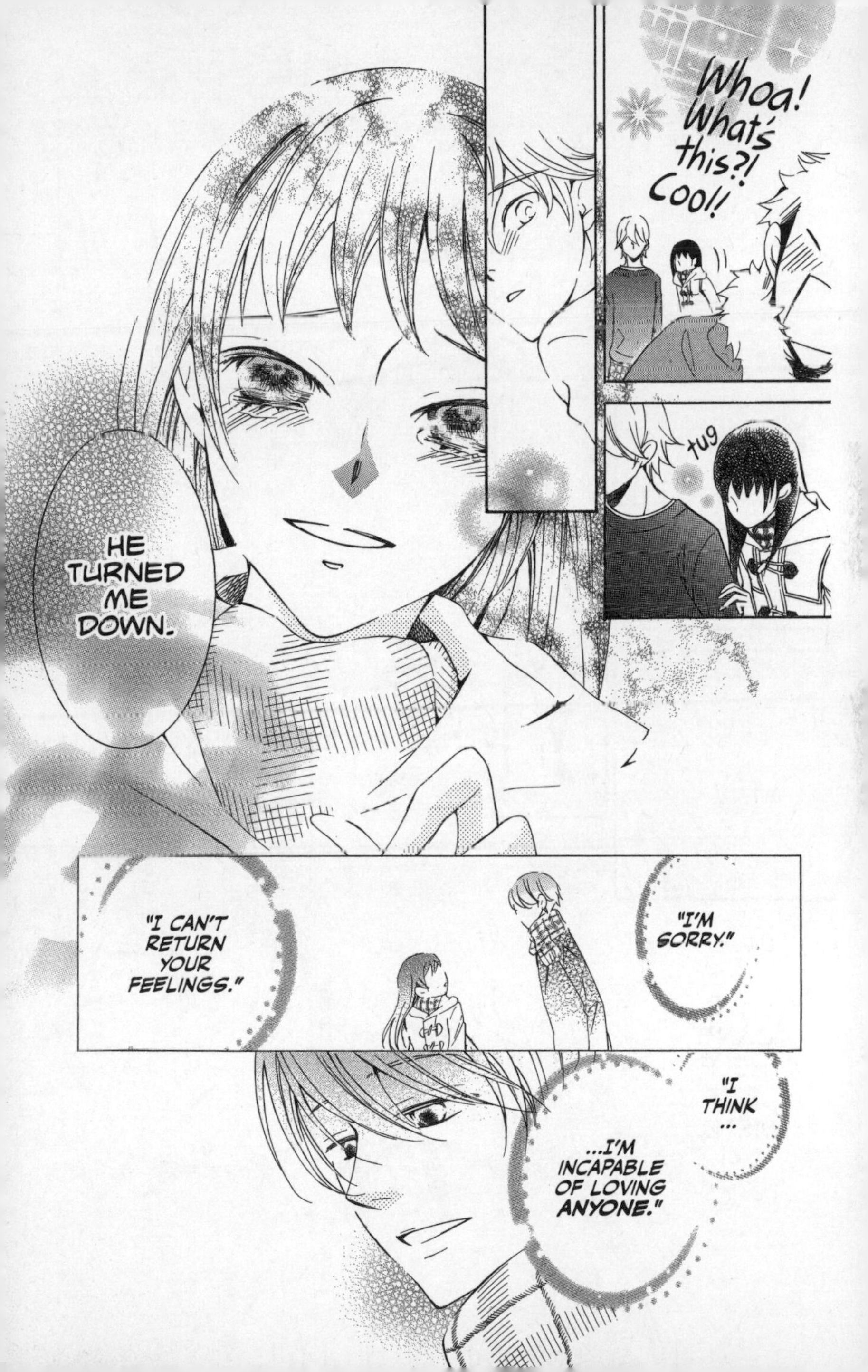
Whoa! What's this?! Cool!
tug
HE TURNED ME DOWN.
"I'M SORRY."
"I CAN'T RETURN YOUR FEELINGS."
"I THINK...
...I'M INCAPABLE OF LOVING ANYONE."

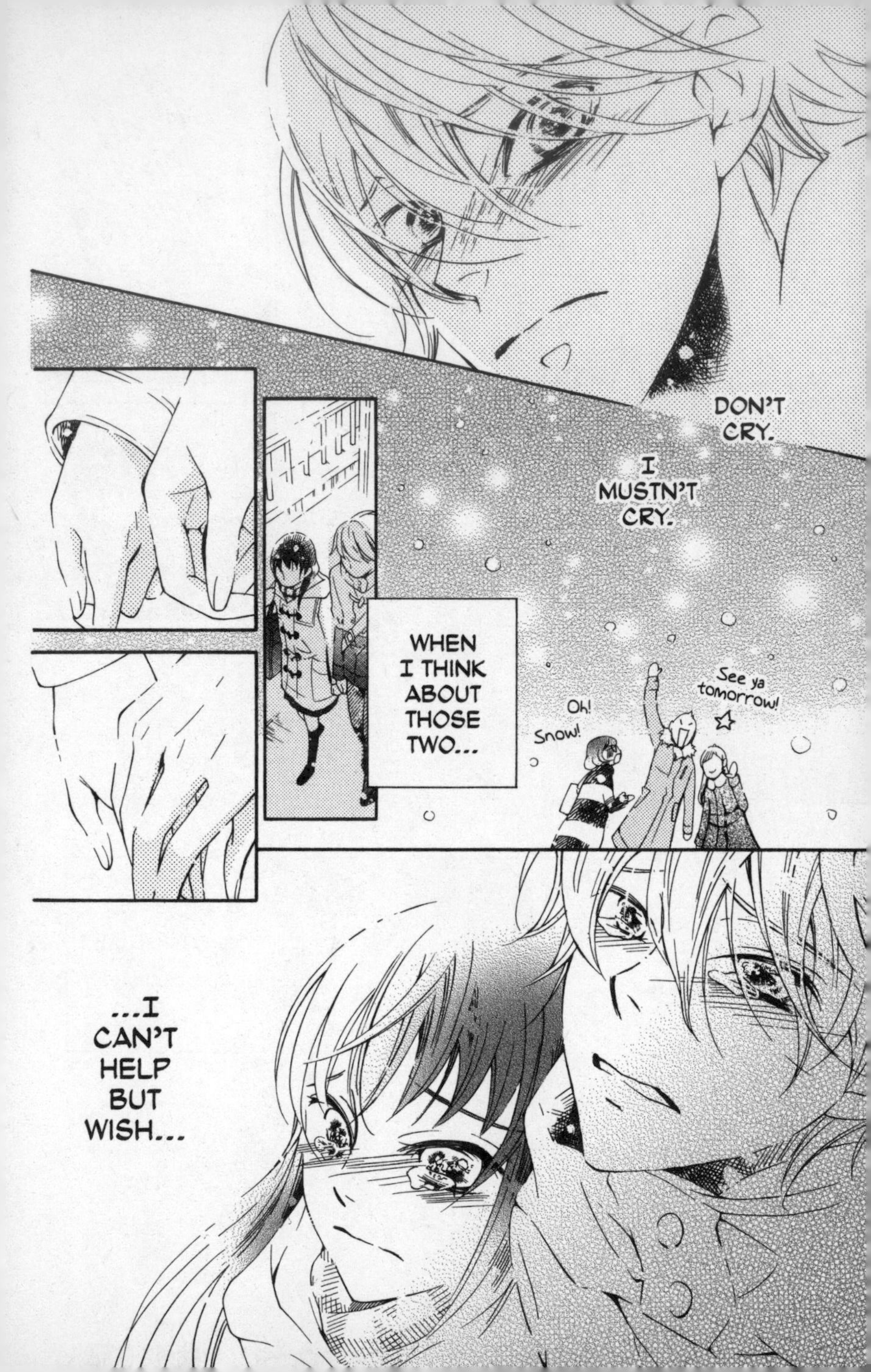
DON'T CRY.
I MUSTN'T CRY.
See ya tomorrow!
Oh! Snow!
WHEN I THINK ABOUT THOSE TWO...
...I CAN'T HELP BUT WISH...

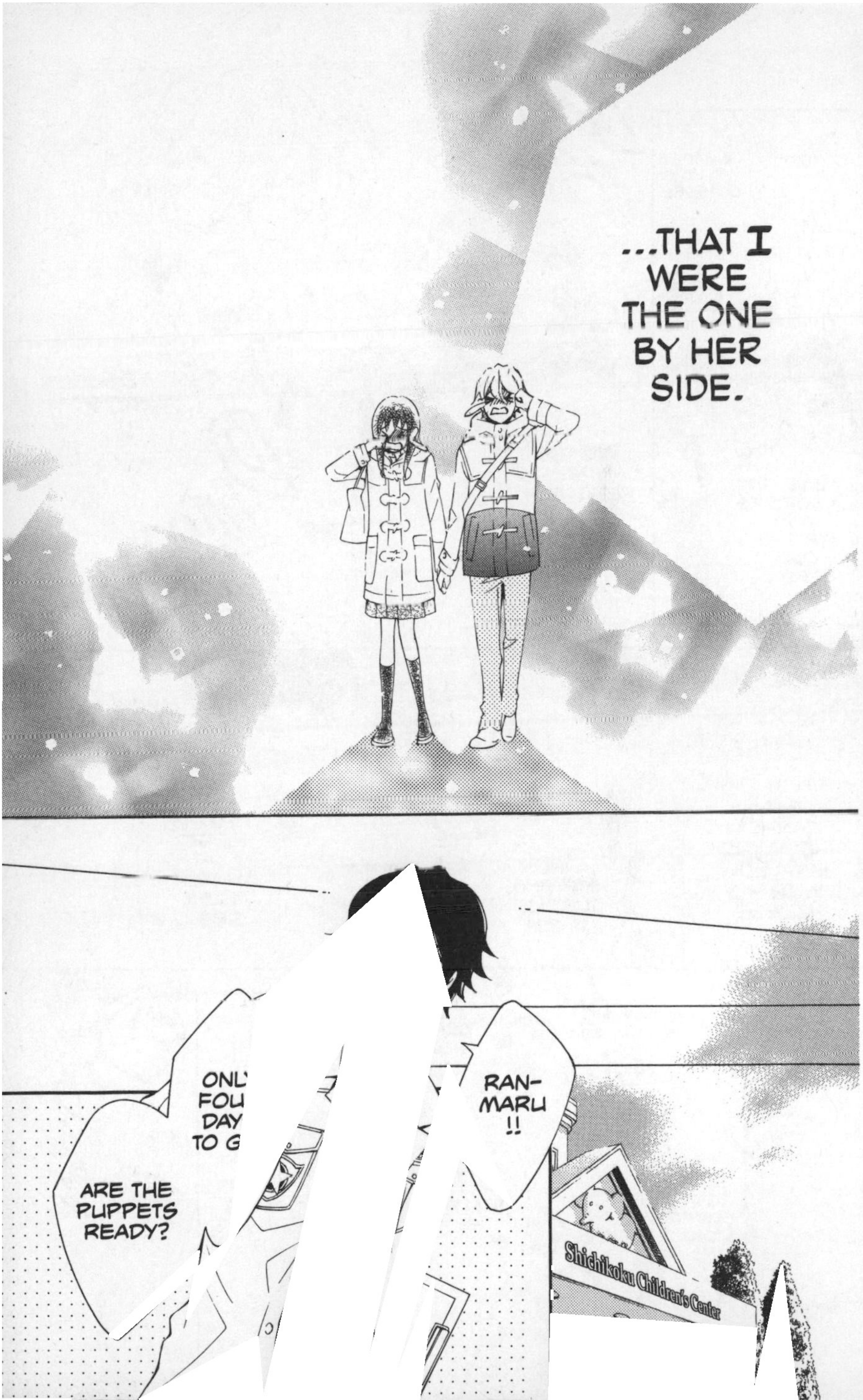
...THAT I WERE THE ONE BY HER SIDE.
RAN-MARU !!
ONLY FOU DAY TO G
ARE THE PUPPETS READY?
Shichikoku Children's Center

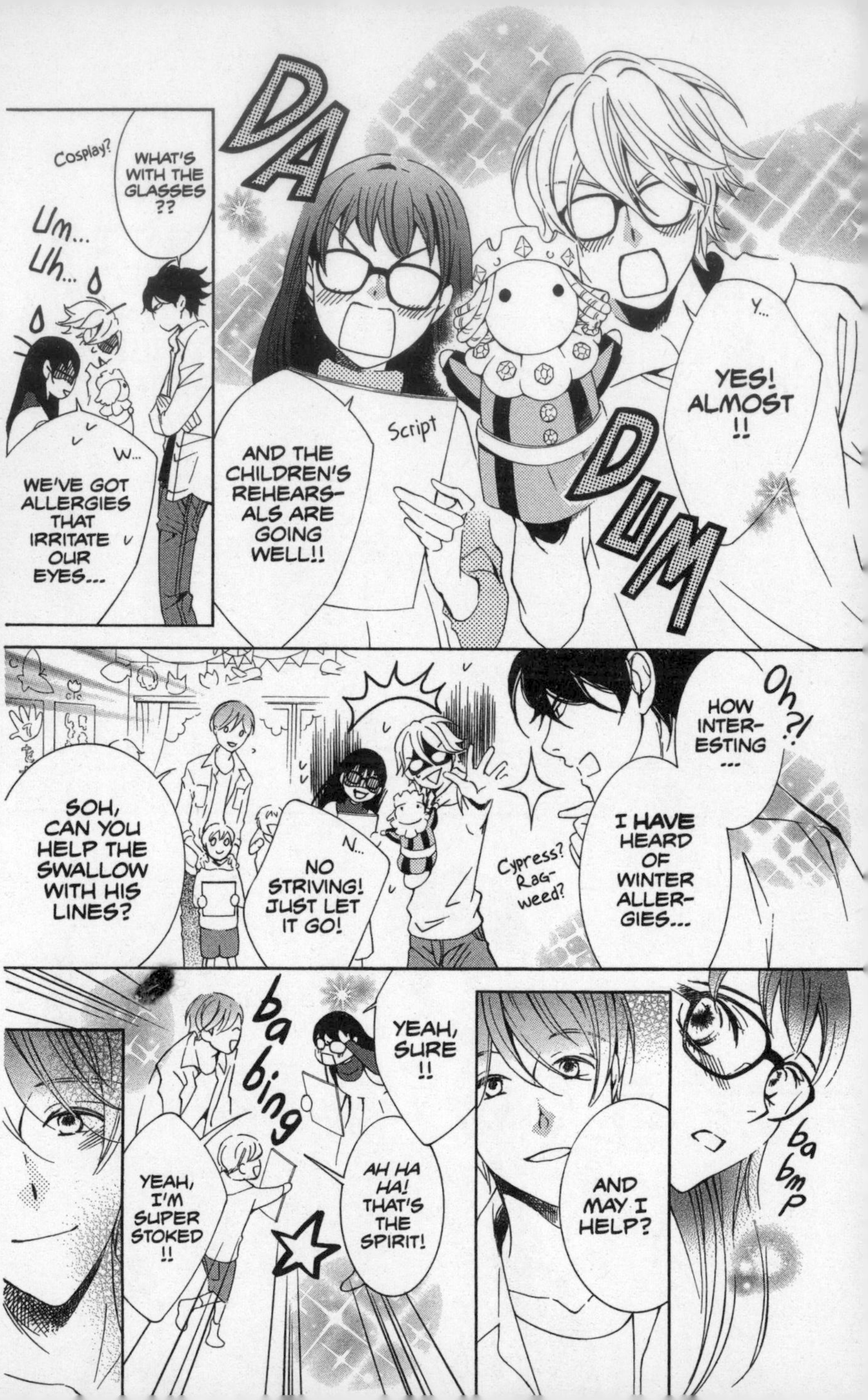
DA
Y...
YES! ALMOST!!
DUM
Script
AND THE CHILDREN'S REHEARS-ALS ARE GOING WELL!!
Cosplay?
WHAT'S WITH THE GLASSES??
Um... Uh...
W...
WE'VE GOT ALLERGIES THAT IRRITATE OUR EYES...
Oh?!
HOW INTER-ESTING...
I HAVE HEARD OF WINTER ALLER-GIES...
Cypress? Rag-weed?
N...
NO STRIVING! JUST LET IT GO!
SOH, CAN YOU HELP THE SWALLOW WITH HIS LINES?
ba bmp
AND MAY I HELP?
YEAH, SURE!!
ba bing
AH HA HA! THAT'S THE SPIRIT!
YEAH, I'M SUPER STOKED!!

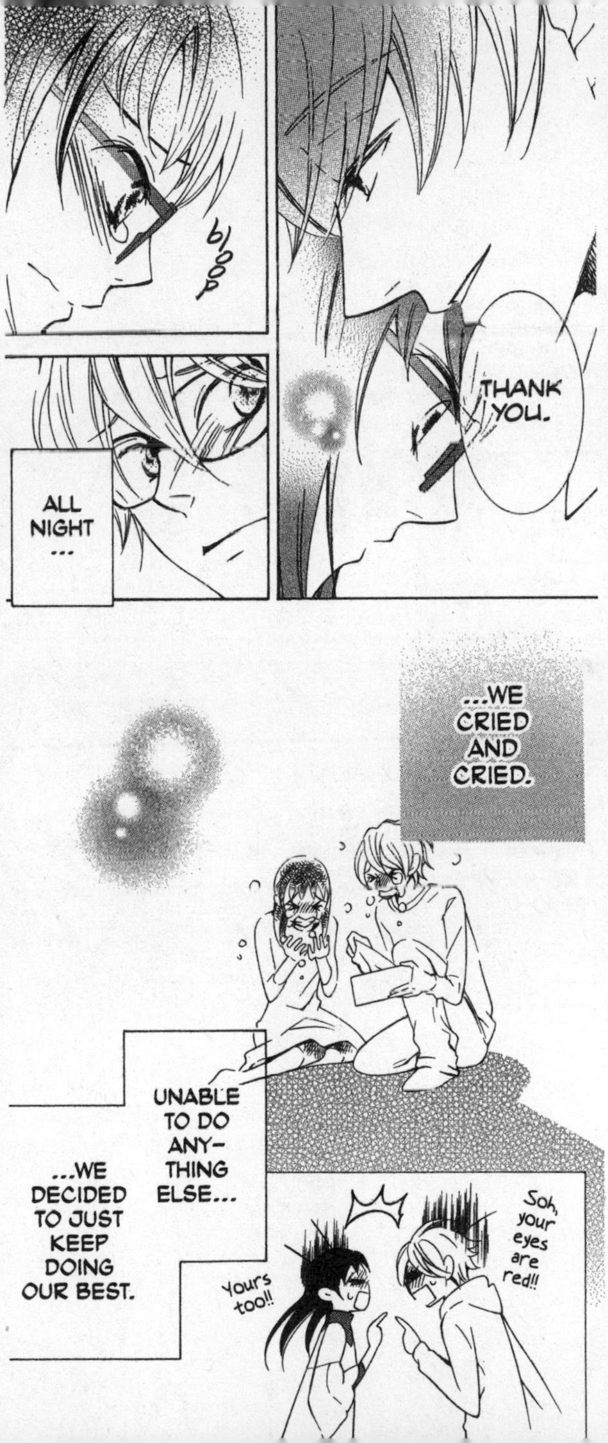
THANK YOU.
bloop
ALL NIGHT...
...WE CRIED AND CRIED.
UNABLE TO DO ANYTHING ELSE...
...WE DECIDED TO JUST KEEP DOING OUR BEST.
Soh, your eyes are red!!
Yours too!!

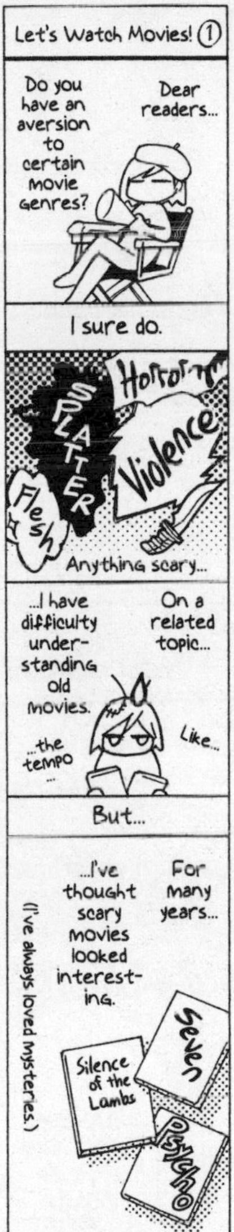
Let's Watch Movies! ①
Dear readers...
Do you have an aversion to certain movie genres?
I sure do.
Horror
SPLATTER
Violence
Flesh
Anything scary...
On a related topic...
...I have difficulty under-standing old movies.
Like...
...the tempo...
But...
For many years...
...I've thought scary movies looked interest-ing.
(I've always loved mysteries.)
Seven
Silence of the Lambs
Psycho
It'd be great if I understood old masterpieces!

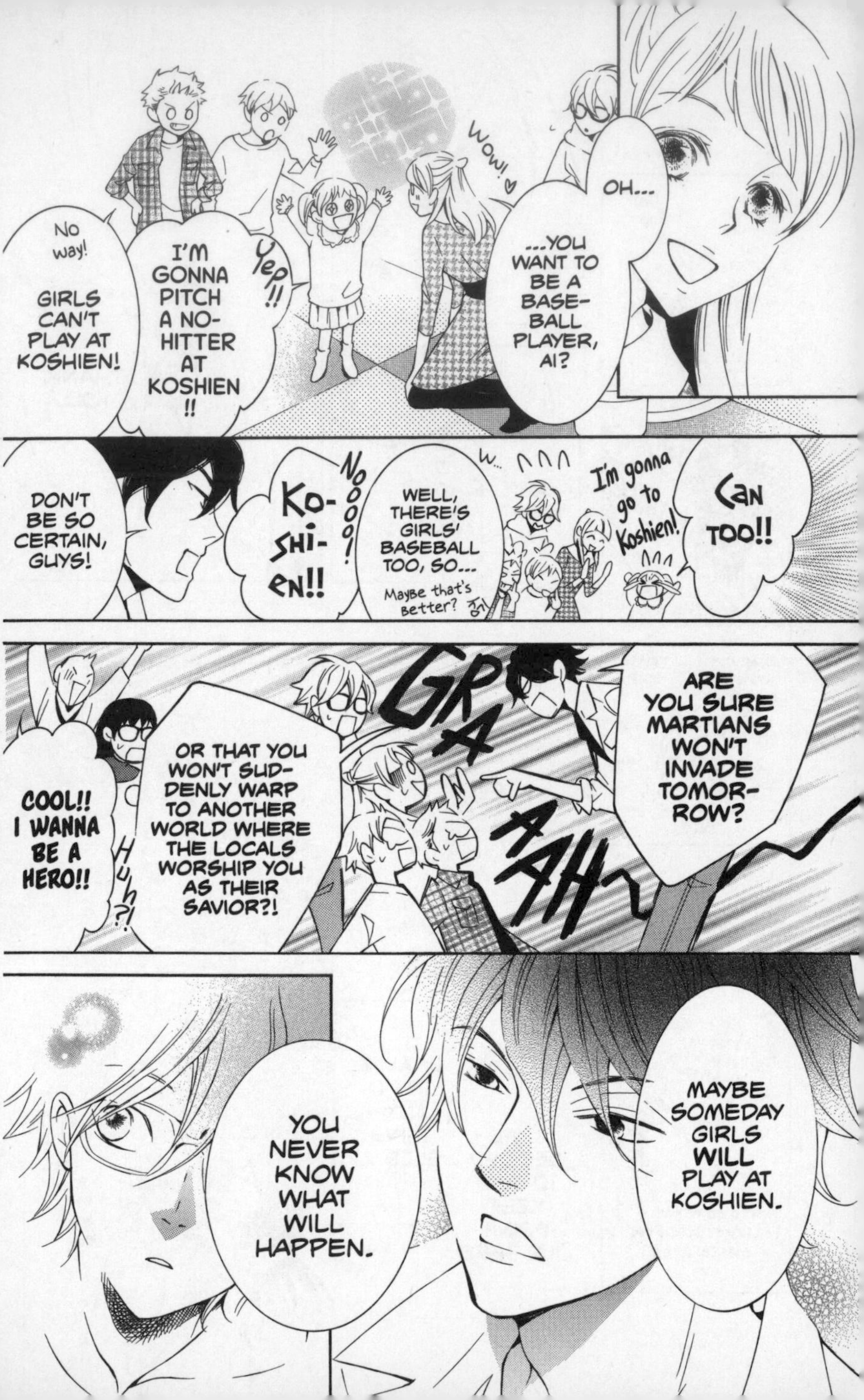
OH...
...YOU WANT TO BE A BASE-BALL PLAYER, AI?
WOW! ♥
YEP!!
I'M GONNA PITCH A NO-HITTER AT KOSHIEN!!
No way!
GIRLS CAN'T PLAY AT KOSHIEN!
CAN TOO!!
I'm gonna go to Koshien!
WELL, THERE'S GIRLS' BASEBALL TOO, SO...
Maybe that's better?
W...
NOOOOO!
KO-SHI-EN!!
DON'T BE SO CERTAIN, GUYS!
ARE YOU SURE MARTIANS WON'T INVADE TOMOR-ROW?
GRAAAH~
OR THAT YOU WON'T SUD-DENLY WARP TO ANOTHER WORLD WHERE THE LOCALS WORSHIP YOU AS THEIR SAVIOR?!
Huh?!
COOL!! I WANNA BE A HERO!!
MAYBE SOMEDAY GIRLS WILL PLAY AT KOSHIEN.
YOU NEVER KNOW WHAT WILL HAPPEN.

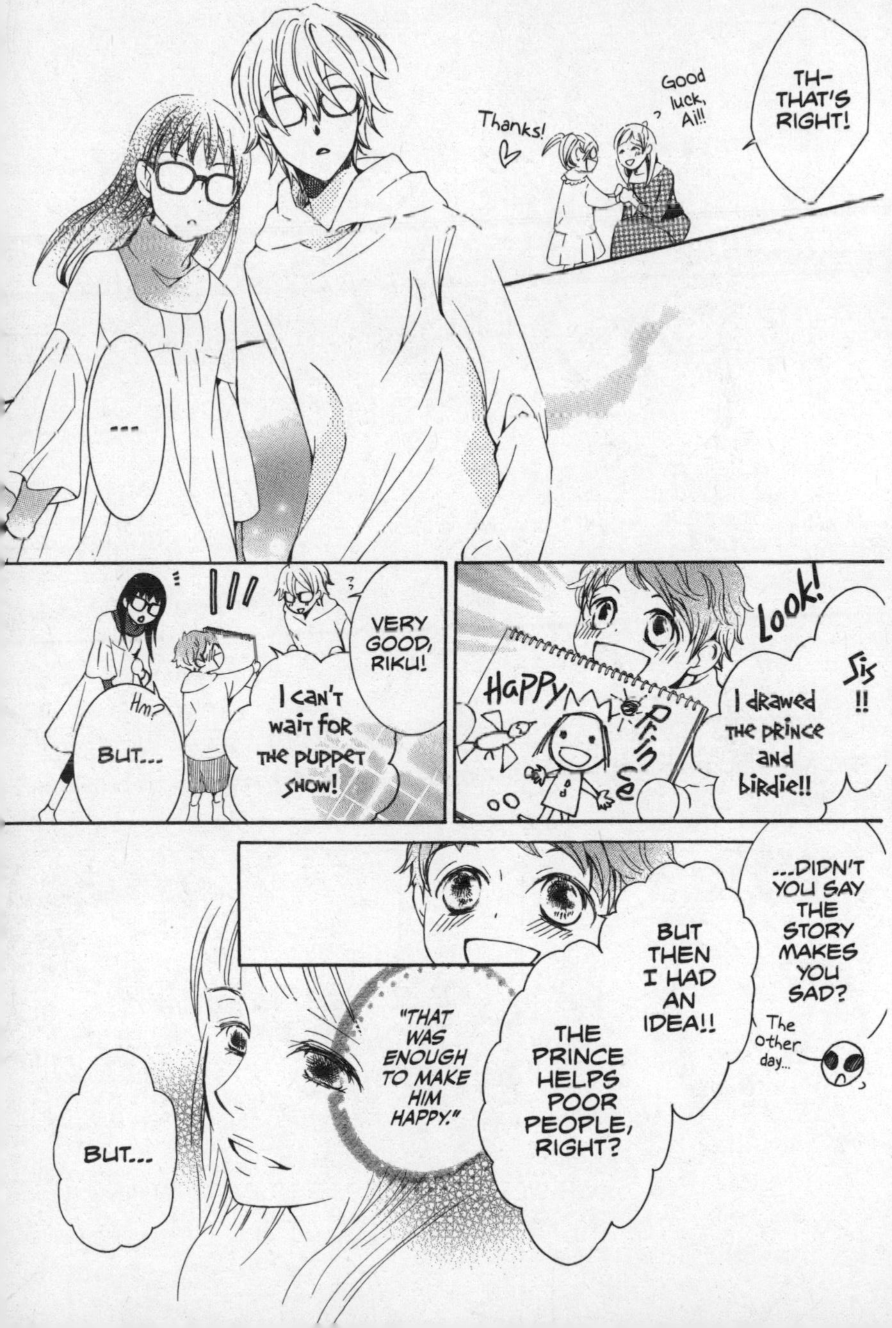
TH-THAT'S RIGHT!
Good luck, Ai!!
Thanks!
...
Look!
Sis!!
I drawed the prince and birdie!!
Happy Prince
VERY GOOD, RIKU!
I can't wait for the puppet show!
Hm?
BUT...
...DIDN'T YOU SAY THE STORY MAKES YOU SAD?
The other day...
BUT THEN I HAD AN IDEA!!
THE PRINCE HELPS POOR PEOPLE, RIGHT?
"THAT WAS ENOUGH TO MAKE HIM HAPPY."
BUT...

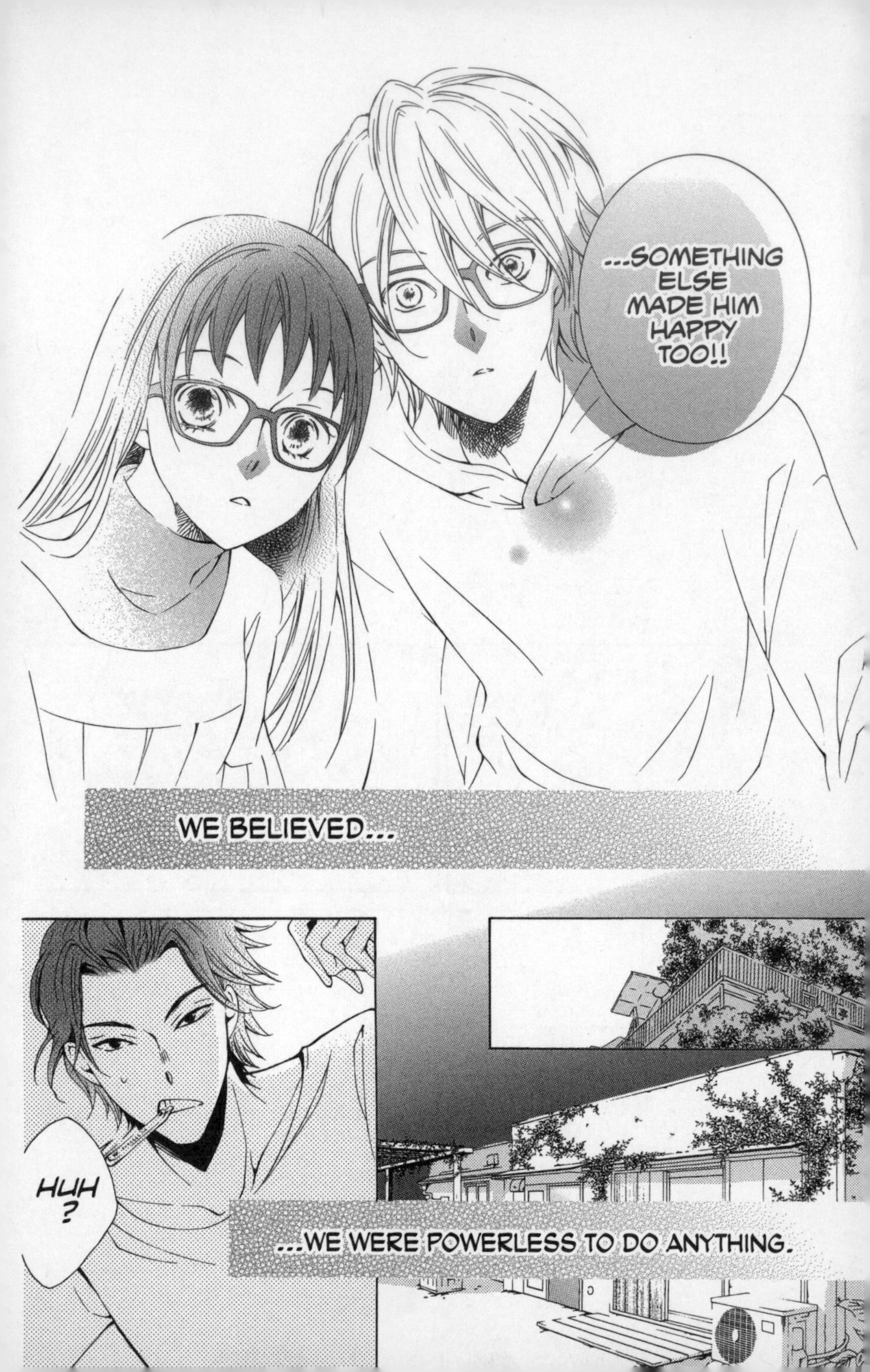
...SOMETHING ELSE MADE HIM HAPPY TOO!!
WE BELIEVED...
...WE WERE POWERLESS TO DO ANYTHING.
HUH?

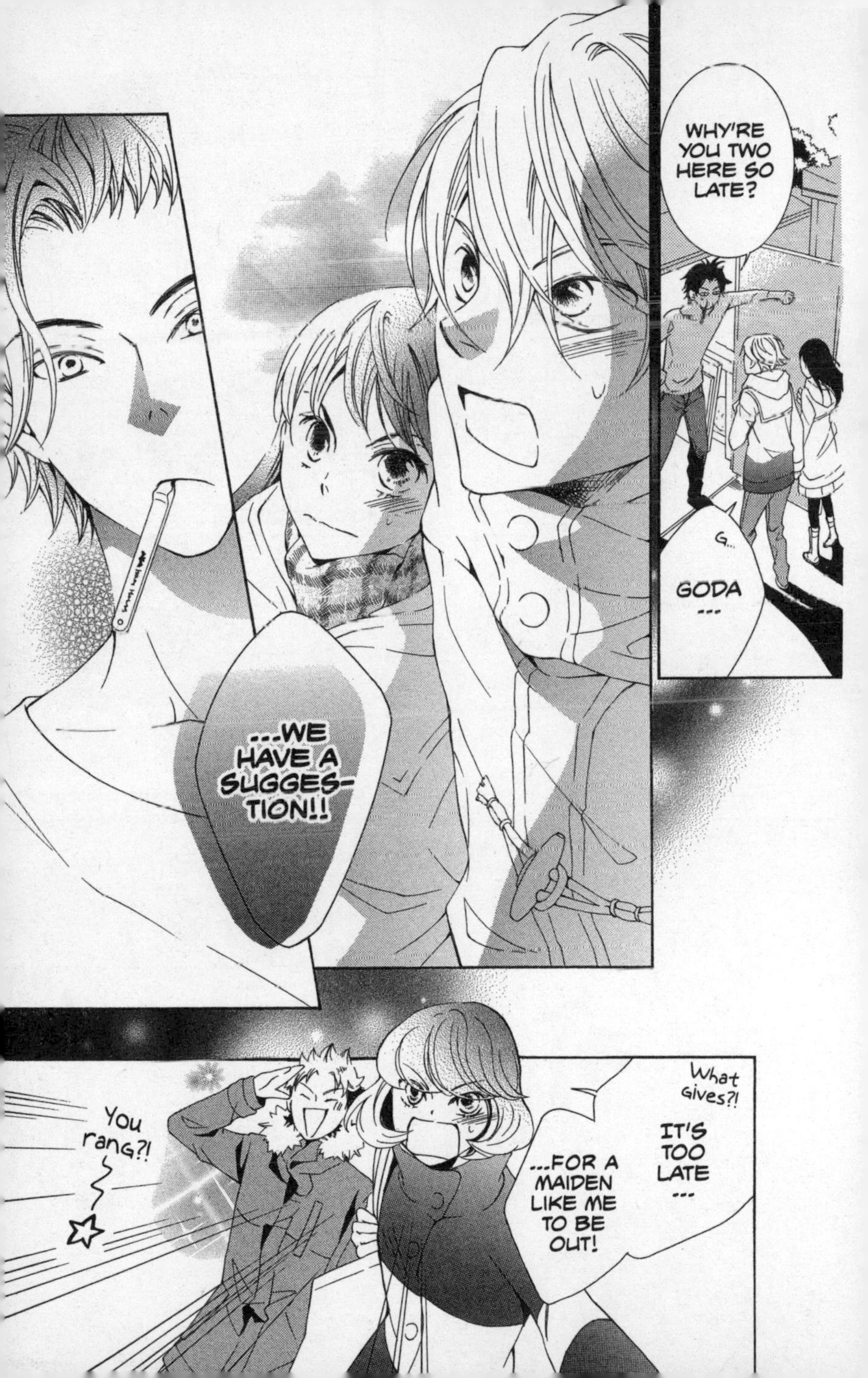
WHY'RE YOU TWO HERE SO LATE?
G...
GODA...
...WE HAVE A SUGGESTION!!
What gives?!
IT'S TOO LATE...
...FOR A MAIDEN LIKE ME TO BE OUT!
You rang?!

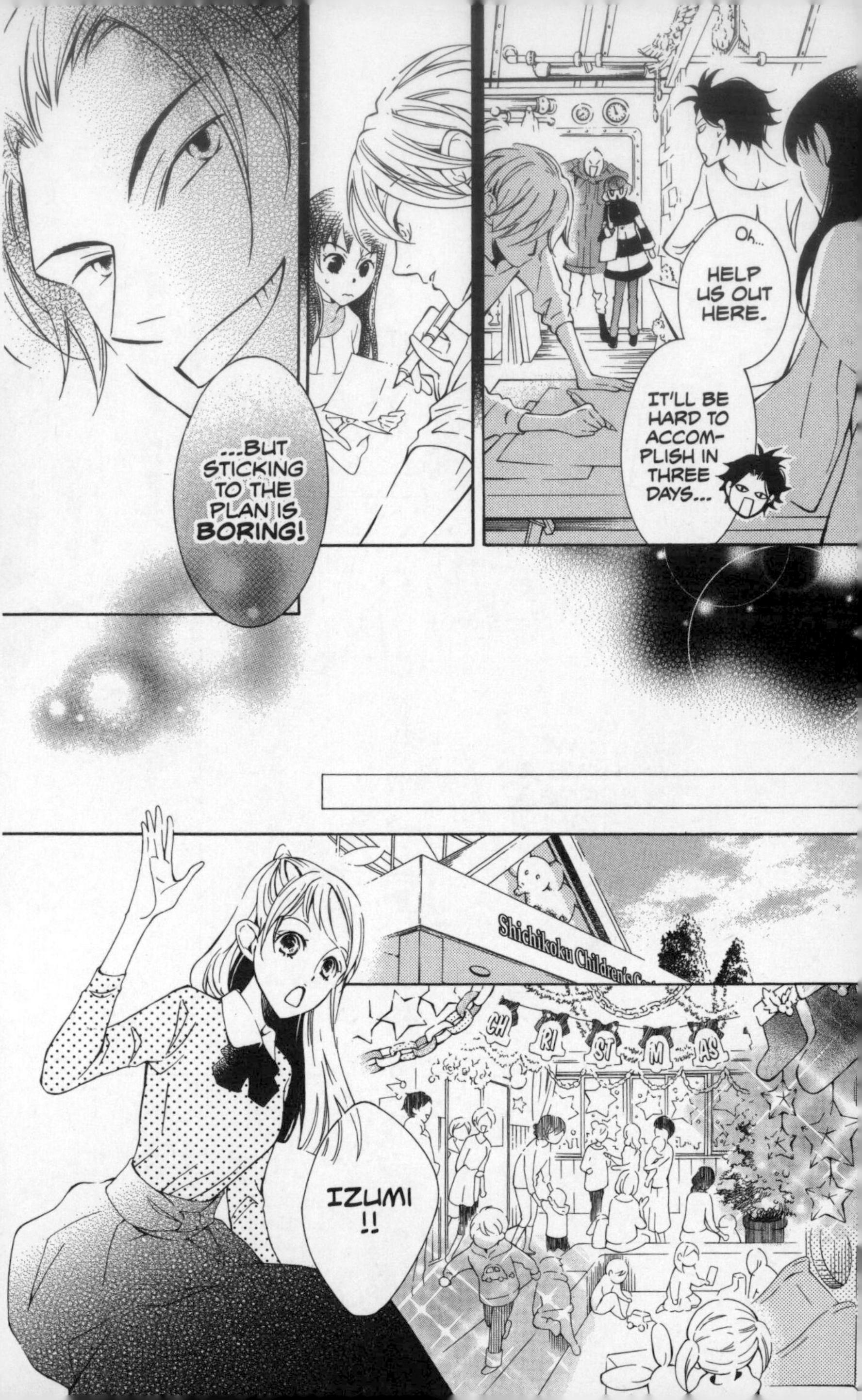
Oh...
HELP US OUT HERE.
IT'LL BE HARD TO ACCOMPLISH IN THREE DAYS...
...BUT STICKING TO THE PLAN IS BORING!
Shichikoku Children's
CH RI ST M AS
IZUMI !!

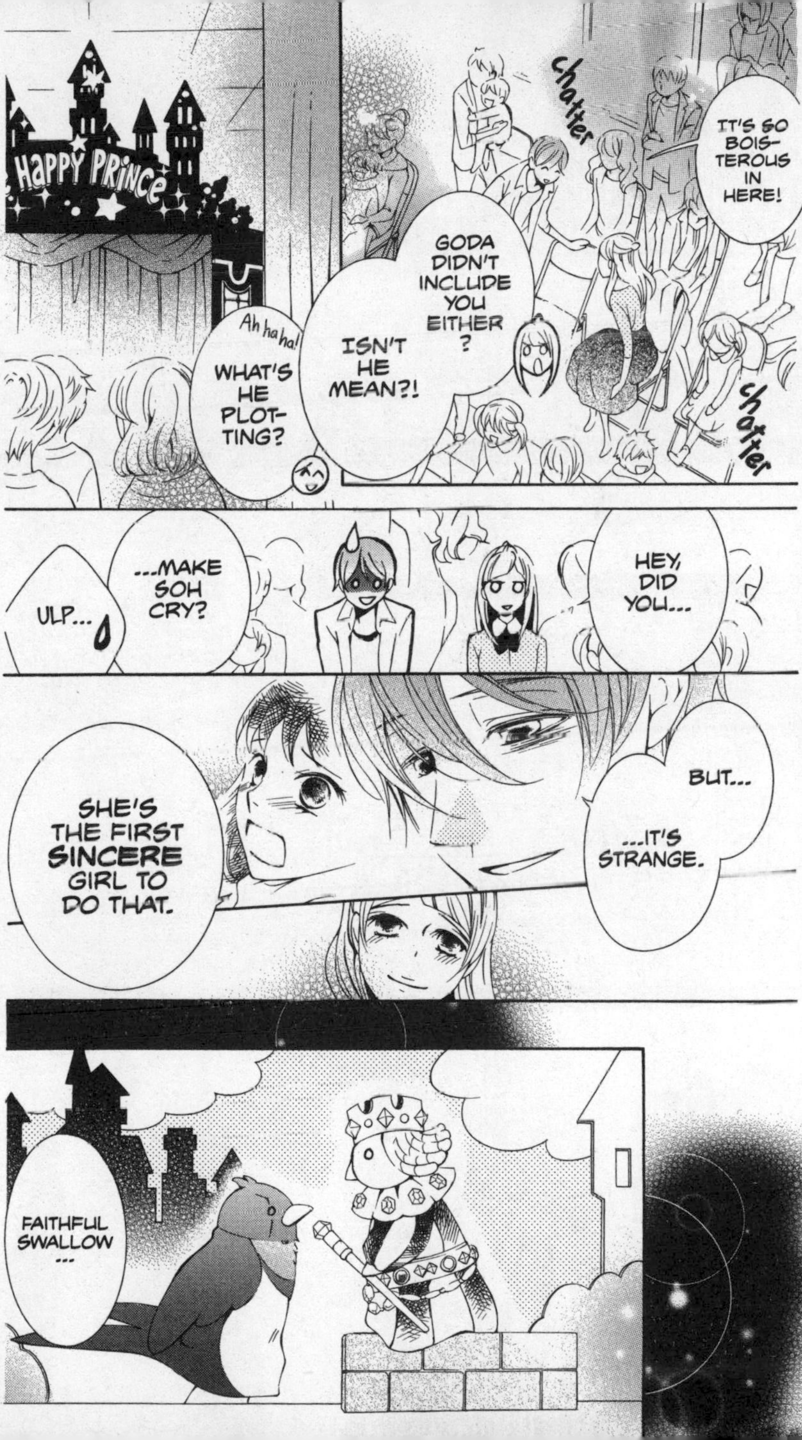
chatter
IT'S SO BOIS-TEROUS IN HERE!
chatter
GODA DIDN'T INCLUDE YOU EITHER?
ISN'T HE MEAN?!
HAPPY PRINCE
Ah ha ha!
WHAT'S HE PLOT-TING?
HEY, DID YOU...
...MAKE SOH CRY?
ULP...
BUT...
...IT'S STRANGE.
SHE'S THE FIRST SINCERE GIRL TO DO THAT.
FAITHFUL SWALLOW...

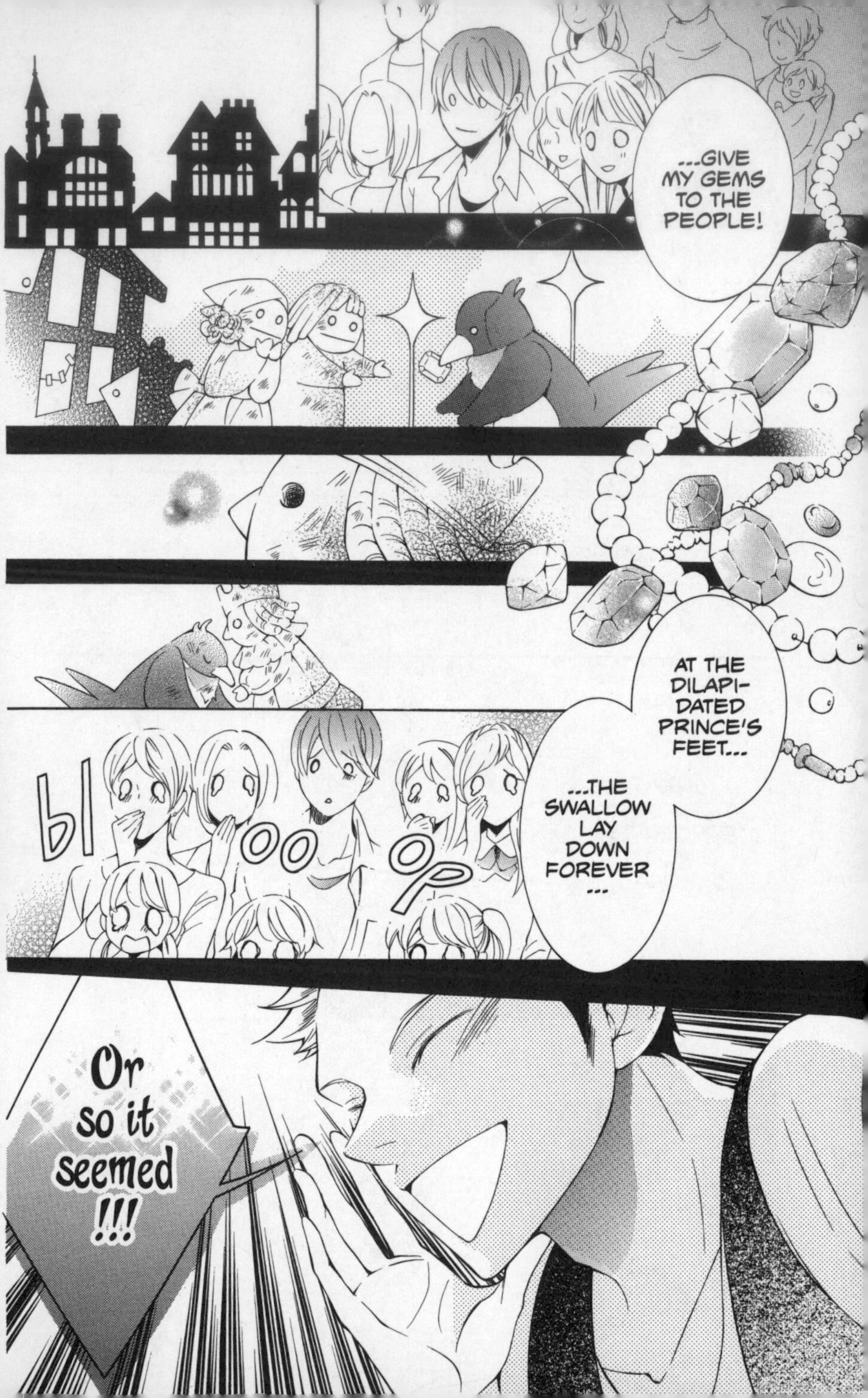
...GIVE MY GEMS TO THE PEOPLE!
AT THE DILAPI-DATED PRINCE'S FEET...
...THE SWALLOW LAY DOWN FOREVER ...
bl oo op
Or so it seemed !!!

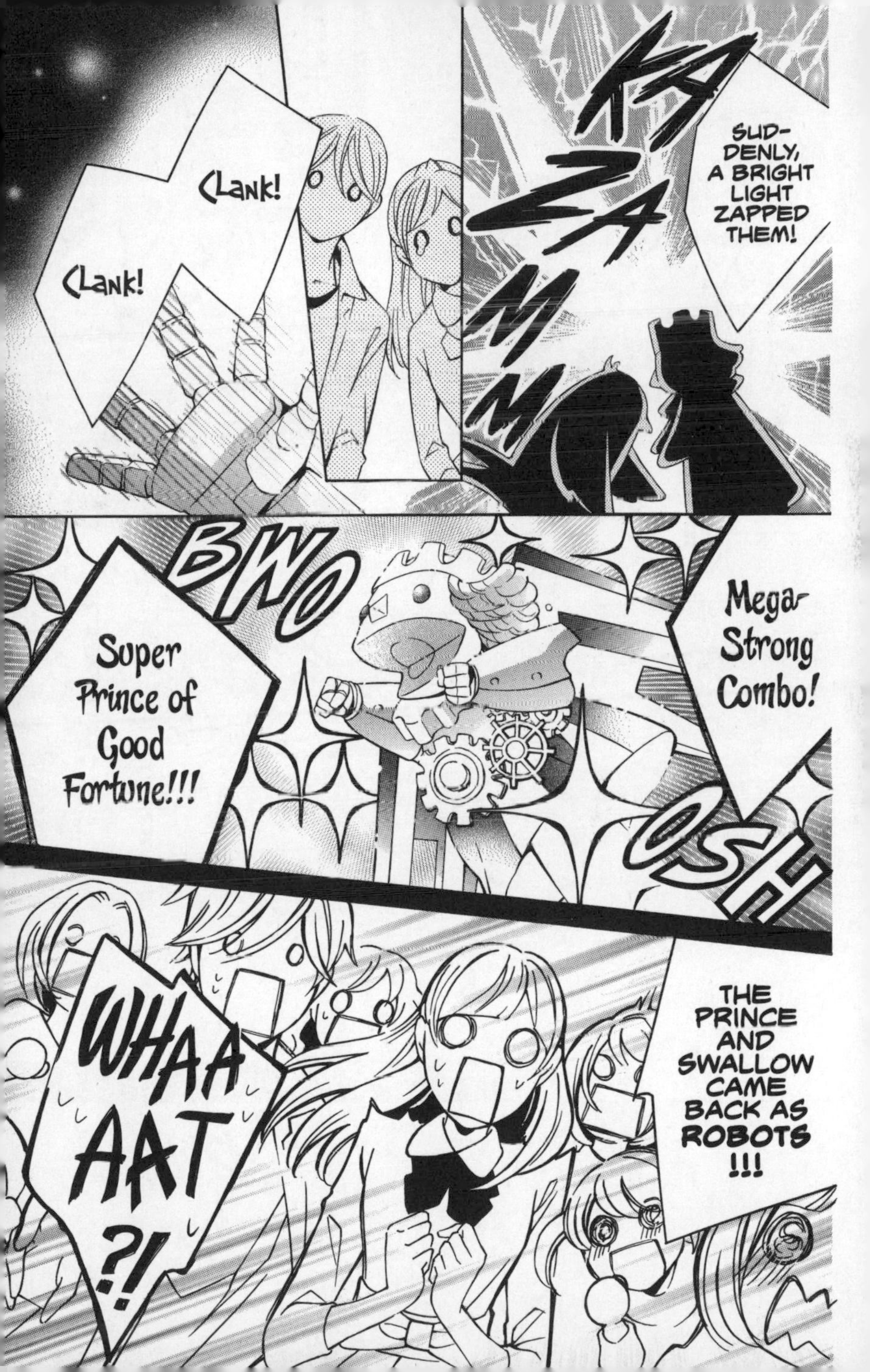
KAZAMMM
SUDDENLY, A BRIGHT LIGHT ZAPPED THEM!
CLANK!
CLANK!
Mega-Strong Combo!
BWO
OSH
Super Prince of Good Fortune!!!
THE PRINCE AND SWALLOW CAME BACK AS ROBOTS!!!
WHAAAAT?!

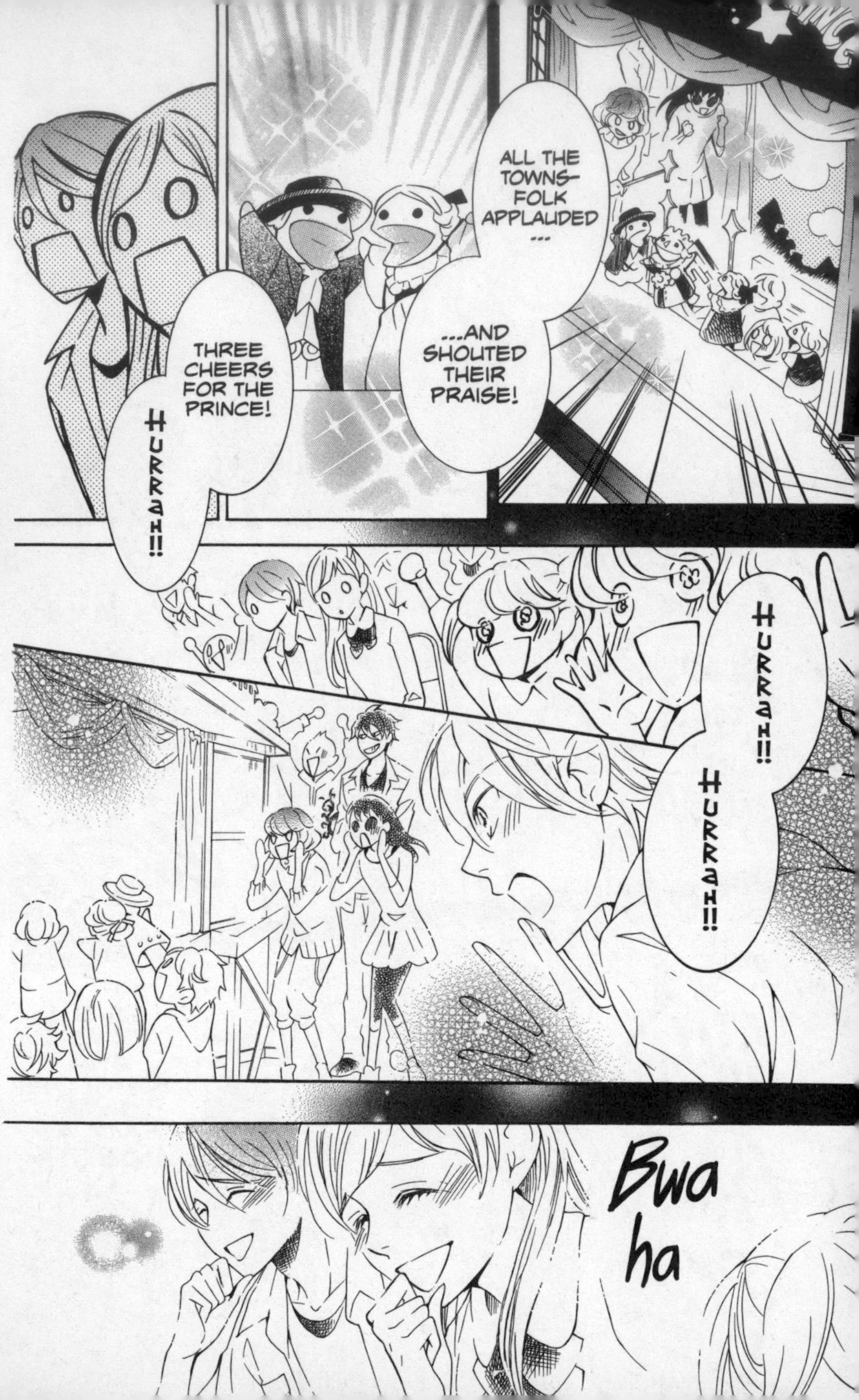
ALL THE TOWNS-FOLK APPLAUDED ...
...AND SHOUTED THEIR PRAISE!
THREE CHEERS FOR THE PRINCE!
HURRAH!!
HURRAH!!
HURRAH!!
Bwa ha

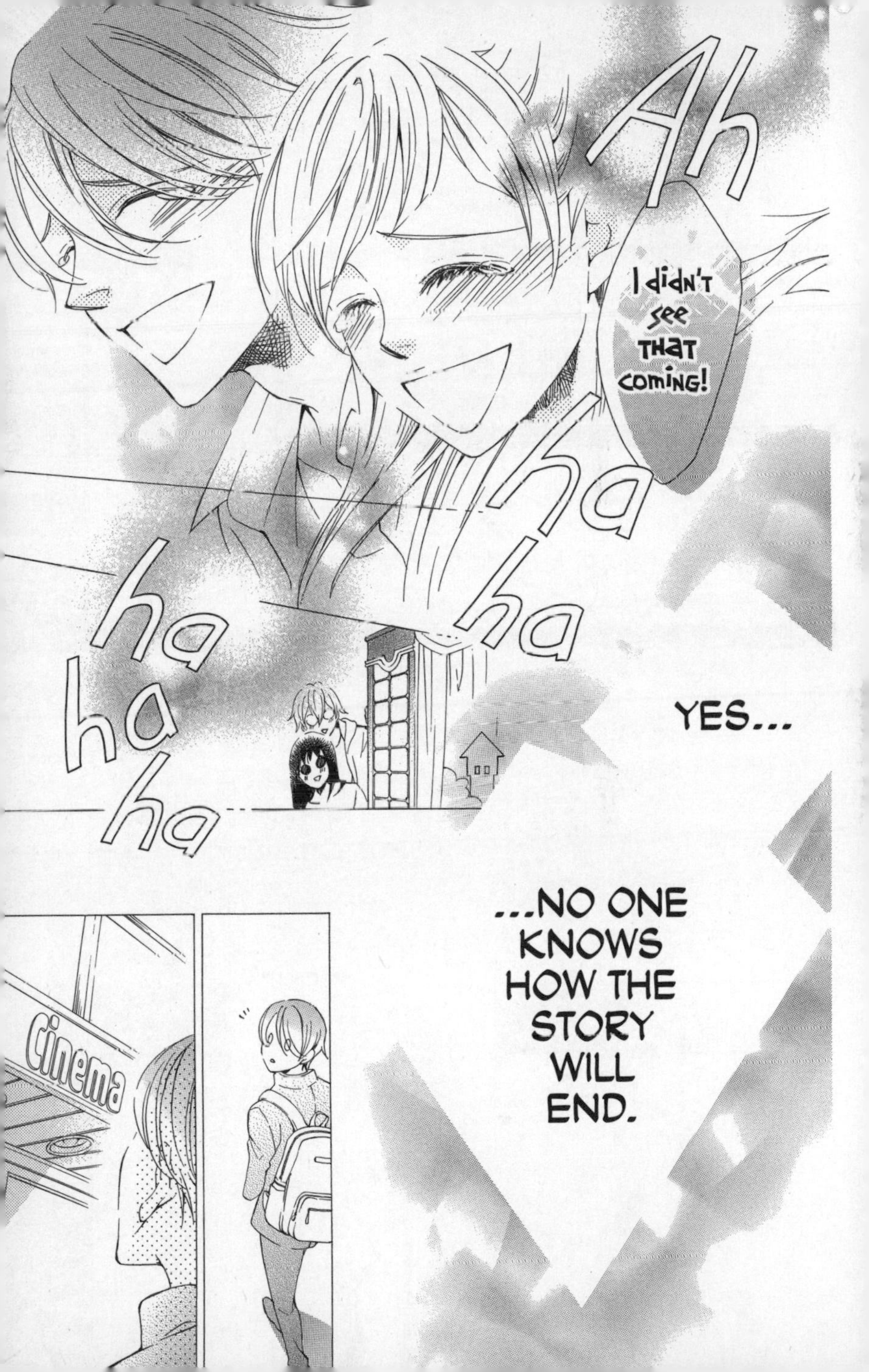
Ah ha ha ha ha ha...
I didn't see that coming!
YES...
...NO ONE KNOWS HOW THE STORY WILL END.
Cinema

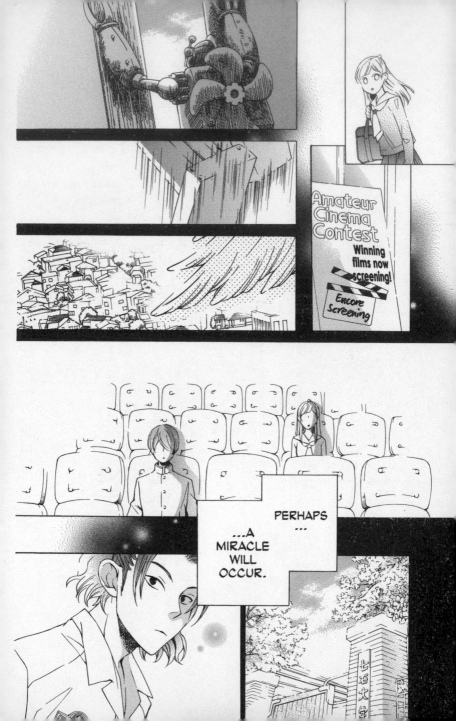

Amateur Cinema Contest
Winning films now screening!

Encore Screening

PERHAPS
...

...A
MIRACLE
WILL
OCCUR.

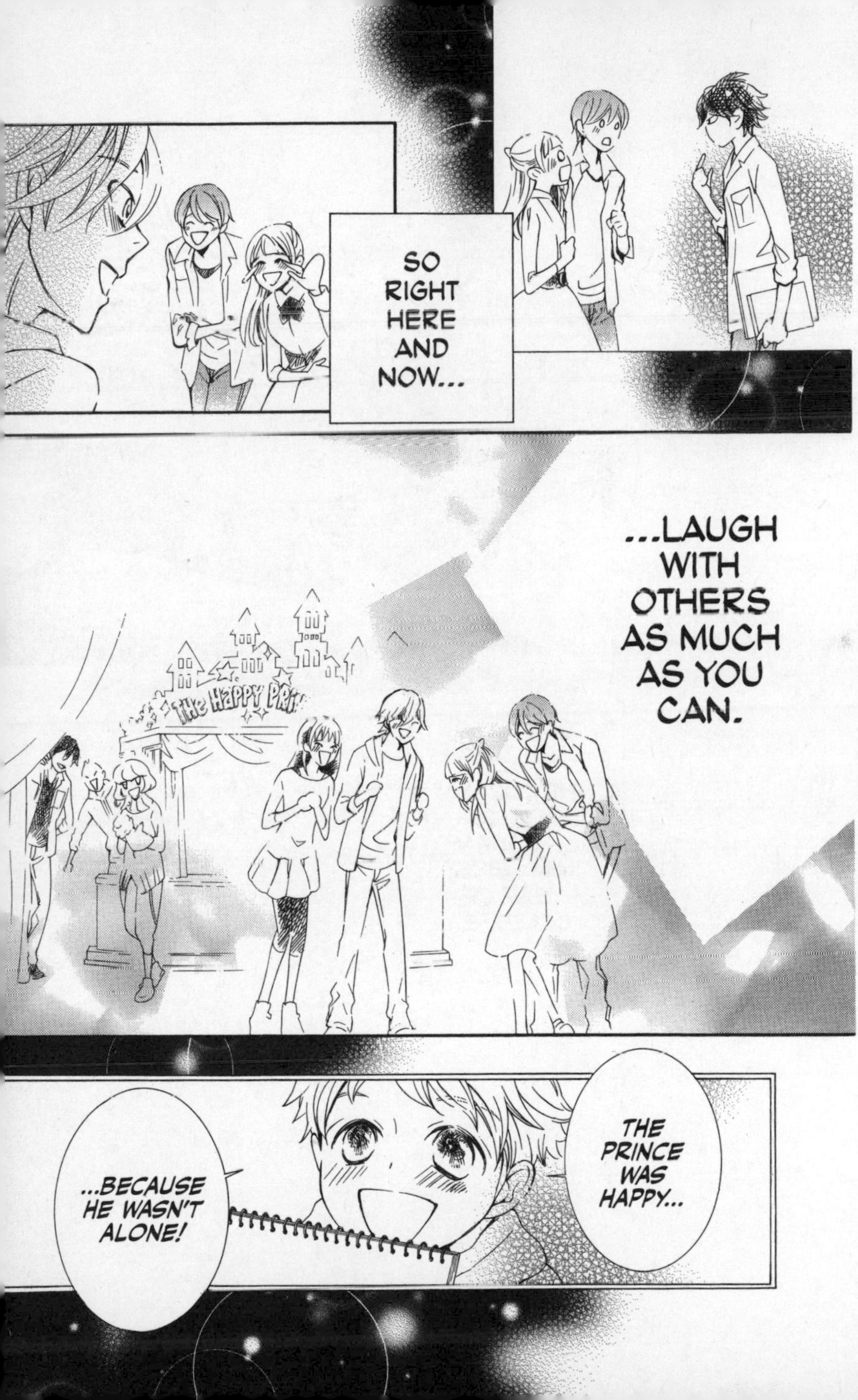
SO RIGHT HERE AND NOW...
...LAUGH WITH OTHERS AS MUCH AS YOU CAN.
THE PRINCE WAS HAPPY...
...BECAUSE HE WASN'T ALONE!

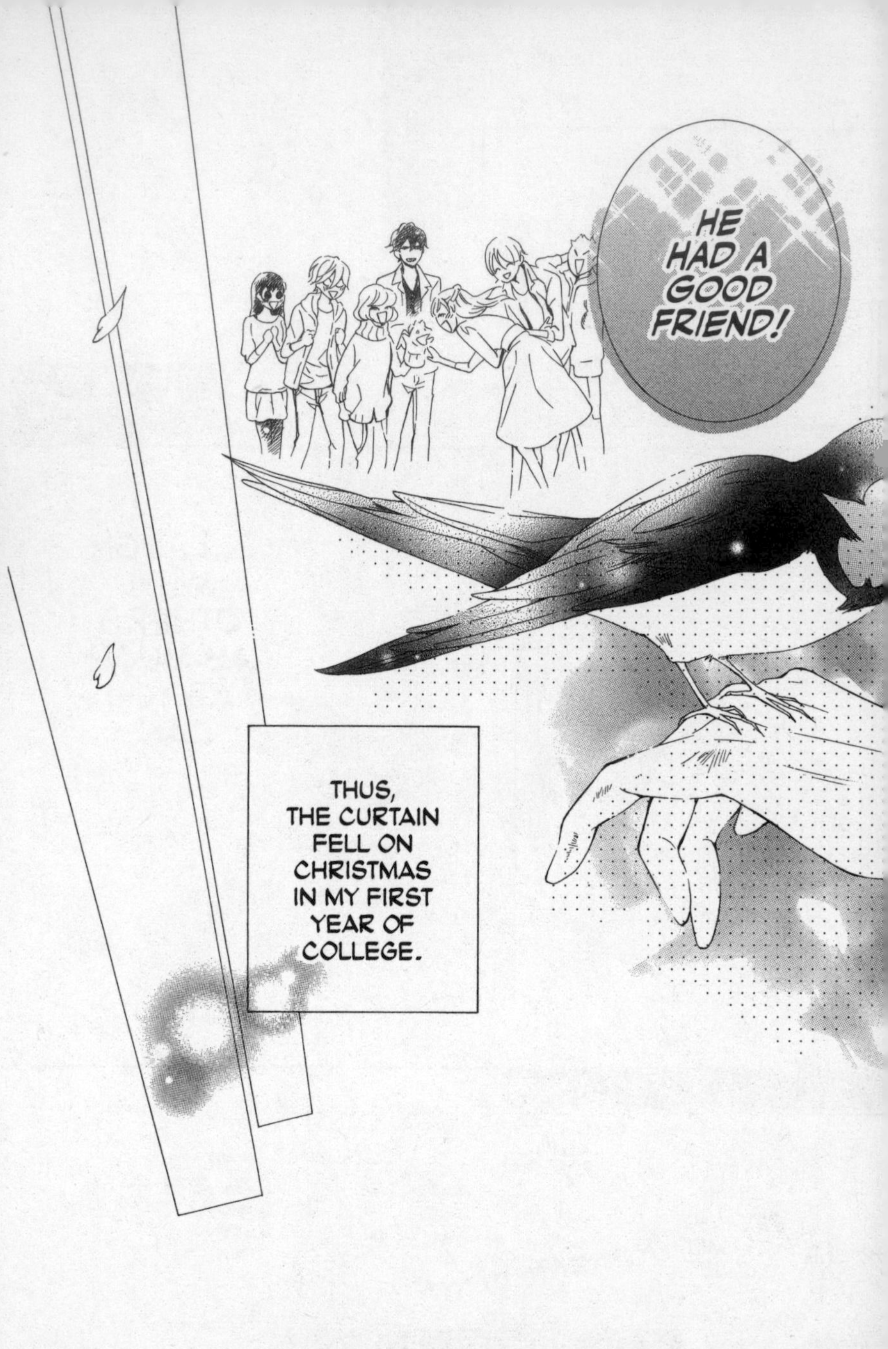
HE HAD A GOOD FRIEND!
THUS, THE CURTAIN FELL ON CHRISTMAS IN MY FIRST YEAR OF COLLEGE.

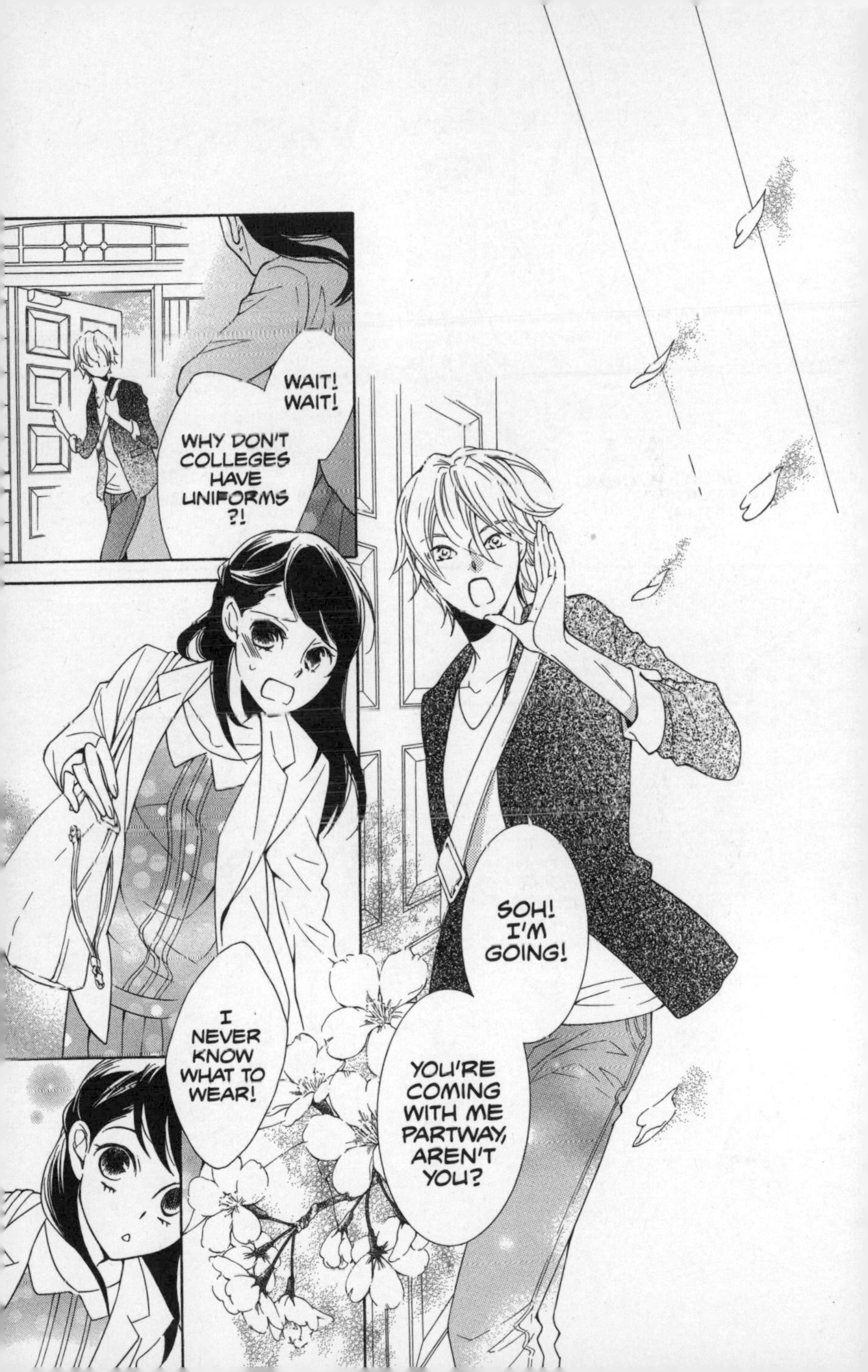
SOH! I'M GOING!
YOU'RE COMING WITH ME PARTWAY, AREN'T YOU?
WAIT! WAIT!
WHY DON'T COLLEGES HAVE UNIFORMS ?!
I NEVER KNOW WHAT TO WEAR!

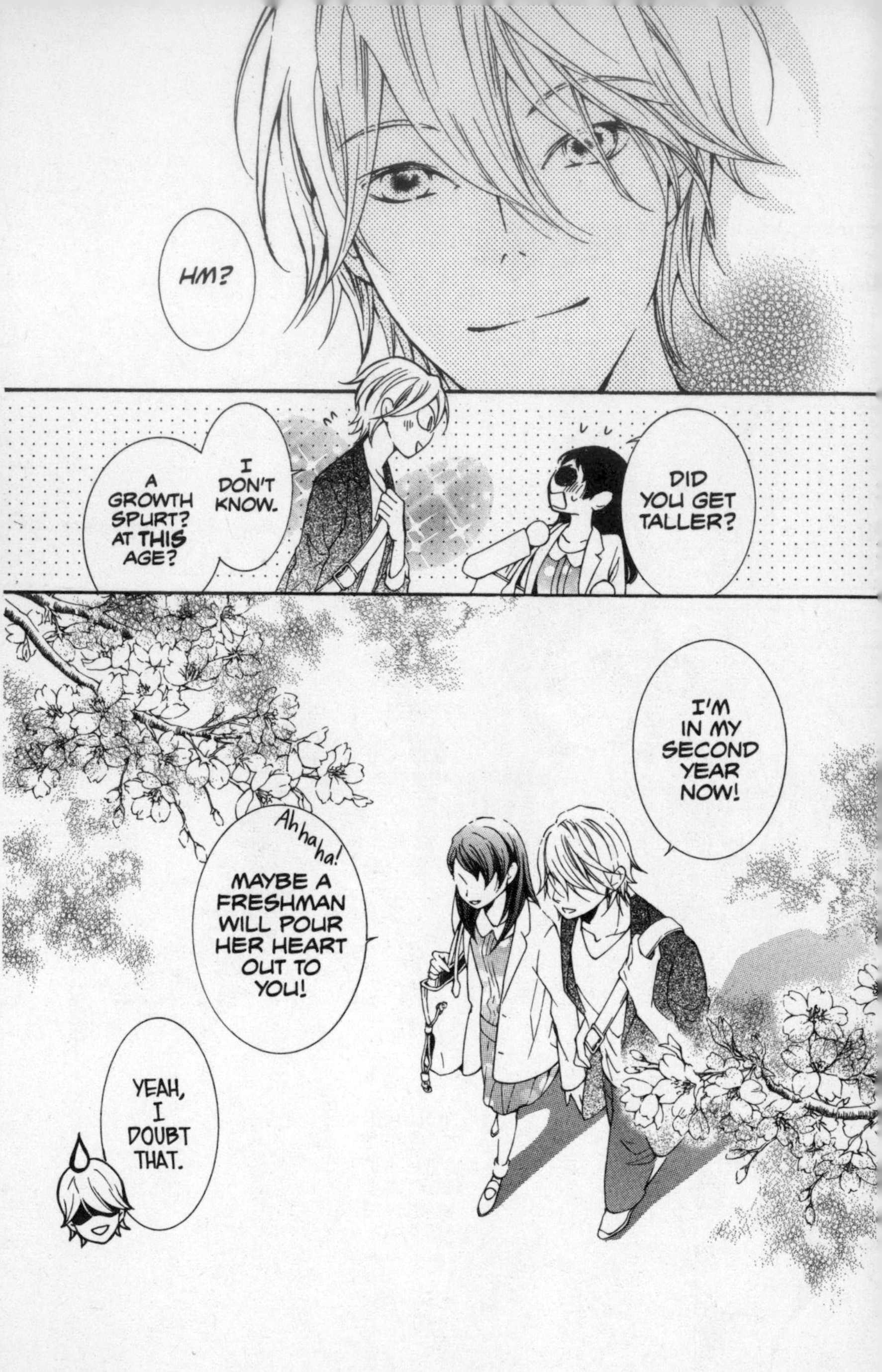
HM?
DID YOU GET TALLER?
I DON'T KNOW.
A GROWTH SPURT? AT THIS AGE?
I'M IN MY SECOND YEAR NOW!
Ahhaha!
MAYBE A FRESHMAN WILL POUR HER HEART OUT TO YOU!
YEAH, I DOUBT THAT.

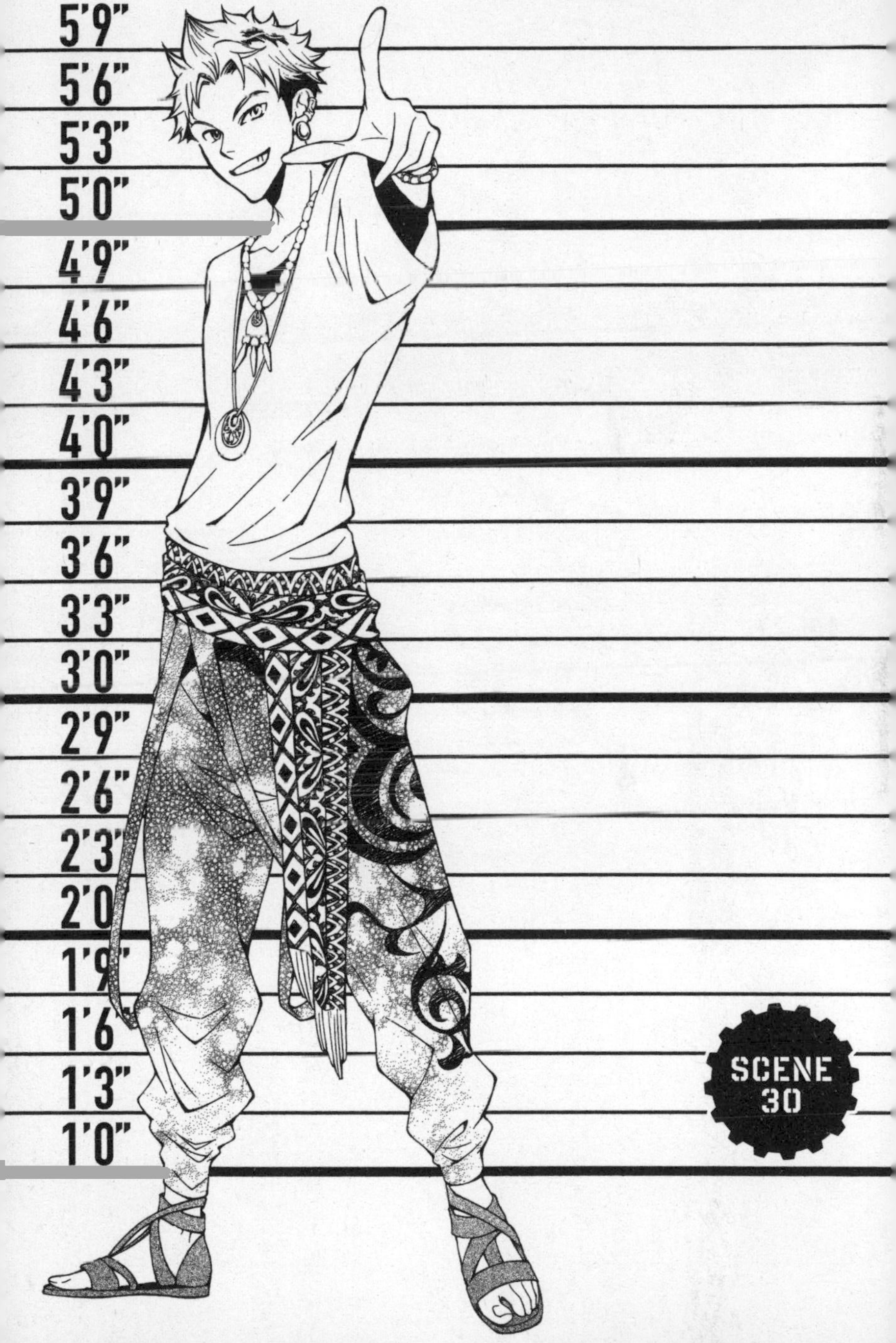
5'9"
5'6"
5'3"
5'0"
4'9"
4'6"
4'3"
4'0"
3'9"
3'6"
3'3"
3'0"
2'9"
2'6"
2'3"
2'0
1'9
1'6
1'3"
1'0"
SCENE 30

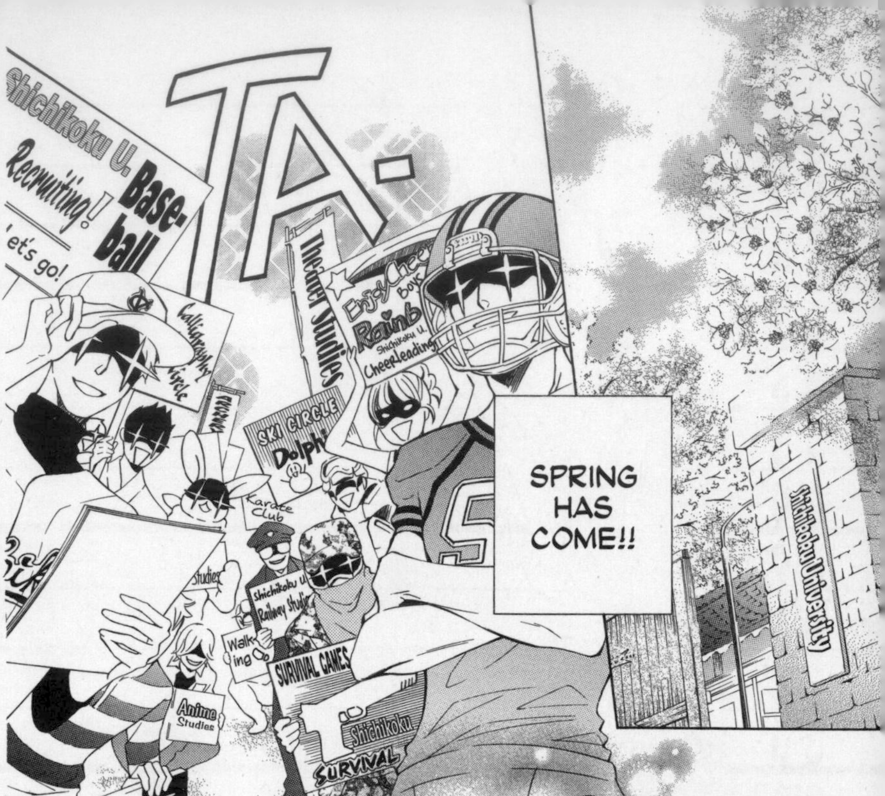

TA-
SPRING HAS COME!!
Shichikoku University
Enjoy Cheer Boys
Shichikoku U. Cheerleading
SKI CIRCLE
Karate Club
Shichikoku U. Railway Studies
SURVIVAL GAMES
Shichikoku
SURVIVAL
Walking
Anime Studies
Studies
Shichikoku U. Baseball
Recruiting!
'et's go!
Rugby Club
Freshmen Welcome
DUM

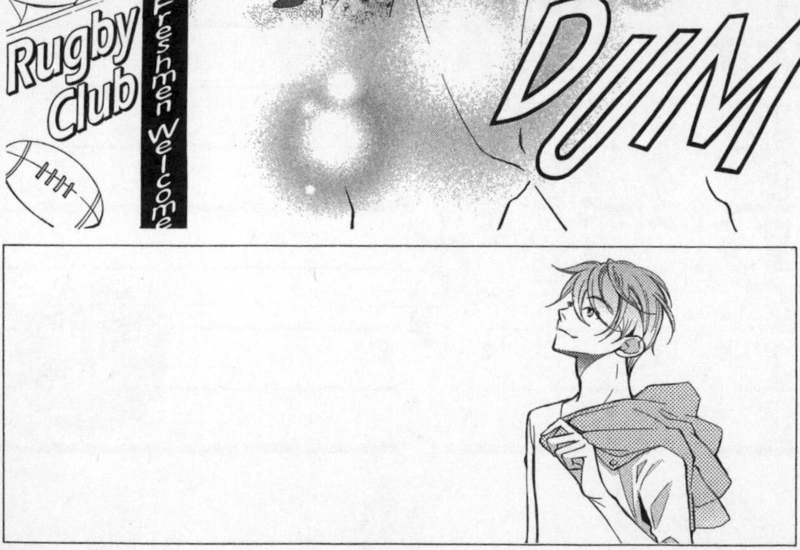

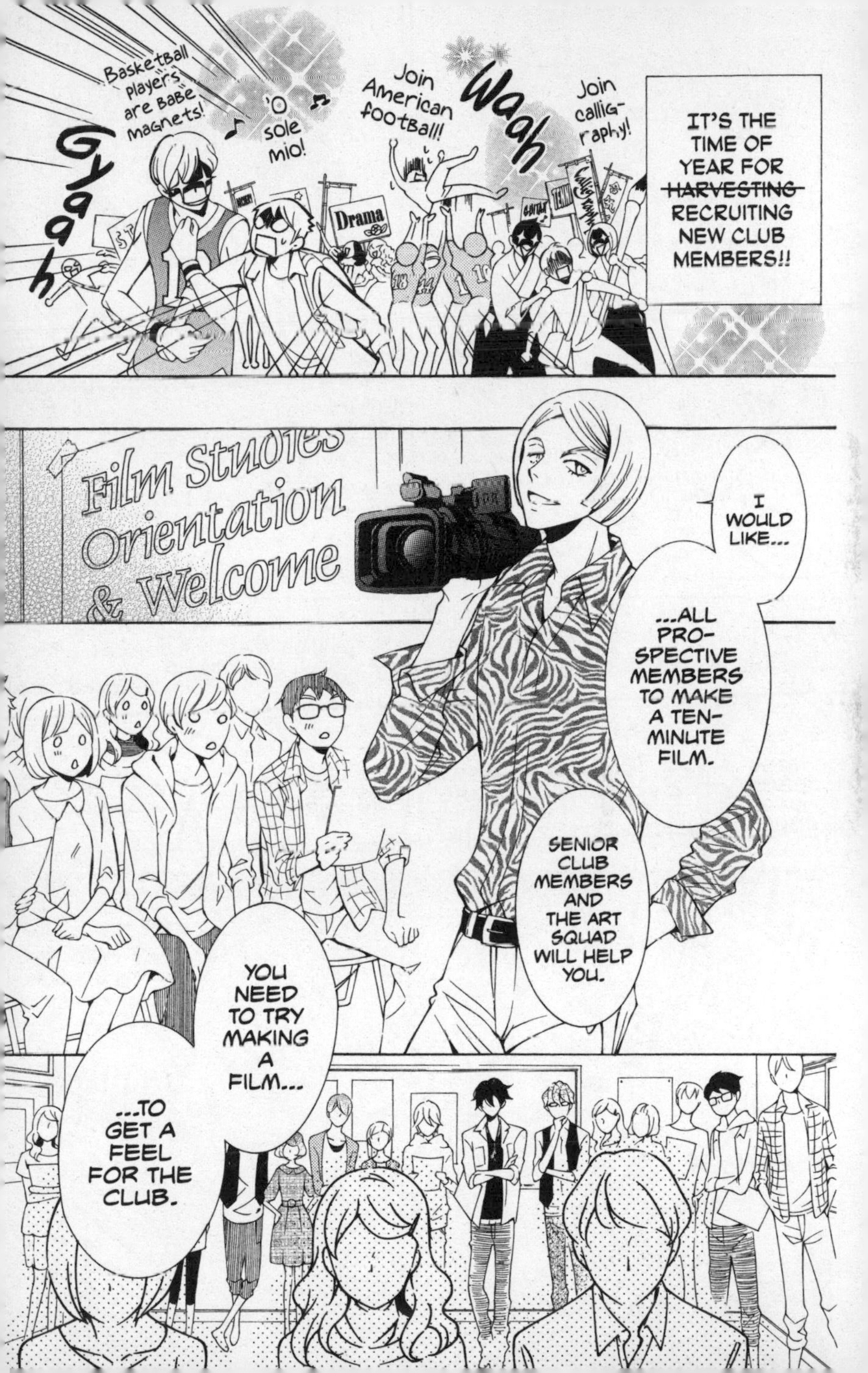
IT'S THE TIME OF YEAR FOR ~~HARVESTING~~ RECRUITING NEW CLUB MEMBERS!!
Join calligraphy!
Waah
Join American football!
'O sole mio!
Basketball players are babe magnets!
Gyaaah
Drama
Film Studies Orientation & Welcome
I WOULD LIKE...
...ALL PROSPECTIVE MEMBERS TO MAKE A TEN-MINUTE FILM.
SENIOR CLUB MEMBERS AND THE ART SQUAD WILL HELP YOU.
YOU NEED TO TRY MAKING A FILM...
...TO GET A FEEL FOR THE CLUB.

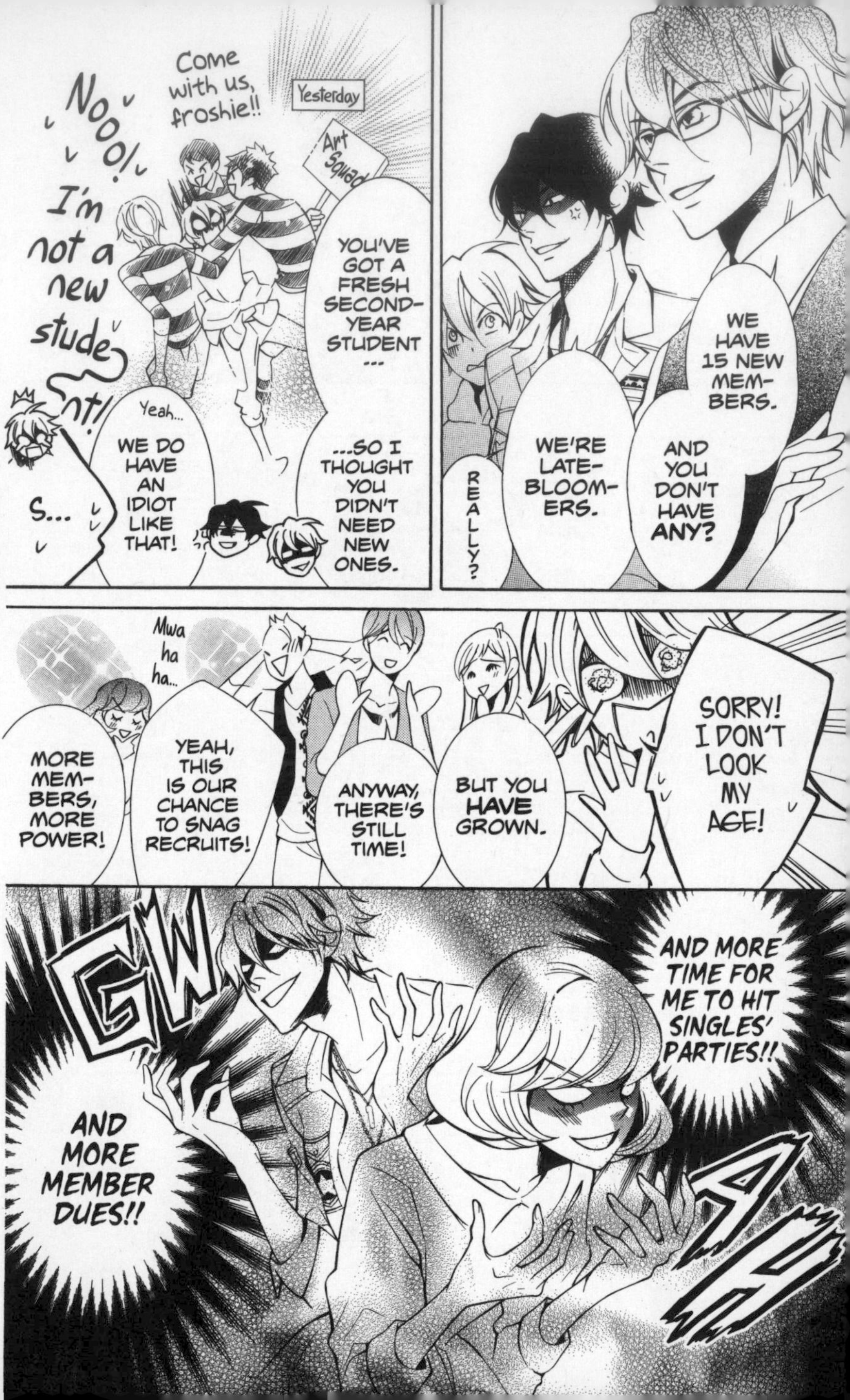
WE HAVE 15 NEW MEMBERS.
AND YOU DON'T HAVE ANY?
WE'RE LATE-BLOOMERS.
REALLY?
Yesterday
Come with us, froshie!!
Art Squad
Noooo! I'm not a new student!
YOU'VE GOT A FRESH SECOND-YEAR STUDENT...
...SO I THOUGHT YOU DIDN'T NEED NEW ONES.
Yeah... WE DO HAVE AN IDIOT LIKE THAT!
S...
SORRY! I DON'T LOOK MY AGE!
BUT YOU HAVE GROWN.
ANYWAY, THERE'S STILL TIME!
YEAH, THIS IS OUR CHANCE TO SNAG RECRUITS!
Mwa ha ha...
MORE MEMBERS, MORE POWER!
AND MORE TIME FOR ME TO HIT SINGLES' PARTIES!!
GWAH
AND MORE MEMBER DUES!!

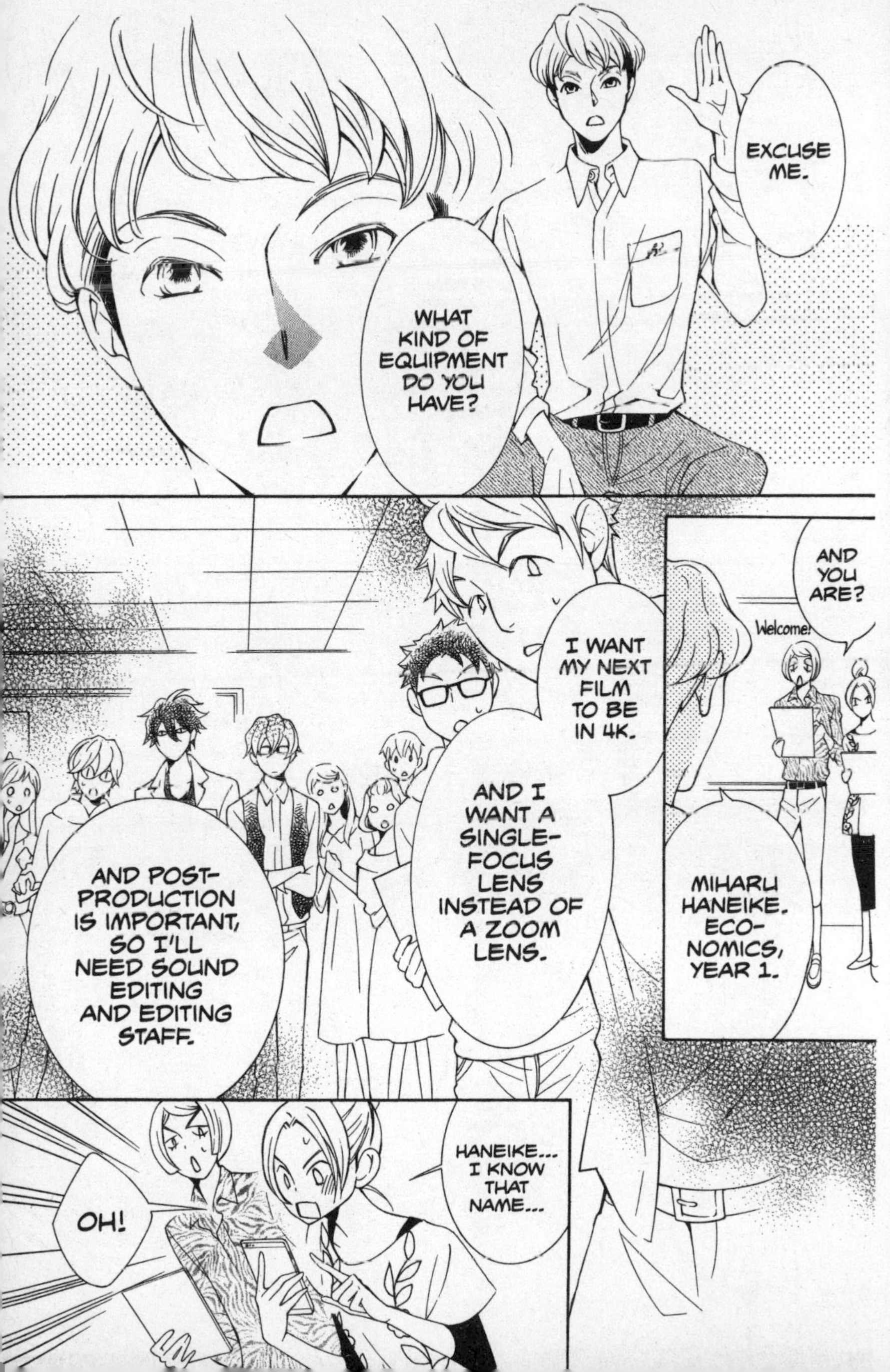
EXCUSE ME.
WHAT KIND OF EQUIPMENT DO YOU HAVE?
AND YOU ARE?
Welcome!
MIHARU HANEIKE. ECO-NOMICS, YEAR 1.
I WANT MY NEXT FILM TO BE IN 4K.
AND I WANT A SINGLE-FOCUS LENS INSTEAD OF A ZOOM LENS.
AND POST-PRODUCTION IS IMPORTANT, SO I'LL NEED SOUND EDITING AND EDITING STAFF.
HANEIKE... I KNOW THAT NAME...
OH!

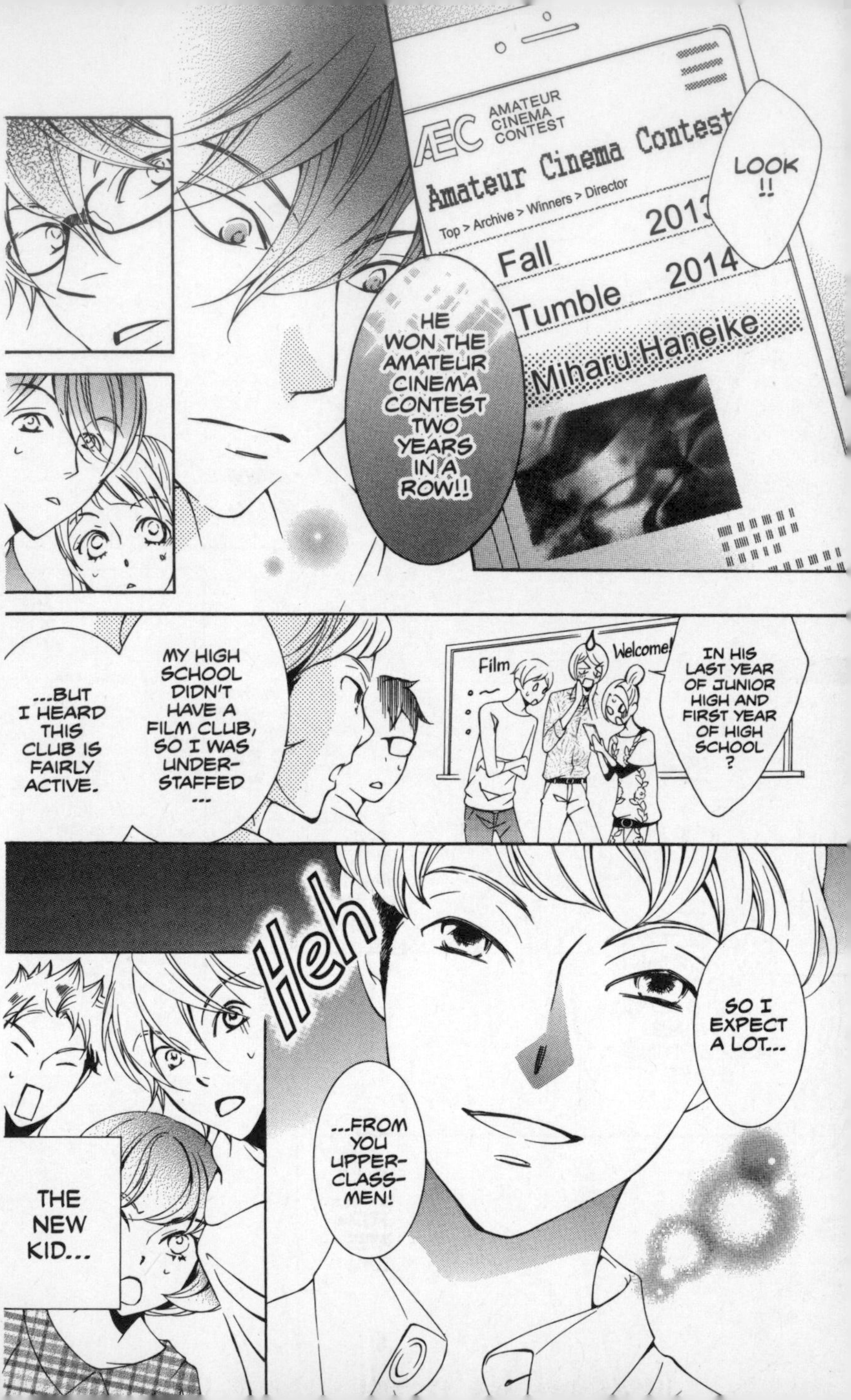
AMATEUR CINEMA CONTEST
Amateur Cinema Contest
Top > Archive > Winners > Director
2013
Fall
2014
Tumble
Miharu Haneike
LOOK!!
HE WON THE AMATEUR CINEMA CONTEST TWO YEARS IN A ROW!!
Welcome!
Film
IN HIS LAST YEAR OF JUNIOR HIGH AND FIRST YEAR OF HIGH SCHOOL?
MY HIGH SCHOOL DIDN'T HAVE A FILM CLUB, SO I WAS UNDER-STAFFED...
...BUT I HEARD THIS CLUB IS FAIRLY ACTIVE.
SO I EXPECT A LOT...
...FROM YOU UPPER-CLASS-MEN!
Heh
THE NEW KID...

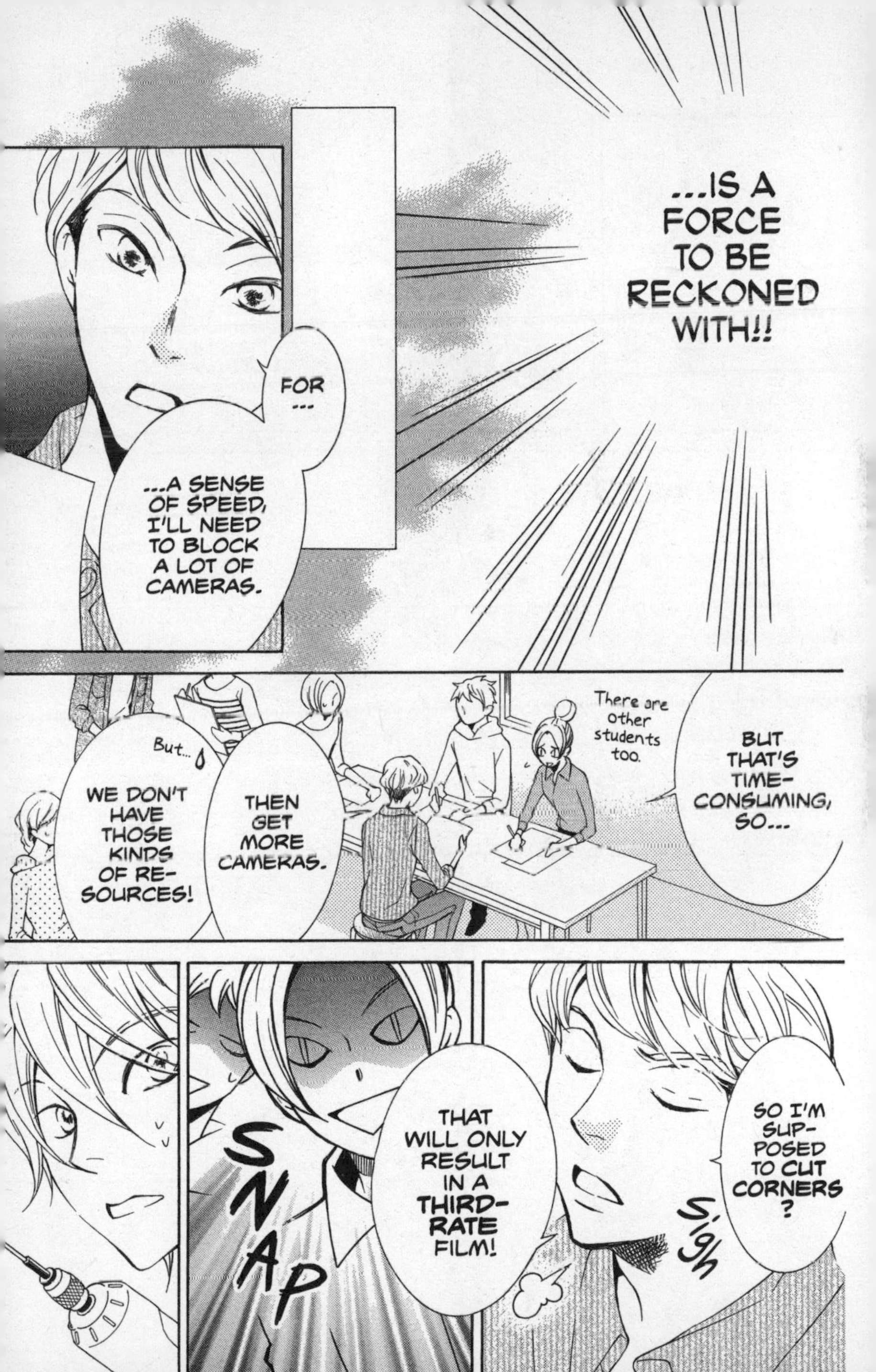
...IS A FORCE TO BE RECKONED WITH!!
FOR...
...A SENSE OF SPEED, I'LL NEED TO BLOCK A LOT OF CAMERAS.
BUT THAT'S TIME-CONSUMING, SO...
There are other students too.
THEN GET MORE CAMERAS.
But...
WE DON'T HAVE THOSE KINDS OF RE-SOURCES!
SO I'M SUP-POSED TO CUT CORNERS?
Sigh
THAT WILL ONLY RESULT IN A THIRD-RATE FILM!
SNAP

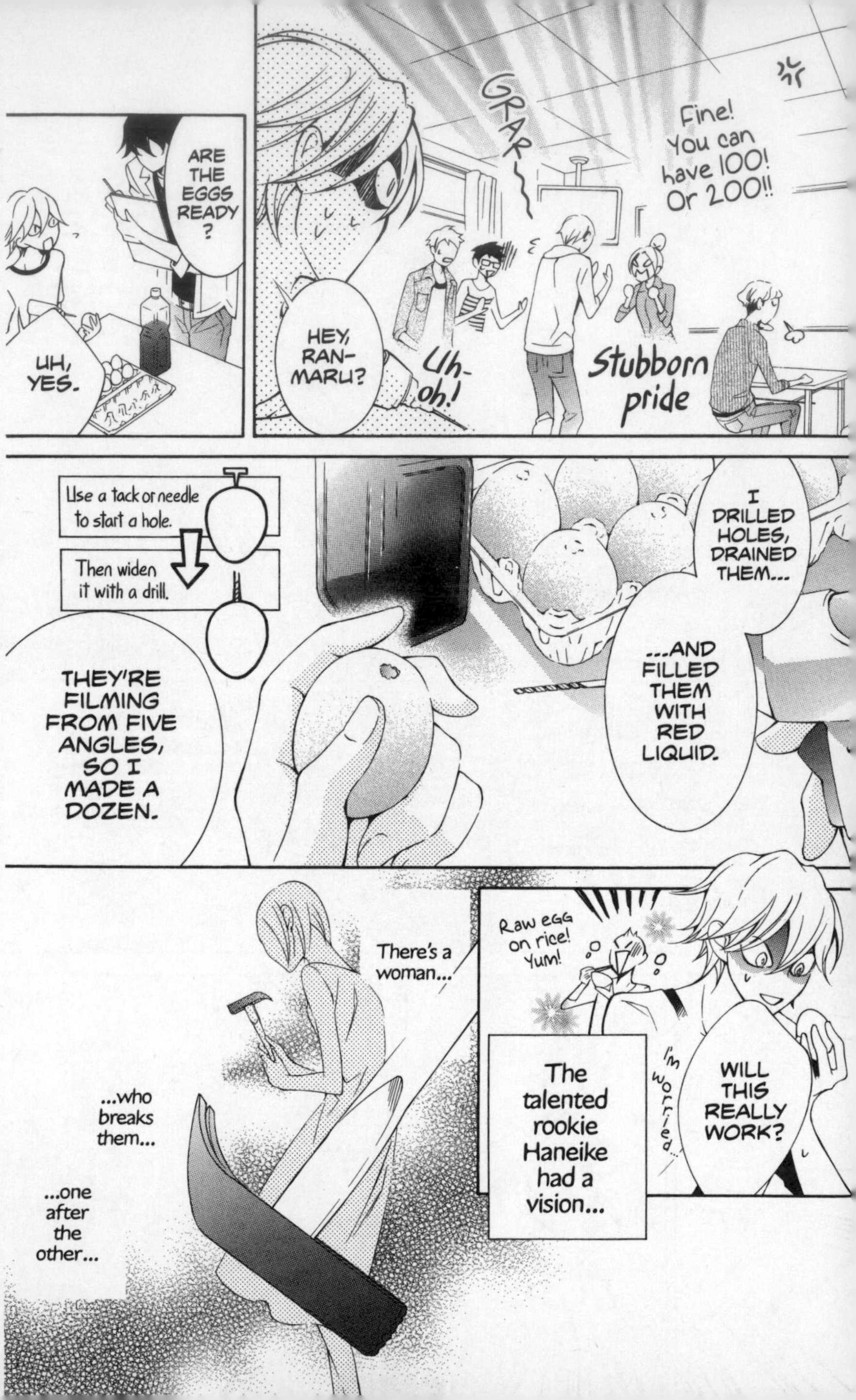
GRAR
Fine! You can have 100! Or 200!!
Stubborn pride
Uh-oh!
HEY, RAN-MARU?
ARE THE EGGS READY?
UH, YES.
I DRILLED HOLES, DRAINED THEM...
...AND FILLED THEM WITH RED LIQUID.
Use a tack or needle to start a hole.
Then widen it with a drill.
THEY'RE FILMING FROM FIVE ANGLES, SO I MADE A DOZEN.
Raw egg on rice! Yum!
WILL THIS REALLY WORK?
I'm worried...
The talented rookie Haneike had a vision...
There's a woman...
...who breaks them...
...one after the other...

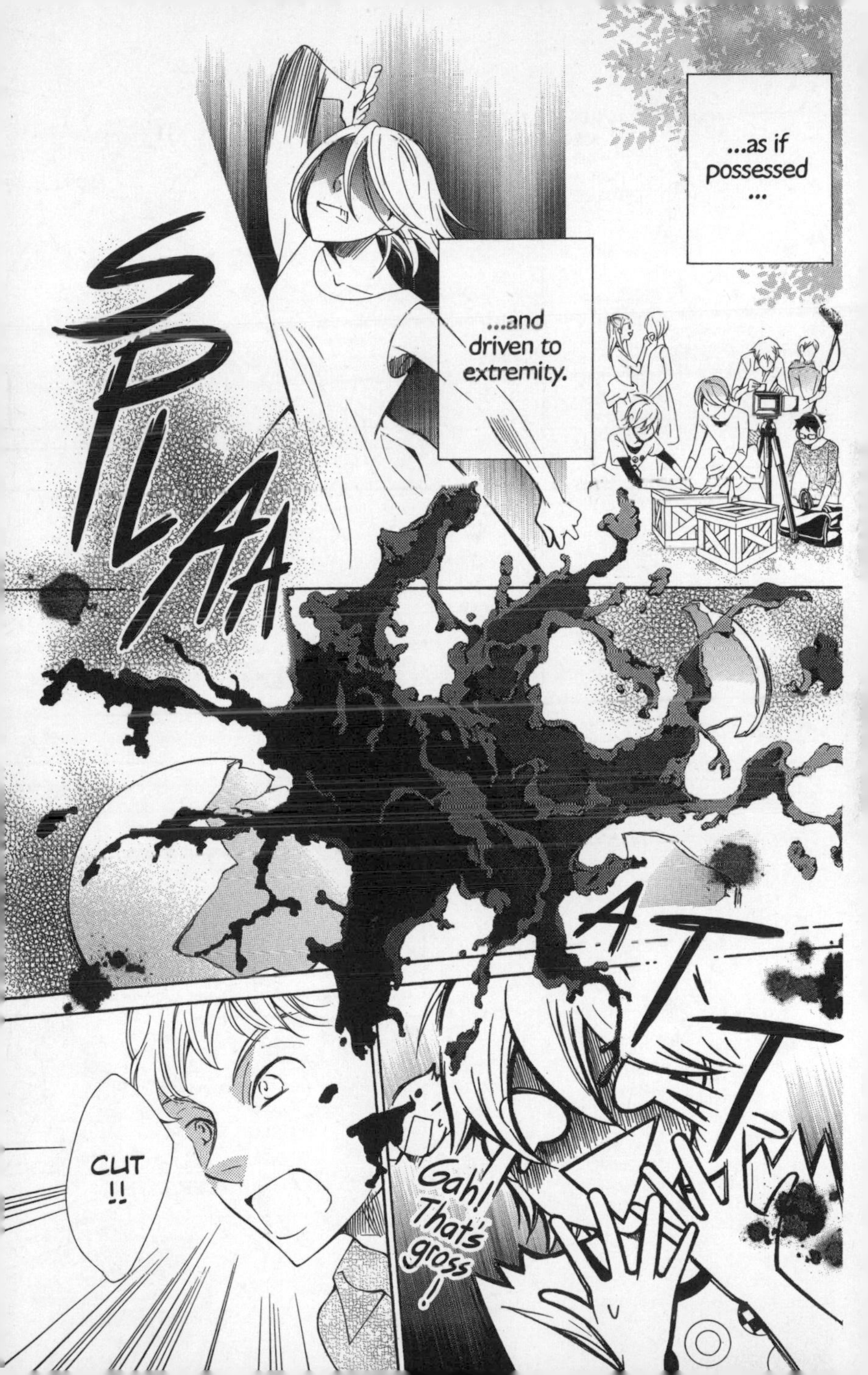
...as if possessed ...
...and driven to extremity.
SPLAA
ATT
Gah! That's gross!
CUT!!

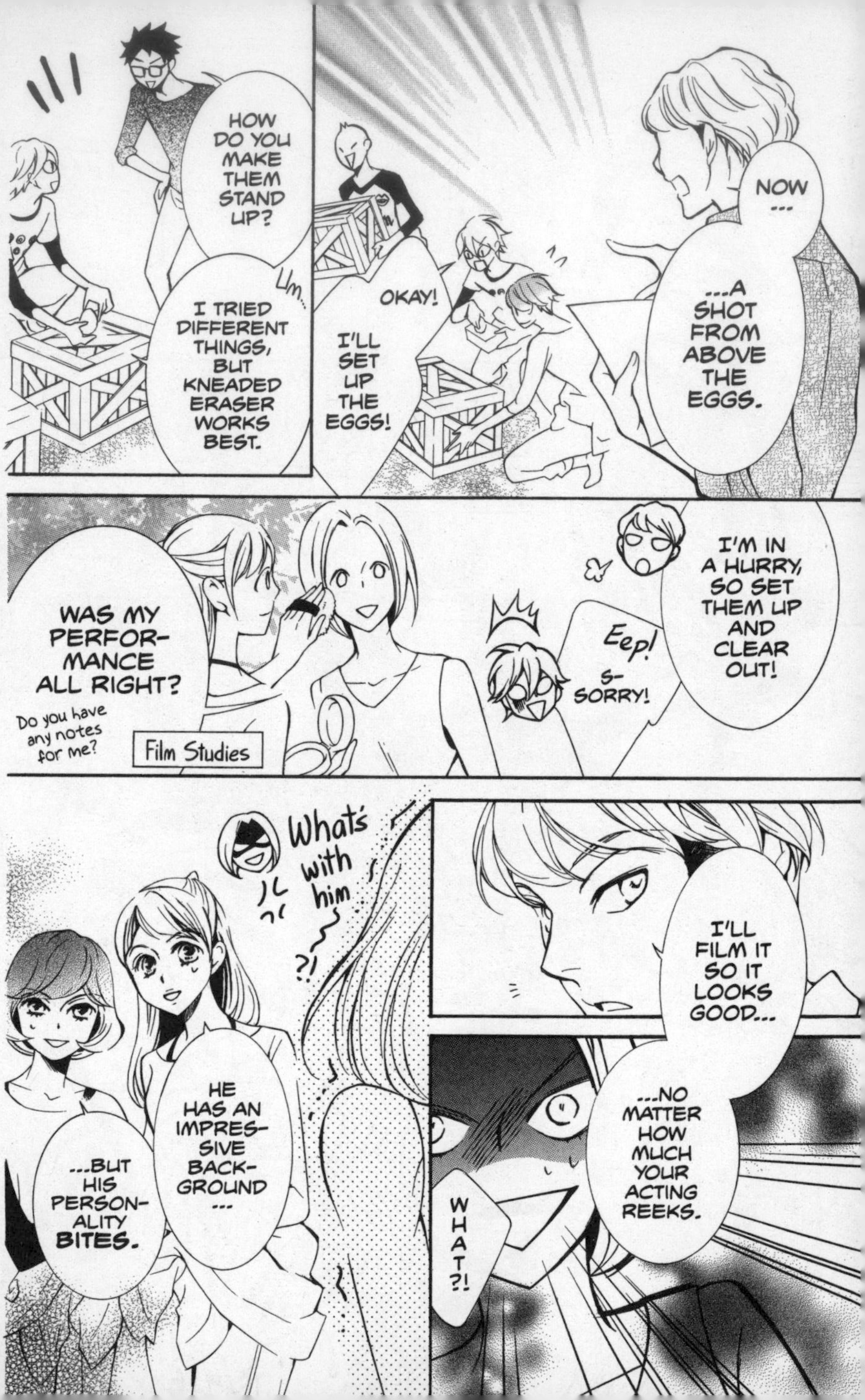

NOW...
...A SHOT FROM ABOVE THE EGGS.
OKAY!
I'LL SET UP THE EGGS!
HOW DO YOU MAKE THEM STAND UP?
Um...
I TRIED DIFFERENT THINGS, BUT KNEADED ERASER WORKS BEST.
I'M IN A HURRY, SO SET THEM UP AND CLEAR OUT!
Eep!
S-SORRY!
WAS MY PERFORMANCE ALL RIGHT?
Do you have any notes for me?
Film Studies
I'LL FILM IT SO IT LOOKS GOOD...
...NO MATTER HOW MUCH YOUR ACTING REEKS.
WHAT?!
What's with him ?!
HE HAS AN IMPRESSIVE BACKGROUND...
...BUT HIS PERSONALITY BITES.

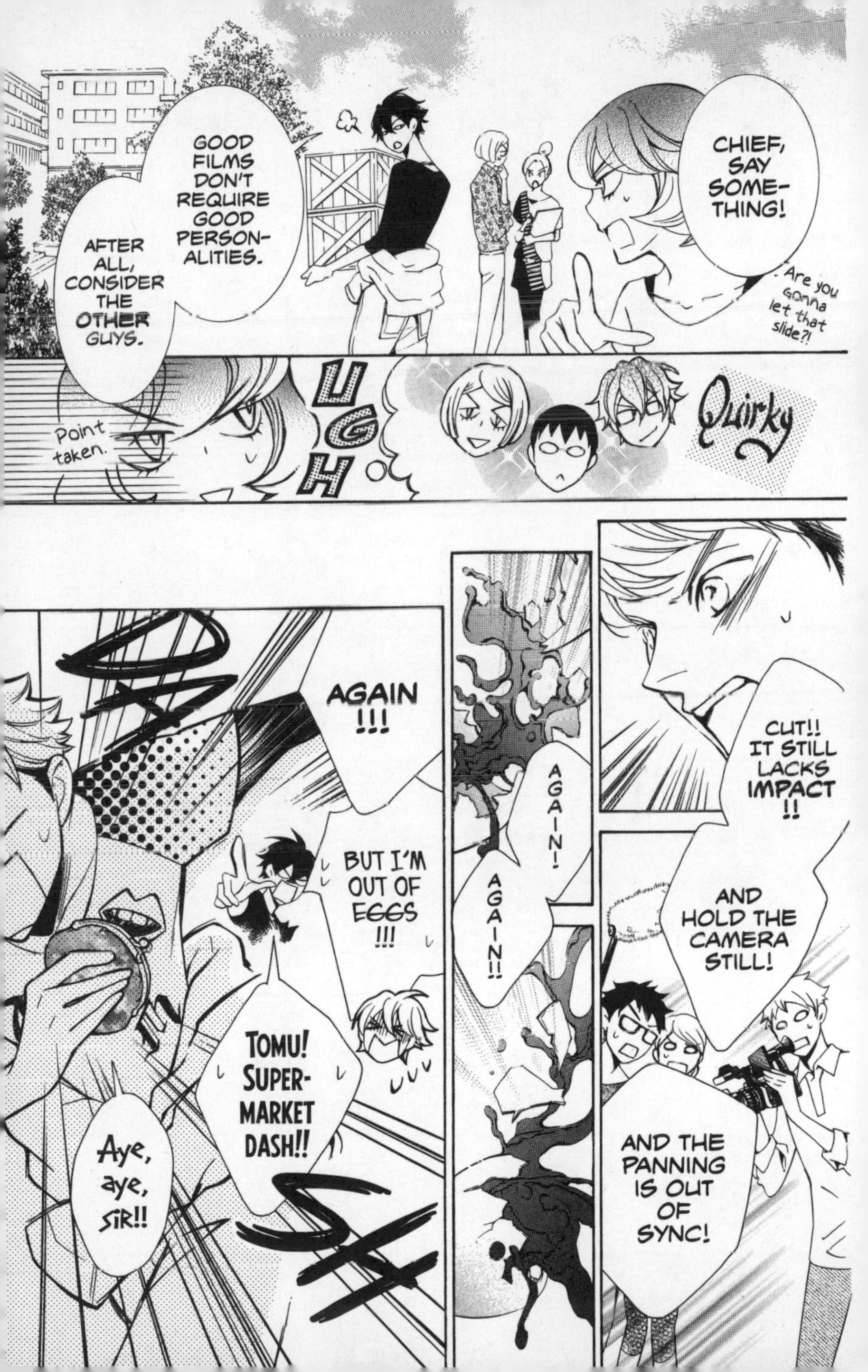
CHIEF, SAY SOME-THING!
Are you gonna let that slide?!
GOOD FILMS DON'T REQUIRE GOOD PERSON-ALITIES.
AFTER ALL, CONSIDER THE OTHER GUYS.
Quirky
UGH
Point taken.
CUT!! IT STILL LACKS IMPACT!!
AND HOLD THE CAMERA STILL!
AND THE PANNING IS OUT OF SYNC!
AGAIN!
AGAIN!!
AGAIN!!!
BUT I'M OUT OF EGGS!!!
TOMU! SUPER-MARKET DASH!!
Aye, aye, sir!!

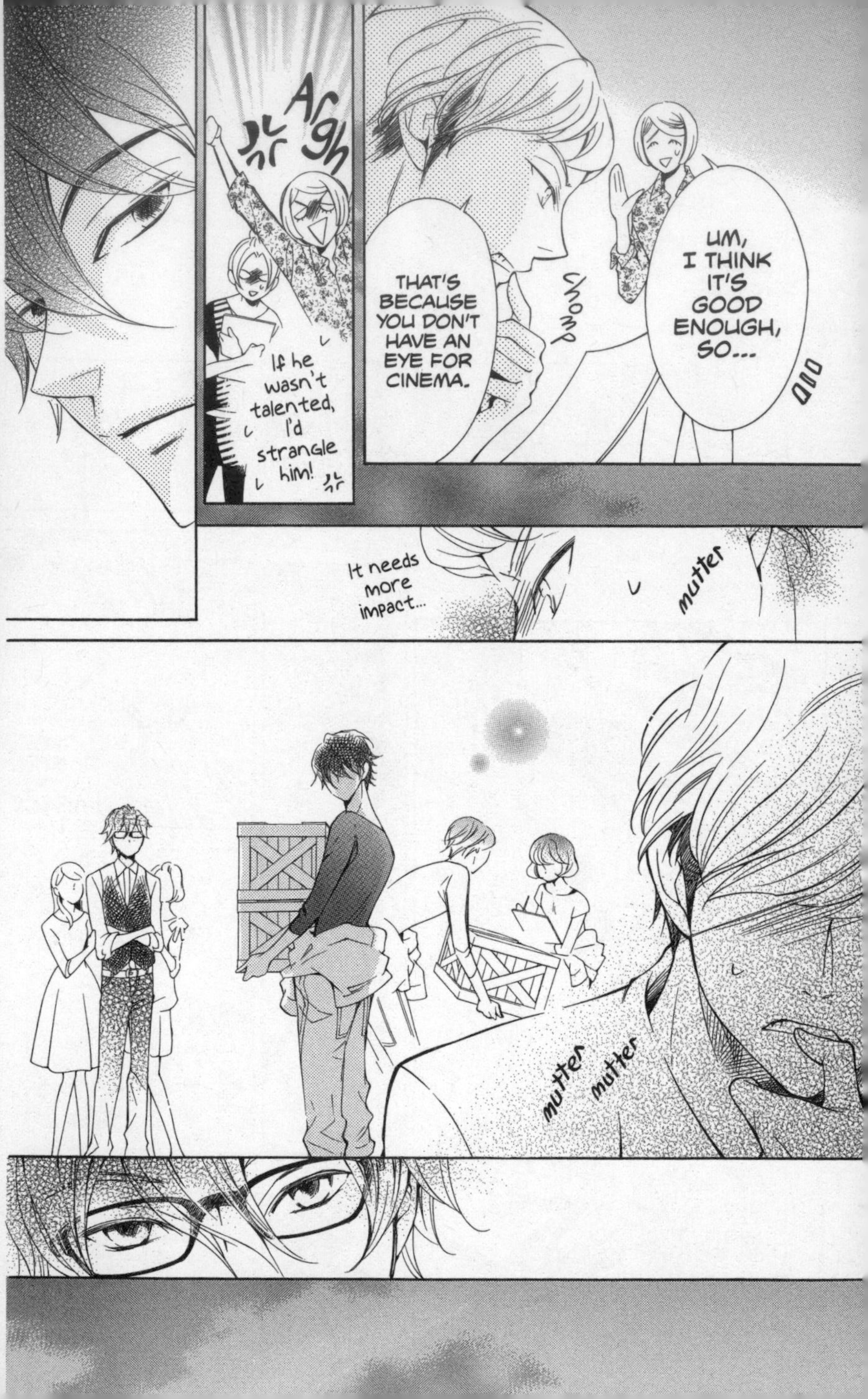

UM, I THINK IT'S GOOD ENOUGH, SO...
chomp
THAT'S BECAUSE YOU DON'T HAVE AN EYE FOR CINEMA.
Argh
If he wasn't talented, I'd strangle him!
mutter
It needs more impact...
mutter mutter

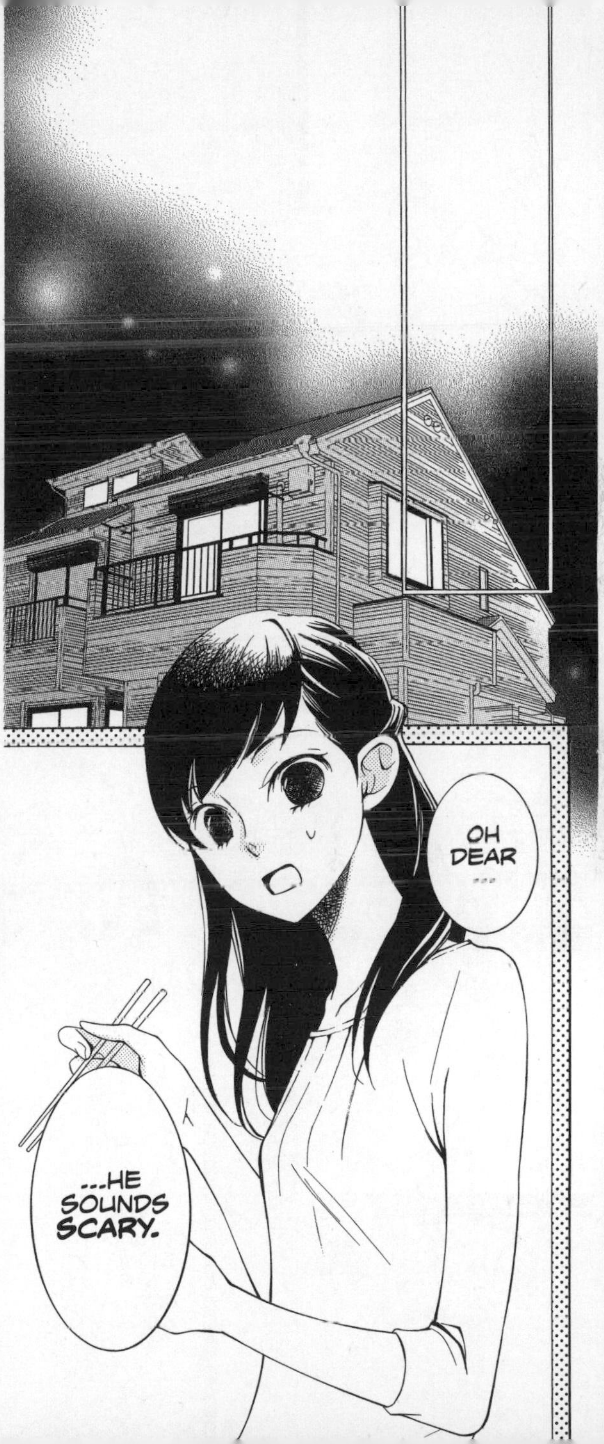

OH DEAR ...
...HE SOUNDS SCARY.

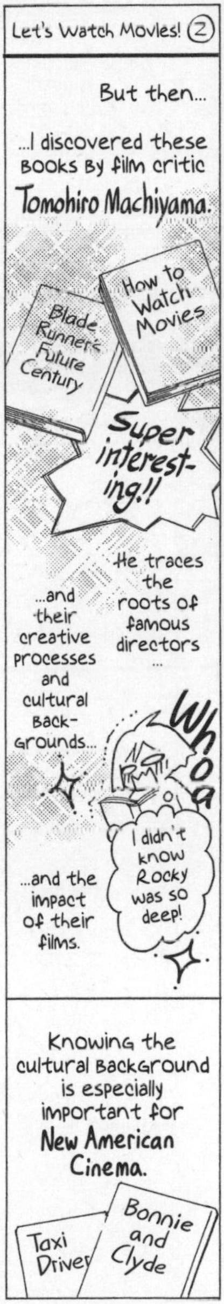

Let's Watch Movies! 2
But then...
...I discovered these books by film critic Tomohiro Machiyama.
How to Watch Movies
Blade Runner's Future Century
Super interesting!!
He traces the roots of famous directors ...
...and their creative processes and cultural back-grounds...
Whoa
I didn't know Rocky was so deep!
...and the impact of their films.
Knowing the cultural background is especially important for New American Cinema.
Bonnie and Clyde
Taxi Driver

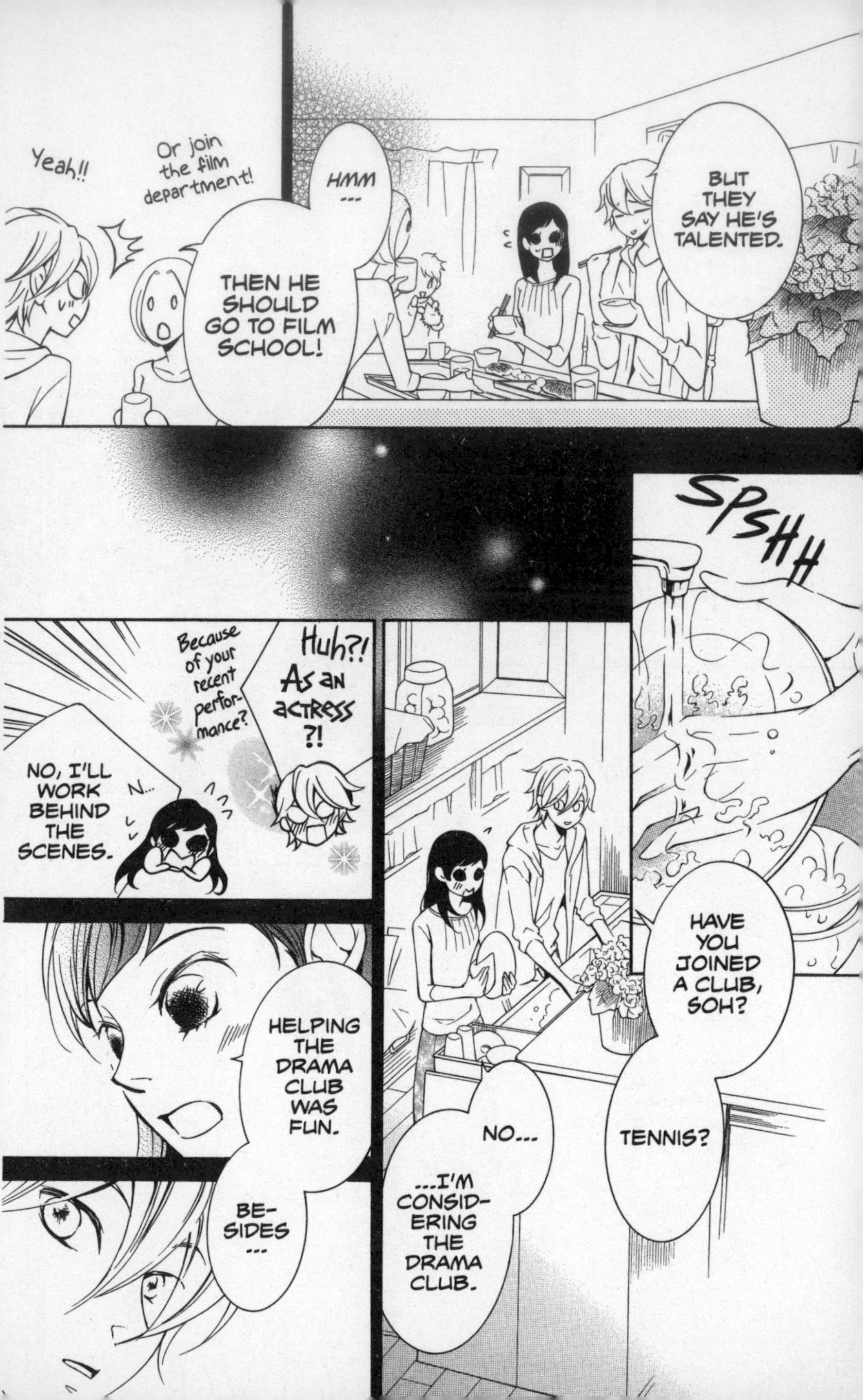
BUT THEY SAY HE'S TALENTED.
HMM...
THEN HE SHOULD GO TO FILM SCHOOL!
Or join the film department!
Yeah!!
SPSHH
HAVE YOU JOINED A CLUB, SOH?
TENNIS?
NO...
...I'M CONSIDERING THE DRAMA CLUB.
Huh?! As an actress?!
Because of your recent performance?
N...
NO, I'LL WORK BEHIND THE SCENES.
HELPING THE DRAMA CLUB WAS FUN.
BESIDES...

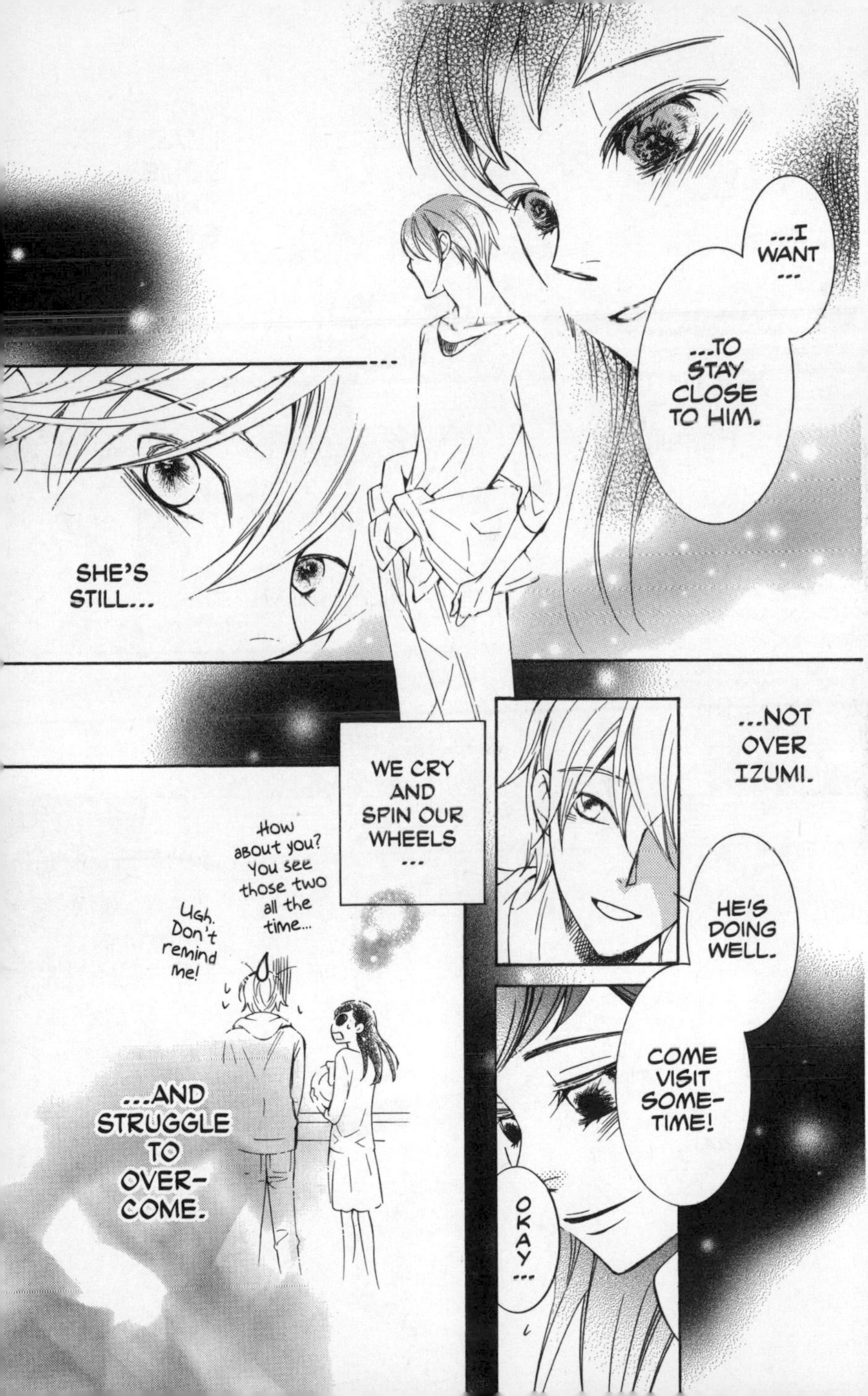
...I WANT...
...TO STAY CLOSE TO HIM.
SHE'S STILL...
...NOT OVER IZUMI.
HE'S DOING WELL.
COME VISIT SOME-TIME!
OKAY...
WE CRY AND SPIN OUR WHEELS...
How about you? You see those two all the time...
Ugh. Don't remind me!
...AND STRUGGLE TO OVER-COME.

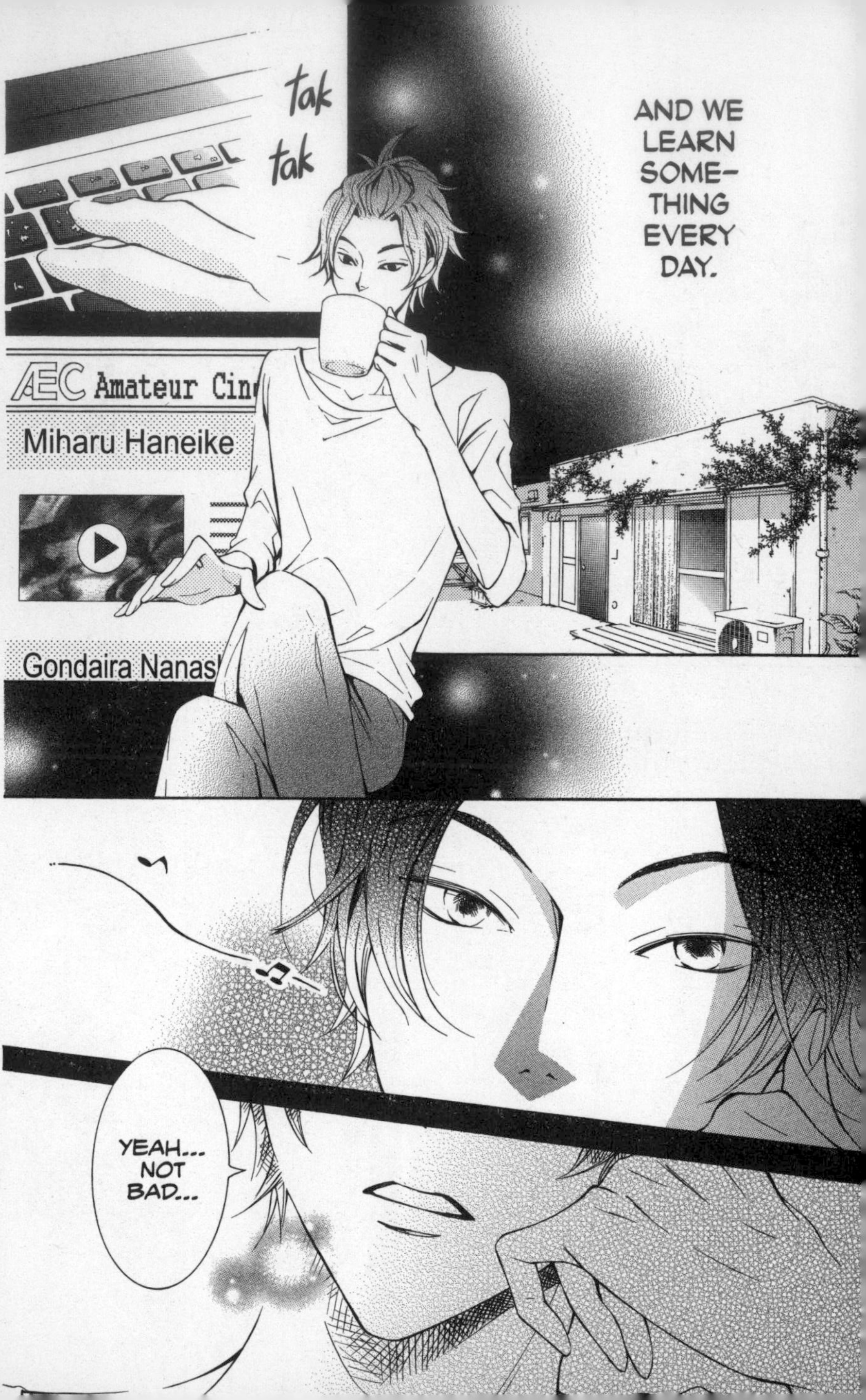
AND WE LEARN SOME-THING EVERY DAY.
tak
tak
ÆC Amateur Cin
Miharu Haneike
Gondaira Nanas
YEAH... NOT BAD...

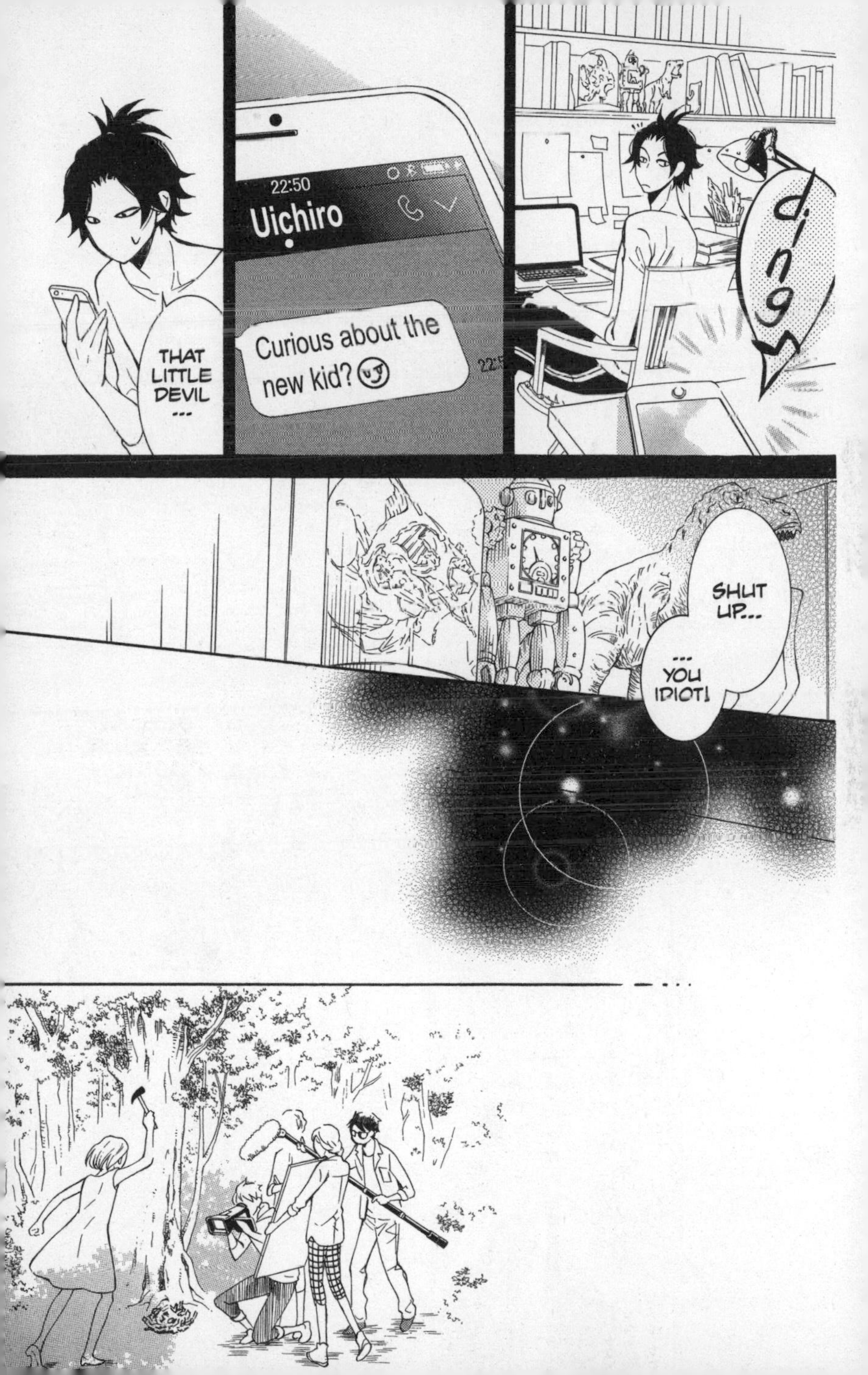
ding
22:50
Uichiro
Curious about the new kid?
THAT LITTLE DEVIL ---
SHUT UP...
--- YOU IDIOT!

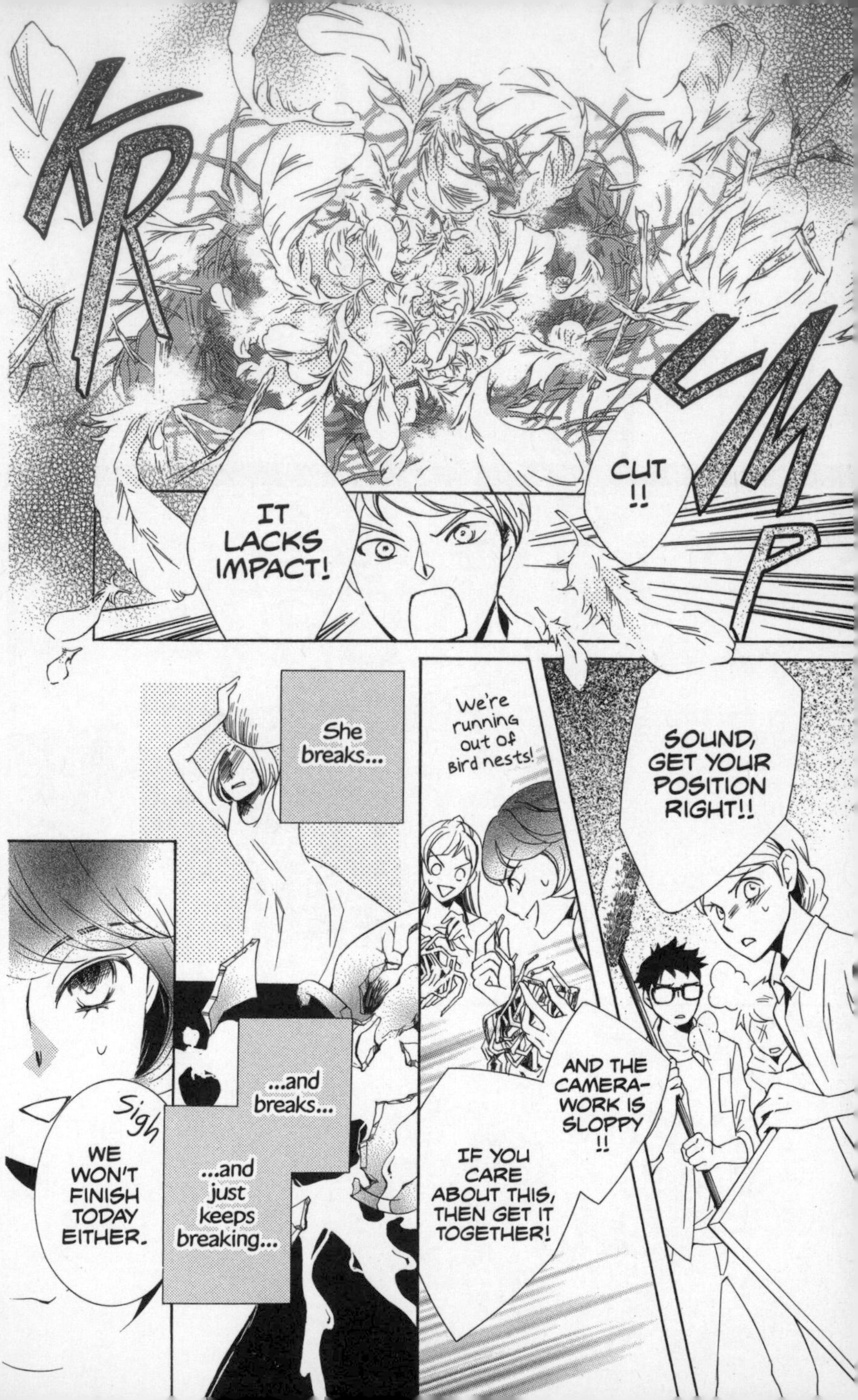
KRUMP
CUT !!
IT LACKS IMPACT!
SOUND, GET YOUR POSITION RIGHT!!
We're running out of bird nests!
AND THE CAMERA-WORK IS SLOPPY !!
IF YOU CARE ABOUT THIS, THEN GET IT TOGETHER!
She breaks...
...and breaks...
...and just keeps breaking...
Sigh
WE WON'T FINISH TODAY EITHER.

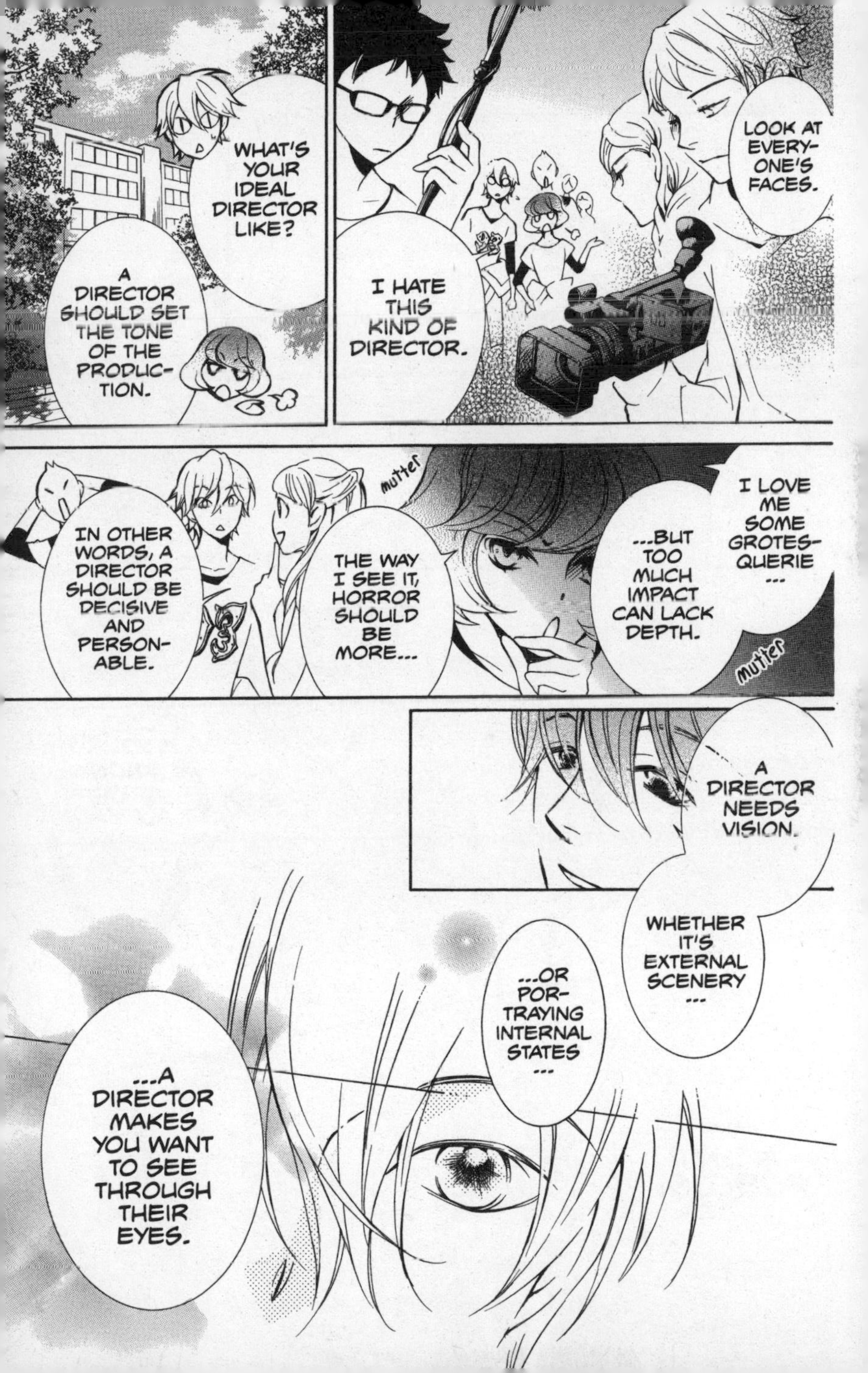
LOOK AT EVERYONE'S FACES.
I HATE THIS KIND OF DIRECTOR.
WHAT'S YOUR IDEAL DIRECTOR LIKE?
A DIRECTOR SHOULD SET THE TONE OF THE PRODUCTION.
I LOVE ME SOME GROTESQUERIE...
mutter
...BUT TOO MUCH IMPACT CAN LACK DEPTH.
mutter
THE WAY I SEE IT, HORROR SHOULD BE MORE...
IN OTHER WORDS, A DIRECTOR SHOULD BE DECISIVE AND PERSONABLE.
A DIRECTOR NEEDS VISION.
WHETHER IT'S EXTERNAL SCENERY...
...OR PORTRAYING INTERNAL STATES...
...A DIRECTOR MAKES YOU WANT TO SEE THROUGH THEIR EYES.

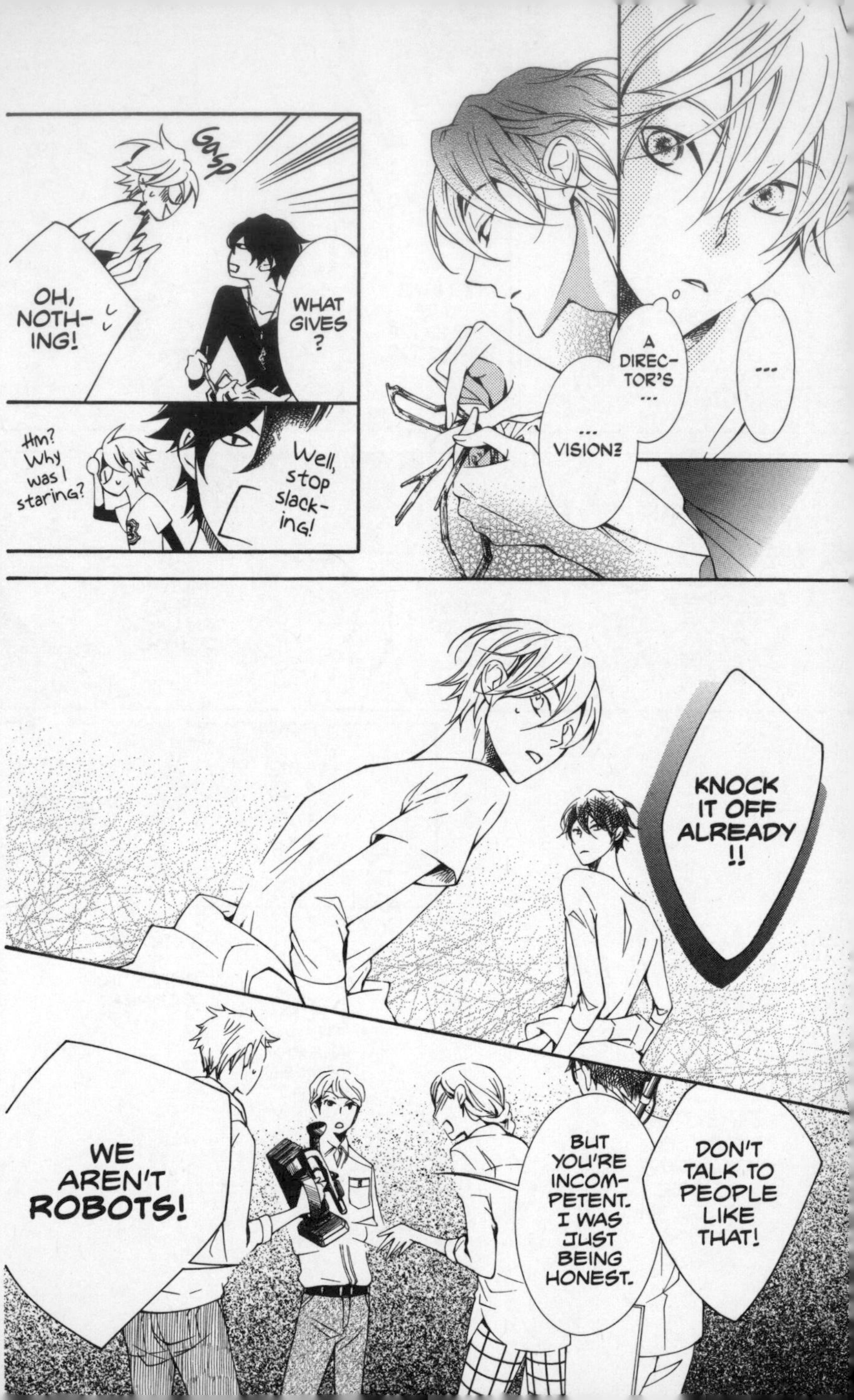
...
A DIRECTOR'S ...
... VISION?
Gasp
WHAT GIVES?
OH, NOTHING!
Well, stop slacking!
Hm? Why was I staring?
KNOCK IT OFF ALREADY!!
DON'T TALK TO PEOPLE LIKE THAT!
BUT YOU'RE INCOMPETENT. I WAS JUST BEING HONEST.
WE AREN'T ROBOTS!

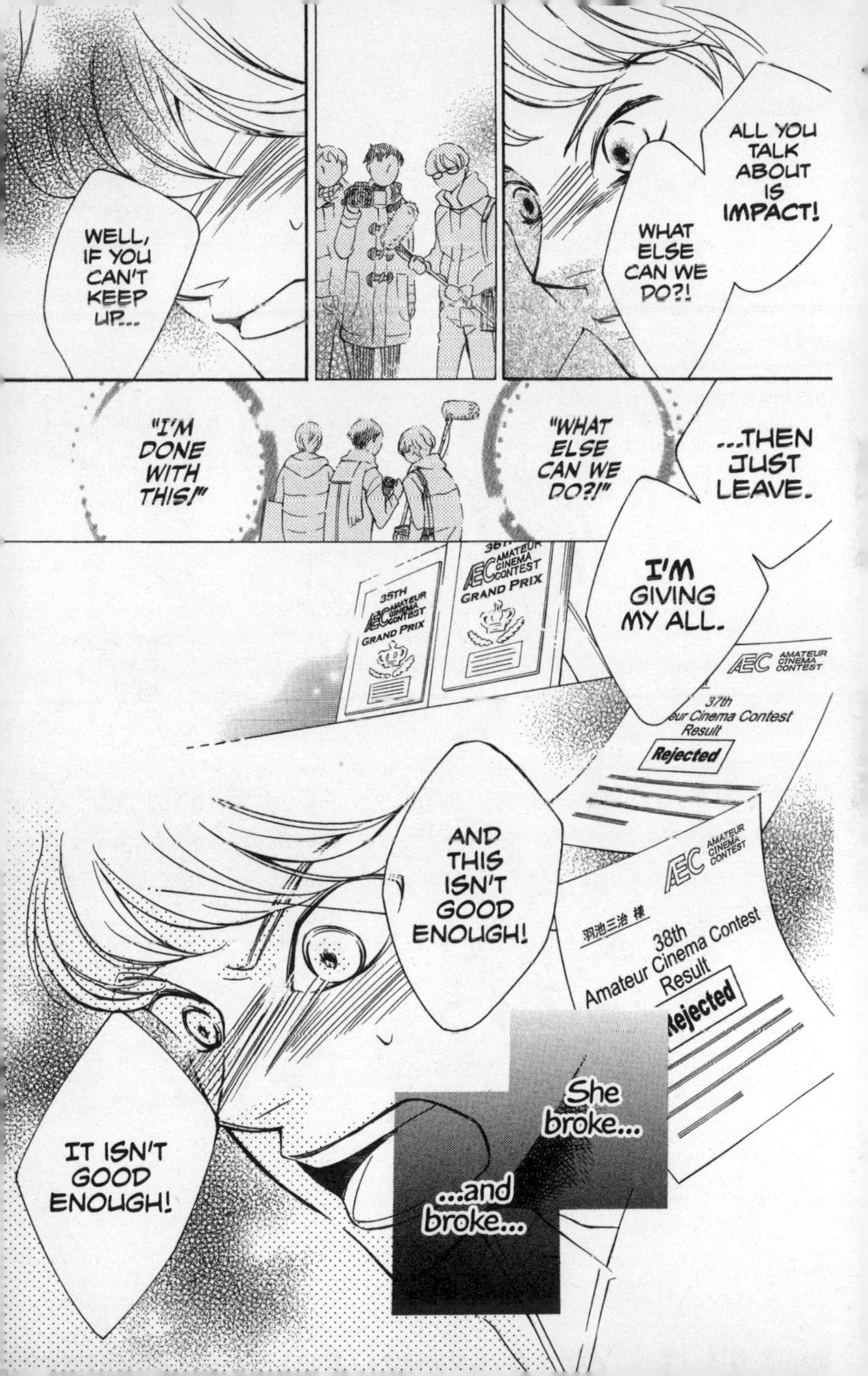
ALL YOU TALK ABOUT IS IMPACT!
WHAT ELSE CAN WE DO?!
WELL, IF YOU CAN'T KEEP UP...
...THEN JUST LEAVE.
"WHAT ELSE CAN WE DO?!"
"I'M DONE WITH THIS!"
I'M GIVING MY ALL.
36TH AEC AMATEUR CINEMA CONTEST GRAND PRIX
35TH AEC AMATEUR CINEMA CONTEST GRAND PRIX
AEC AMATEUR CINEMA CONTEST
37th
eur Cinema Contest
Result
Rejected
AEC AMATEUR CINEMA CONTEST
羽池三治 様
38th
Amateur Cinema Contest
Result
Rejected
AND THIS ISN'T GOOD ENOUGH!
IT ISN'T GOOD ENOUGH!
She broke...
...and broke...

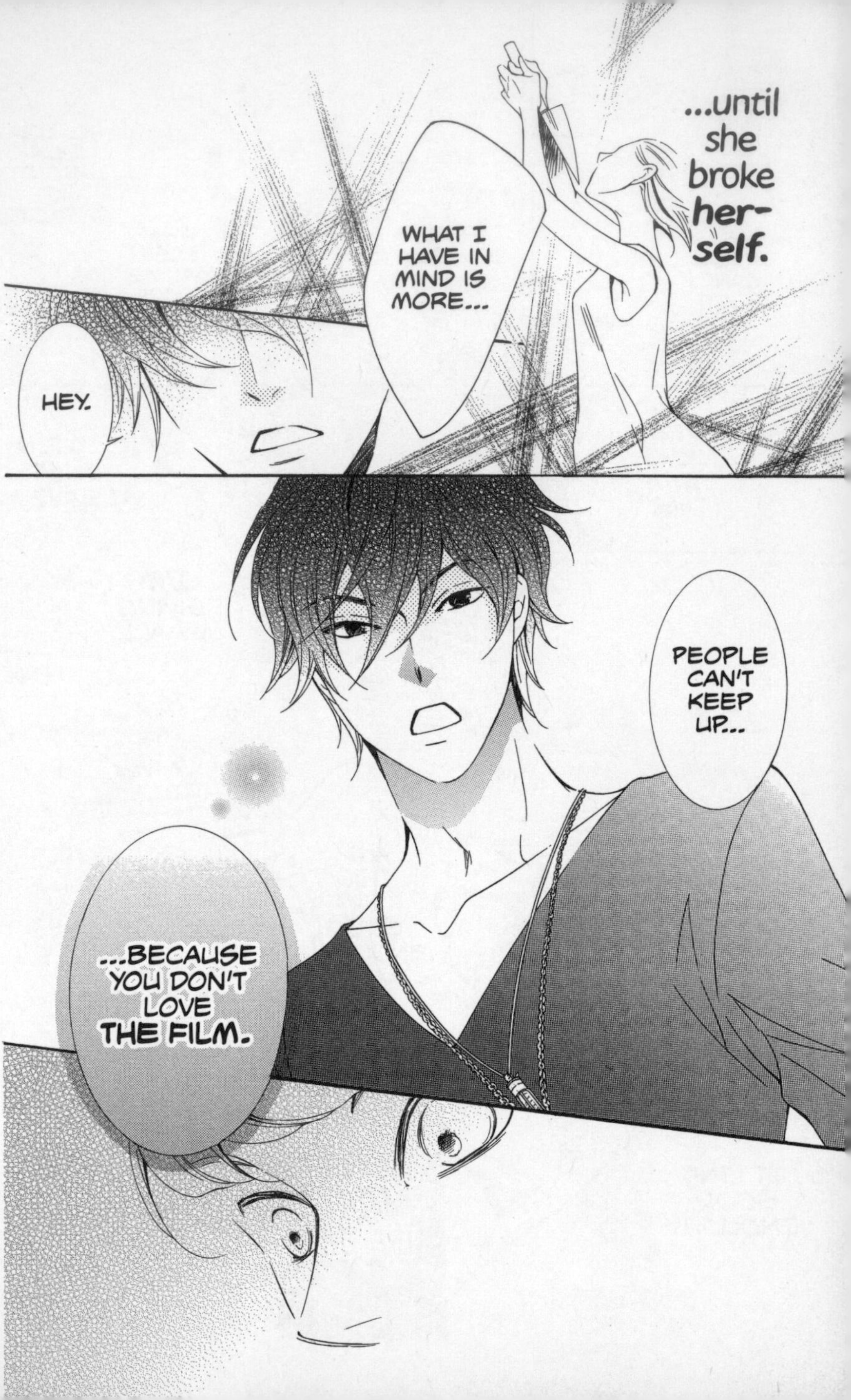
...until she broke her-self.
WHAT I HAVE IN MIND IS MORE...
HEY.
PEOPLE CAN'T KEEP UP...
...BECAUSE YOU DON'T LOVE THE FILM.

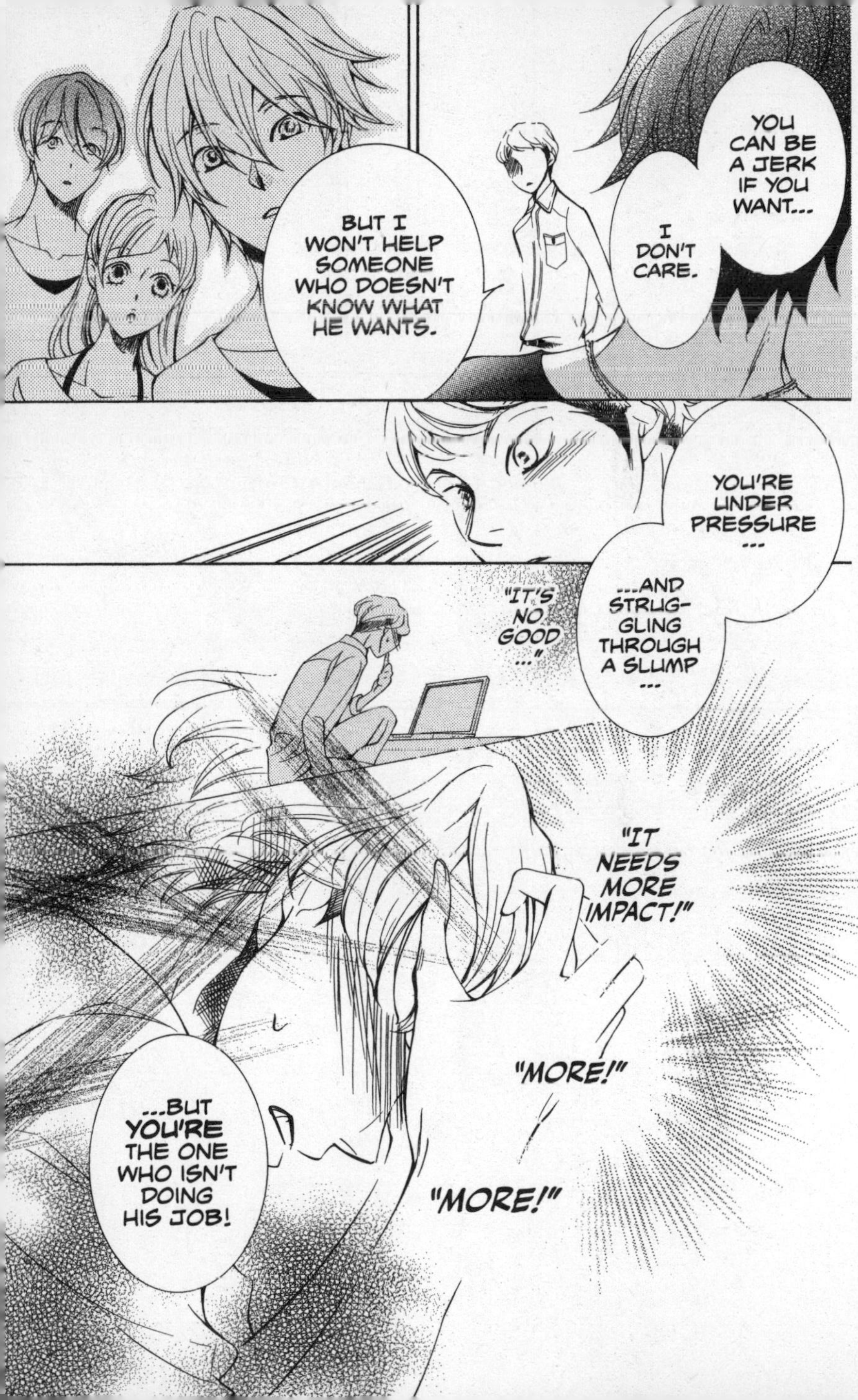
YOU CAN BE A JERK IF YOU WANT...
I DON'T CARE.
BUT I WON'T HELP SOMEONE WHO DOESN'T KNOW WHAT HE WANTS.
YOU'RE UNDER PRESSURE...
...AND STRUGGLING THROUGH A SLUMP...
"IT'S NO GOOD..."
"IT NEEDS MORE IMPACT!"
"MORE!"
"MORE!"
...BUT YOU'RE THE ONE WHO ISN'T DOING HIS JOB!

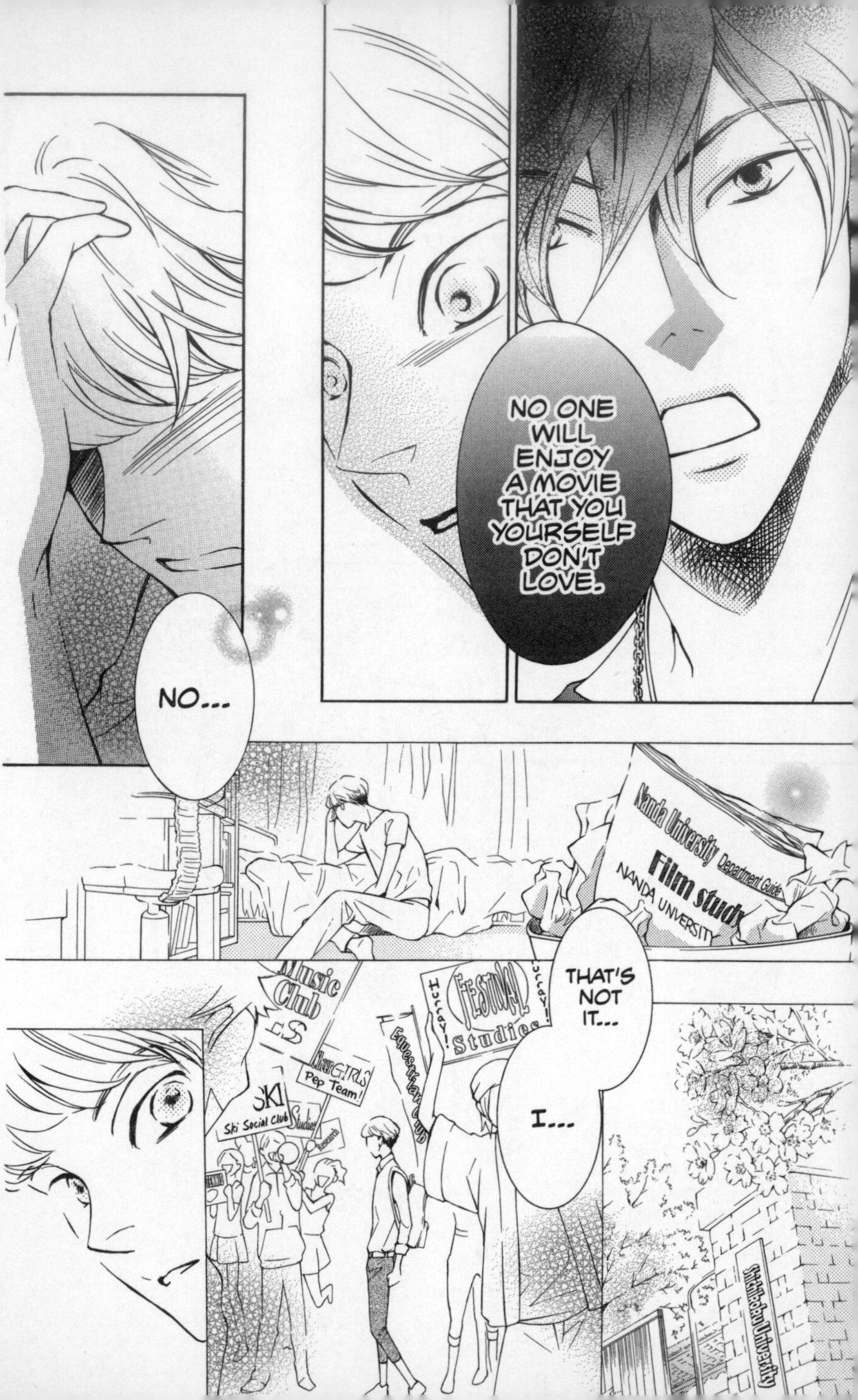
NO ONE WILL ENJOY A MOVIE THAT YOU YOURSELF DON'T LOVE.
NO...
Nanda University Department Guide
Film study
NANDA UNIVERSITY
THAT'S NOT IT...
I...
Music Club
Pep Team!
Ski Social Club
Hurray!
Studies

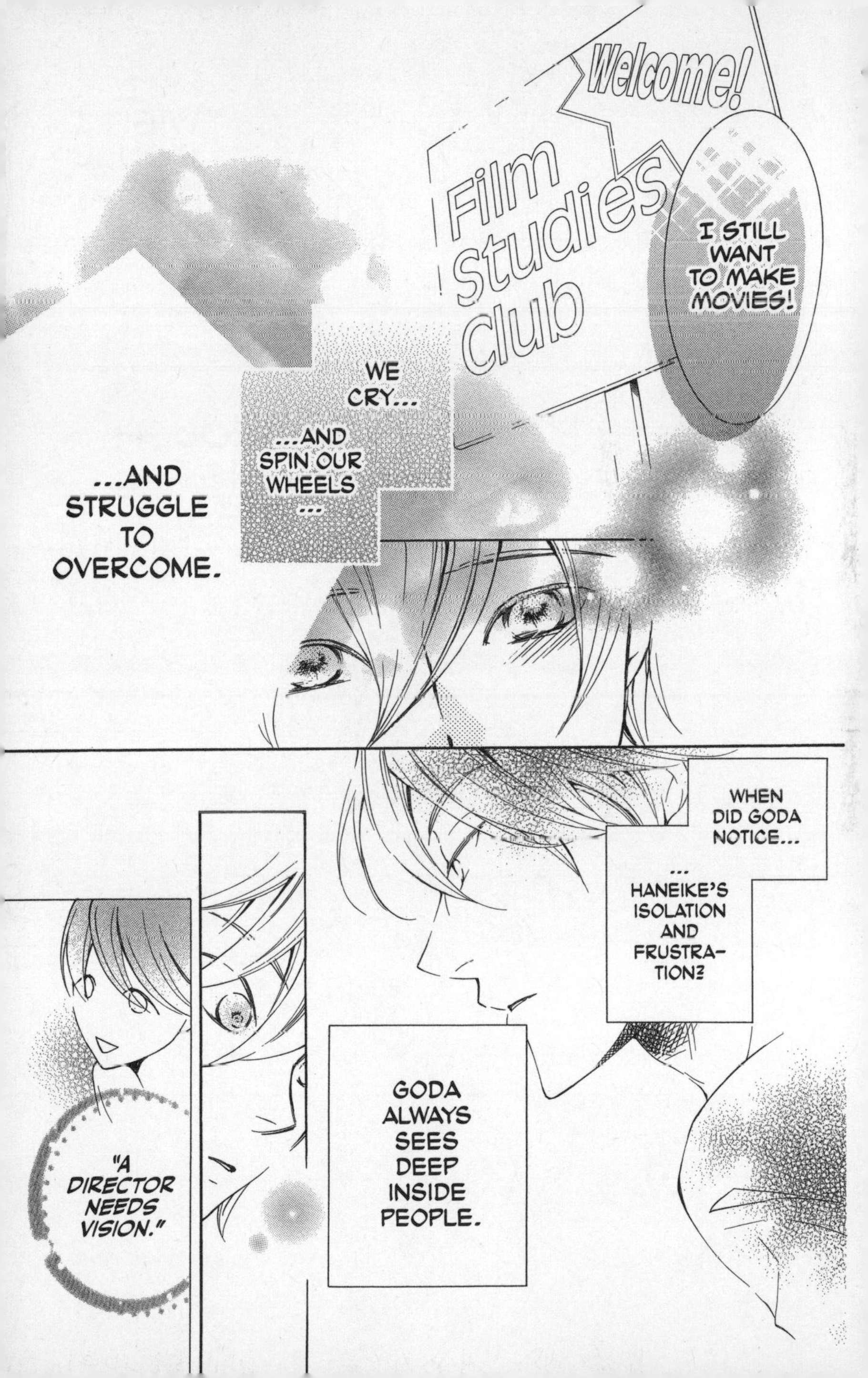
Welcome!
Film Studies Club
I STILL WANT TO MAKE MOVIES!
WE CRY...
...AND SPIN OUR WHEELS...
...AND STRUGGLE TO OVERCOME.
WHEN DID GODA NOTICE...
...HANEIKE'S ISOLATION AND FRUSTRATION?
GODA ALWAYS SEES DEEP INSIDE PEOPLE.
"A DIRECTOR NEEDS VISION."

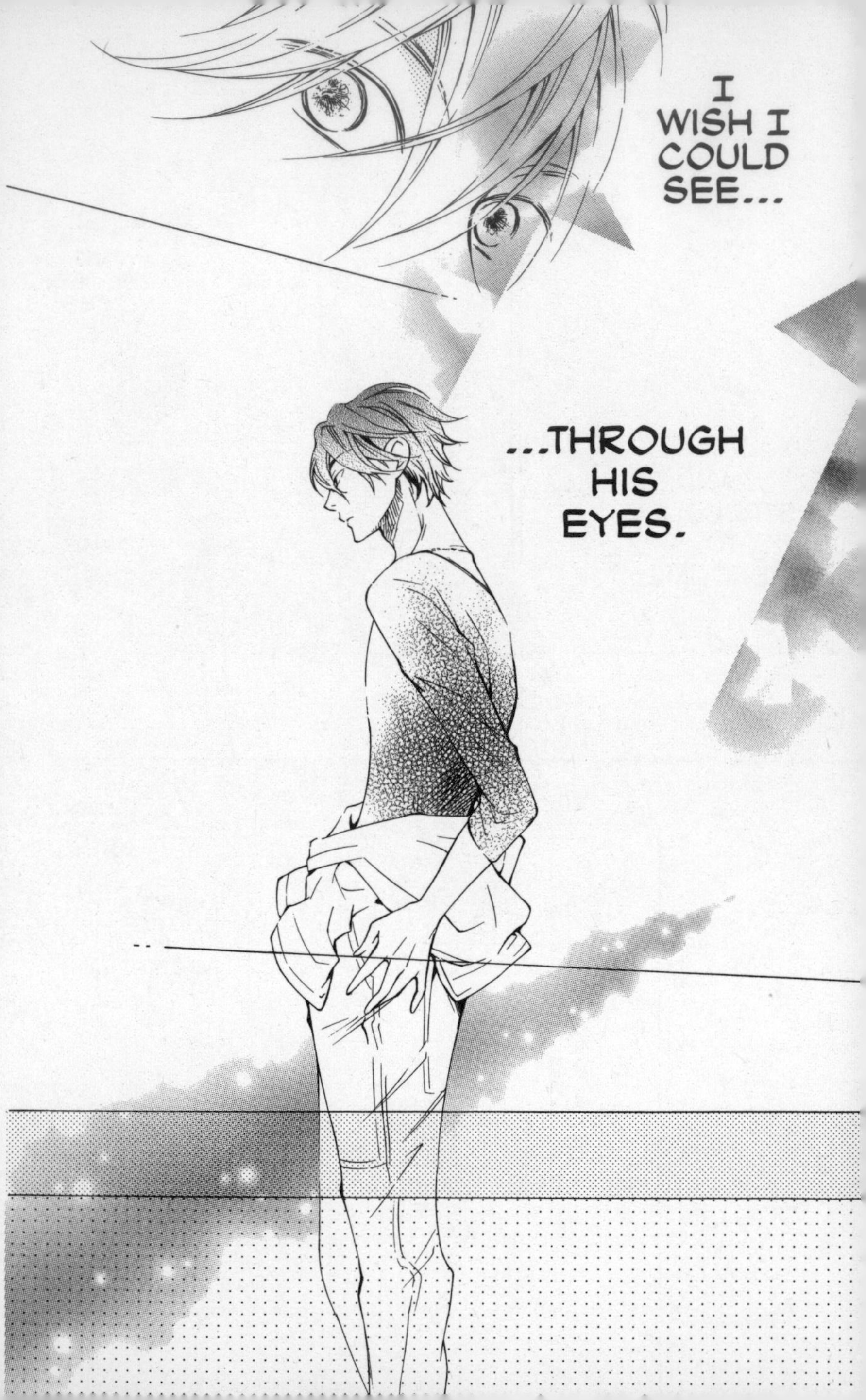
I WISH I COULD SEE...
...THROUGH HIS EYES.

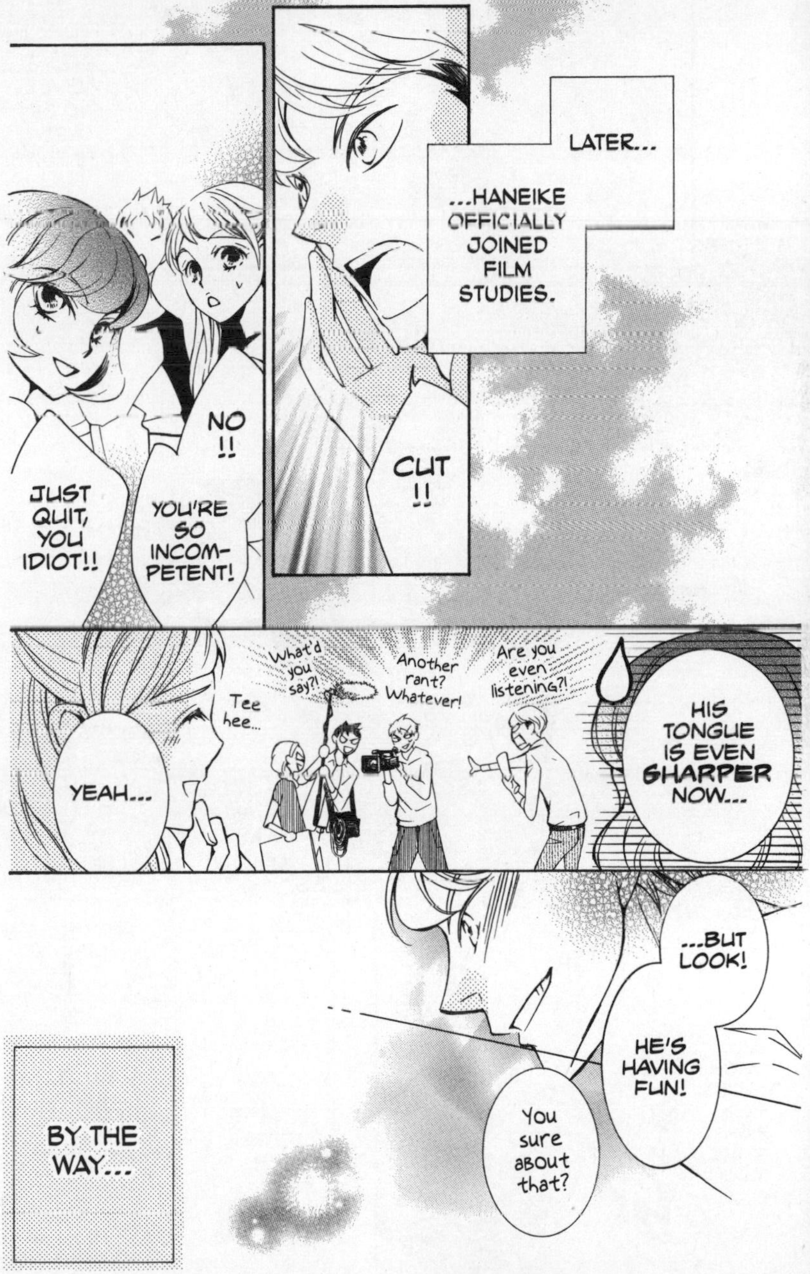
LATER...
...HANEIKE OFFICIALLY JOINED FILM STUDIES.
CUT!!
NO!!
YOU'RE SO INCOMPETENT!
JUST QUIT, YOU IDIOT!!
HIS TONGUE IS EVEN SHARPER NOW...
Are you even listening?!
Another rant? Whatever!
What'd you say?!
Tee hee...
YEAH...
...BUT LOOK!
HE'S HAVING FUN!
You sure about that?
BY THE WAY...

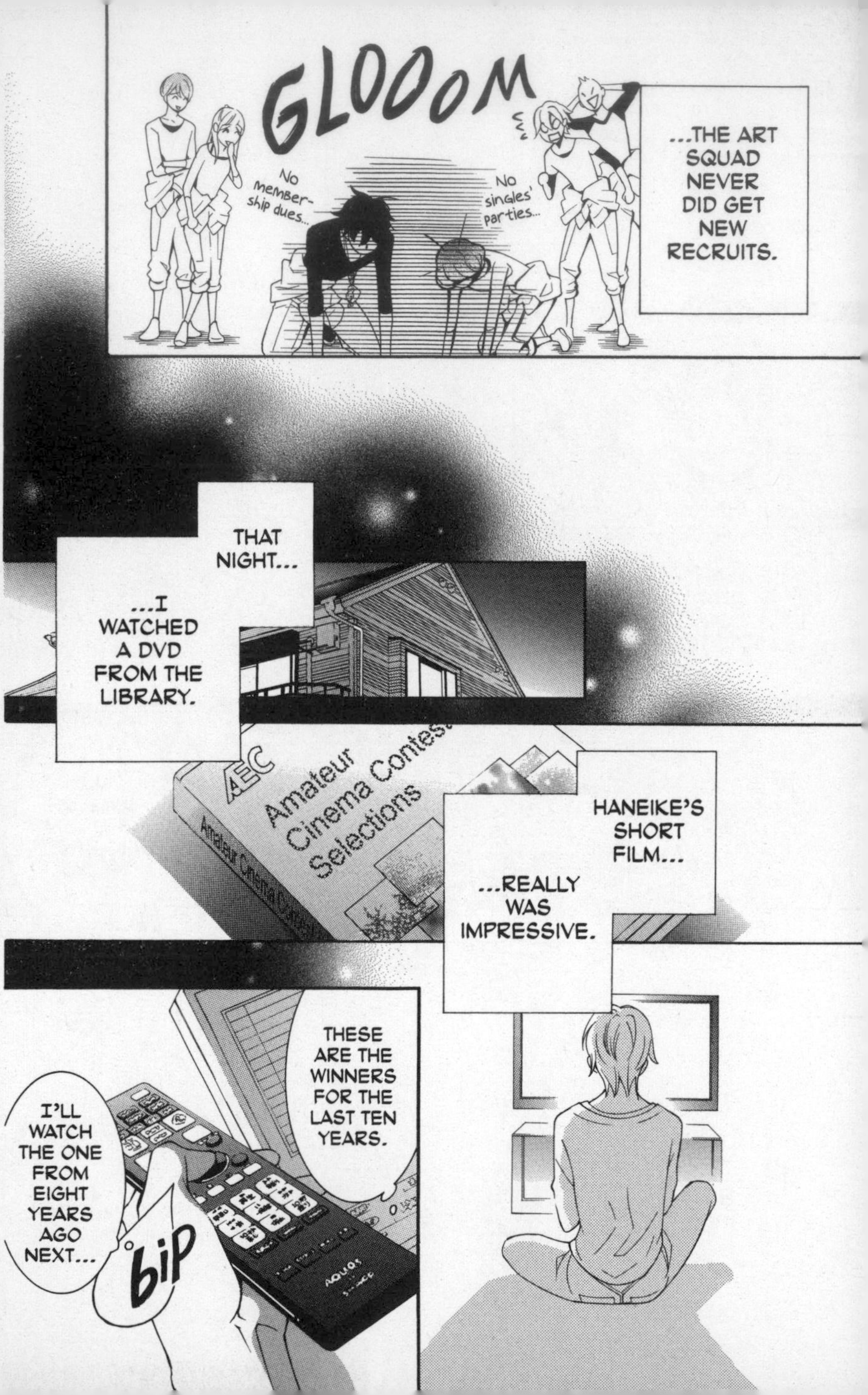
...THE ART SQUAD NEVER DID GET NEW RECRUITS.
GLOOOM
No singles' parties...
No membership dues...
THAT NIGHT...
...I WATCHED A DVD FROM THE LIBRARY.
HANEIKE'S SHORT FILM...
...REALLY WAS IMPRESSIVE.
AEC
Amateur Cinema Contest Selections
THESE ARE THE WINNERS FOR THE LAST TEN YEARS.
I'LL WATCH THE ONE FROM EIGHT YEARS AGO NEXT...
bip
AQUOS

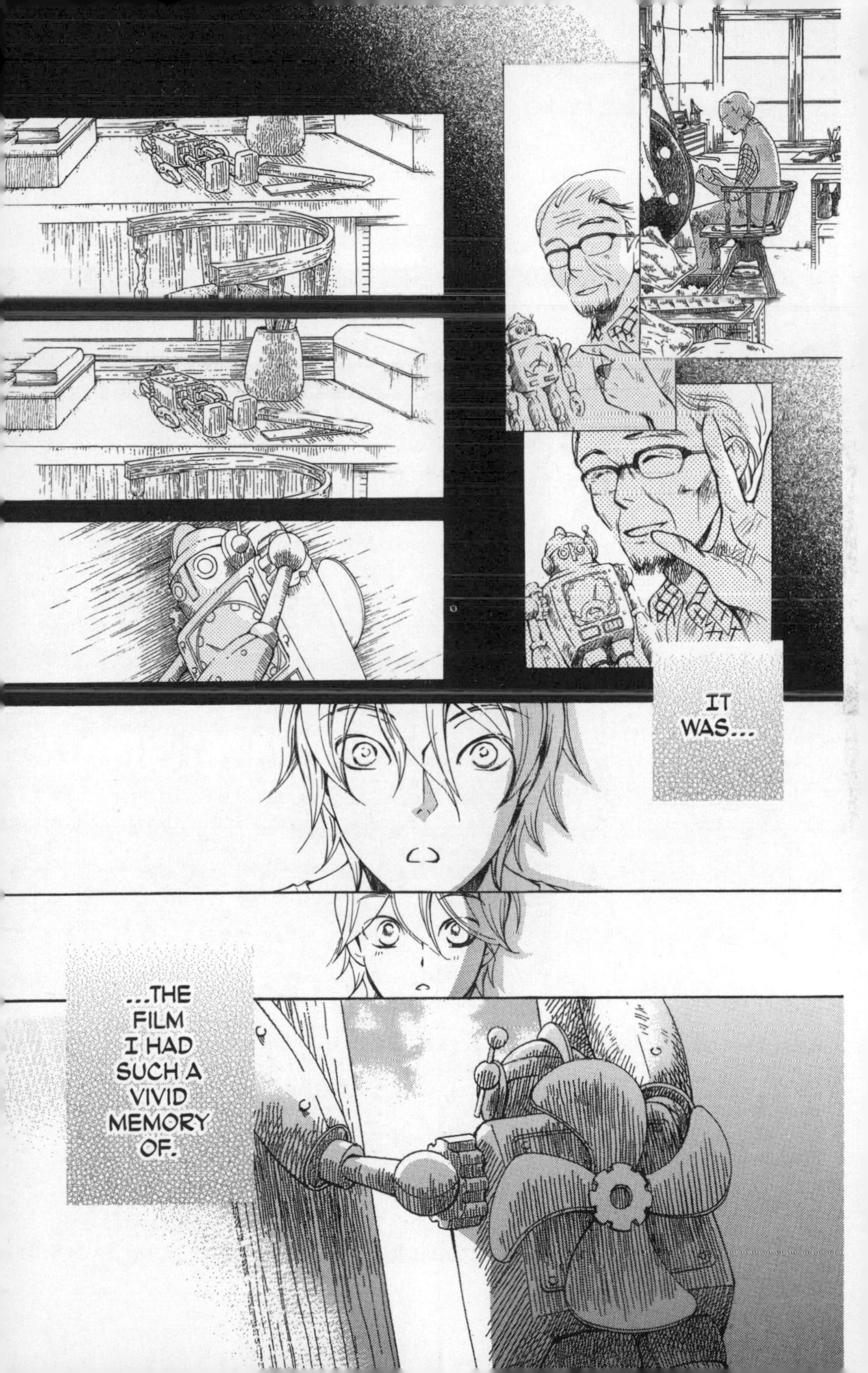
IT WAS...
...THE FILM I HAD SUCH A VIVID MEMORY OF.

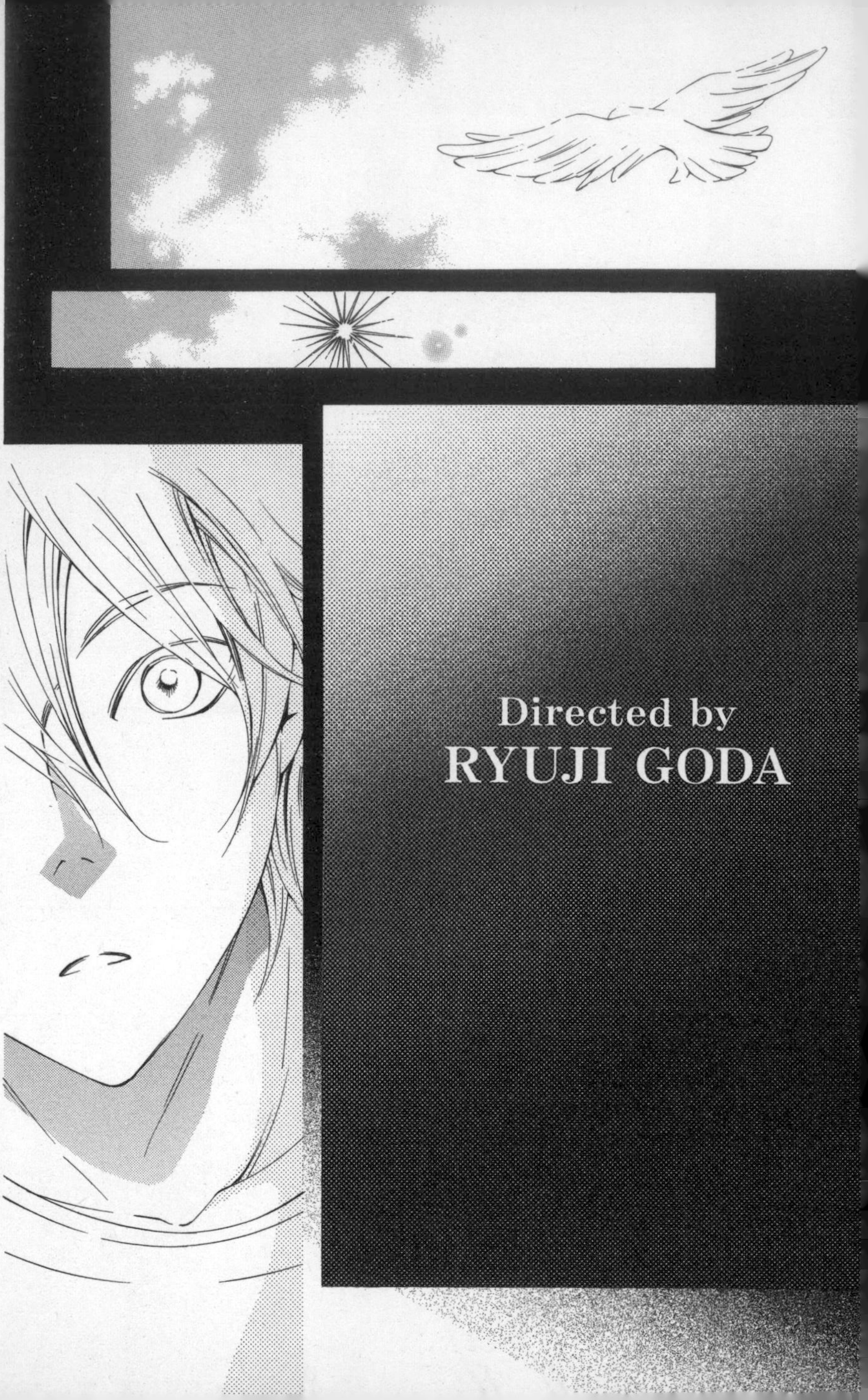
Directed by
RYUJI GODA

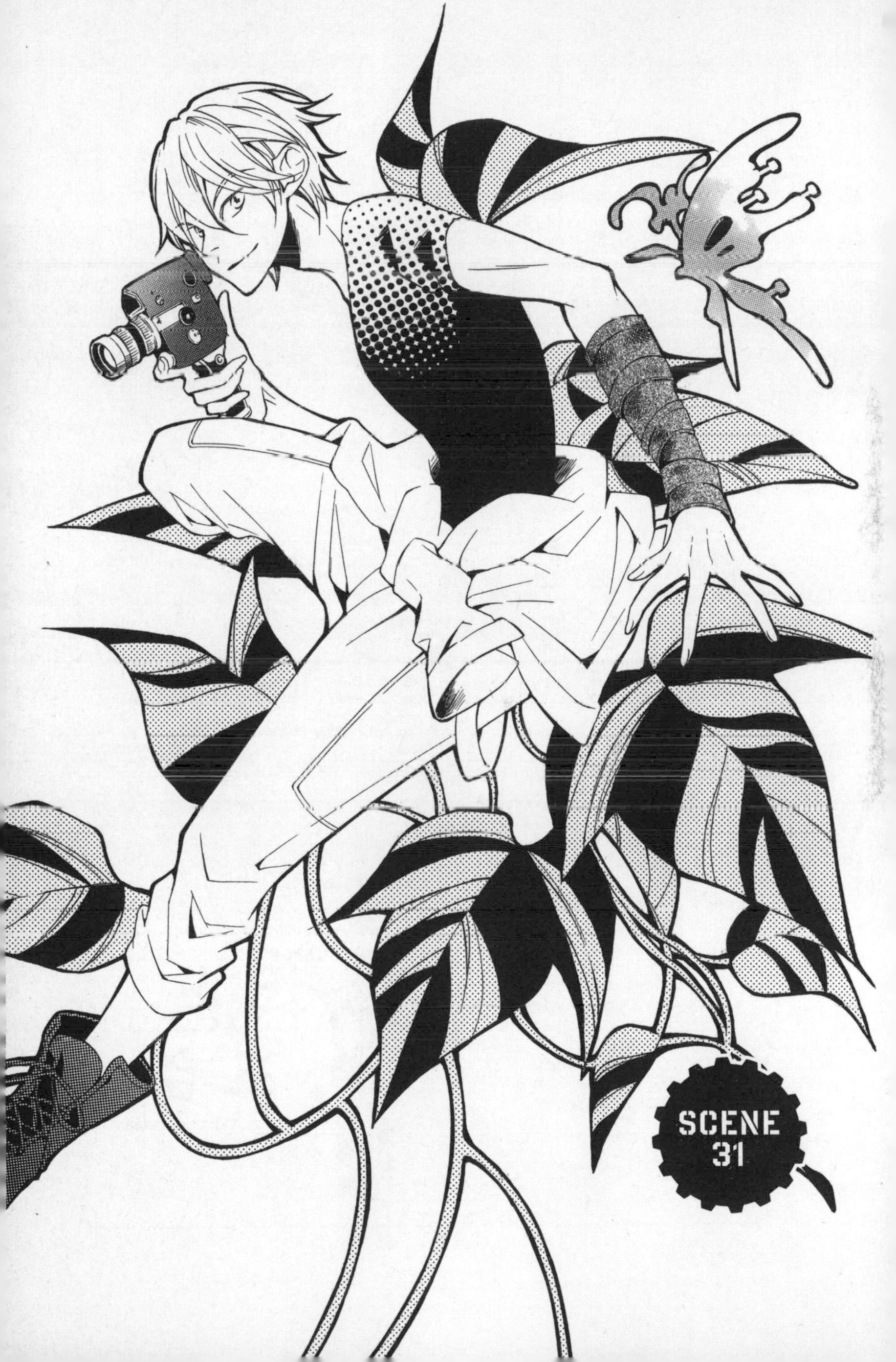
SCENE
31

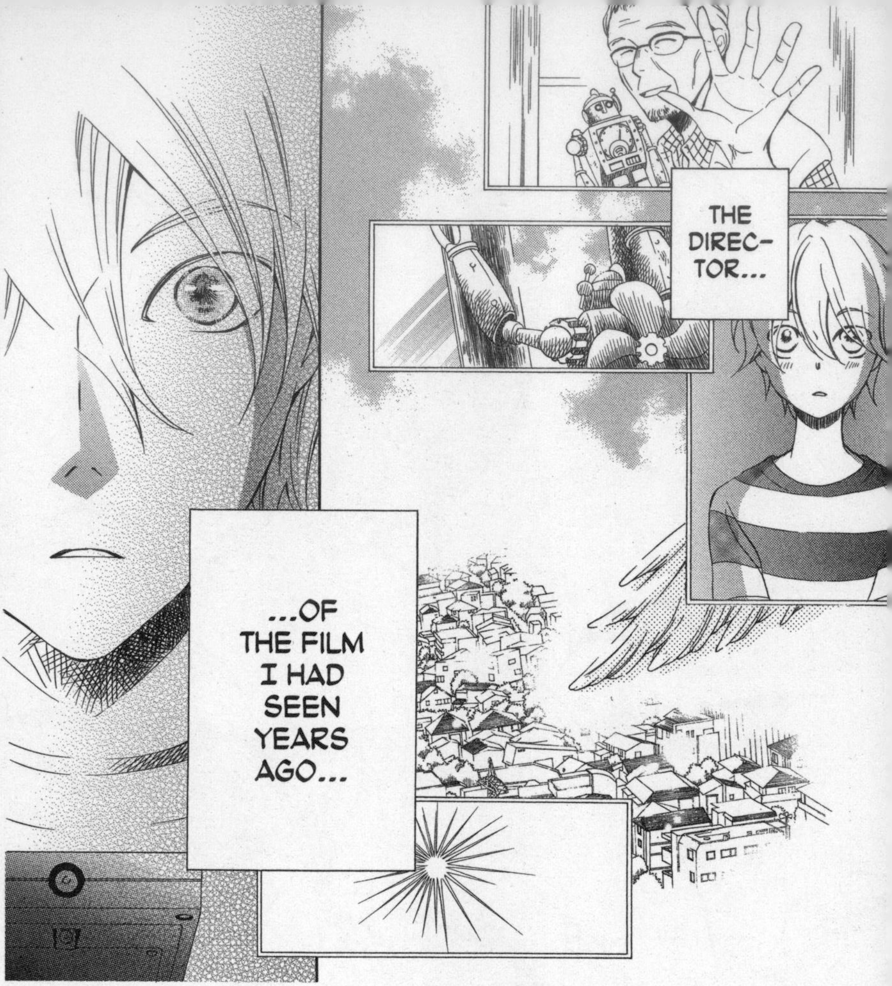
THE DIRECTOR...
...OF THE FILM I HAD SEEN YEARS AGO...

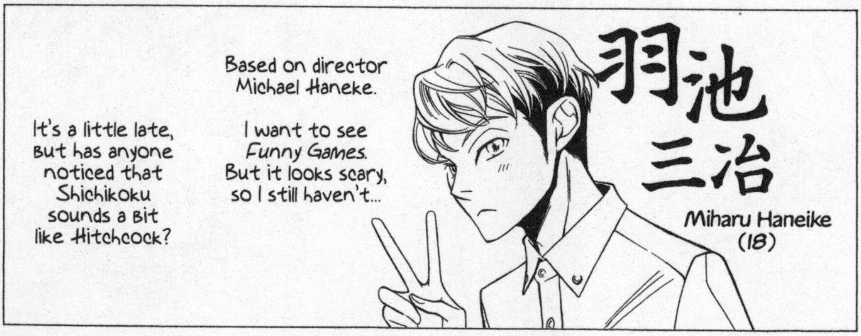
羽池三治
Miharu Haneike (18)
Based on director Michael Haneke.
I want to see *Funny Games*. But it looks scary, so I still haven't...
It's a little late, but has anyone noticed that Shichikoku sounds a bit like Hitchcock?

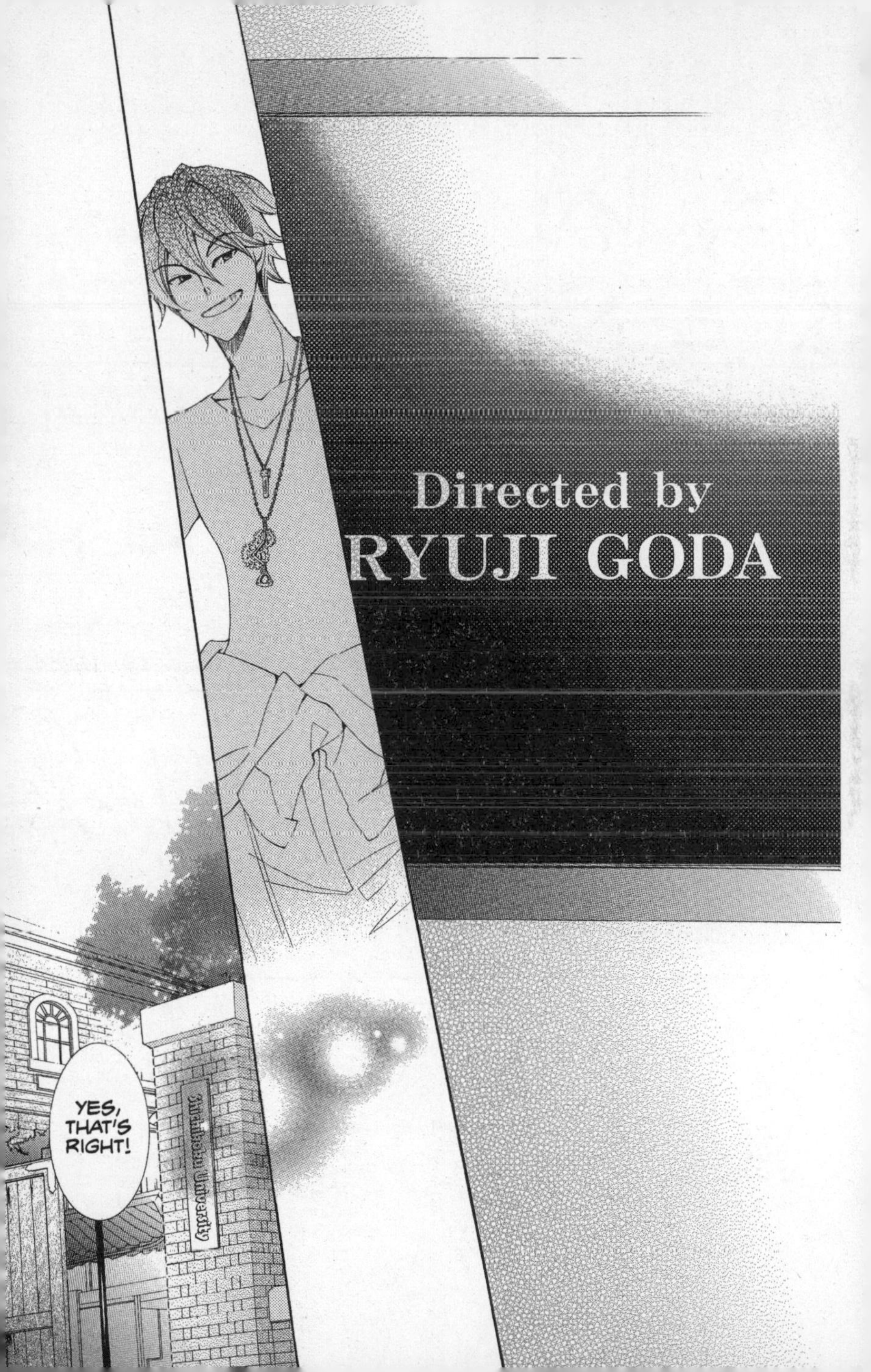
Directed by
RYUJI GODA
YES, THAT'S RIGHT!

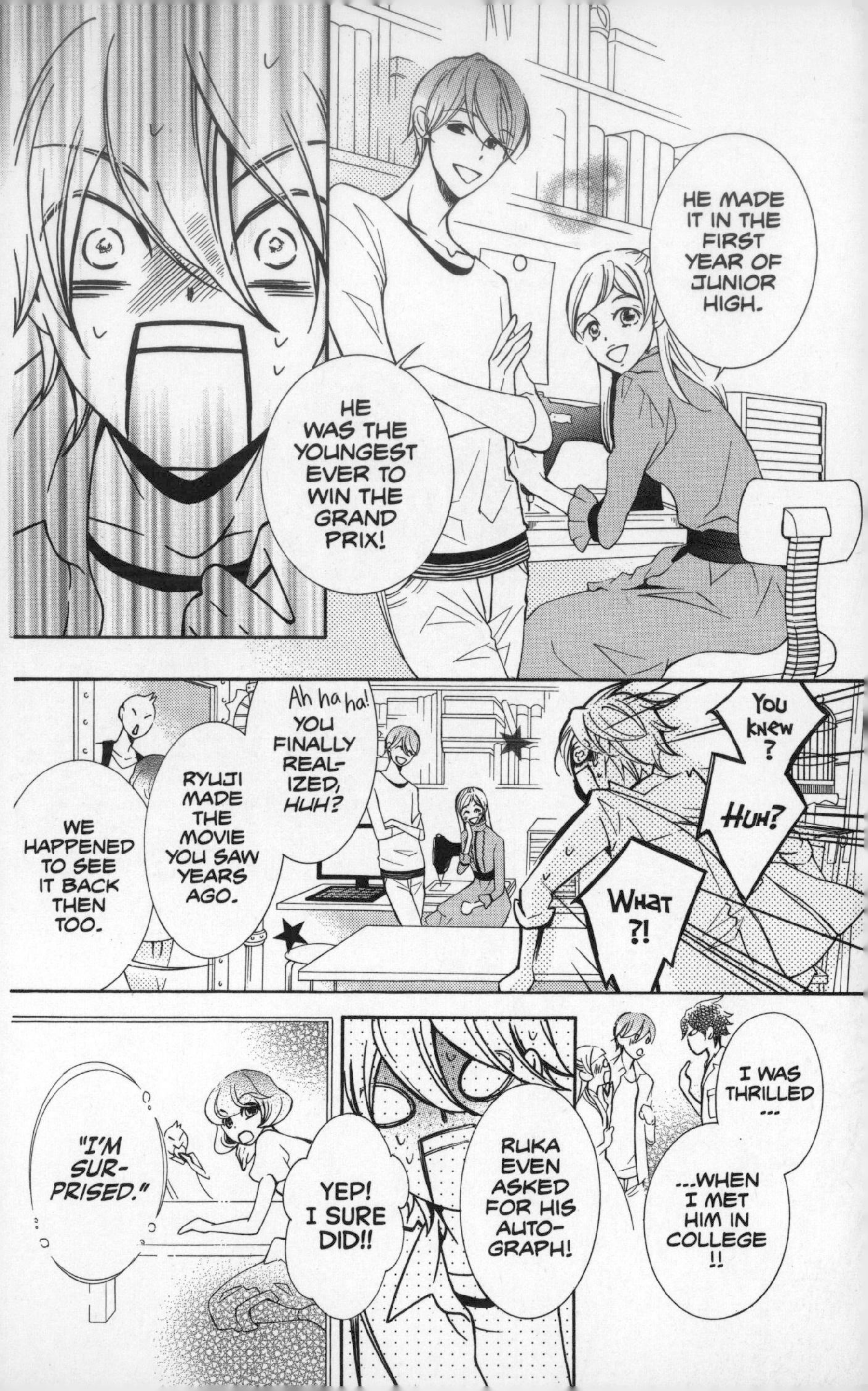
HE MADE IT IN THE FIRST YEAR OF JUNIOR HIGH.
HE WAS THE YOUNGEST EVER TO WIN THE GRAND PRIX!
You knew?
HUH?
WHAT?!
Ah ha ha! YOU FINALLY REAL-IZED, HUH?
RYUJI MADE THE MOVIE YOU SAW YEARS AGO.
WE HAPPENED TO SEE IT BACK THEN TOO.
I WAS THRILLED...
...WHEN I MET HIM IN COLLEGE!!
RUKA EVEN ASKED FOR HIS AUTO-GRAPH!
YEP! I SURE DID!!
"I'M SUR-PRISED."

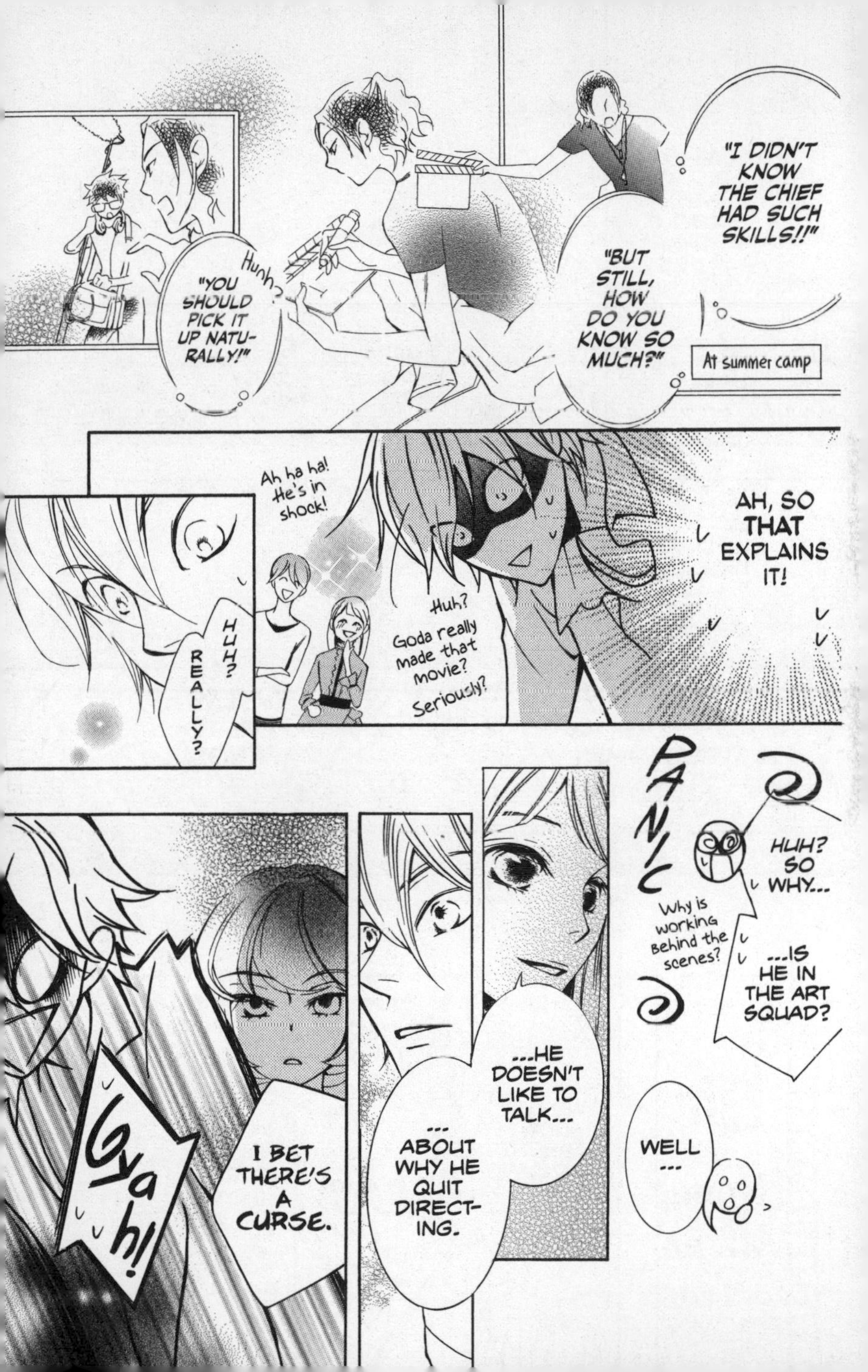
At summer camp
"I DIDN'T KNOW THE CHIEF HAD SUCH SKILLS!!"
"BUT STILL, HOW DO YOU KNOW SO MUCH?"
Hunh?
"YOU SHOULD PICK IT UP NATU-RALLY!"
AH, SO THAT EXPLAINS IT!
Huh? Goda really made that movie? Seriously?
Ah ha ha! He's in shock!
HUH? REALLY?
PANIC
HUH? SO WHY...
...IS HE IN THE ART SQUAD?
Why is working behind the scenes?
WELL...
...HE DOESN'T LIKE TO TALK...
...ABOUT WHY HE QUIT DIRECT-ING.
I BET THERE'S A CURSE.
Gyah!

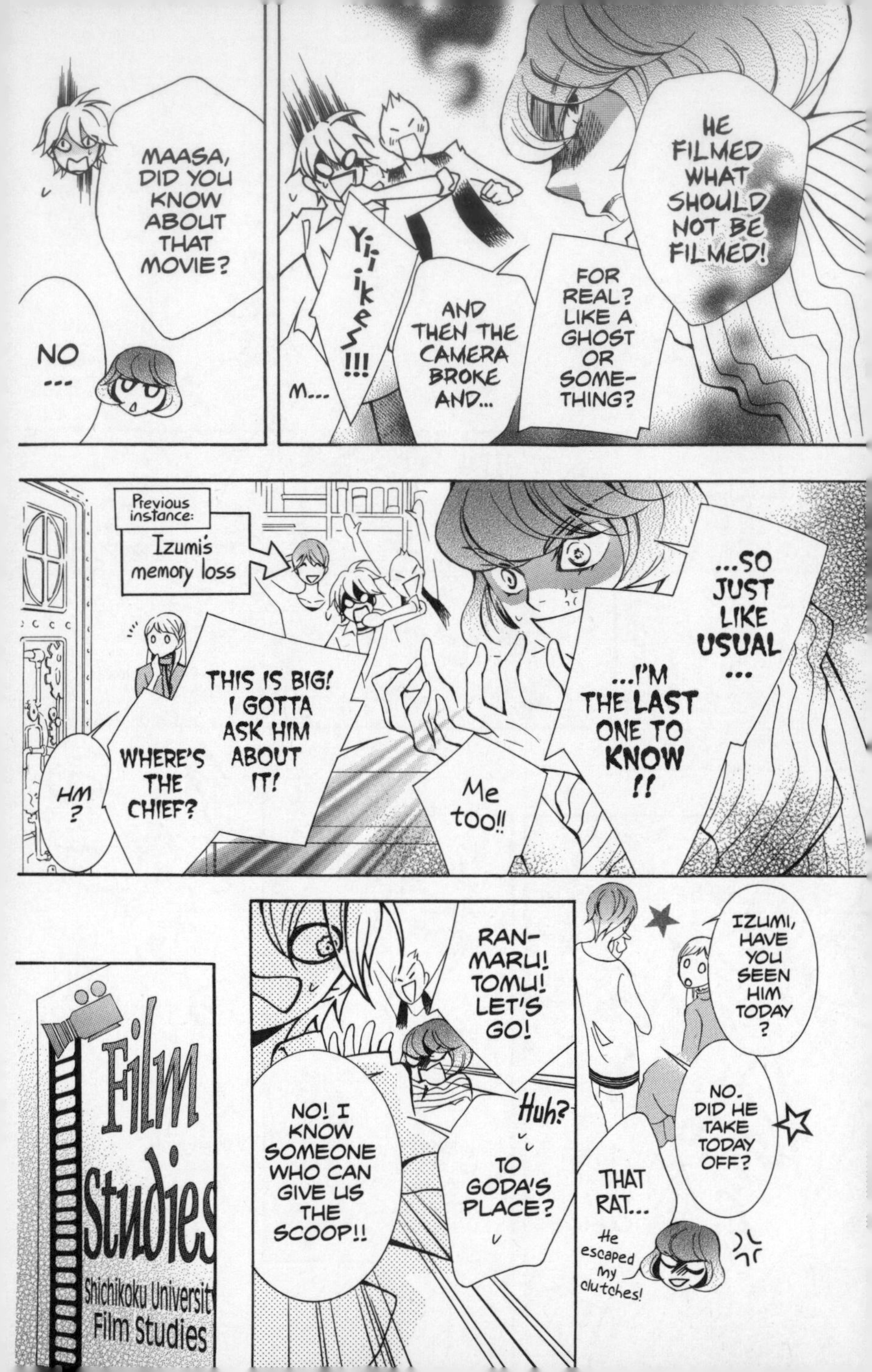
HE FILMED WHAT SHOULD NOT BE FILMED!
FOR REAL? LIKE A GHOST OR SOME-THING?
AND THEN THE CAMERA BROKE AND...
Yiiikes!!!
M...
MAASA, DID YOU KNOW ABOUT THAT MOVIE?
NO ---
...SO JUST LIKE USUAL...
...I'M THE LAST ONE TO KNOW!!
Me too!!
THIS IS BIG! I GOTTA ASK HIM ABOUT IT!
WHERE'S THE CHIEF?
HM?
Previous instance:
Izumi's memory loss
IZUMI, HAVE YOU SEEN HIM TODAY?
NO. DID HE TAKE TODAY OFF?
THAT RAT...
He escaped my clutches!
RAN-MARU! TOMU! LET'S GO!
Huh?
TO GODA'S PLACE?
NO! I KNOW SOMEONE WHO CAN GIVE US THE SCOOP!!
Film Studies
Shichikoku University
Film Studies

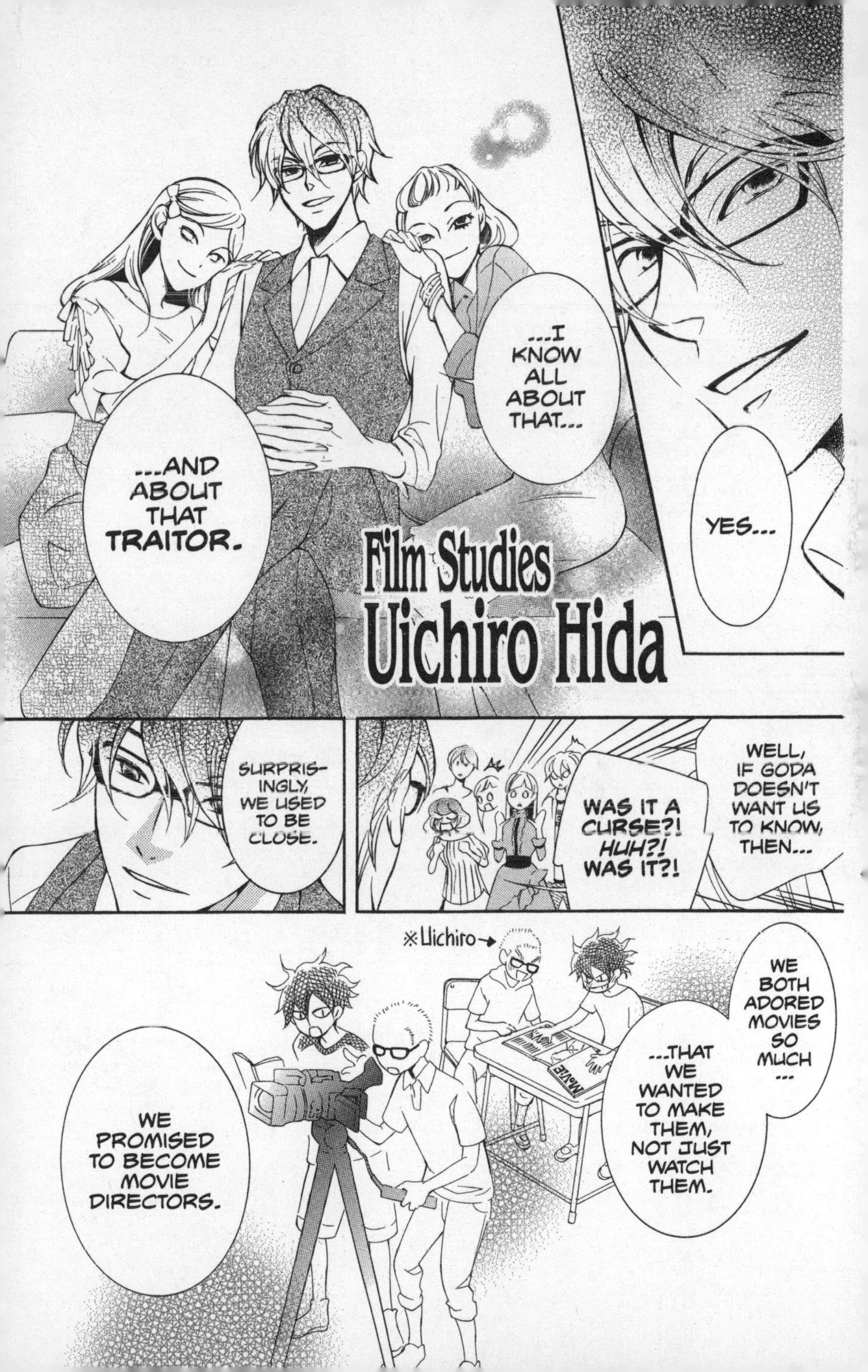
YES...
...I KNOW ALL ABOUT THAT...
...AND ABOUT THAT TRAITOR.
Film Studies
Uichiro Hida
WELL, IF GODA DOESN'T WANT US TO KNOW, THEN...
WAS IT A CURSE?! HUH?! WAS IT?!
SURPRIS-INGLY, WE USED TO BE CLOSE.
※Uichiro
WE BOTH ADORED MOVIES SO MUCH...
...THAT WE WANTED TO MAKE THEM, NOT JUST WATCH THEM.
MOVIE
WE PROMISED TO BECOME MOVIE DIRECTORS.

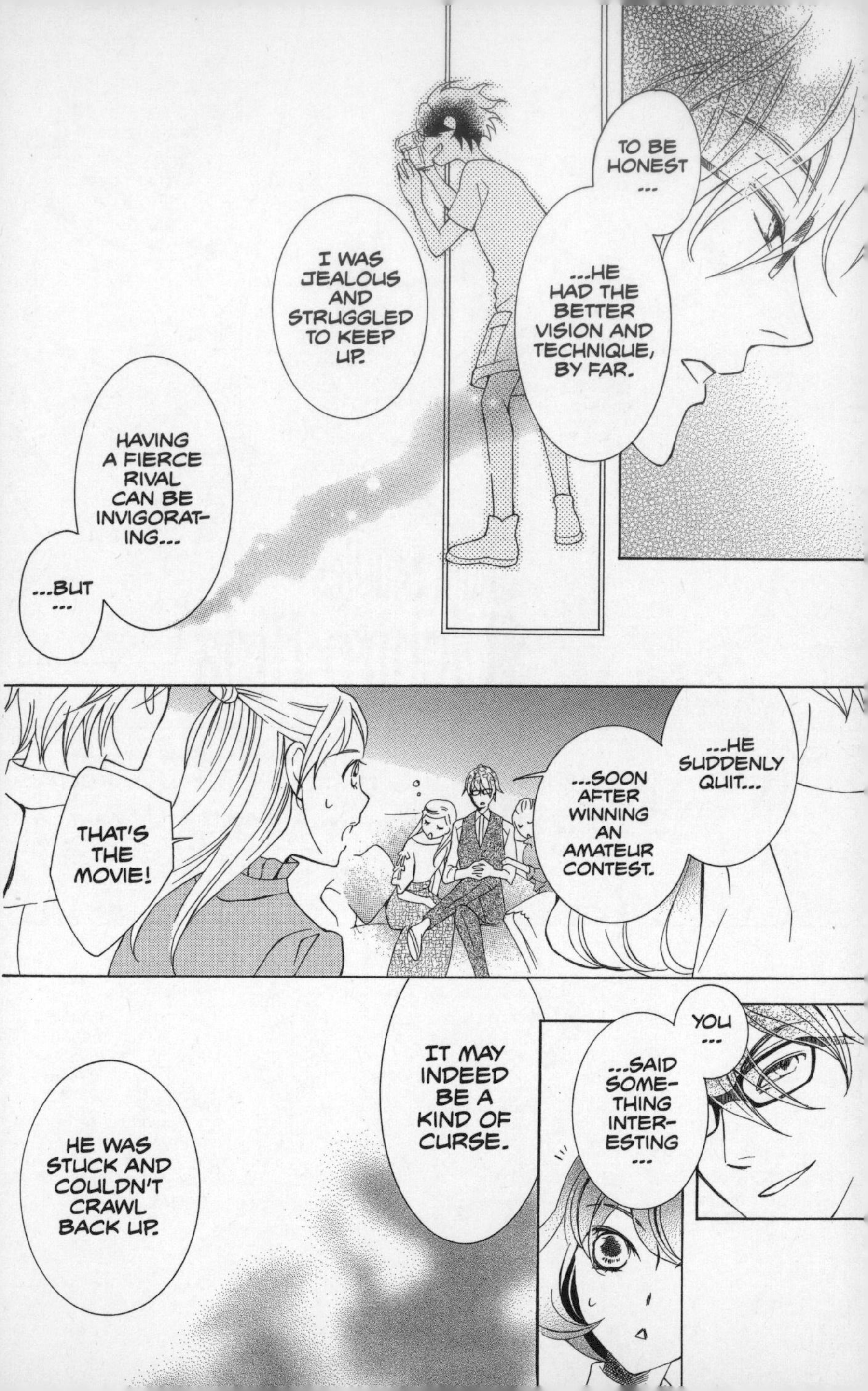
TO BE HONEST...
...HE HAD THE BETTER VISION AND TECHNIQUE, BY FAR.
I WAS JEALOUS AND STRUGGLED TO KEEP UP.
HAVING A FIERCE RIVAL CAN BE INVIGORAT-ING...
...BUT...
...HE SUDDENLY QUIT...
...SOON AFTER WINNING AN AMATEUR CONTEST.
THAT'S THE MOVIE!
YOU...
...SAID SOME-THING INTER-ESTING...
IT MAY INDEED BE A KIND OF CURSE.
HE WAS STUCK AND COULDN'T CRAWL BACK UP.

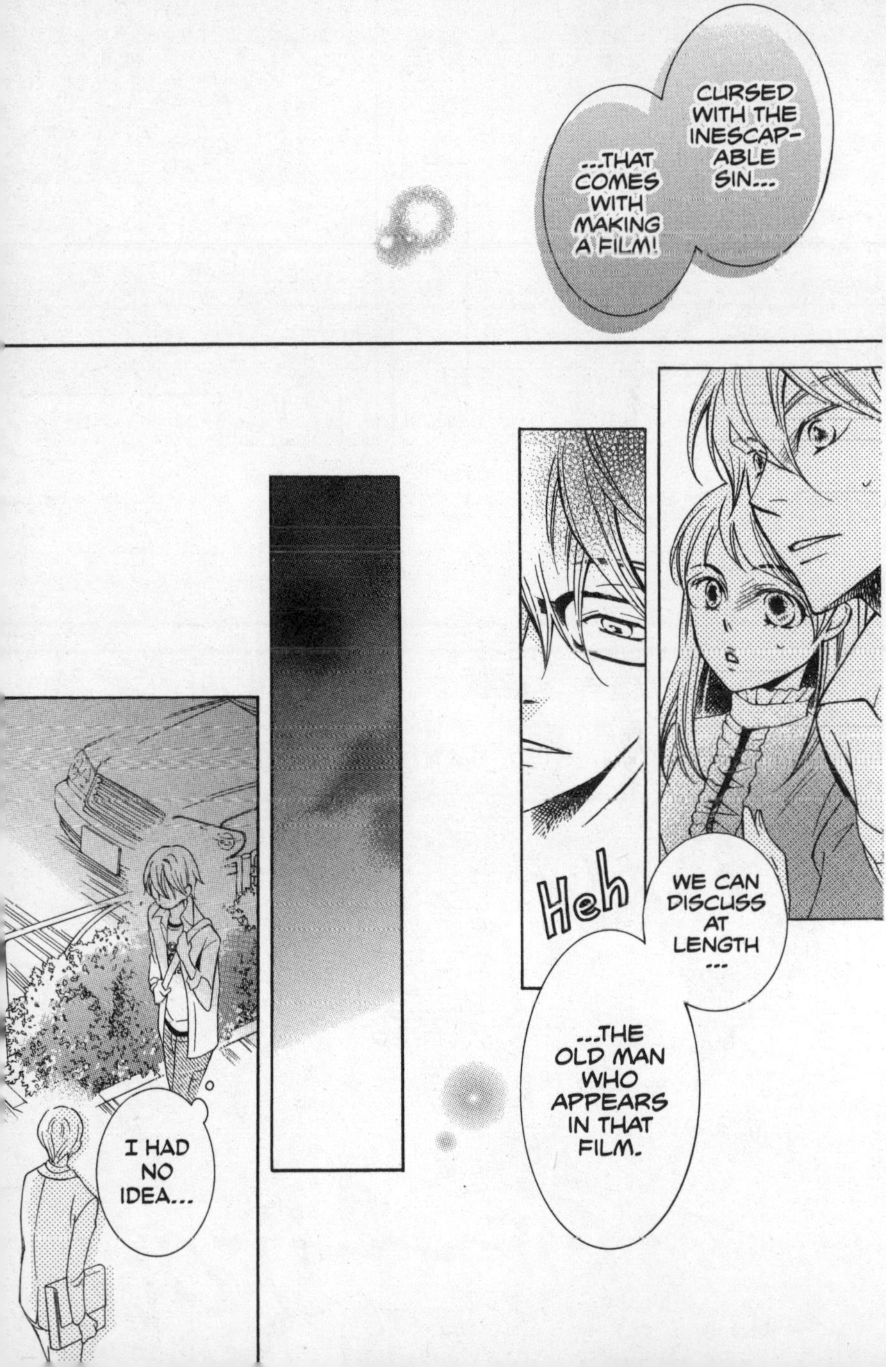
CURSED WITH THE INESCAP-ABLE SIN...
...THAT COMES WITH MAKING A FILM!
Heh
WE CAN DISCUSS AT LENGTH ...
...THE OLD MAN WHO APPEARS IN THAT FILM.
I HAD NO IDEA...

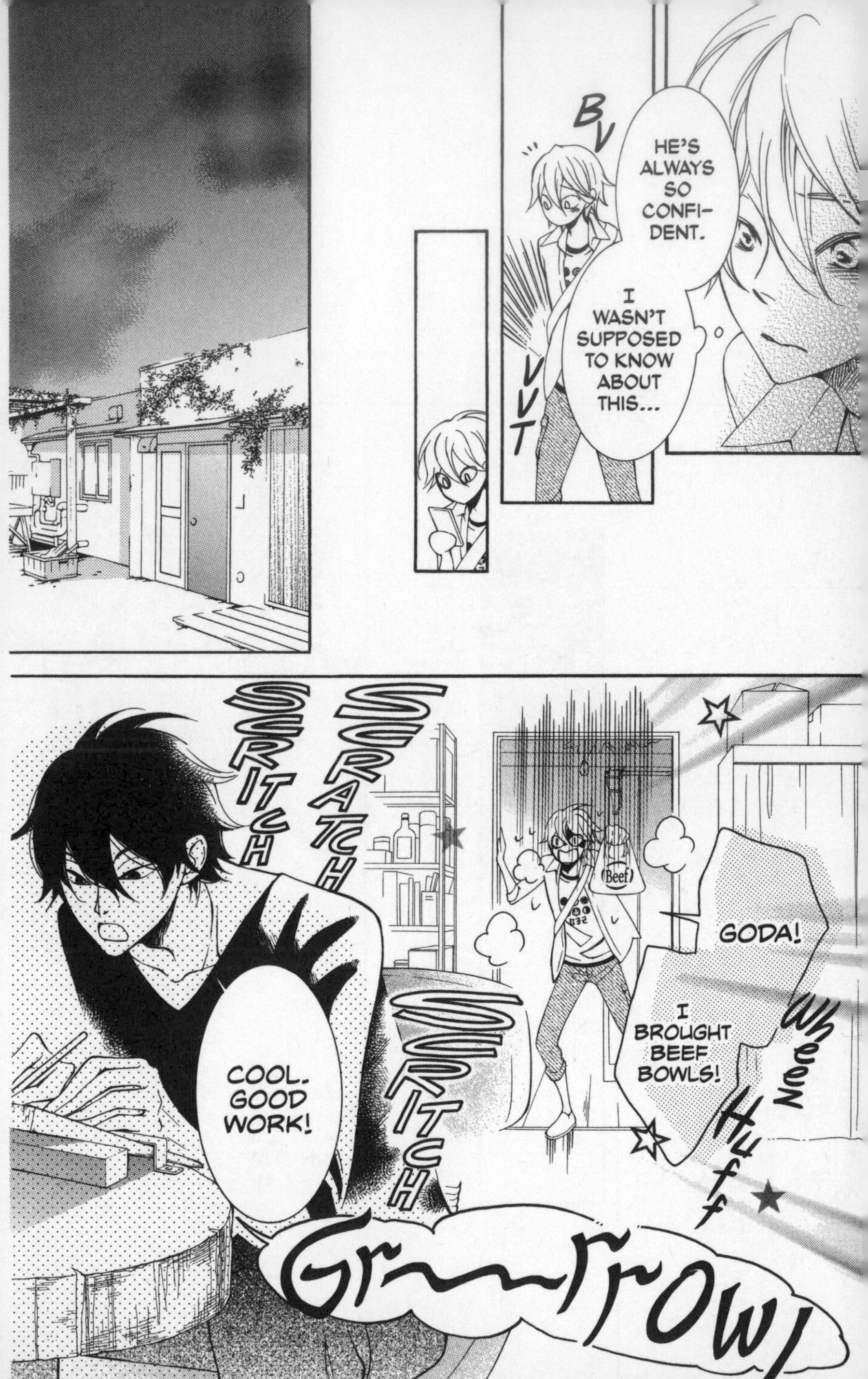
BVVVT
HE'S ALWAYS SO CONFIDENT.
I WASN'T SUPPOSED TO KNOW ABOUT THIS...
GODA!
I BROUGHT BEEF BOWLS!
Beef
Wheeez
Huff
SCRATCH
SCRITCH
COOL. GOOD WORK!
SCRITCH
Gr~~rowl

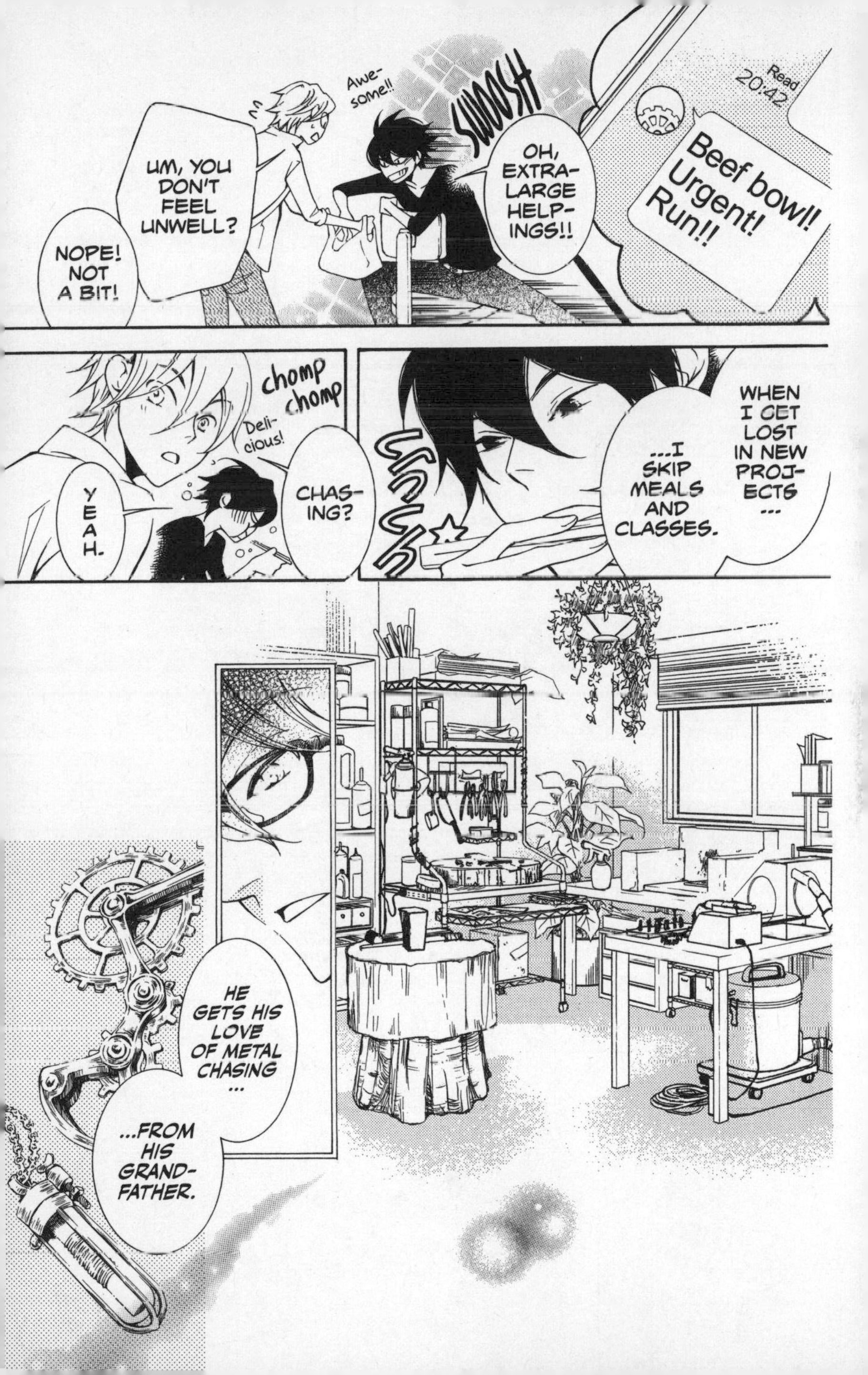
Read 20:42
Beef bowl!! Urgent! Run!!
OH, EXTRA-LARGE HELP-INGS!!
SWOOSH
Awe-some!!
UM, YOU DON'T FEEL UNWELL?
NOPE! NOT A BIT!
WHEN I GET LOST IN NEW PROJ-ECTS...
...I SKIP MEALS AND CLASSES.
chomp chomp
Deli-cious!
CHAS-ING?
YEAH.
HE GETS HIS LOVE OF METAL CHASING...
...FROM HIS GRAND-FATHER.

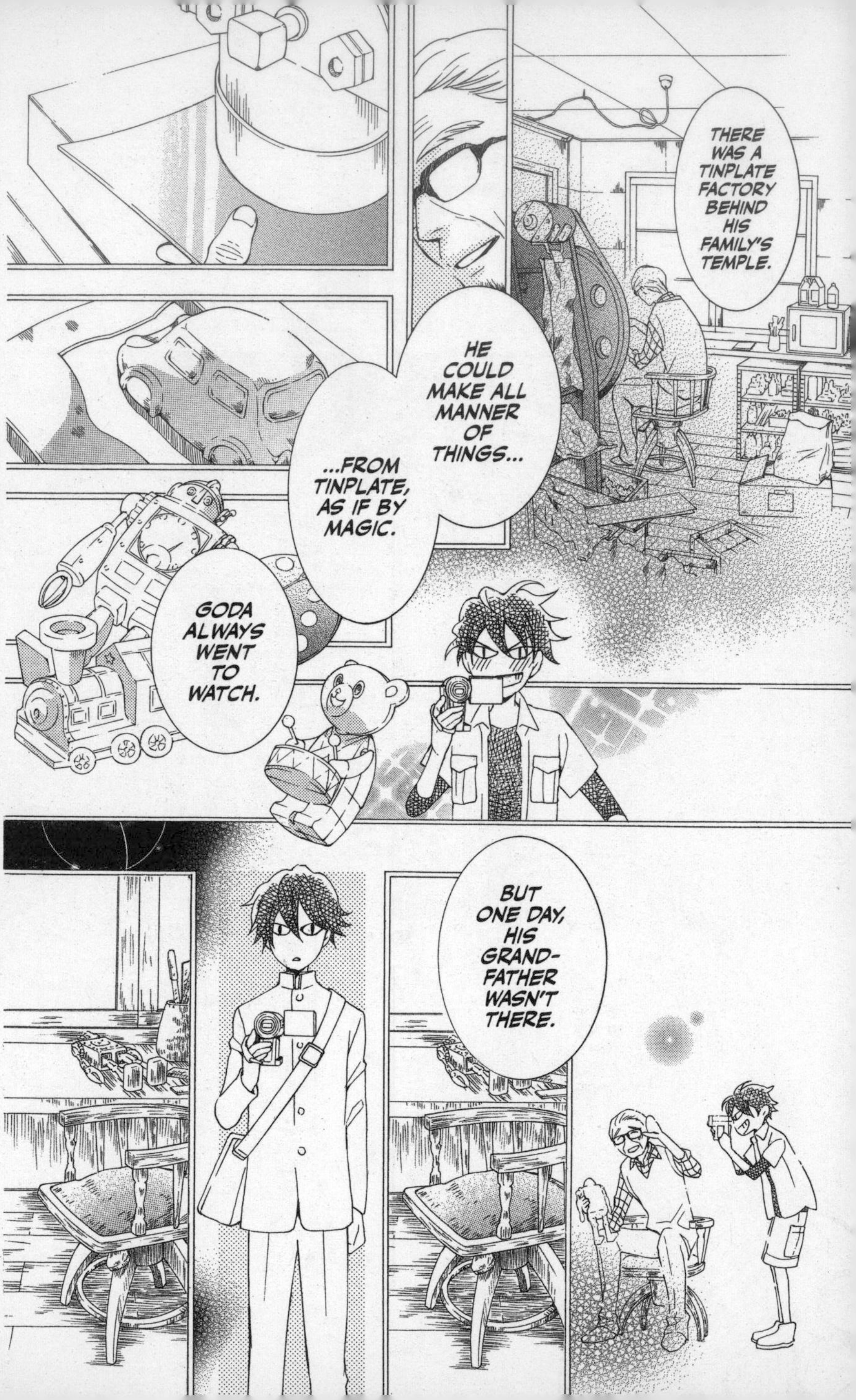
THERE WAS A TINPLATE FACTORY BEHIND HIS FAMILY'S TEMPLE.
HE COULD MAKE ALL MANNER OF THINGS...
...FROM TINPLATE, AS IF BY MAGIC.
GODA ALWAYS WENT TO WATCH.
BUT ONE DAY, HIS GRAND-FATHER WASN'T THERE.

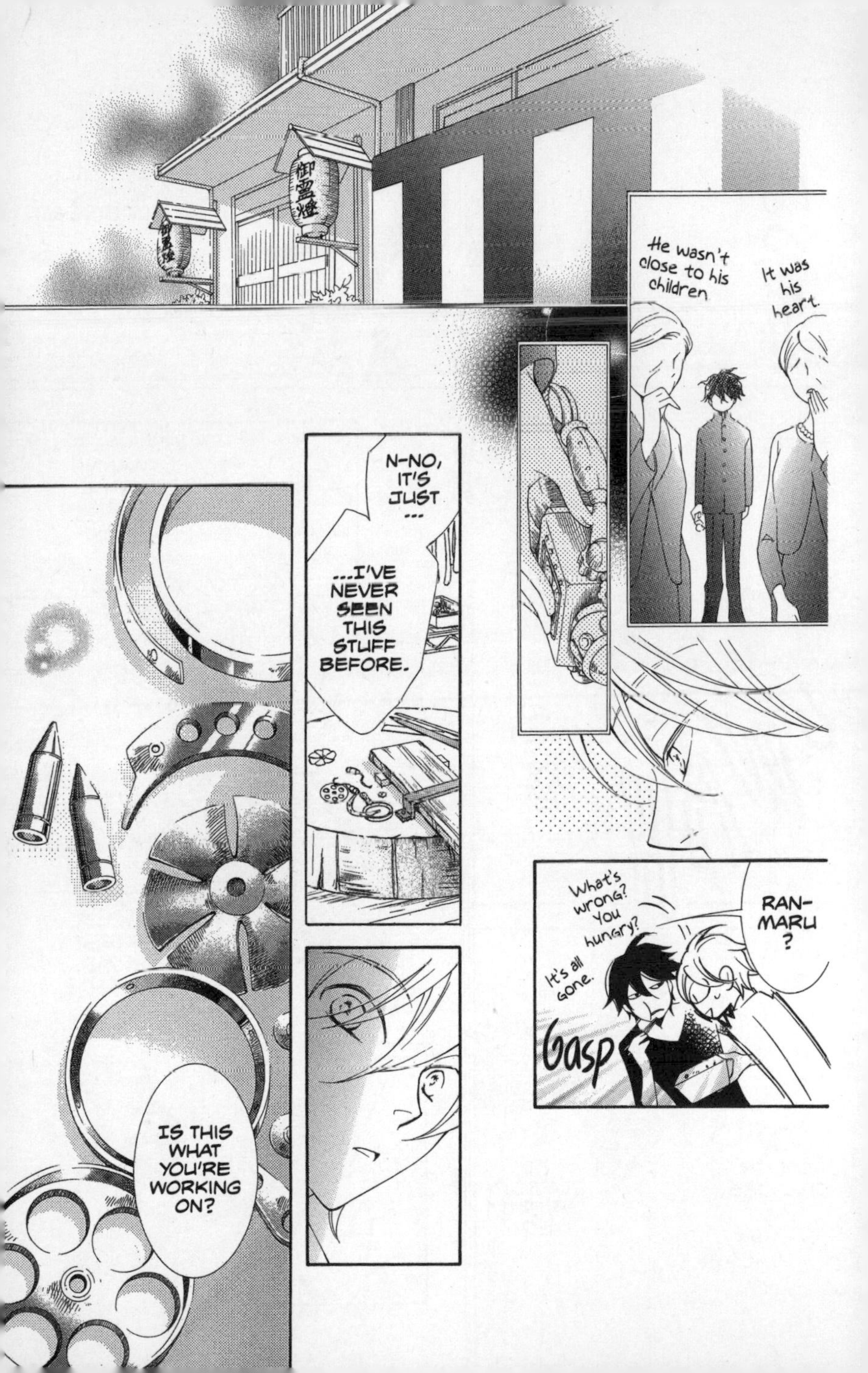
御霊燈
御霊燈
It was his heart.
He wasn't close to his children
RAN-MARU?
What's wrong? You hungry?
It's all gone.
Gasp
N-NO, IT'S JUST ...
...I'VE NEVER SEEN THIS STUFF BEFORE.
IS THIS WHAT YOU'RE WORKING ON?

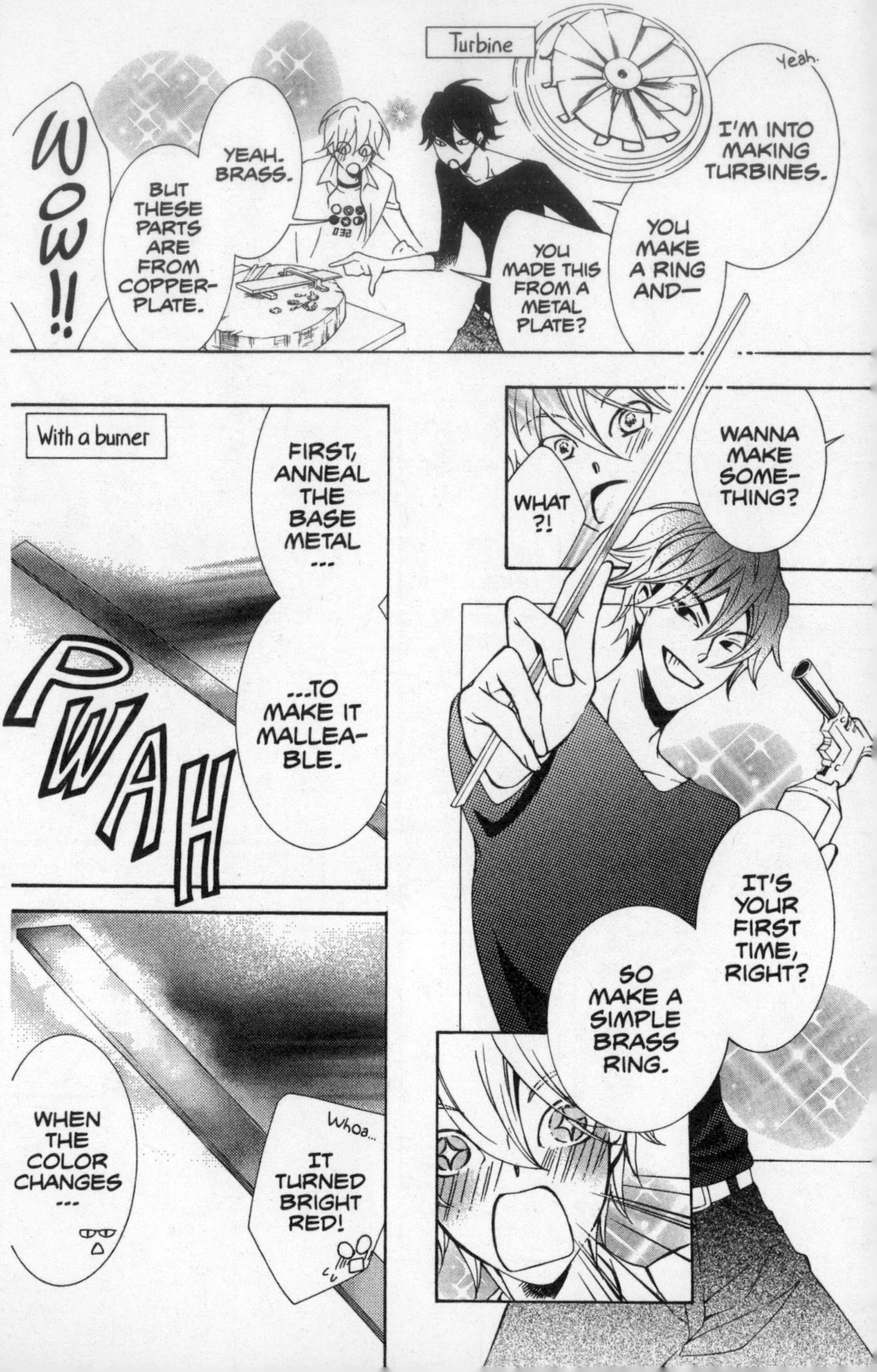
Yeah.
I'M INTO MAKING TURBINES.
Turbine
YOU MAKE A RING AND—
YOU MADE THIS FROM A METAL PLATE?
YEAH. BRASS.
BUT THESE PARTS ARE FROM COPPER-PLATE.
WOW!!
WANNA MAKE SOME-THING?
WHAT ?!
IT'S YOUR FIRST TIME, RIGHT?
SO MAKE A SIMPLE BRASS RING.
With a burner
FIRST, ANNEAL THE BASE METAL ---
...TO MAKE IT MALLEA-BLE.
PWAH
Whoa...
IT TURNED BRIGHT RED!
WHEN THE COLOR CHANGES ---

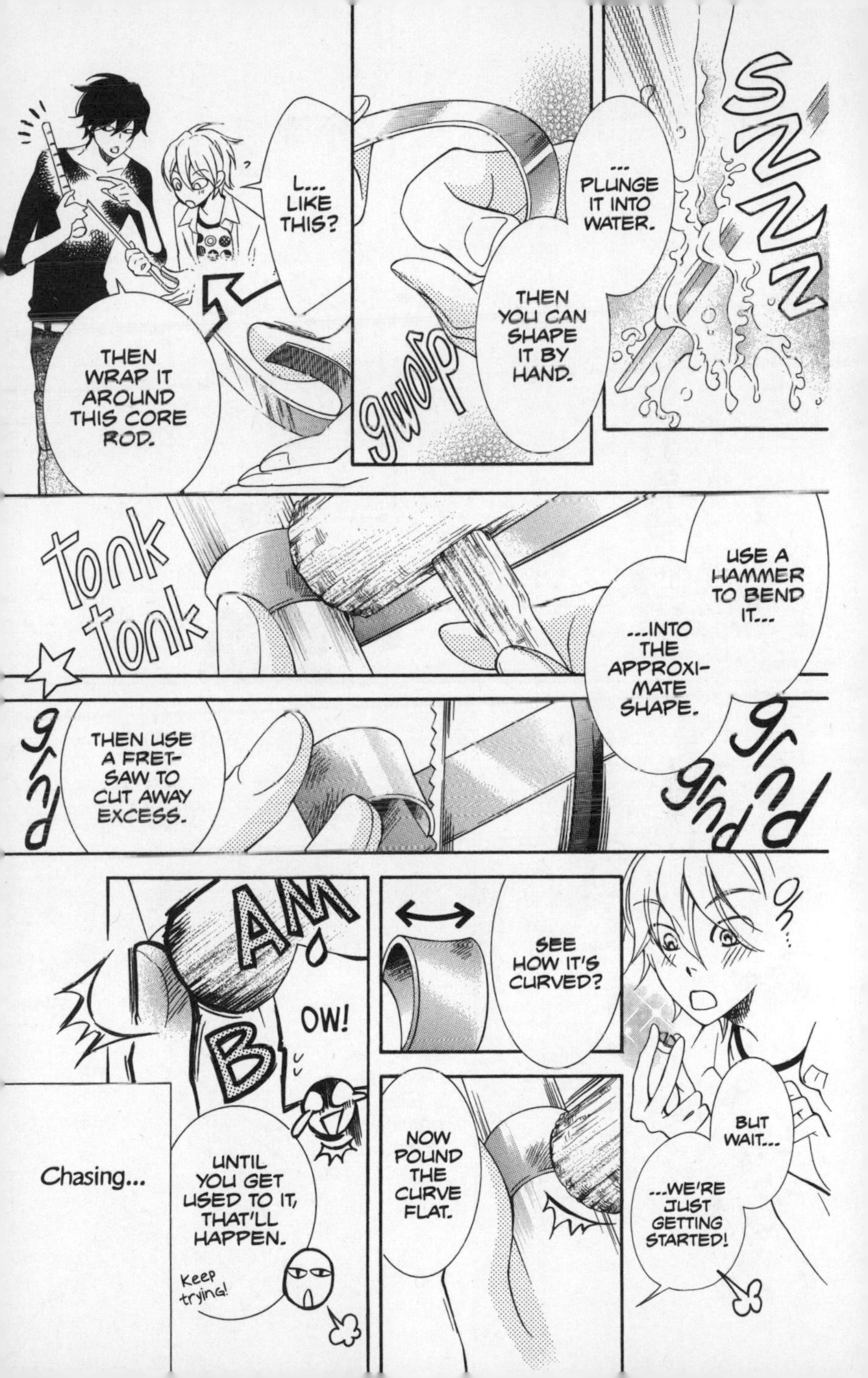
SNNN
...PLUNGE IT INTO WATER.
THEN YOU CAN SHAPE IT BY HAND.
gwolp
L... LIKE THIS?
THEN WRAP IT AROUND THIS CORE ROD.
USE A HAMMER TO BEND IT...
...INTO THE APPROXIMATE SHAPE.
tonk tonk
grind grind
THEN USE A FRET-SAW TO CUT AWAY EXCESS.
grind
Oh...
BUT WAIT...
...WE'RE JUST GETTING STARTED!
SEE HOW IT'S CURVED?
NOW POUND THE CURVE FLAT.
BAM
OW!
UNTIL YOU GET USED TO IT, THAT'LL HAPPEN.
Keep trying!
Chasing...

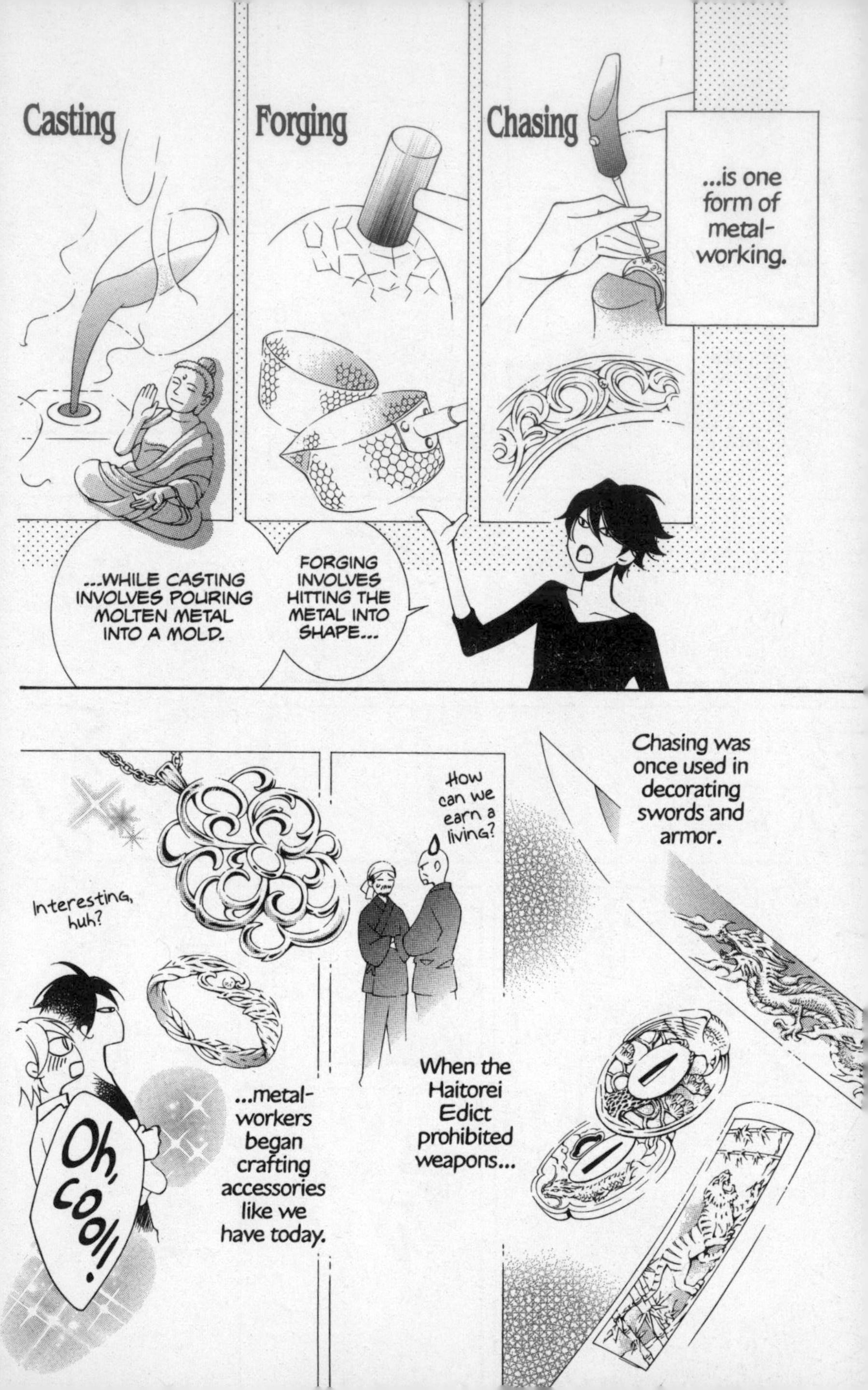
Chasing
...is one form of metal-working.
Forging
Casting
FORGING INVOLVES HITTING THE METAL INTO SHAPE...
...WHILE CASTING INVOLVES POURING MOLTEN METAL INTO A MOLD.
Chasing was once used in decorating swords and armor.
How can we earn a living?
When the Haitorei Edict prohibited weapons...
...metal-workers began crafting accessories like we have today.
Interesting, huh?
Oh, cool!

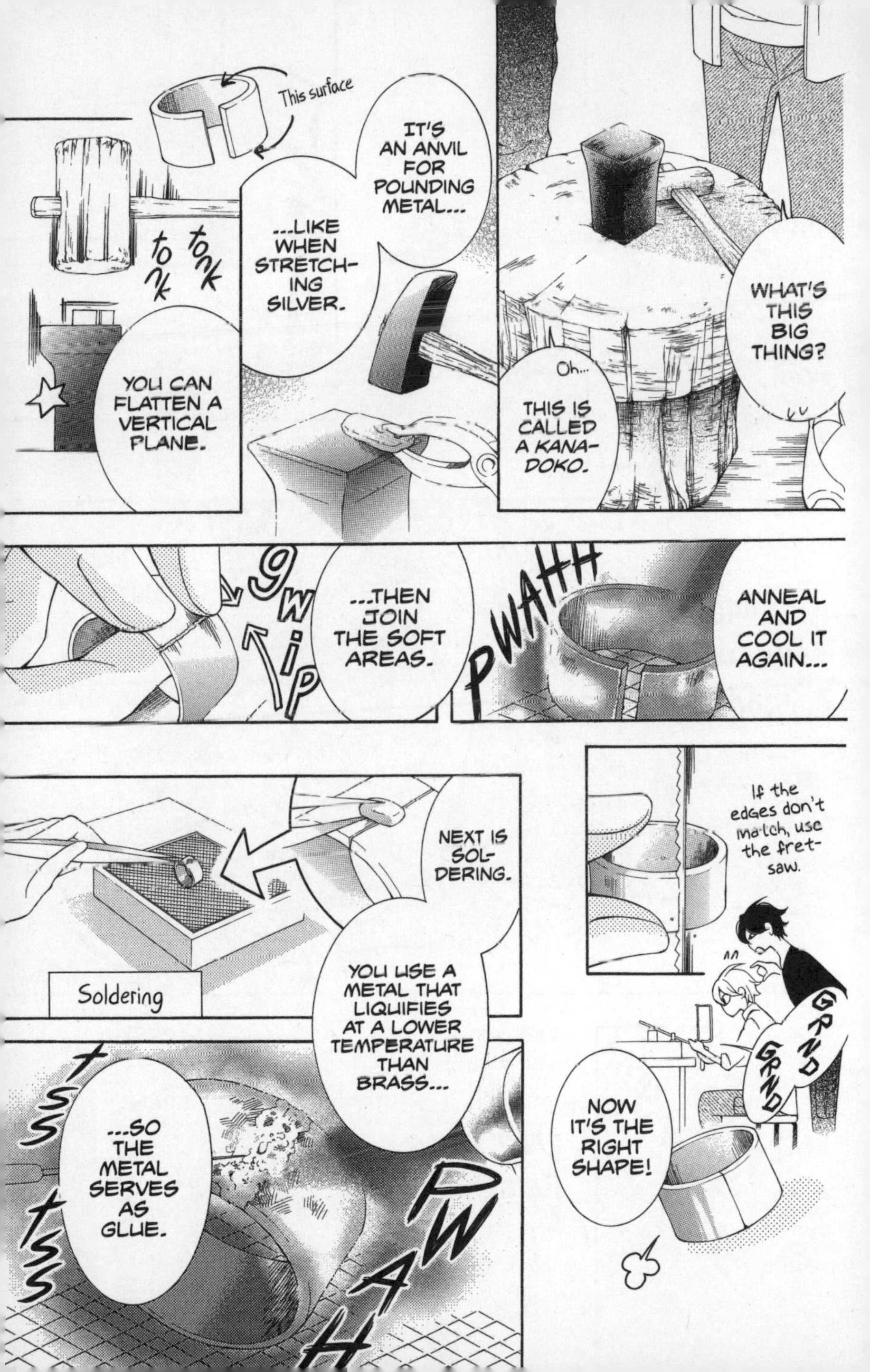
WHAT'S THIS BIG THING?
Oh...
THIS IS CALLED A KANA-DOKO.
IT'S AN ANVIL FOR POUNDING METAL...
...LIKE WHEN STRETCH-ING SILVER.
This surface
tonk tonk
YOU CAN FLATTEN A VERTICAL PLANE.
ANNEAL AND COOL IT AGAIN...
PWAHH
...THEN JOIN THE SOFT AREAS.
gwip
If the edges don't match, use the fret-saw.
GRND GRND
NOW IT'S THE RIGHT SHAPE!
NEXT IS SOL-DERING.
Soldering
YOU USE A METAL THAT LIQUIFIES AT A LOWER TEMPERATURE THAN BRASS...
...SO THE METAL SERVES AS GLUE.
PWAH
TSS TSS

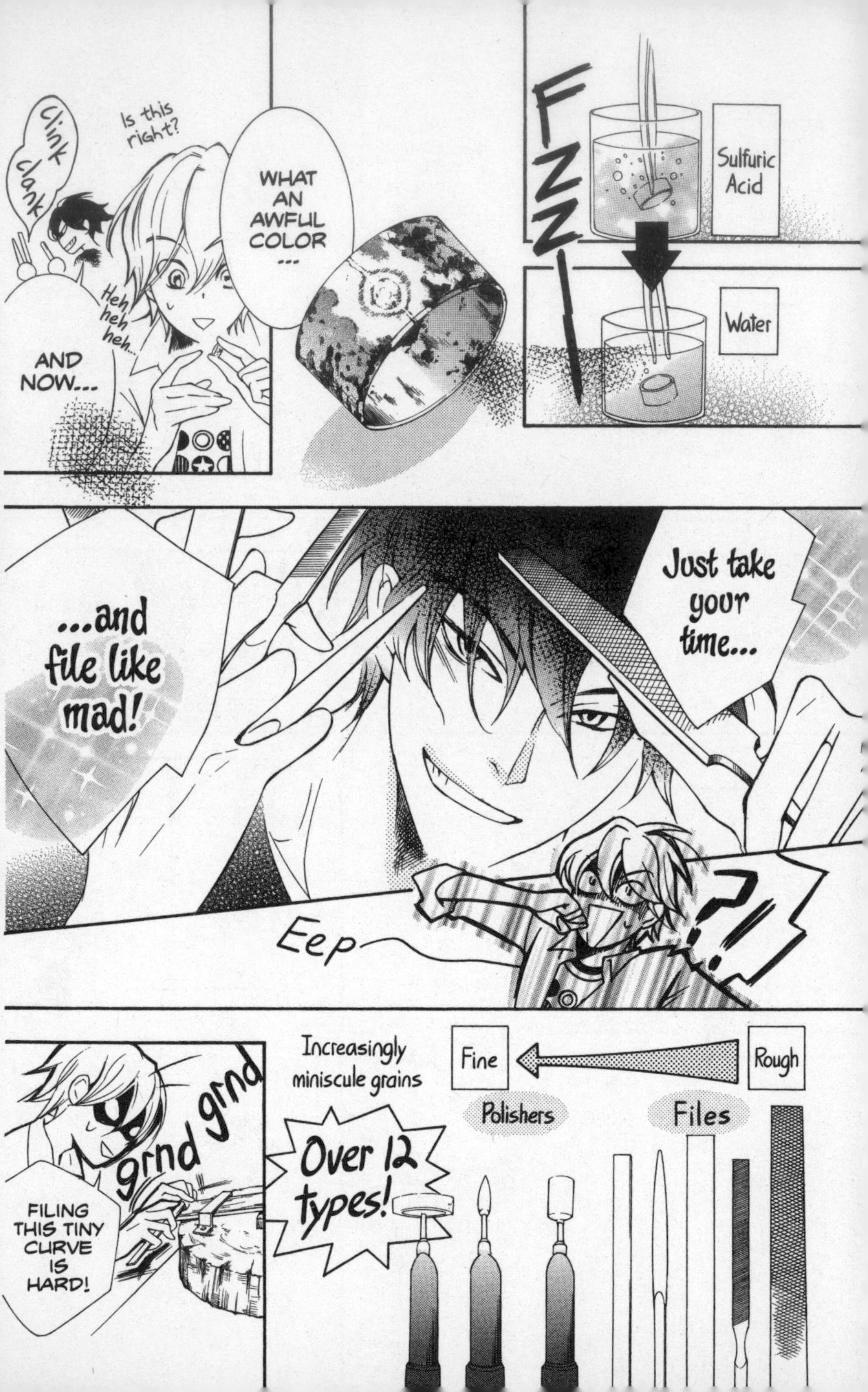
Sulfuric Acid
FZZ
Water
WHAT AN AWFUL COLOR ...
clink clank
Is this right?
Heh heh heh...
AND NOW...
Just take your time...
...and file like mad!
?!
Eep
Rough
Fine
Increasingly miniscule grains
Files
Polishers
Over 12 types!
grnd grnd
FILING THIS TINY CURVE IS HARD!

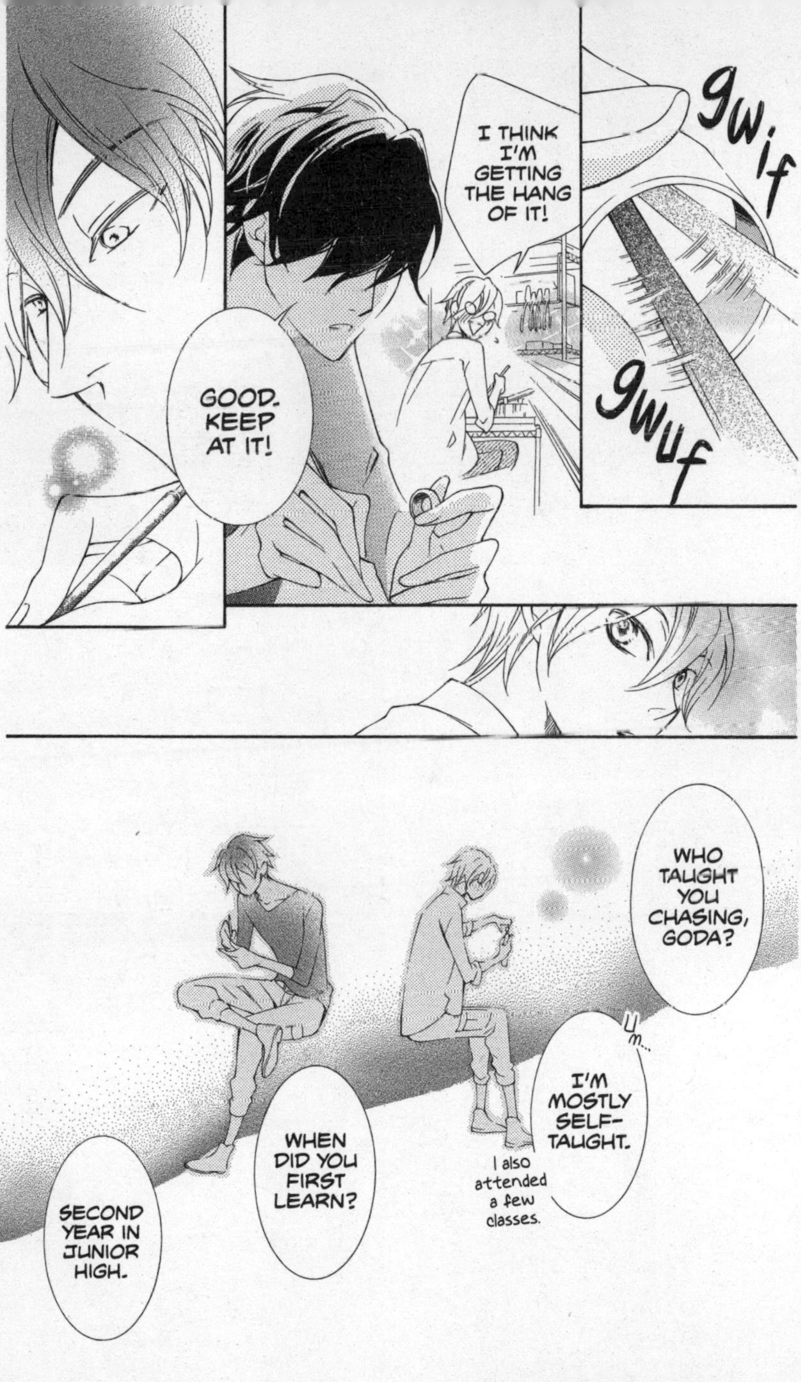
gwif
gwuf
I THINK I'M GETTING THE HANG OF IT!
GOOD. KEEP AT IT!
WHO TAUGHT YOU CHASING, GODA?
Um...
I'M MOSTLY SELF-TAUGHT.
I also attended a few classes.
WHEN DID YOU FIRST LEARN?
SECOND YEAR IN JUNIOR HIGH.

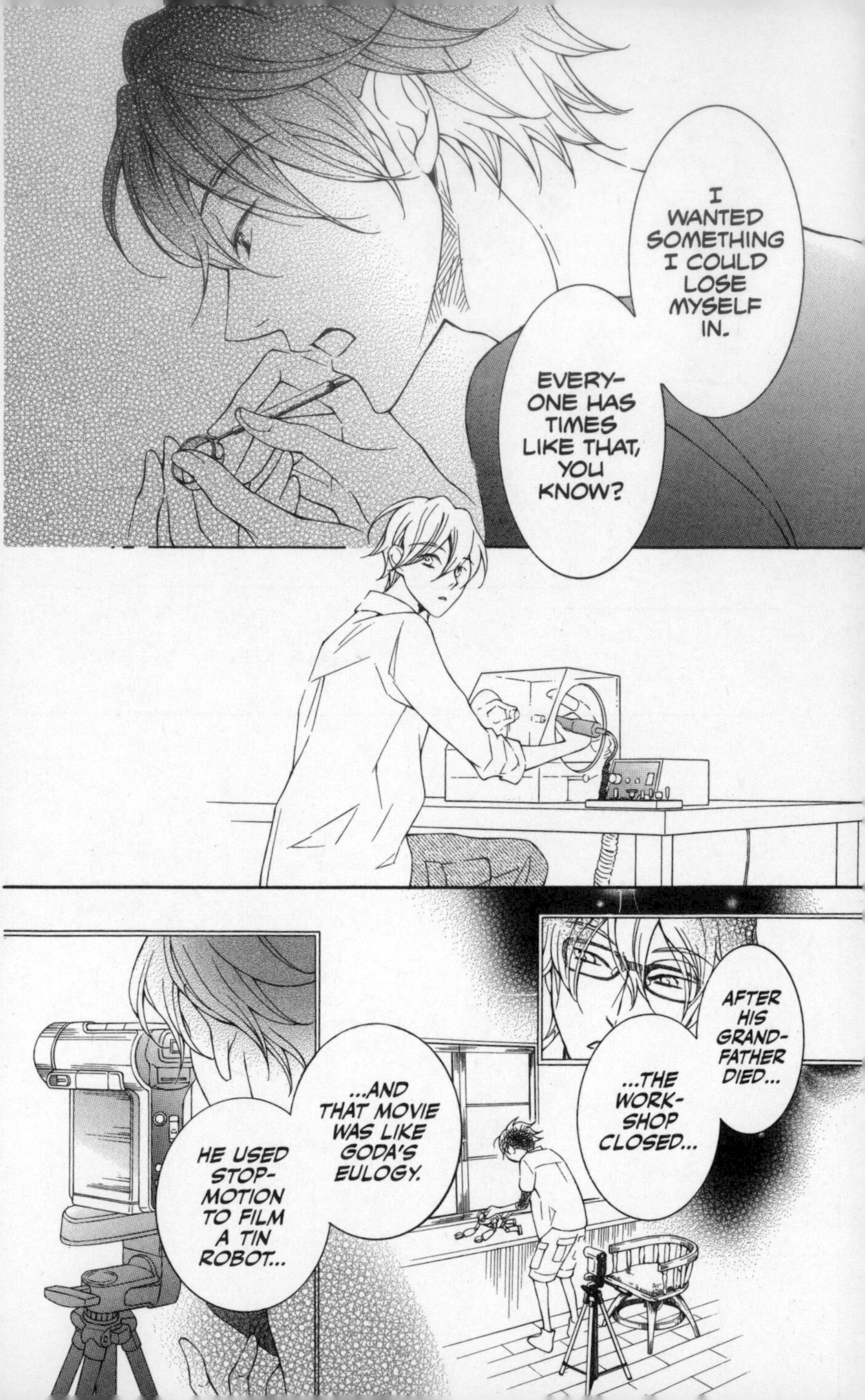
I WANTED SOMETHING I COULD LOSE MYSELF IN.
EVERY-ONE HAS TIMES LIKE THAT, YOU KNOW?
AFTER HIS GRAND-FATHER DIED...
...THE WORK-SHOP CLOSED...
...AND THAT MOVIE WAS LIKE GODA'S EULOGY.
HE USED STOP-MOTION TO FILM A TIN ROBOT...

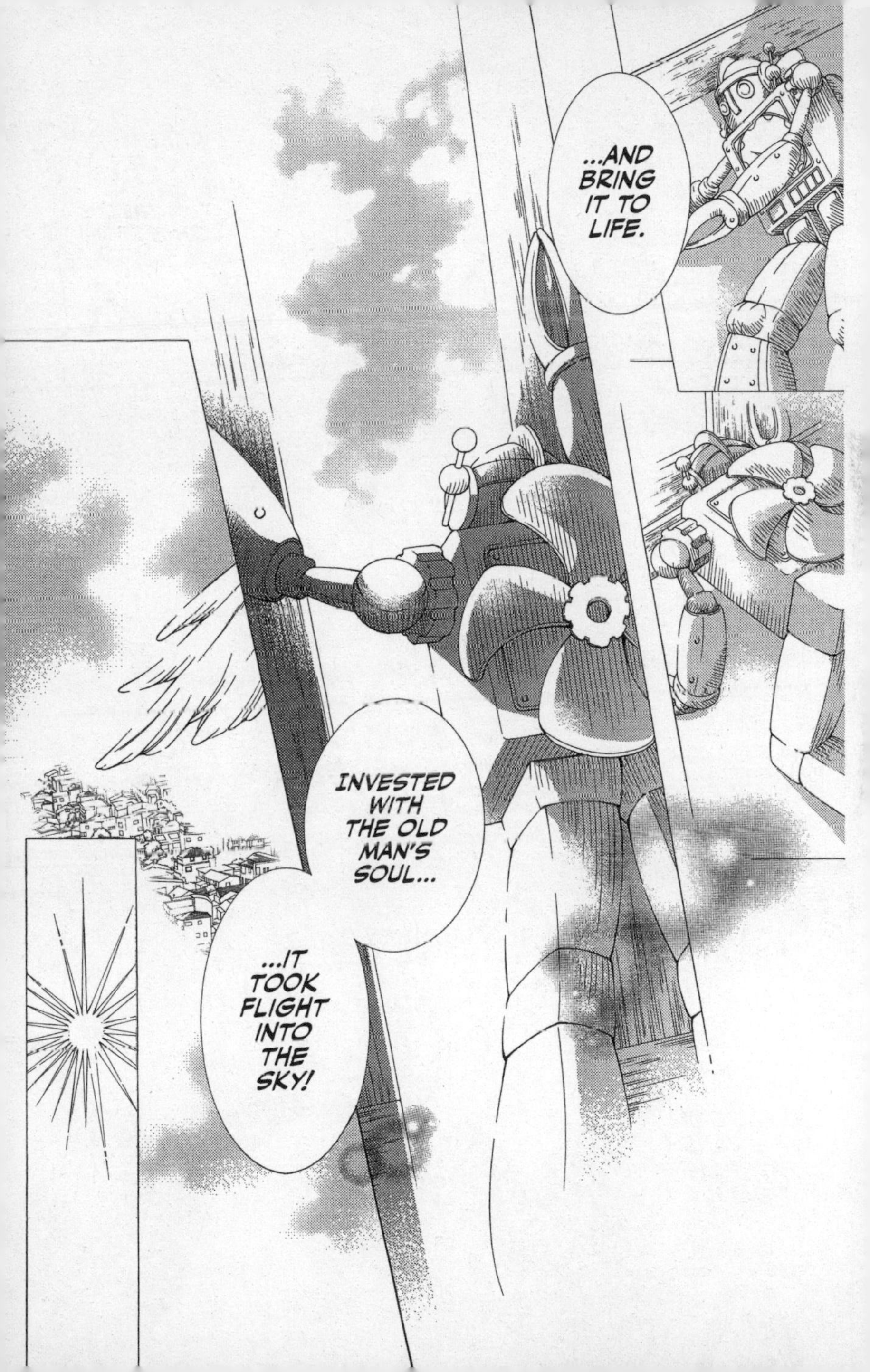
...AND BRING IT TO LIFE.
INVESTED WITH THE OLD MAN'S SOUL...
...IT TOOK FLIGHT INTO THE SKY!

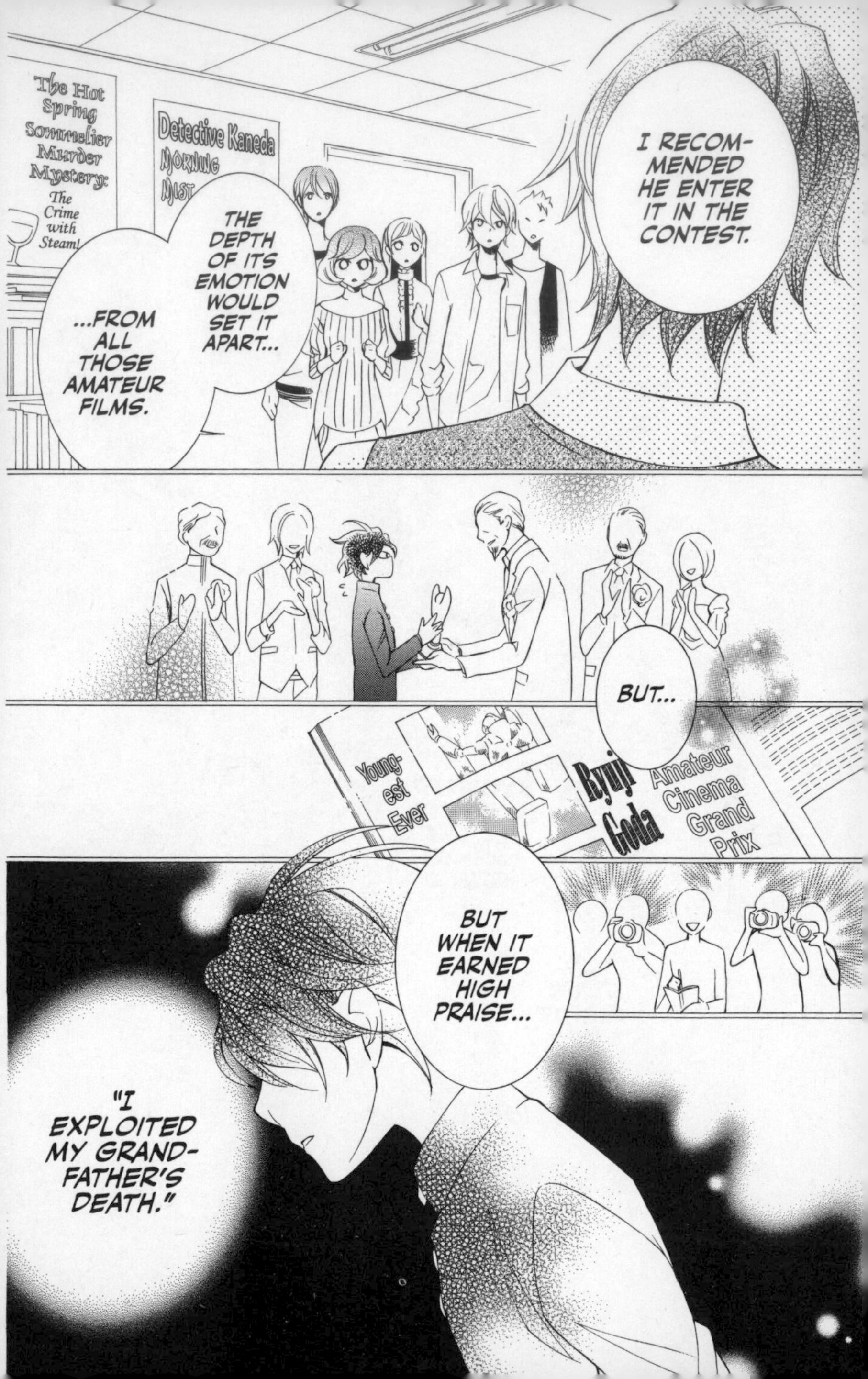
I RECOMMENDED HE ENTER IT IN THE CONTEST.
Detective Kaneda MORNING MIST
The Hot Spring Sommelier Murder Mystery: The Crime with Steam!
THE DEPTH OF ITS EMOTION WOULD SET IT APART...
...FROM ALL THOSE AMATEUR FILMS.
BUT...
Amateur Cinema Grand Prix
Ryuji Goda
Youngest Ever
BUT WHEN IT EARNED HIGH PRAISE...
"I EXPLOITED MY GRANDFATHER'S DEATH."

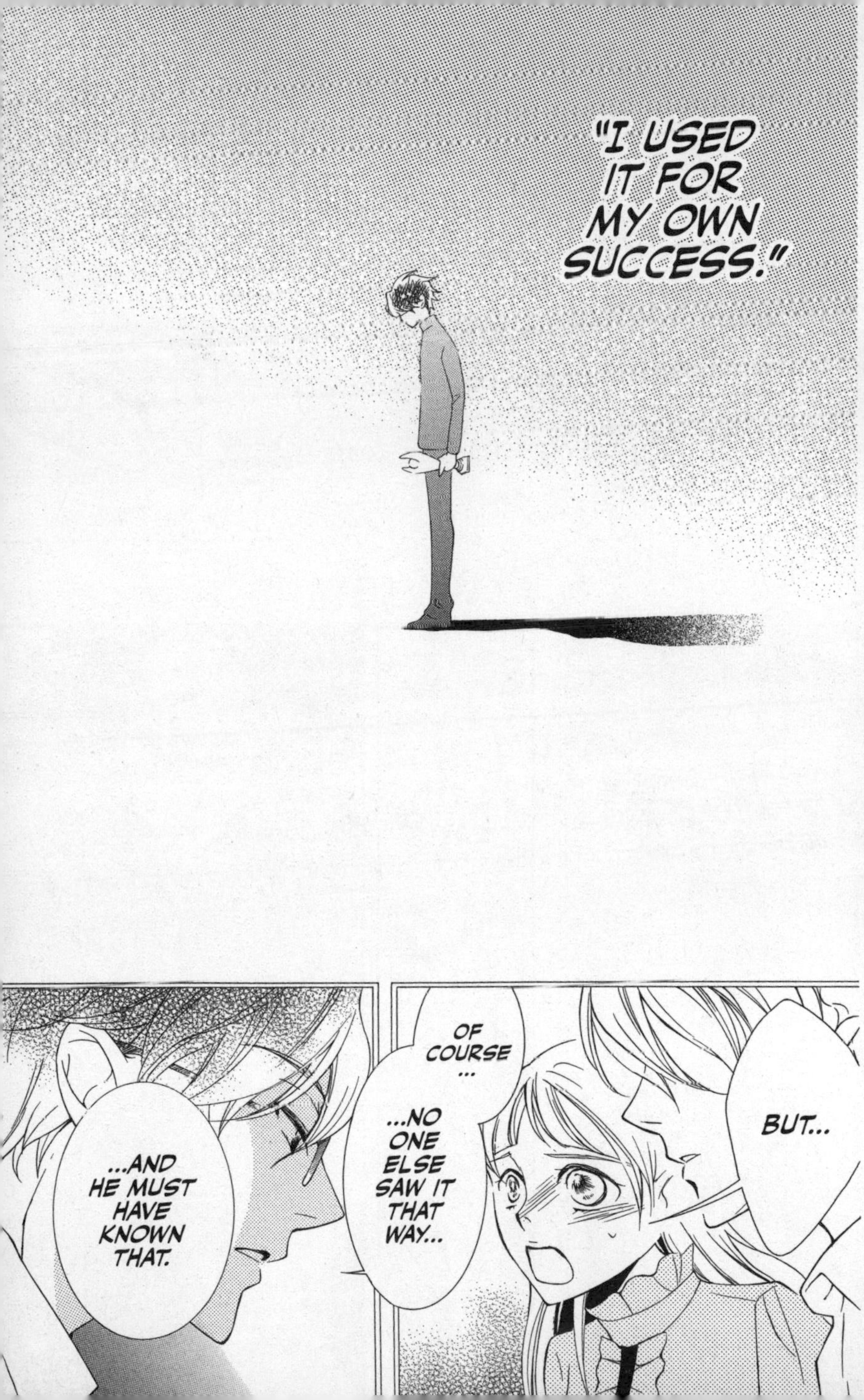
"I USED IT FOR MY OWN SUCCESS."
BUT...
OF COURSE...
...NO ONE ELSE SAW IT THAT WAY...
...AND HE MUST HAVE KNOWN THAT.

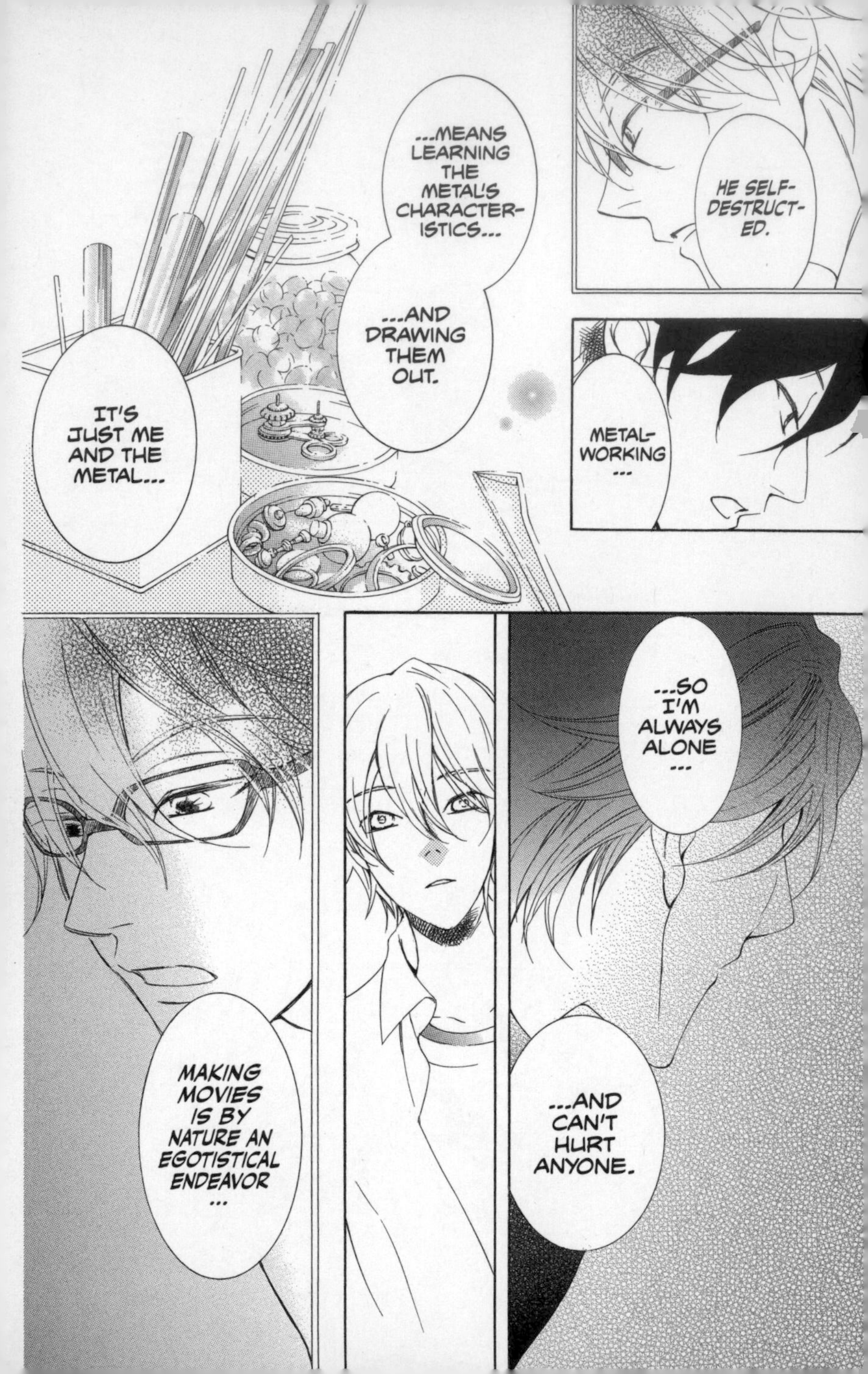
HE SELF-DESTRUCTED.
METAL-WORKING...
...MEANS LEARNING THE METAL'S CHARACTERISTICS...
...AND DRAWING THEM OUT.
IT'S JUST ME AND THE METAL...
...SO I'M ALWAYS ALONE...
...AND CAN'T HURT ANYONE.
MAKING MOVIES IS BY NATURE AN EGOTISTICAL ENDEAVOR...

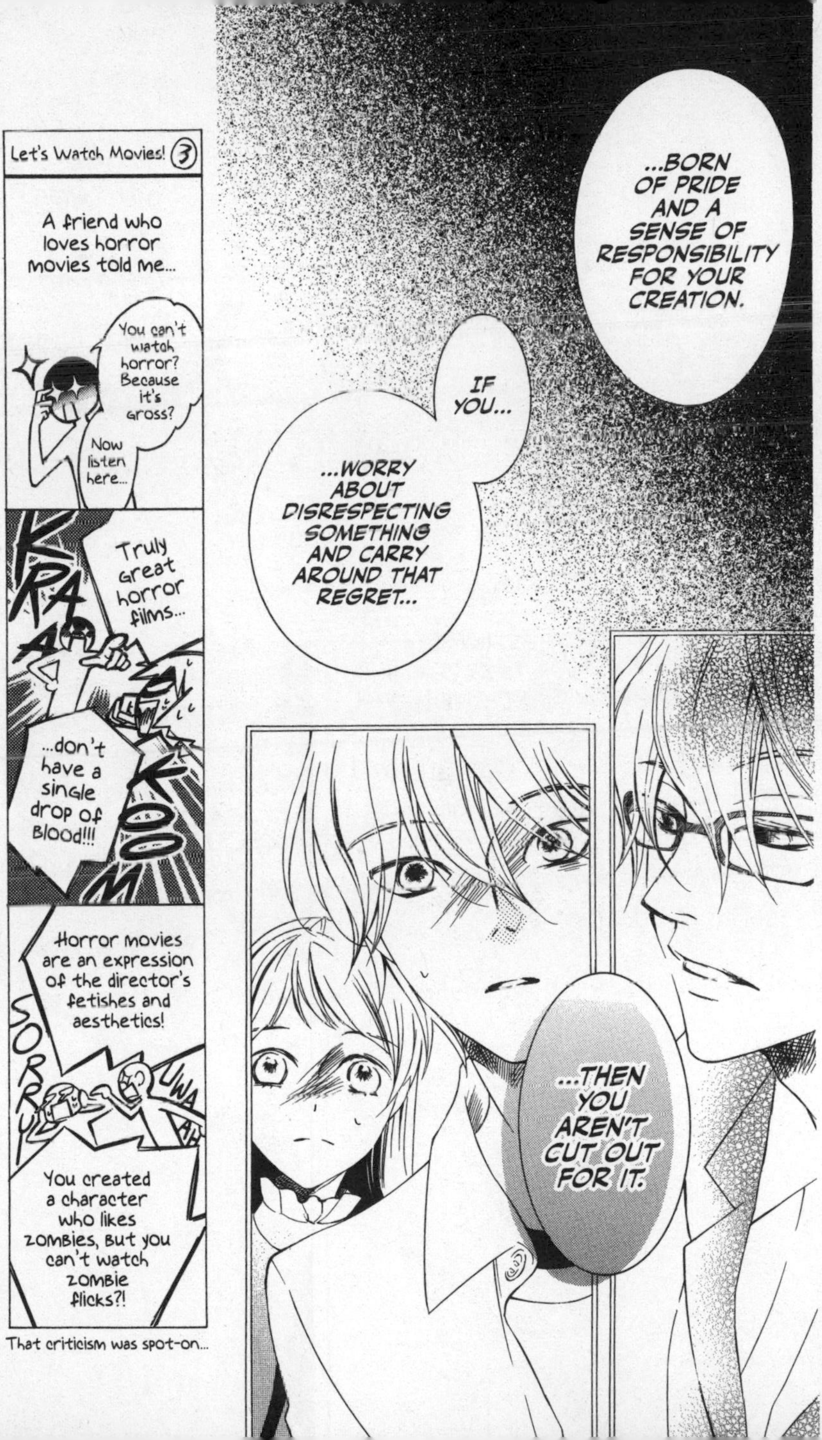
...BORN OF PRIDE AND A SENSE OF RESPONSIBILITY FOR YOUR CREATION.
IF YOU...
...WORRY ABOUT DISRESPECTING SOMETHING AND CARRY AROUND THAT REGRET...
...THEN YOU AREN'T CUT OUT FOR IT.
Let's Watch Movies! 3
A friend who loves horror movies told me...
You can't watch horror? Because it's gross?
Now listen here...
Truly great horror films...
KRAAA
...don't have a single drop of Blood!!!
KOOOM
Horror movies are an expression of the director's fetishes and aesthetics!
SORRY!
UWAAAH
You created a character who likes zombies, but you can't watch zombie flicks?!
That criticism was spot-on...

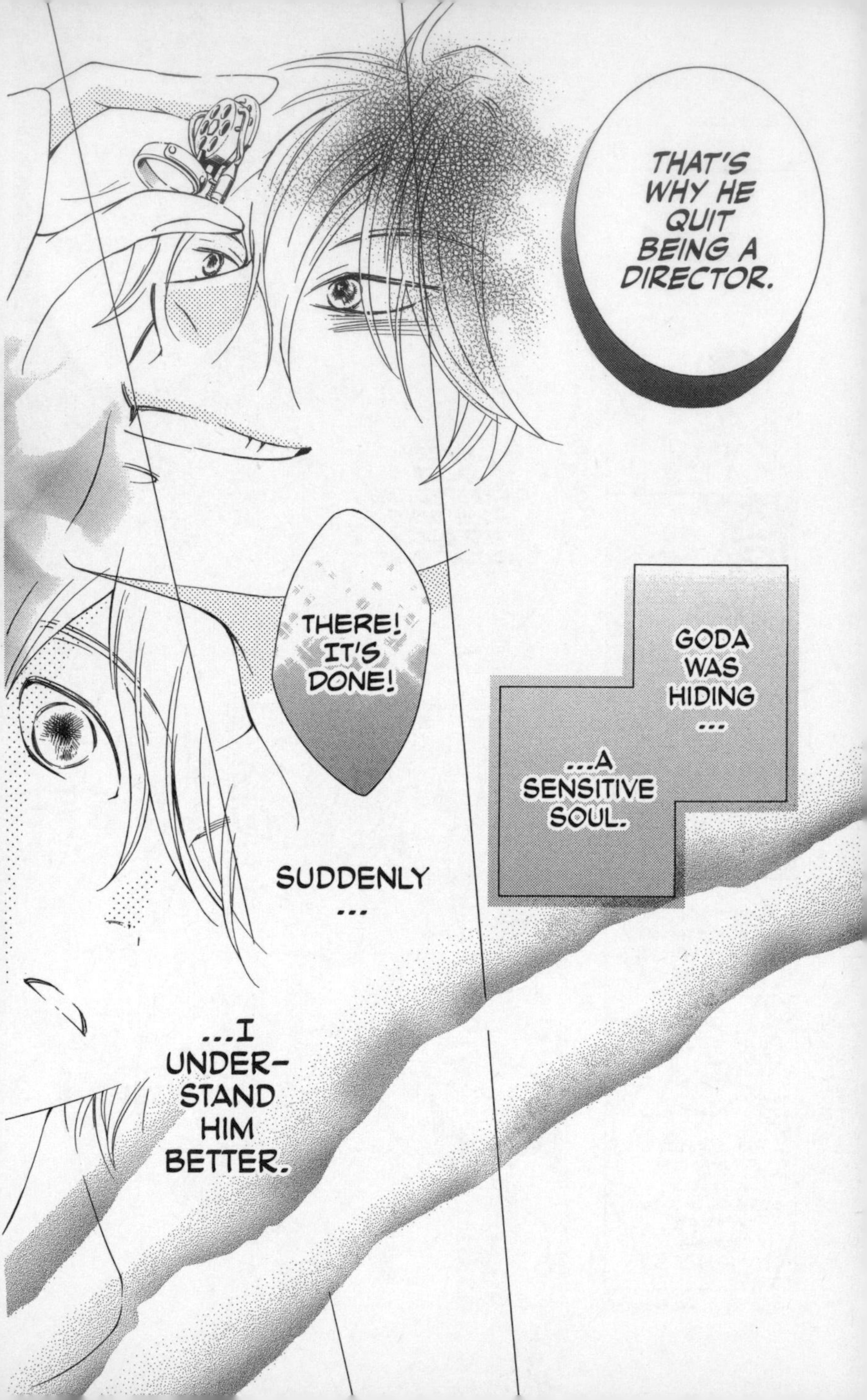
THAT'S WHY HE QUIT BEING A DIRECTOR.
GODA WAS HIDING ...
...A SENSITIVE SOUL.
THERE! IT'S DONE!
SUDDENLY ...
...I UNDER-STAND HIM BETTER.

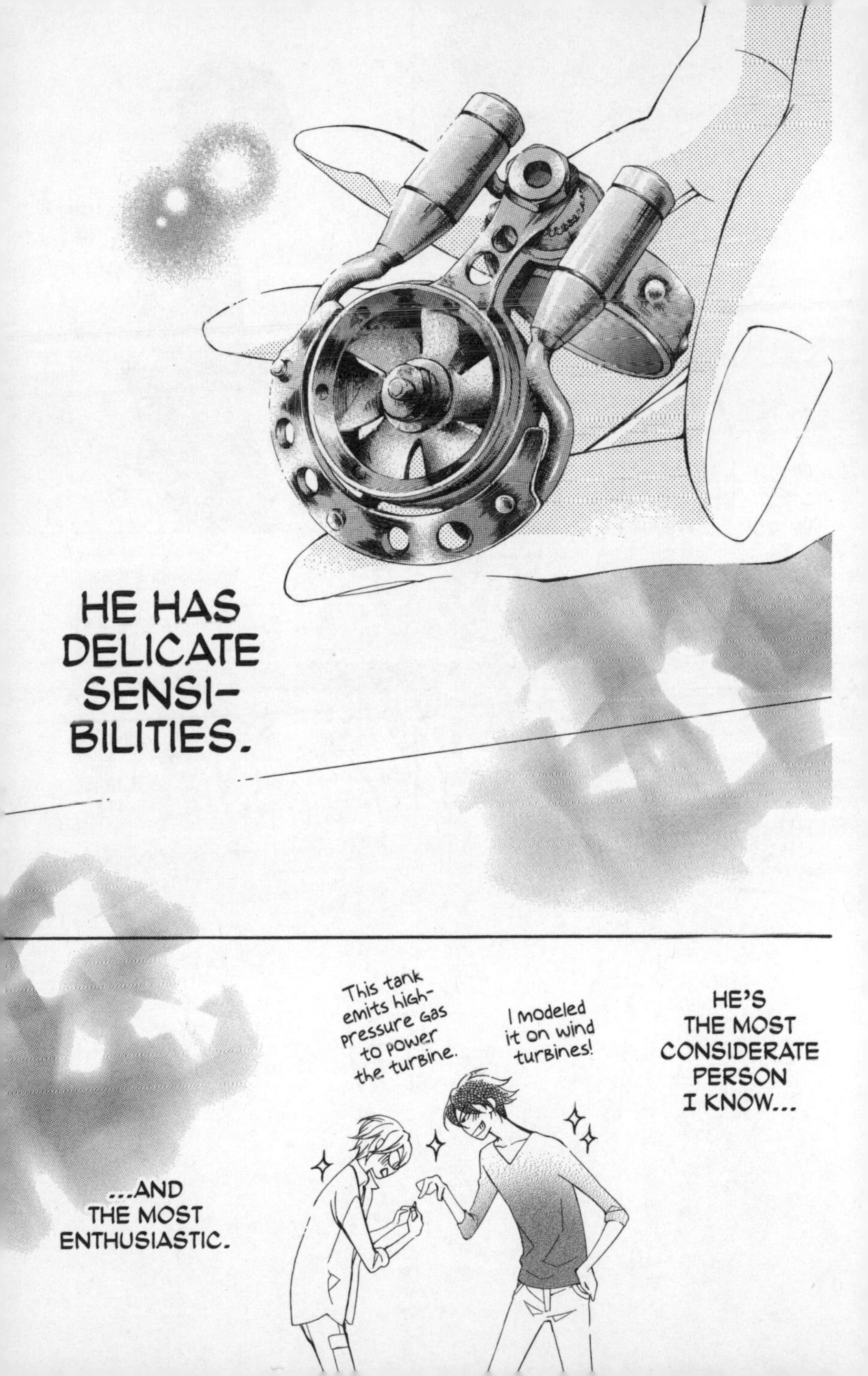
HE HAS DELICATE SENSI-BILITIES.
HE'S THE MOST CONSIDERATE PERSON I KNOW...
I modeled it on wind turbines!
This tank emits high-pressure gas to power the turbine.
...AND THE MOST ENTHUSIASTIC.

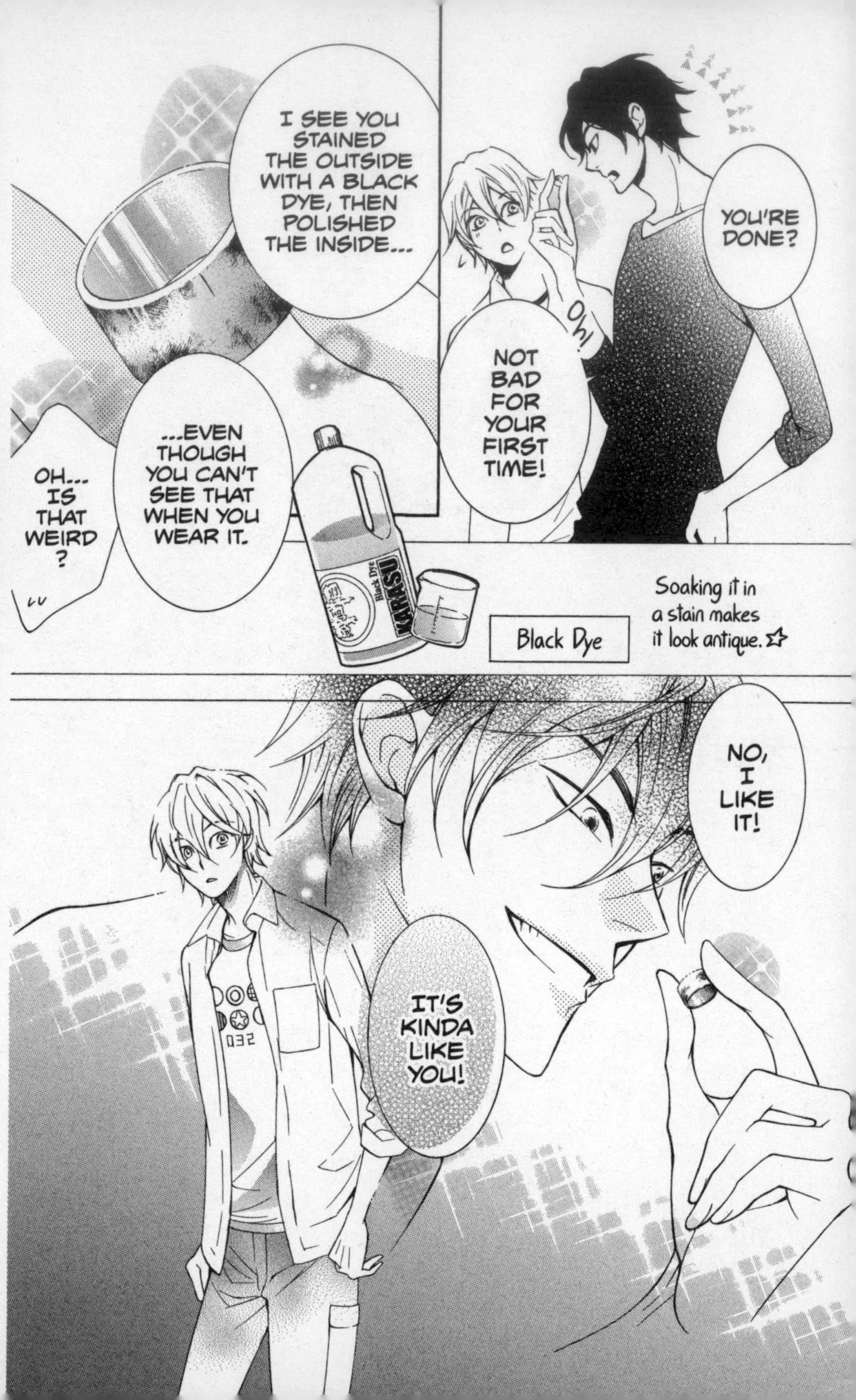
YOU'RE DONE?
Oh!
NOT BAD FOR YOUR FIRST TIME!
I SEE YOU STAINED THE OUTSIDE WITH A BLACK DYE, THEN POLISHED THE INSIDE...
...EVEN THOUGH YOU CAN'T SEE THAT WHEN YOU WEAR IT.
OH... IS THAT WEIRD?
Black Dye
KARASU
Soaking it in a stain makes it look antique. ☆
Black Dye
NO, I LIKE IT!
IT'S KINDA LIKE YOU!

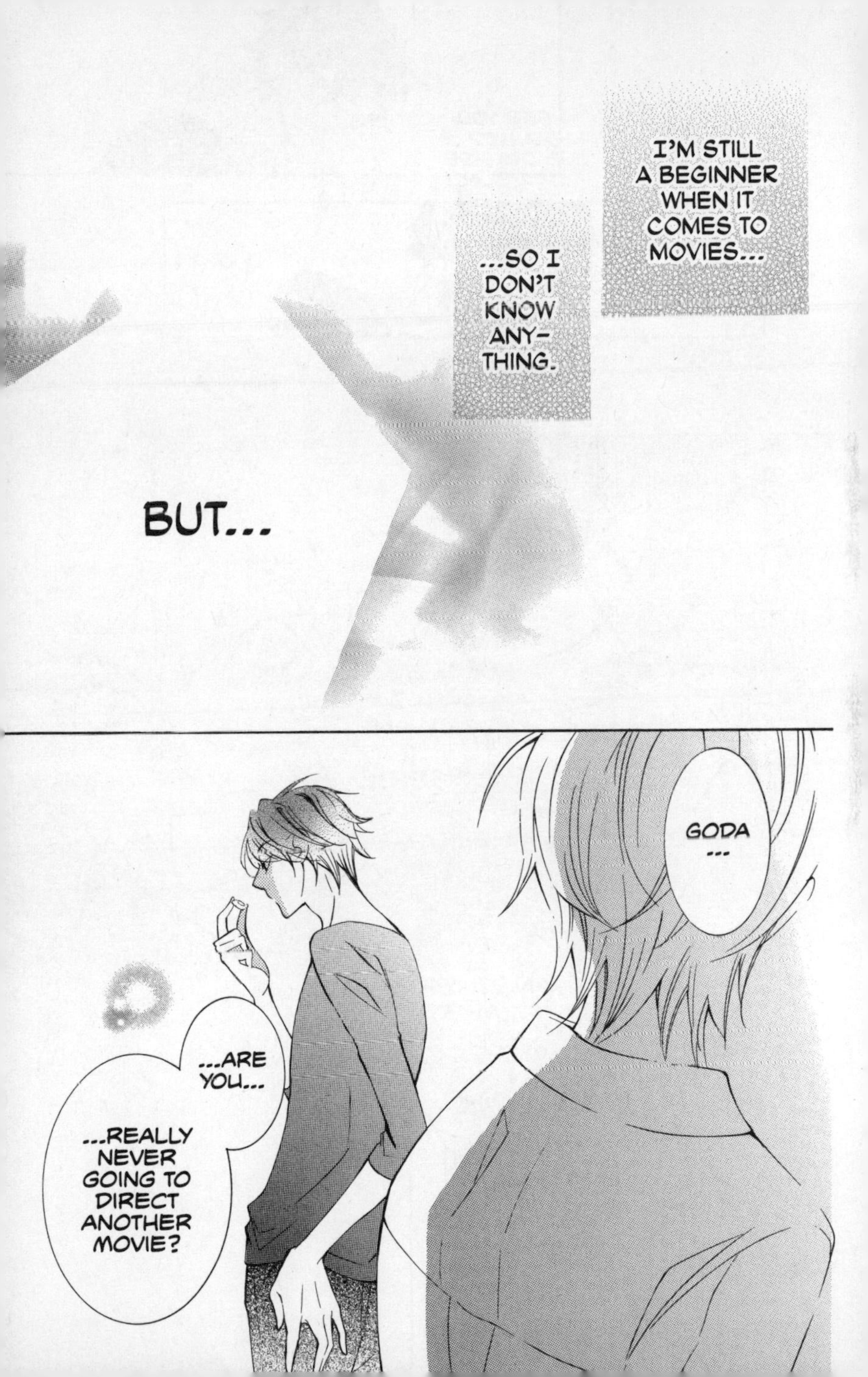
I'M STILL A BEGINNER WHEN IT COMES TO MOVIES...
...SO I DON'T KNOW ANY-THING.
BUT...
GODA ...
...ARE YOU...
...REALLY NEVER GOING TO DIRECT ANOTHER MOVIE?

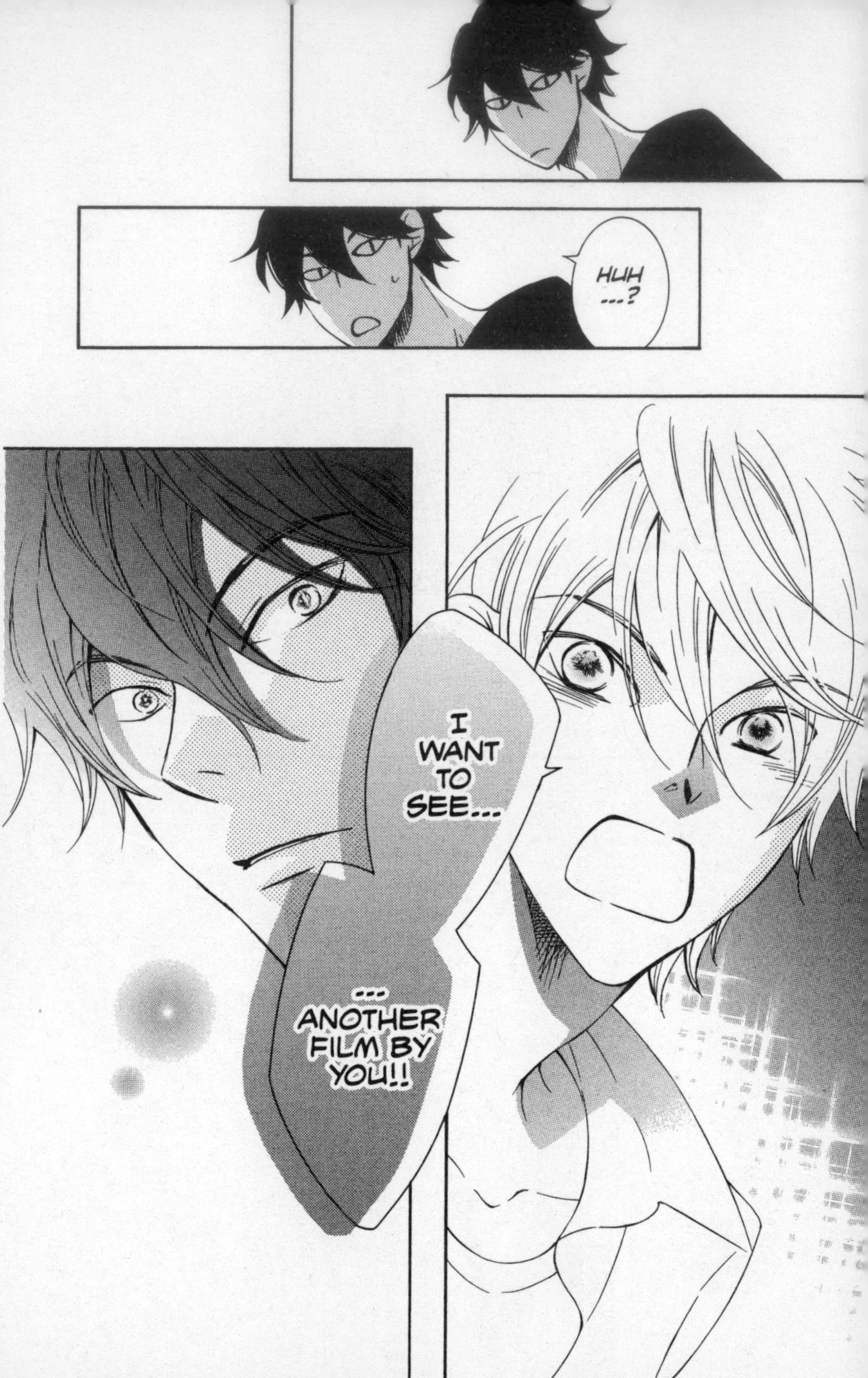
HUH---?
I WANT TO SEE...
...ANOTHER FILM BY YOU!!

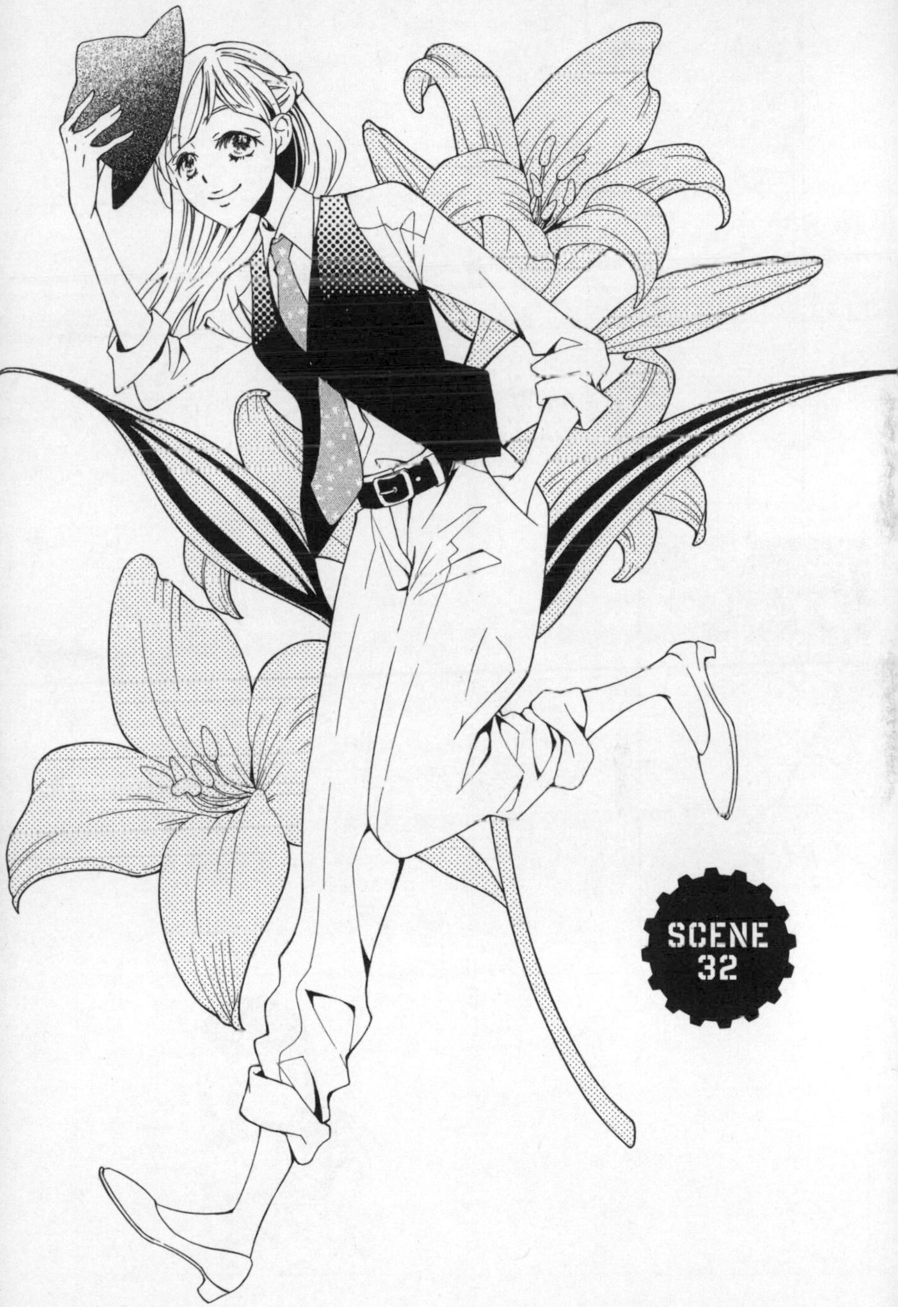
SCENE
32

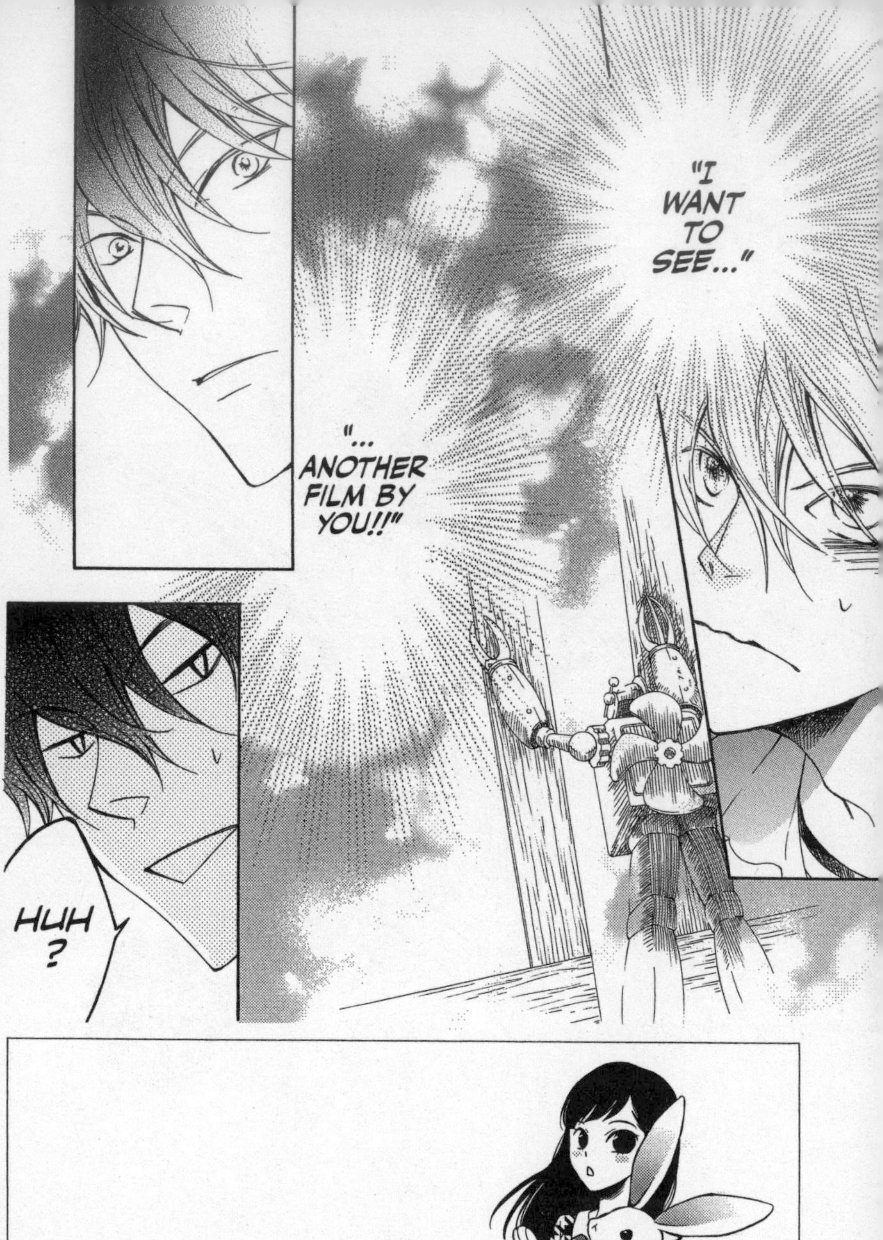
"I WANT TO SEE..."
"...ANOTHER FILM BY YOU!!"
HUH?

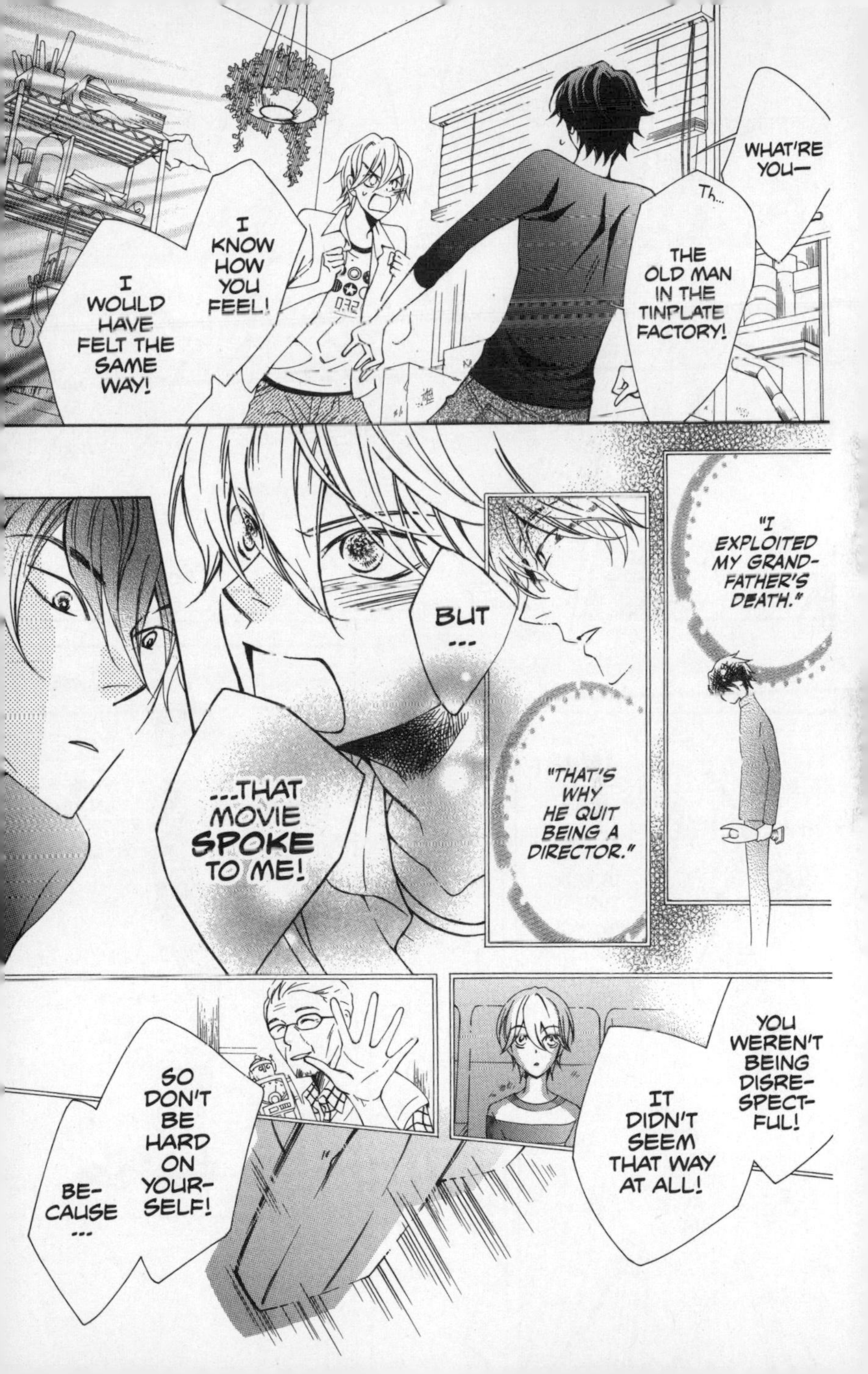
WHAT'RE YOU—
Th...
THE OLD MAN IN THE TINPLATE FACTORY!
I KNOW HOW YOU FEEL!
I WOULD HAVE FELT THE SAME WAY!
"I EXPLOITED MY GRANDFATHER'S DEATH."
"THAT'S WHY HE QUIT BEING A DIRECTOR."
BUT ...
...THAT MOVIE **SPOKE** TO ME!
YOU WEREN'T BEING DISRESPECTFUL!
IT DIDN'T SEEM THAT WAY AT ALL!
SO DON'T BE HARD ON YOURSELF!
BECAUSE ...

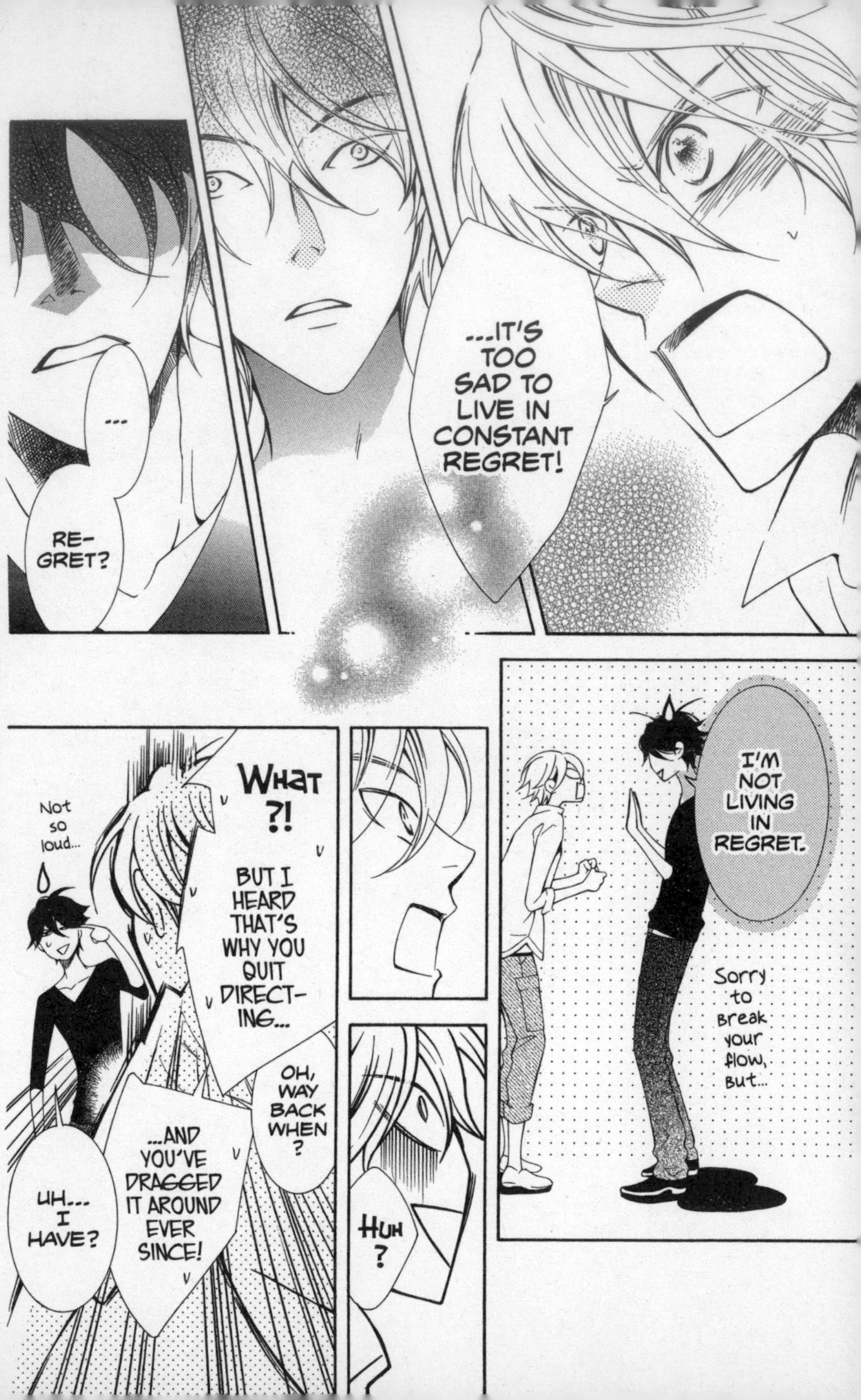
...IT'S TOO SAD TO LIVE IN CONSTANT REGRET!
...
RE-GRET?
I'M NOT LIVING IN REGRET.
Sorry to break your flow, but...
WHAT?!
HUH?
BUT I HEARD THAT'S WHY YOU QUIT DIRECT-ING...
Not so loud...
OH, WAY BACK WHEN?
...AND YOU'VE DRAGGED IT AROUND EVER SINCE!
UH... I HAVE?

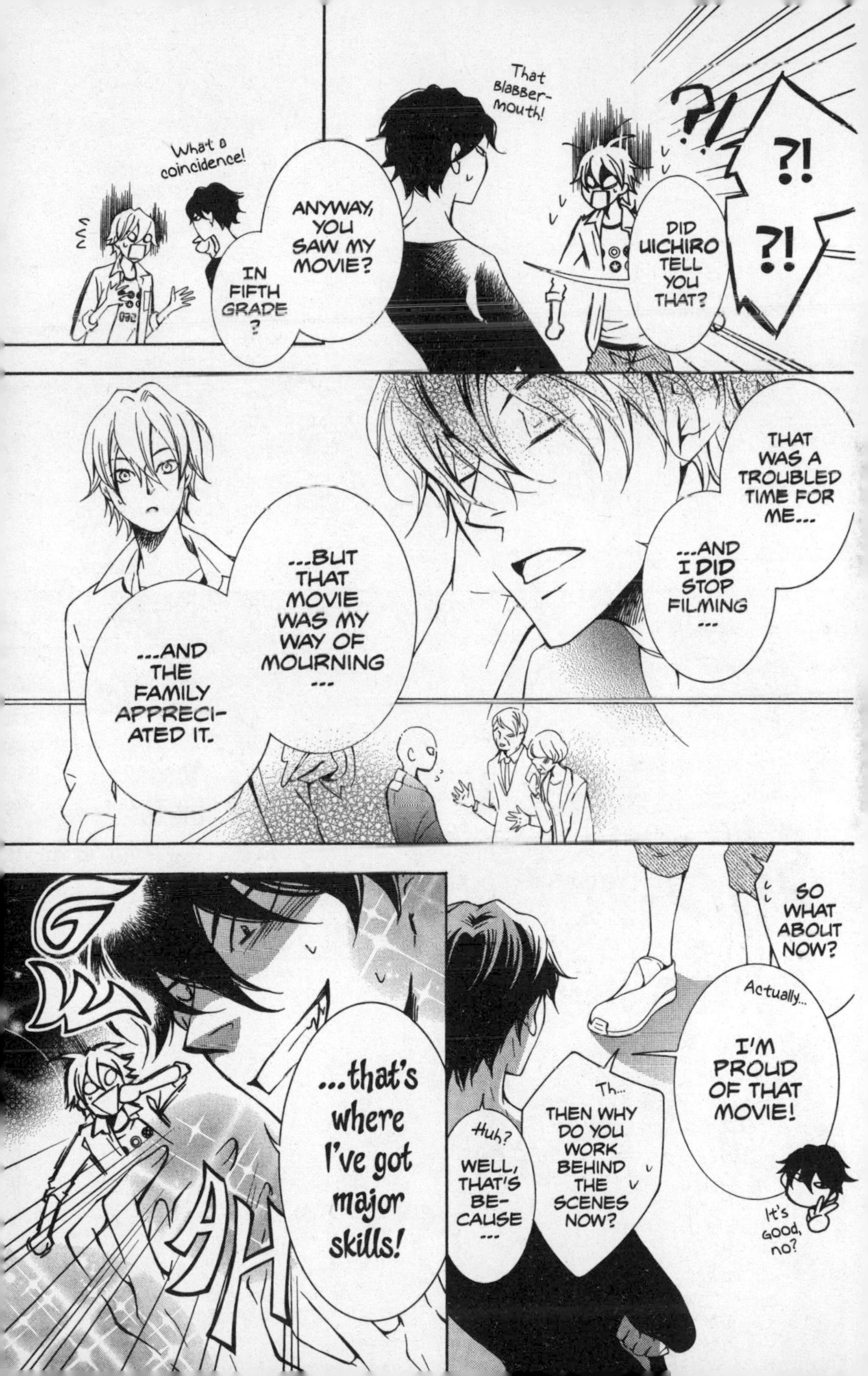
?!
?!
?!
DID UICHIRO TELL YOU THAT?
That blabber-mouth!
ANYWAY, YOU SAW MY MOVIE?
IN FIFTH GRADE?
What a coincidence!
THAT WAS A TROUBLED TIME FOR ME...
...AND I DID STOP FILMING...
...BUT THAT MOVIE WAS MY WAY OF MOURNING...
...AND THE FAMILY APPRECIATED IT.
SO WHAT ABOUT NOW?
Actually...
I'M PROUD OF THAT MOVIE!
It's good, no?
Th...
THEN WHY DO YOU WORK BEHIND THE SCENES NOW?
Huh?
WELL, THAT'S BE-CAUSE...
...that's where I've got major skills!

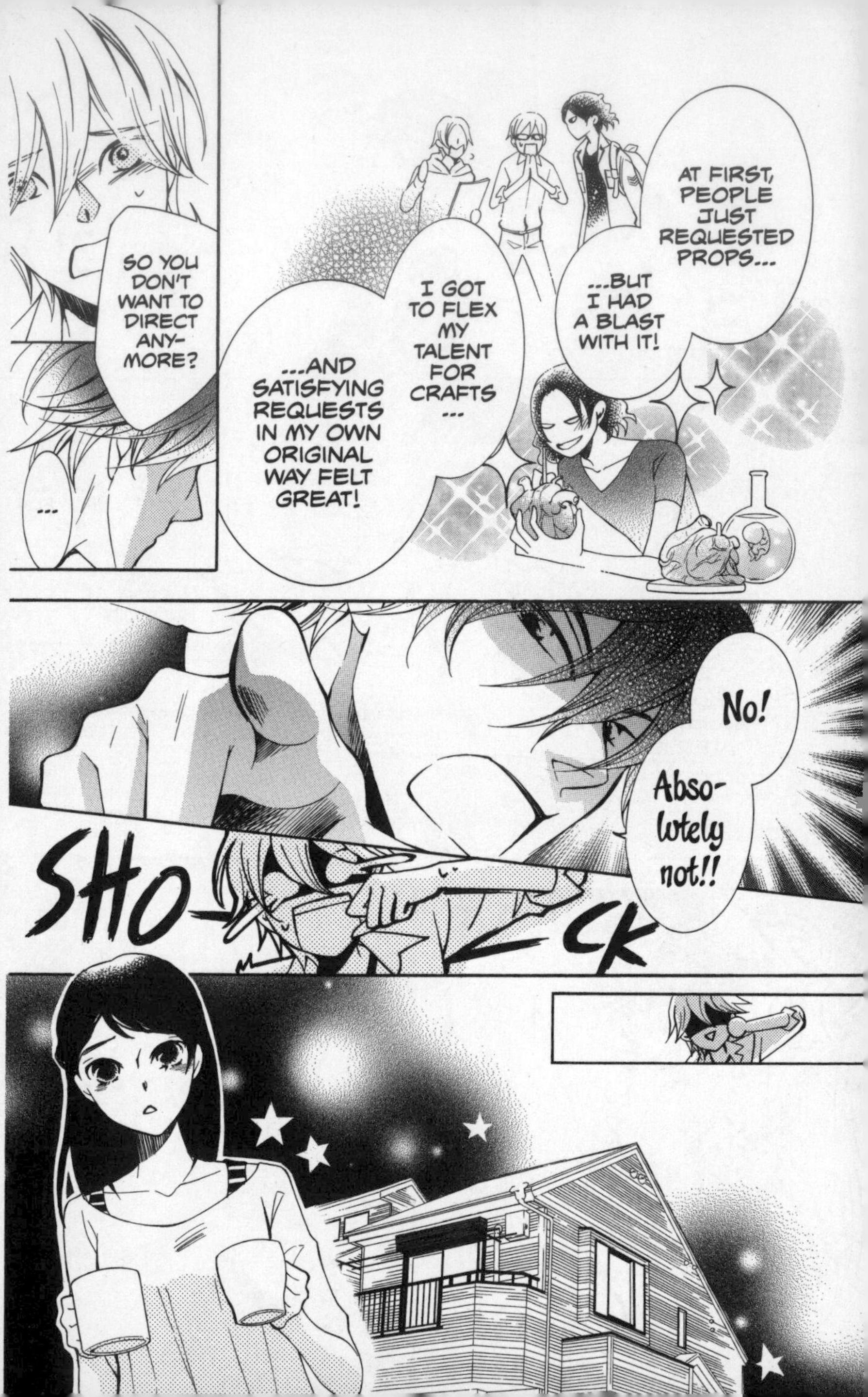
AT FIRST, PEOPLE JUST REQUESTED PROPS...
...BUT I HAD A BLAST WITH IT!
I GOT TO FLEX MY TALENT FOR CRAFTS...
...AND SATISFYING REQUESTS IN MY OWN ORIGINAL WAY FELT GREAT!
SO YOU DON'T WANT TO DIRECT ANY-MORE?
...
No!
Abso-lutely not!!
SHO-CK

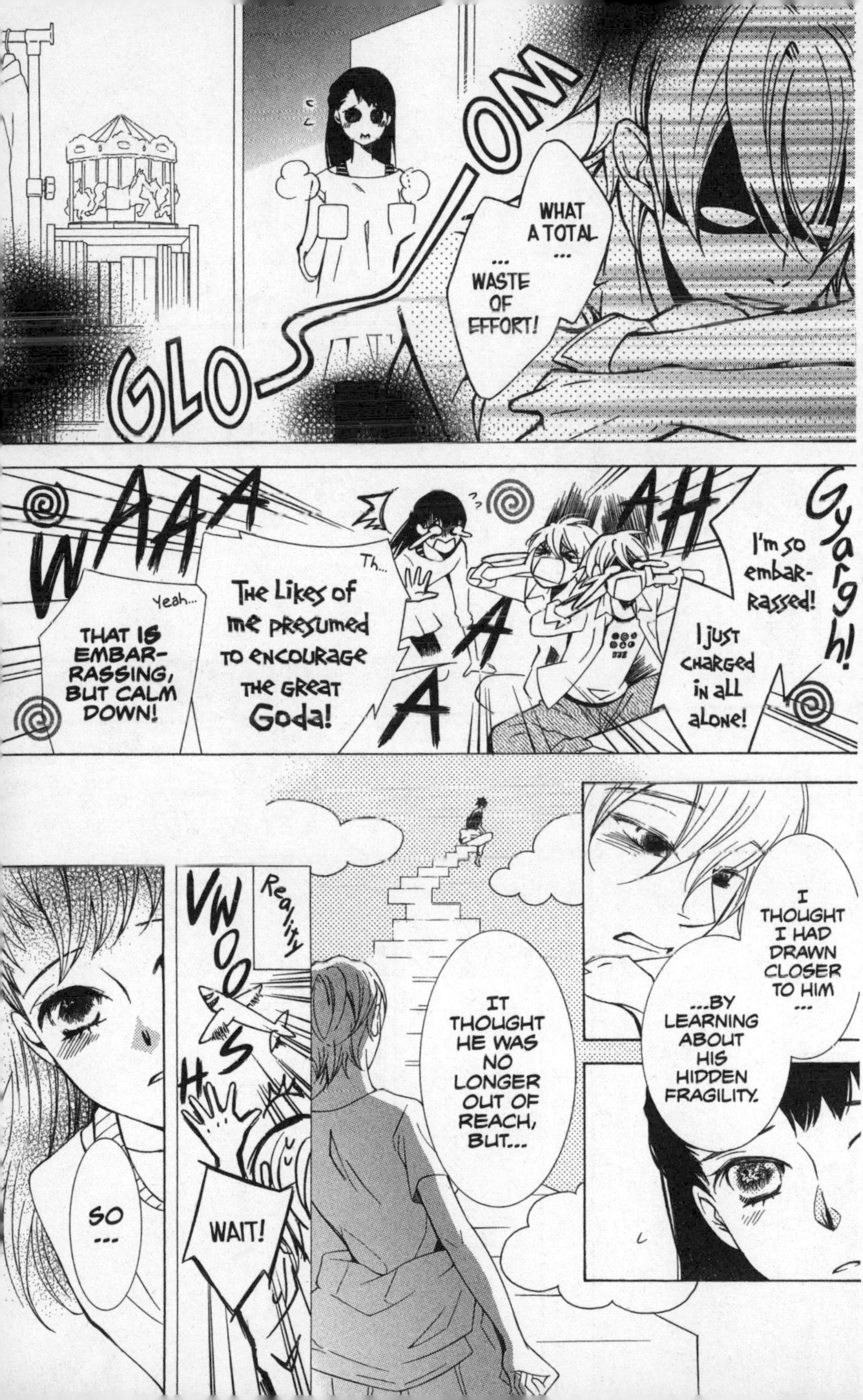
GLO-OM
WHAT A TOTAL ...
... WASTE OF EFFORT!
Gyargh!
I'm so embar-rassed!
I just charged in all alone!
WAAA AAA AH
Th...
The Likes of me presumed to encourage the great Goda!
Yeah...
THAT IS EMBAR-RASSING, BUT CALM DOWN!
I THOUGHT I HAD DRAWN CLOSER TO HIM ...
...BY LEARNING ABOUT HIS HIDDEN FRAGILITY.
IT THOUGHT HE WAS NO LONGER OUT OF REACH, BUT...
Reality
VWOOSH
WAIT!
SO ...

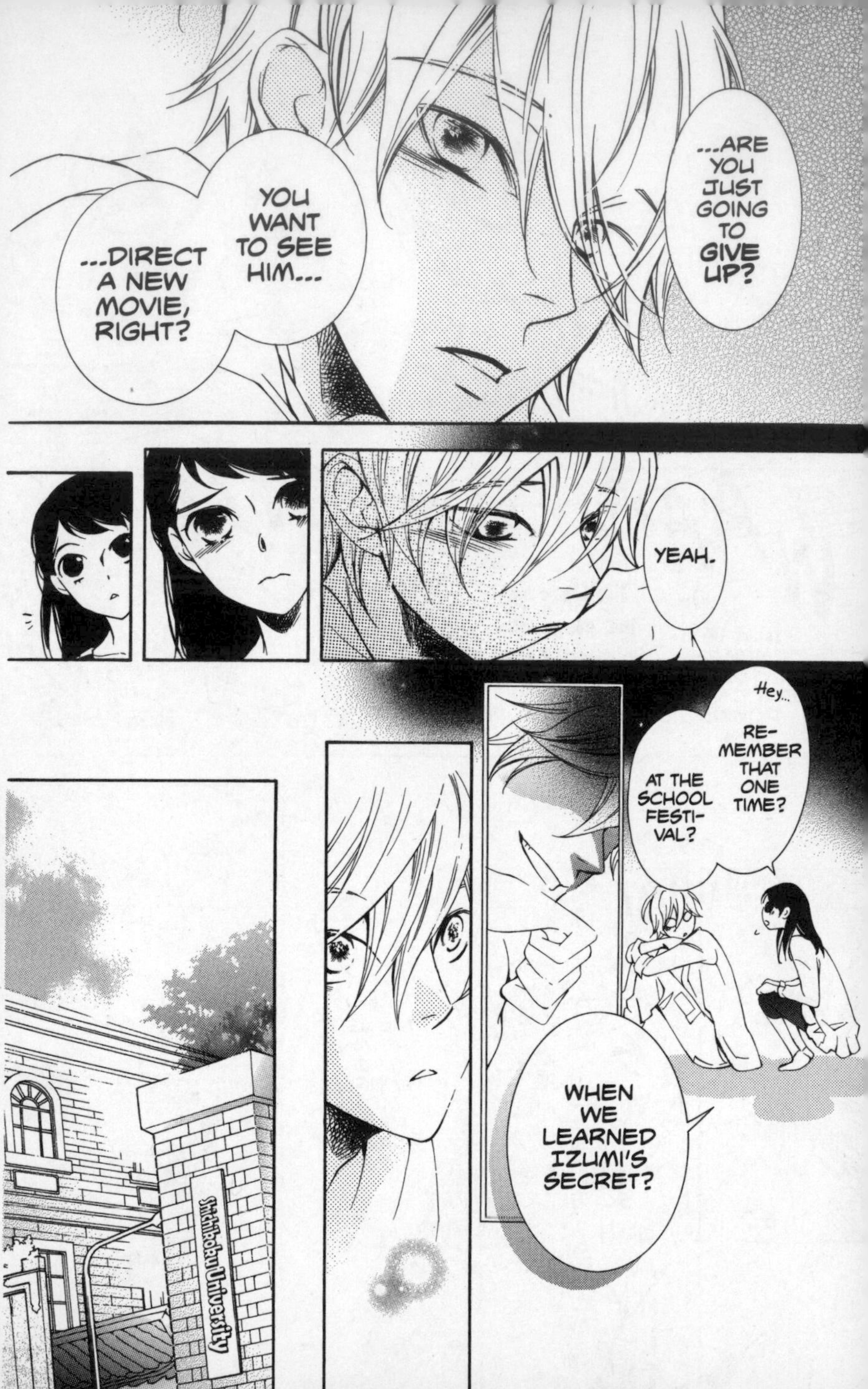
...ARE YOU JUST GOING TO GIVE UP?
YOU WANT TO SEE HIM...
...DIRECT A NEW MOVIE, RIGHT?
YEAH.
Hey...
RE-MEMBER THAT ONE TIME?
AT THE SCHOOL FESTI-VAL?
WHEN WE LEARNED IZUMI'S SECRET?
Shichiboku University

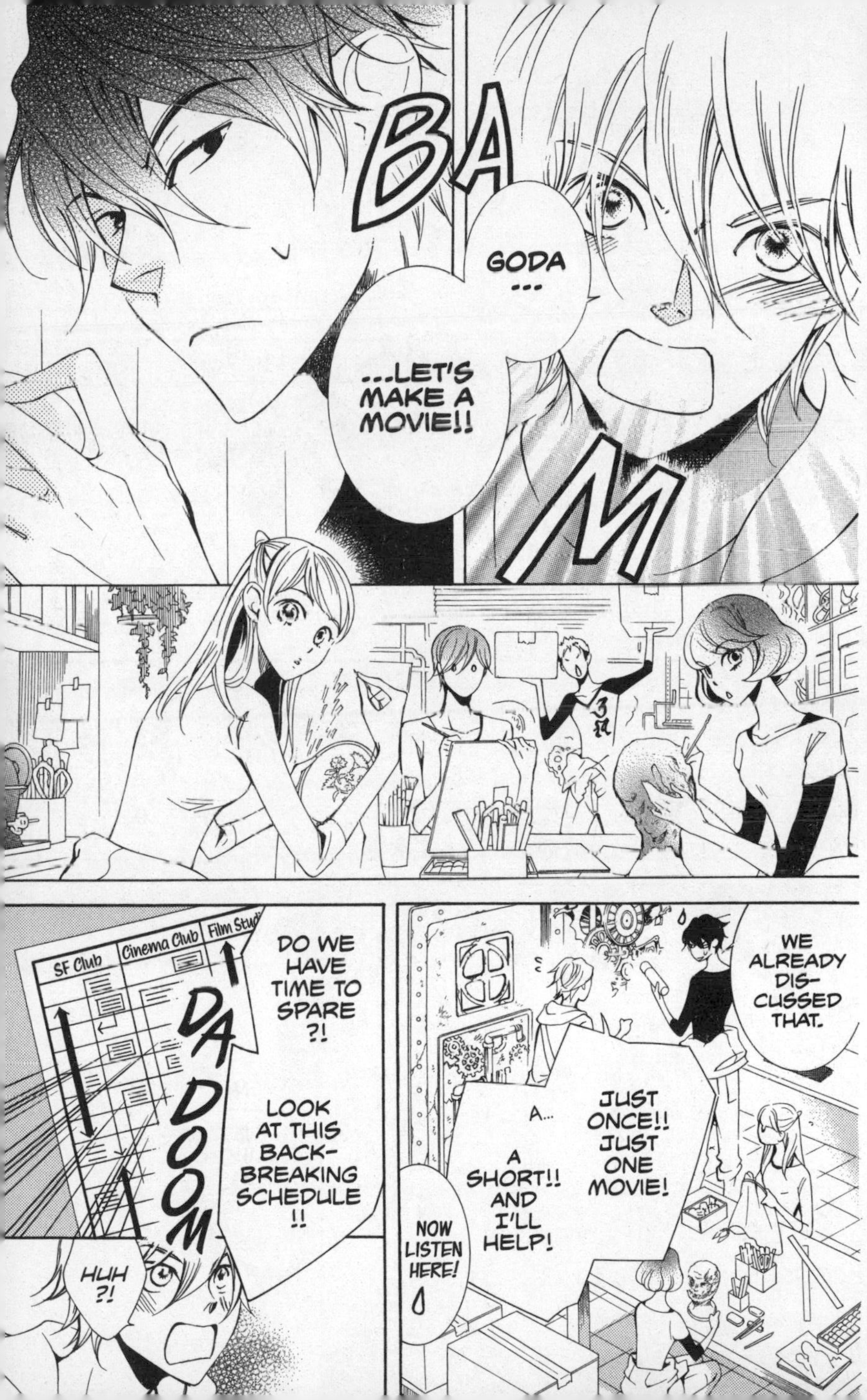
BAM
GODA ...
...LET'S MAKE A MOVIE!!
WE ALREADY DIS-CUSSED THAT.
JUST ONCE!! JUST ONE MOVIE!
A...
A SHORT!! AND I'LL HELP!
NOW LISTEN HERE!
Film Stud
Cinema Club
SF Club
DO WE HAVE TIME TO SPARE?!
DADOOM
LOOK AT THIS BACK-BREAKING SCHEDULE!!
HUH?!

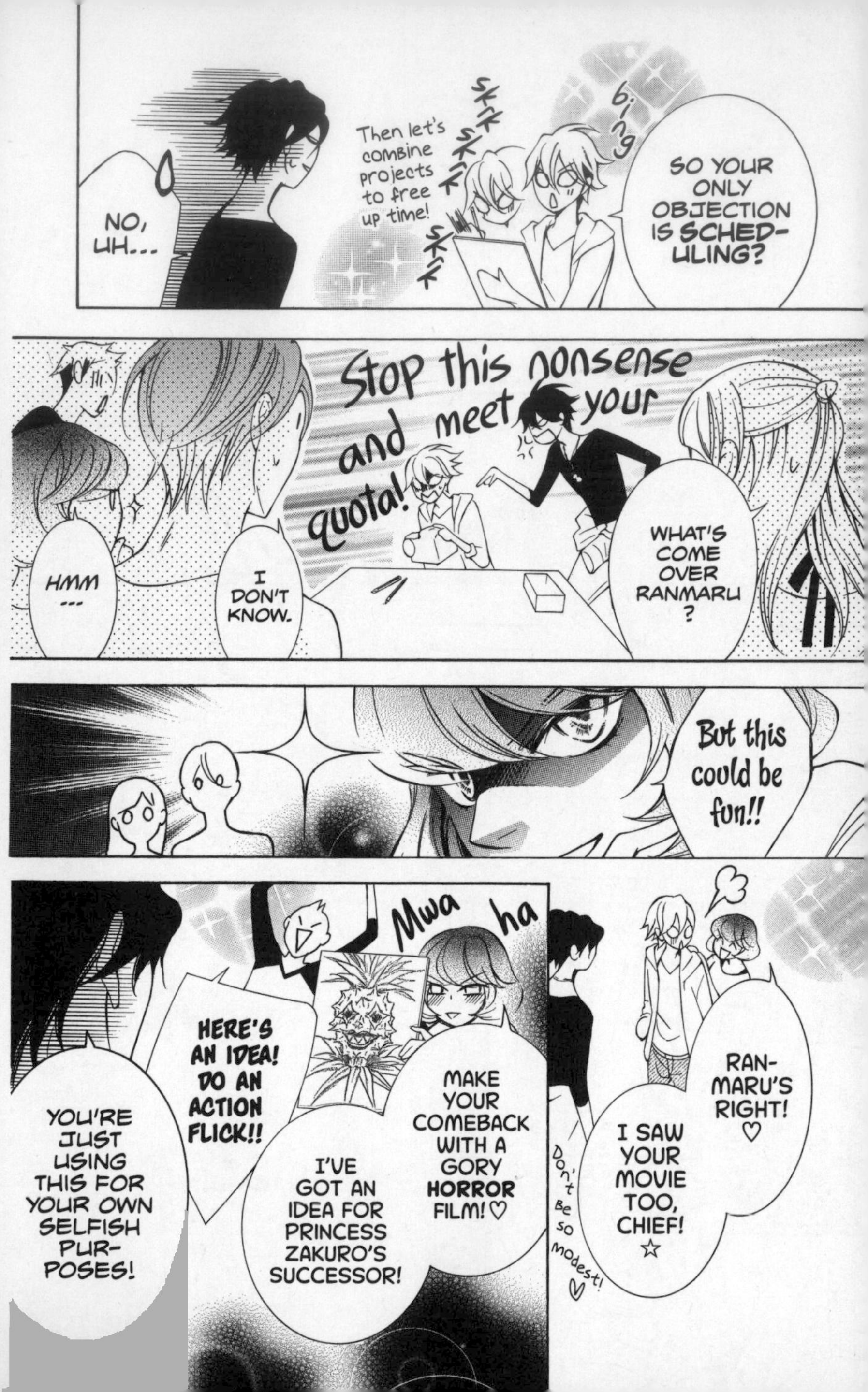
bing
SO YOUR ONLY OBJECTION IS SCHEDULING?
skrik skrik skrik skrik
Then let's combine projects to free up time!
NO, UH...
WHAT'S COME OVER RANMARU?
Stop this nonsense and meet your quota!
I DON'T KNOW.
HMM...
But this could be fun!!
RAN-MARU'S RIGHT! ♡
I SAW YOUR MOVIE TOO, CHIEF! ☆
Don't be so modest! ♡
Mwa ha
MAKE YOUR COMEBACK WITH A GORY HORROR FILM! ♡
HERE'S AN IDEA! DO AN ACTION FLICK!!
I'VE GOT AN IDEA FOR PRINCESS ZAKURO'S SUCCESSOR!
YOU'RE JUST USING THIS FOR YOUR OWN SELFISH PURPOSES!

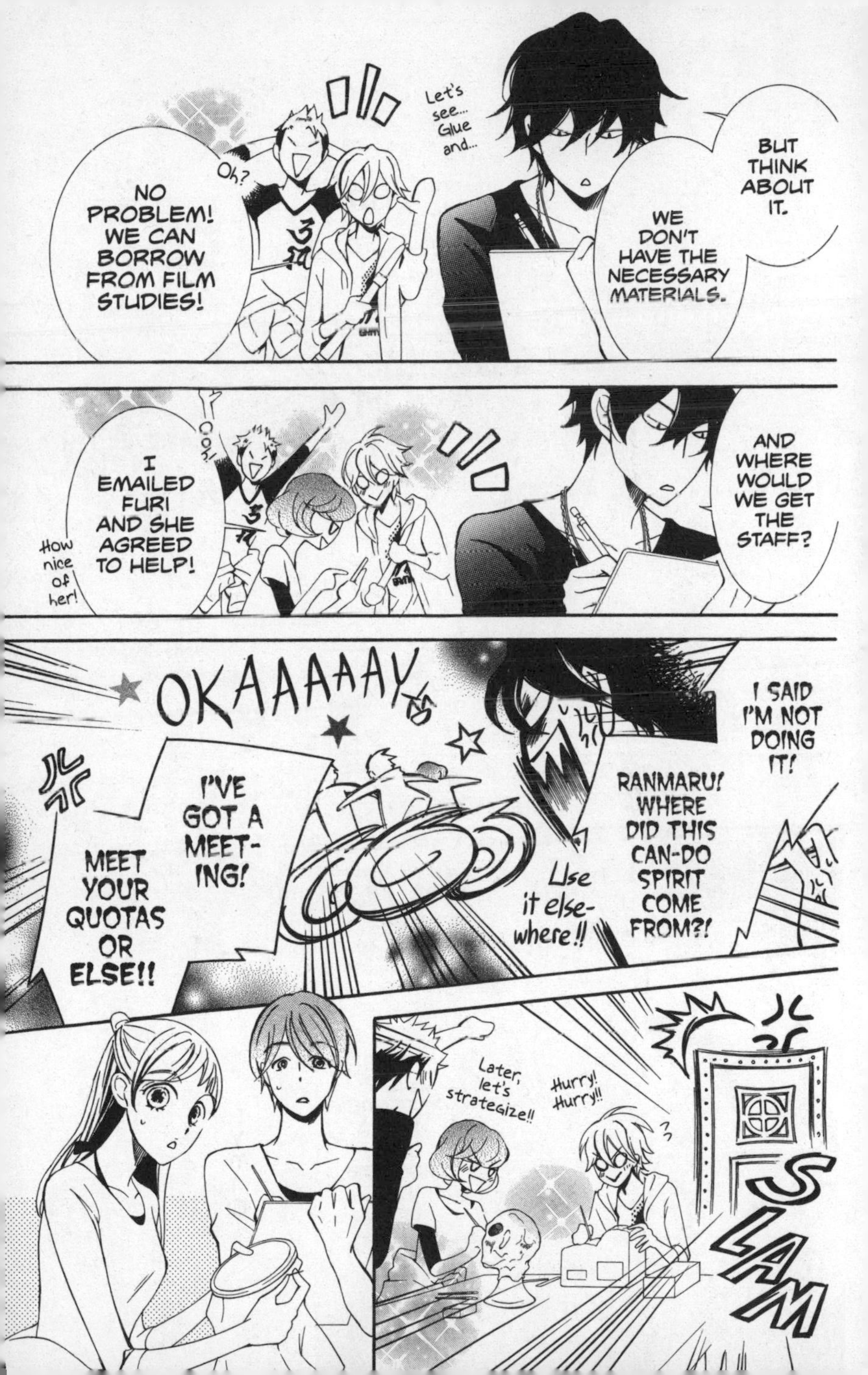
BUT THINK ABOUT IT.
WE DON'T HAVE THE NECESSARY MATERIALS.
Let's see... Glue and...
Oh?
NO PROBLEM! WE CAN BORROW FROM FILM STUDIES!
AND WHERE WOULD WE GET THE STAFF?
Ooh!
I EMAILED FURI AND SHE AGREED TO HELP!
How nice of her!
I SAID I'M NOT DOING IT!
RANMARU! WHERE DID THIS CAN-DO SPIRIT COME FROM?!
Use it elsewhere!!
OKAAAAAY
I'VE GOT A MEETING!
MEET YOUR QUOTAS OR ELSE!!
SLAM
Hurry! Hurry!!
Later, let's strategize!!

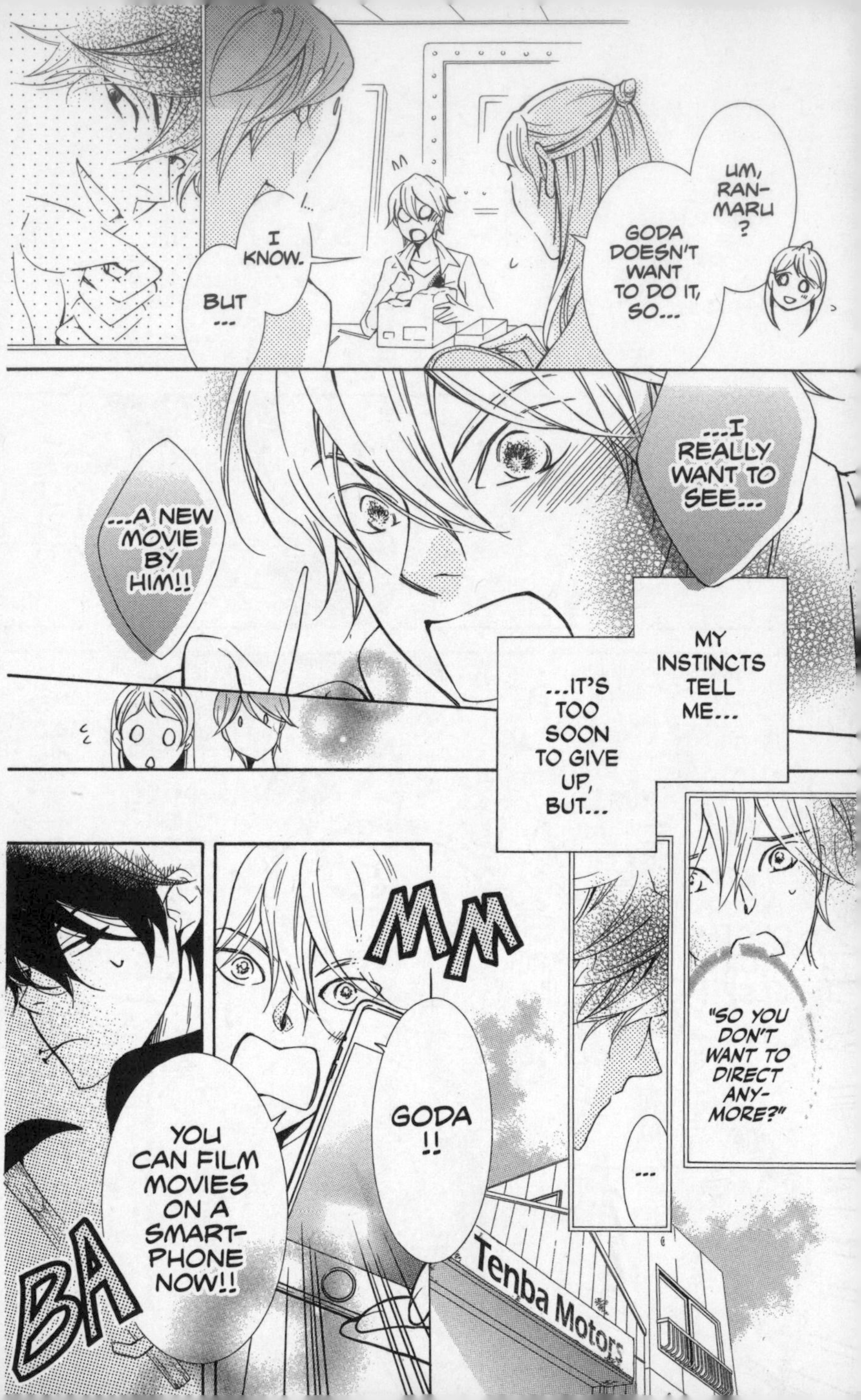
UM, RAN-MARU?
GODA DOESN'T WANT TO DO IT, SO...
I KNOW.
BUT...
...I REALLY WANT TO SEE...
...A NEW MOVIE BY HIM!!
MY INSTINCTS TELL ME...
...IT'S TOO SOON TO GIVE UP, BUT...
"SO YOU DON'T WANT TO DIRECT ANY-MORE?"
...
MM
GODA!!
YOU CAN FILM MOVIES ON A SMART-PHONE NOW!!
BA
Tenba Motors

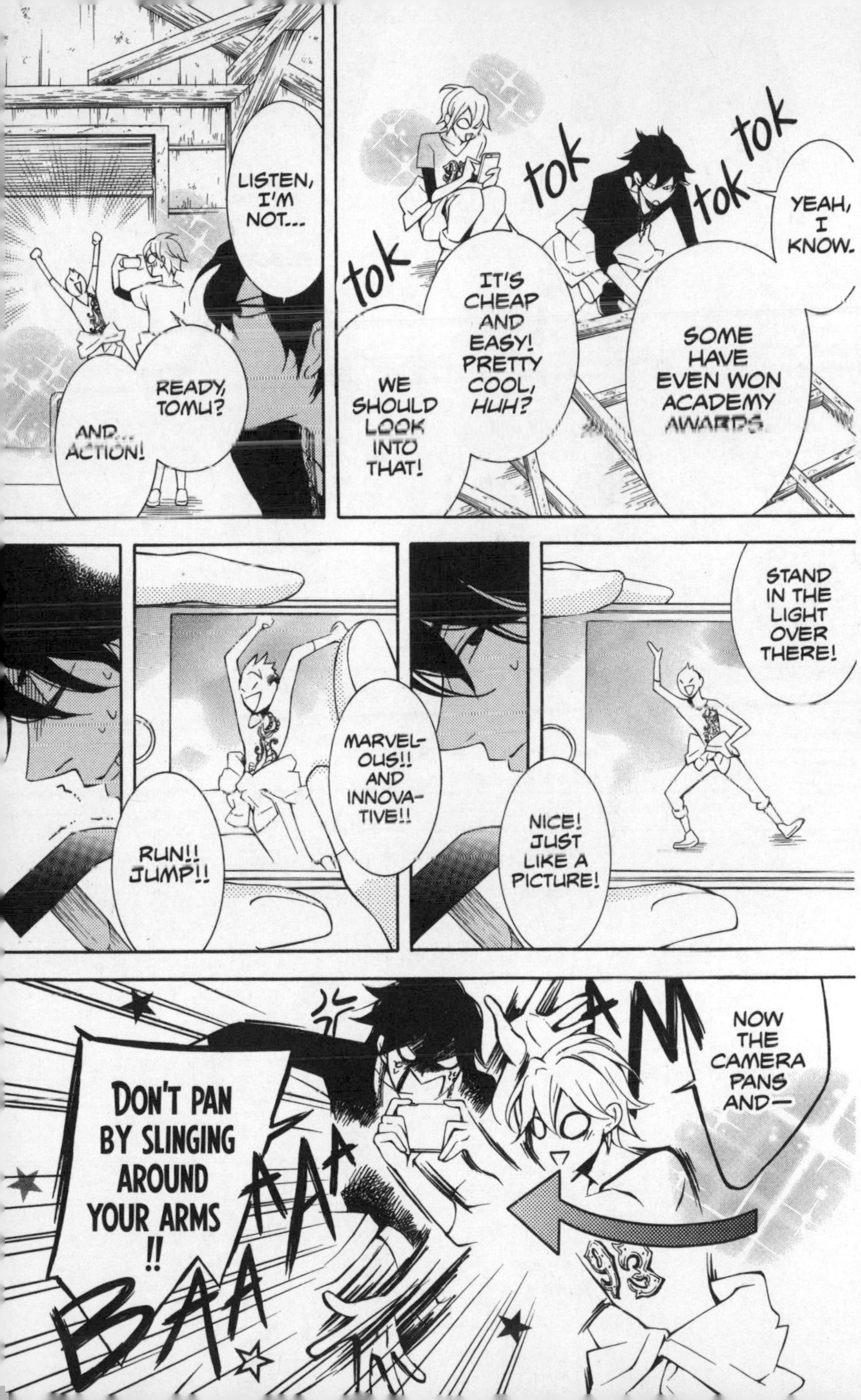
YEAH, I KNOW.
SOME HAVE EVEN WON ACADEMY AWARDS.
tok tok tok tok
IT'S CHEAP AND EASY! PRETTY COOL, HUH?
WE SHOULD LOOK INTO THAT!
LISTEN, I'M NOT...
READY, TOMU?
AND... ACTION!
STAND IN THE LIGHT OVER THERE!
NICE! JUST LIKE A PICTURE!
MARVEL-OUS!! AND INNOVA-TIVE!!
RUN!! JUMP!!
NOW THE CAMERA PANS AND—
DON'T PAN BY SLINGING AROUND YOUR ARMS!!

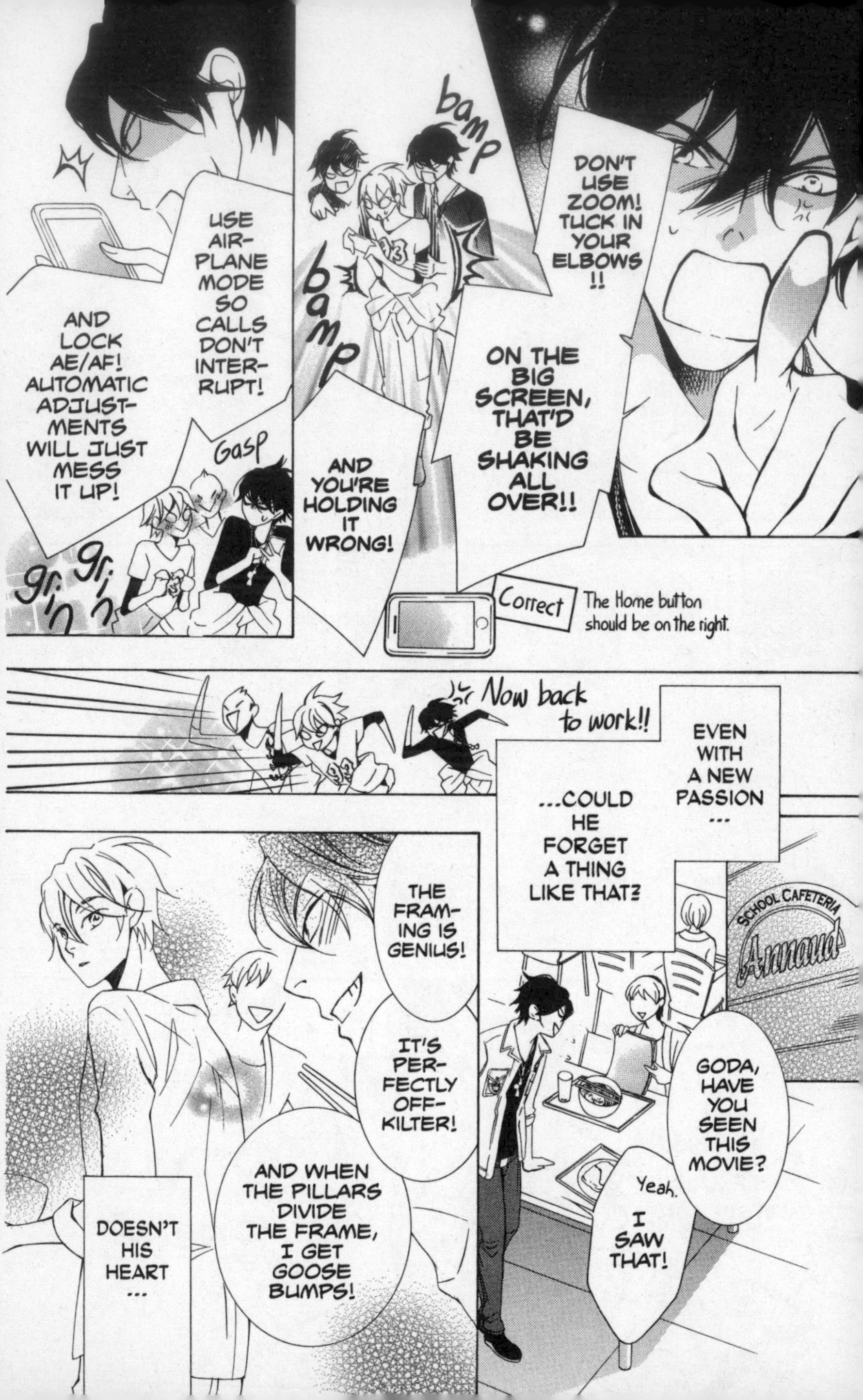
DON'T USE ZOOM! TUCK IN YOUR ELBOWS!!
ON THE BIG SCREEN, THAT'D BE SHAKING ALL OVER!!
bamp
bamp
AND YOU'RE HOLDING IT WRONG!
USE AIR-PLANE MODE SO CALLS DON'T INTER-RUPT!
AND LOCK AE/AF! AUTOMATIC ADJUST-MENTS WILL JUST MESS IT UP!
Gasp
grin grin
Correct
The Home button should be on the right.
Now back to work!!
EVEN WITH A NEW PASSION...
...COULD HE FORGET A THING LIKE THAT?
SCHOOL CAFETERIA
GODA, HAVE YOU SEEN THIS MOVIE?
Yeah.
I SAW THAT!
THE FRAM-ING IS GENIUS!
IT'S PER-FECTLY OFF-KILTER!
AND WHEN THE PILLARS DIVIDE THE FRAME, I GET GOOSE BUMPS!
DOESN'T HIS HEART...

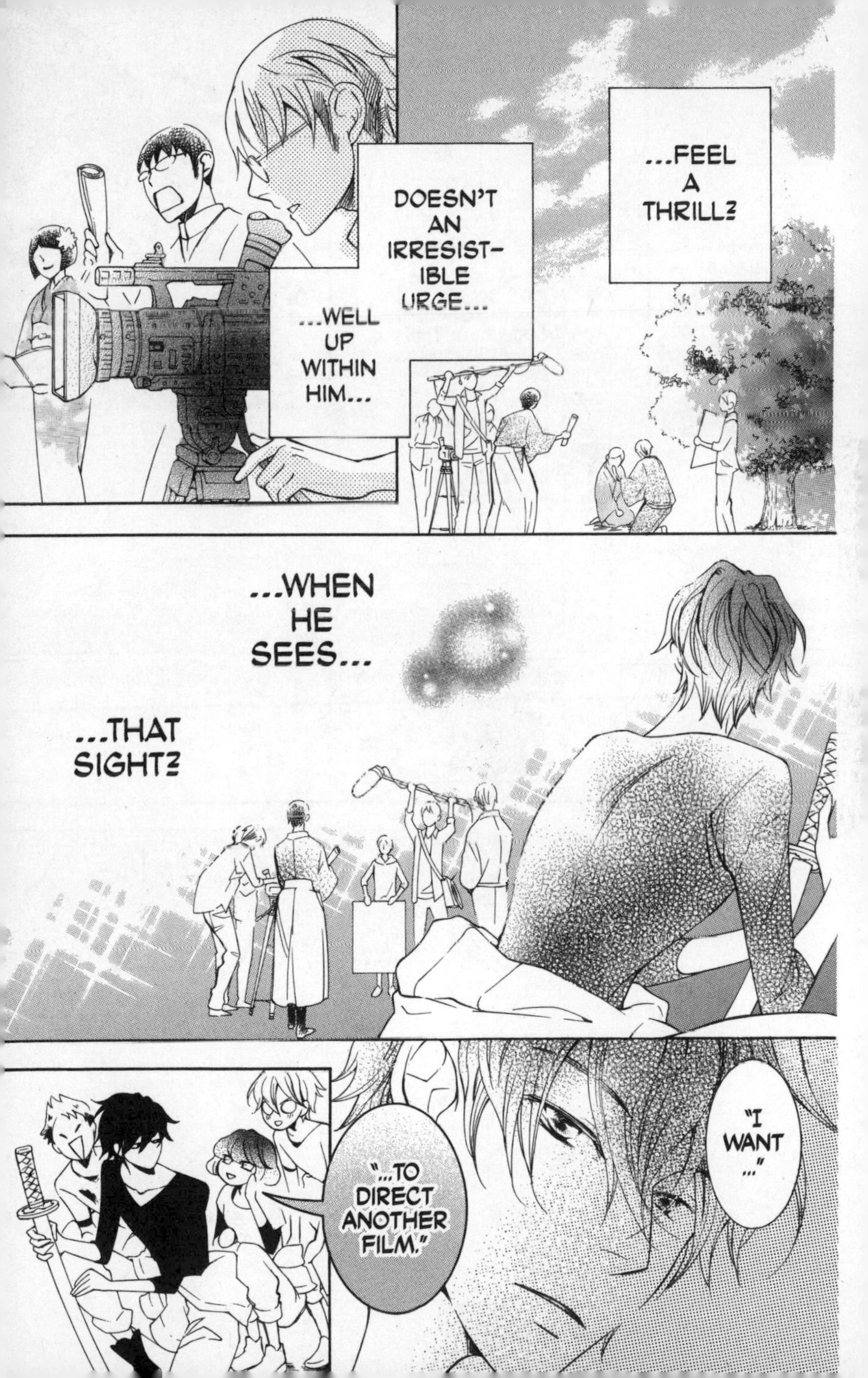
...FEEL A THRILL?
DOESN'T AN IRRESIST-IBLE URGE...
...WELL UP WITHIN HIM...
...WHEN HE SEES...
...THAT SIGHT?
"I WANT..."
"...TO DIRECT ANOTHER FILM."

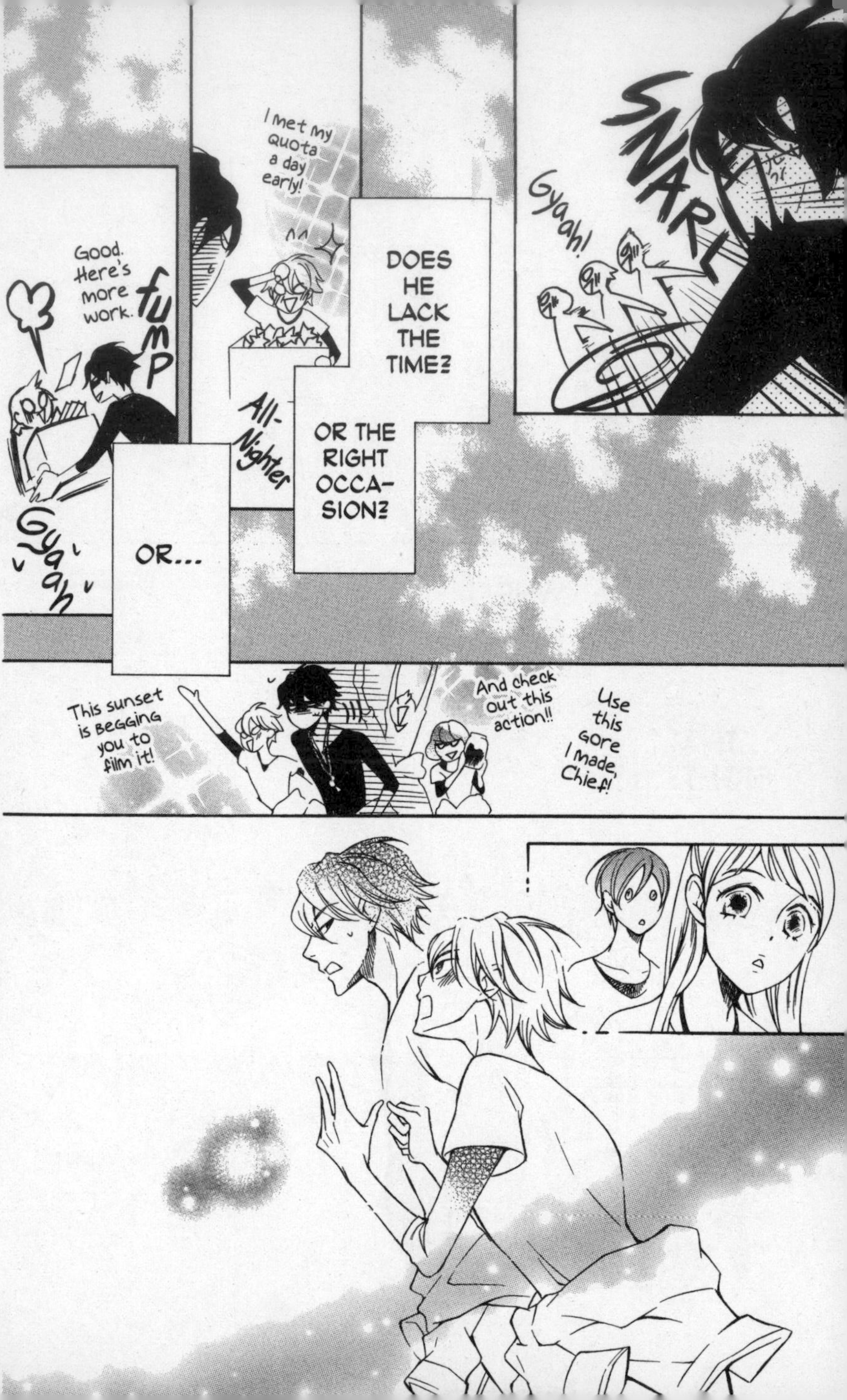
SNARL
Gyaah!
I met my quota a day early!
DOES HE LACK THE TIME?
All-Nighter
Good. Here's more work.
FUMP
Gyaah
OR THE RIGHT OCCASION?
OR...
Use this gore I made, Chief!
And check out this action!!
This sunset is begging you to film it!

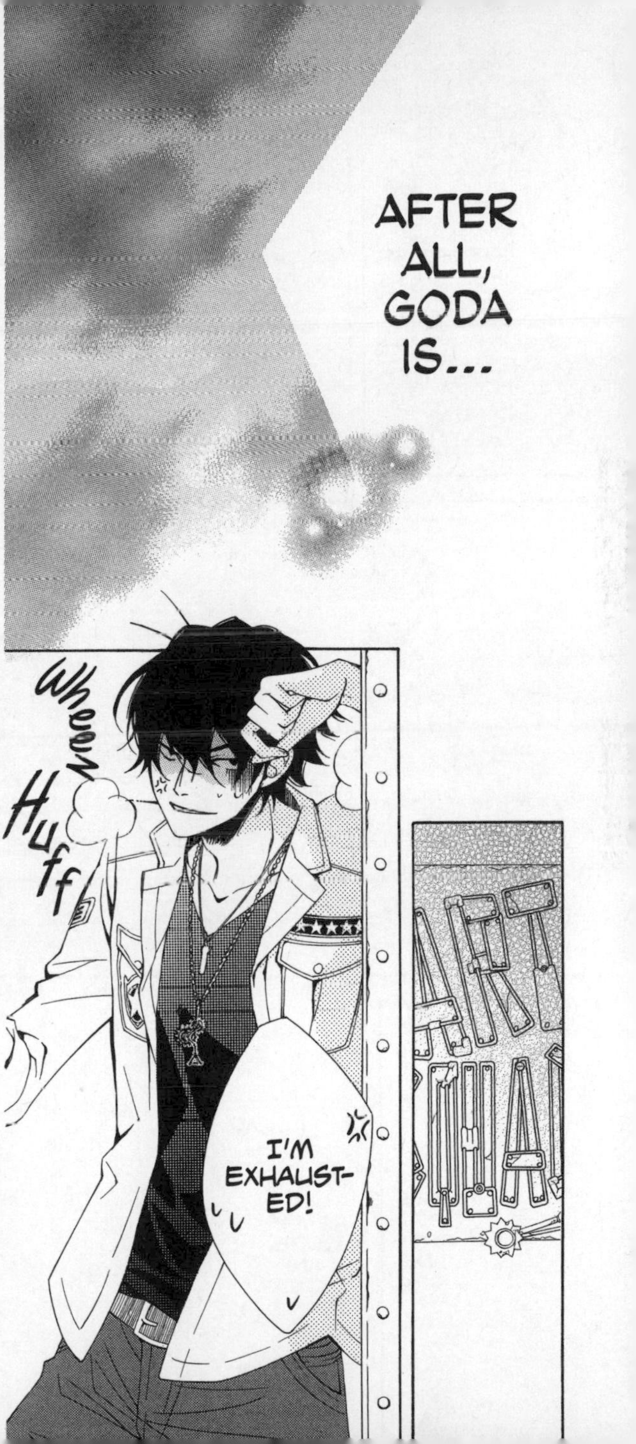
AFTER ALL, GODA IS...
Wheew
Huff
I'M EXHAUST-ED!

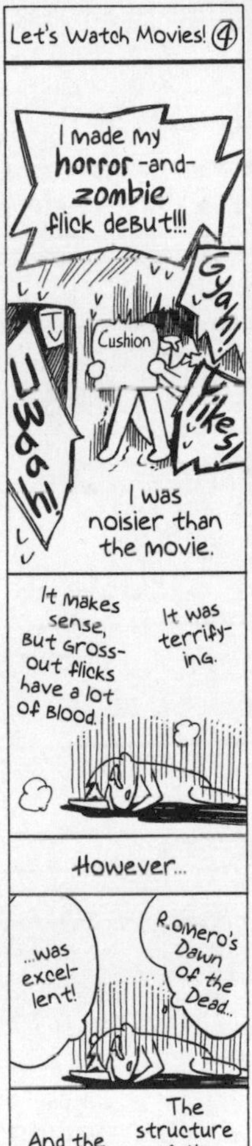
Let's Watch Movies! ④
I made my horror-and-zombie flick debut!!!
Gyah!
Yikes!
Cushion
Uwaah!!
I was noisier than the movie.
It was terrify-ing.
It makes sense, but gross-out flicks have a lot of blood.
However...
Romero's Dawn of the Dead...
...was excel-lent!
The structure of the opening sequence and the use of color were awesome!
And the music and visuals came together splendidly!
I watched the Dario Argento version.

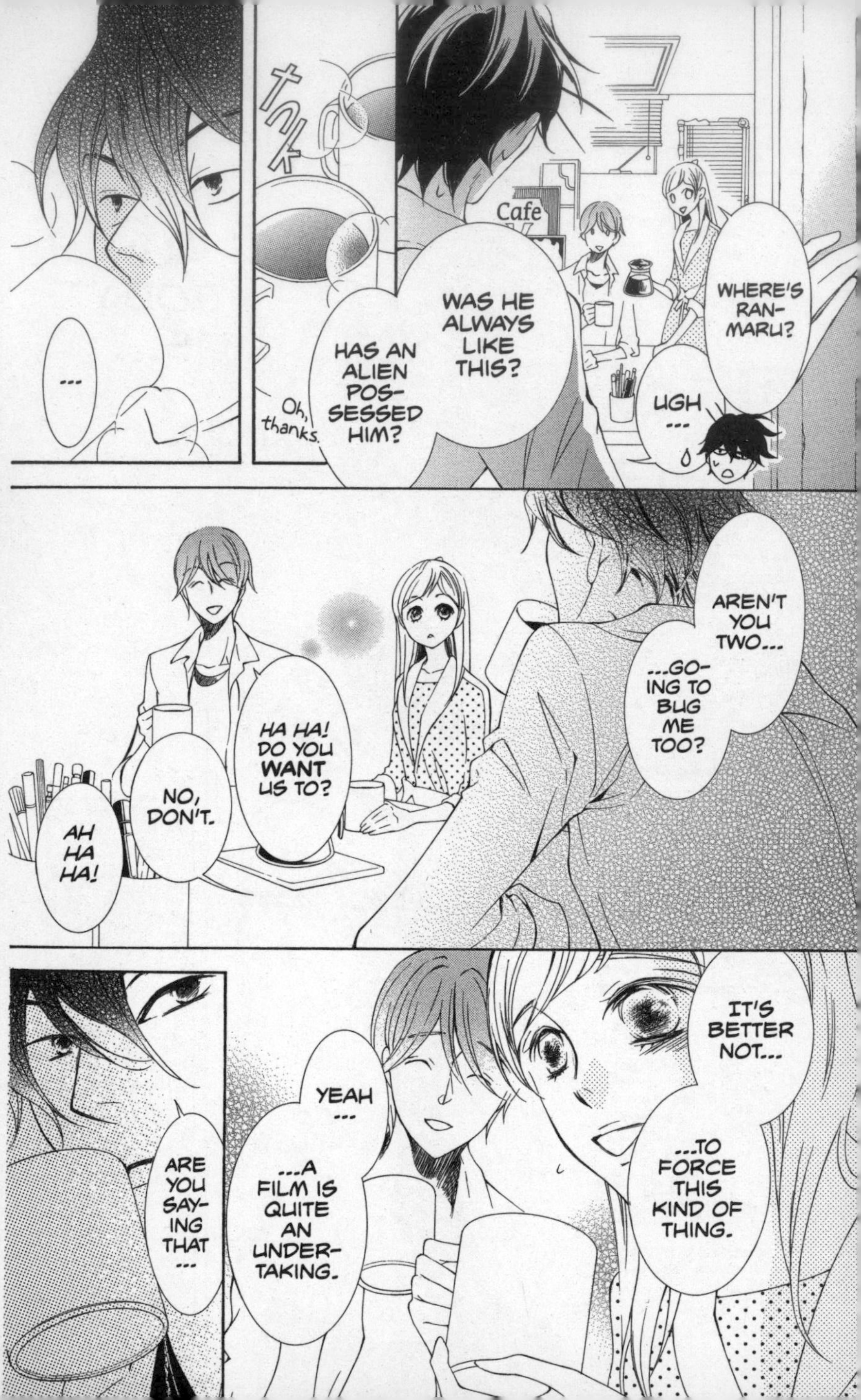
WHERE'S RAN-MARU?
WAS HE ALWAYS LIKE THIS?
UGH...
HAS AN ALIEN POS-SESSED HIM?
Oh, thanks.
...
AREN'T YOU TWO...
...GO-ING TO BUG ME TOO?
HA HA! DO YOU WANT US TO?
NO, DON'T.
AH HA HA!
IT'S BETTER NOT...
...TO FORCE THIS KIND OF THING.
YEAH...
...A FILM IS QUITE AN UNDER-TAKING.
ARE YOU SAY-ING THAT...

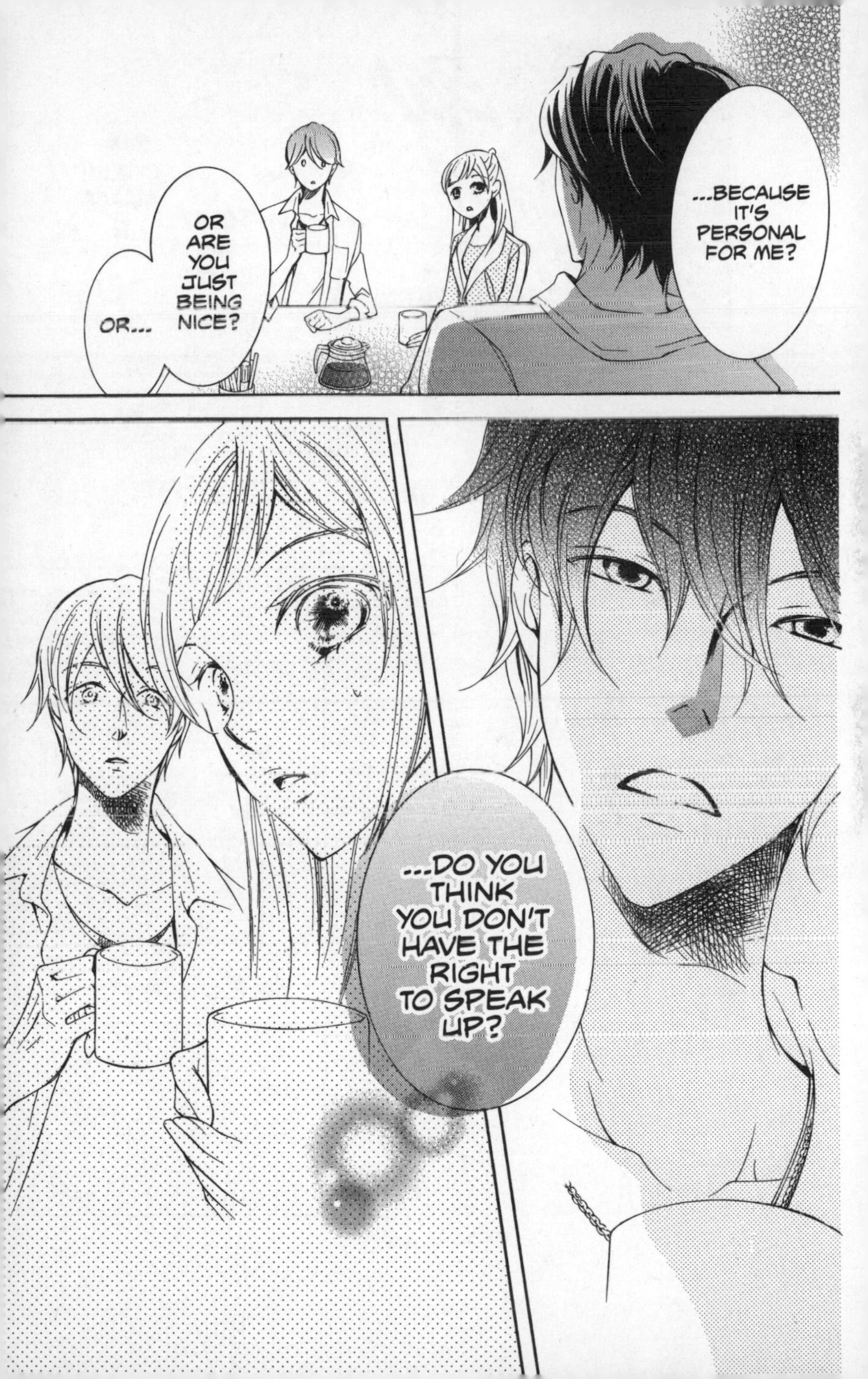
...BECAUSE IT'S PERSONAL FOR ME?
OR ARE YOU JUST BEING NICE?
OR...
...DO YOU THINK YOU DON'T HAVE THE RIGHT TO SPEAK UP?

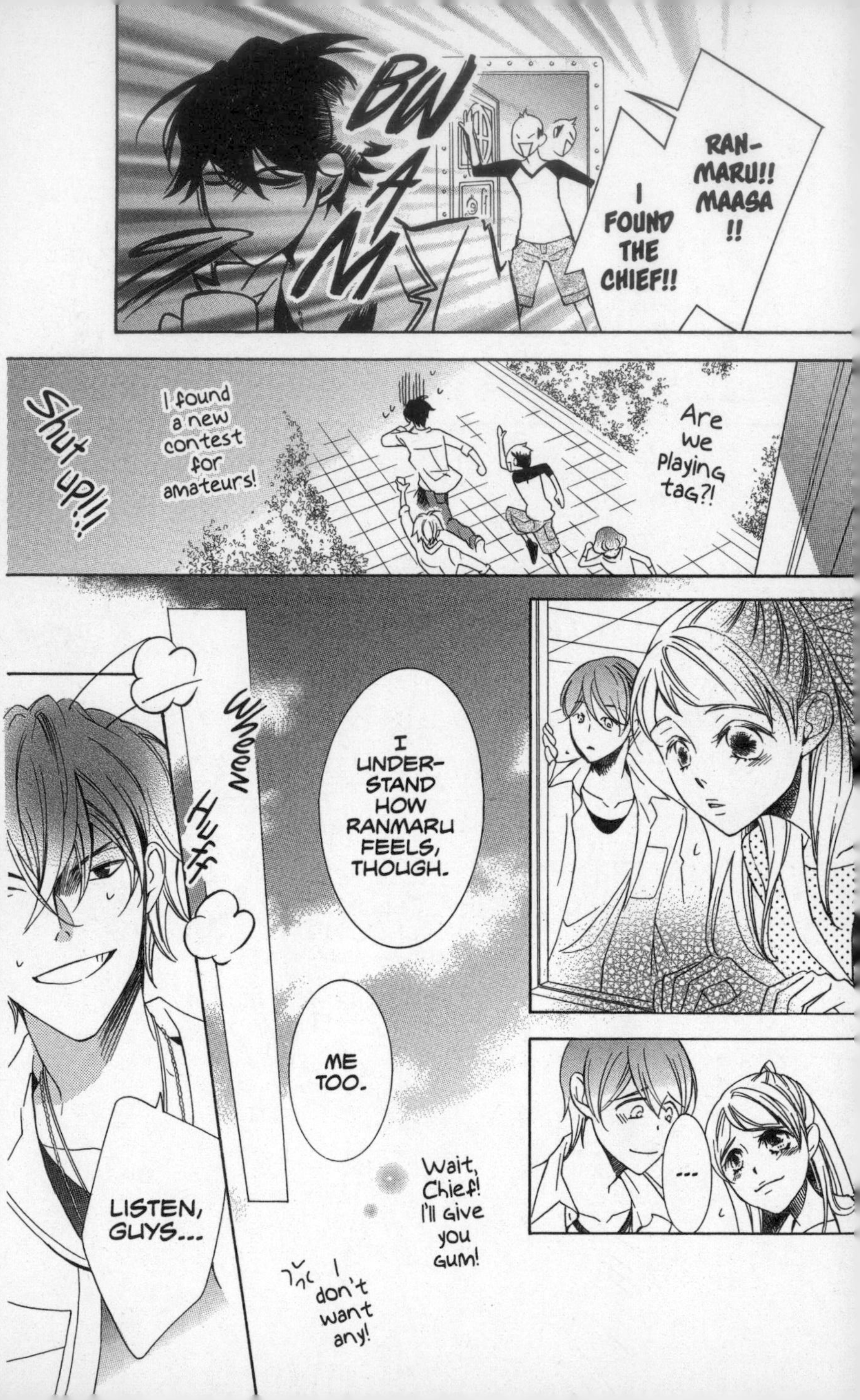
BWAM
RAN-MARU!! MAASA!!
I FOUND THE CHIEF!!
Are we playing tag?!
I found a new contest for amateurs!
Shut up!!!
I UNDER-STAND HOW RANMARU FEELS, THOUGH.
ME TOO.
...
Wait, Chief! I'll give you gum!
I don't want any!
Wheeew
Huff
LISTEN, GUYS...

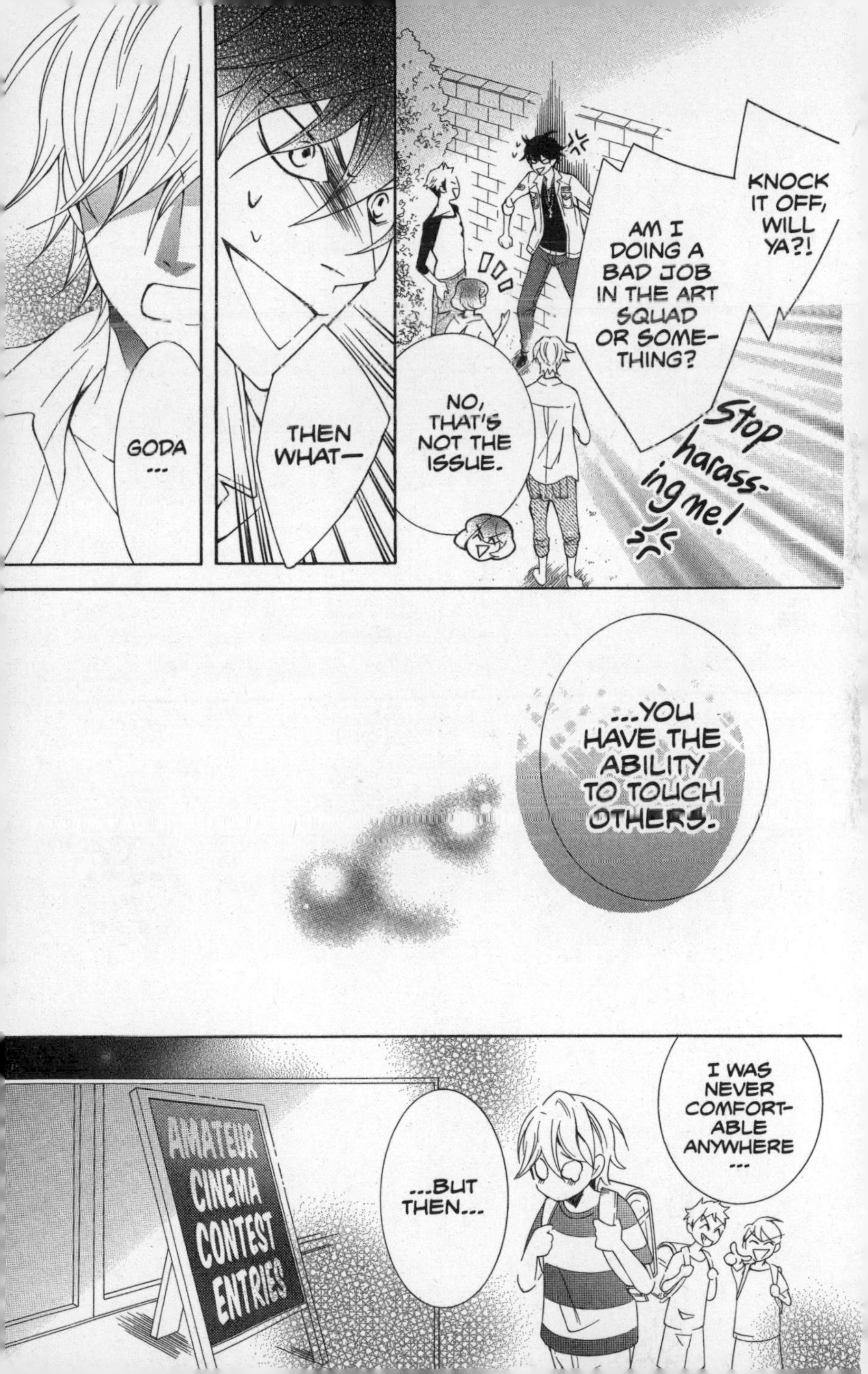
KNOCK IT OFF, WILL YA?!
AM I DOING A BAD JOB IN THE ART SQUAD OR SOMETHING?
Stop harassing me!
NO, THAT'S NOT THE ISSUE.
THEN WHAT—
GODA...
...YOU HAVE THE ABILITY TO TOUCH OTHERS.
I WAS NEVER COMFORTABLE ANYWHERE...
...BUT THEN...
AMATEUR CINEMA CONTEST ENTRIES

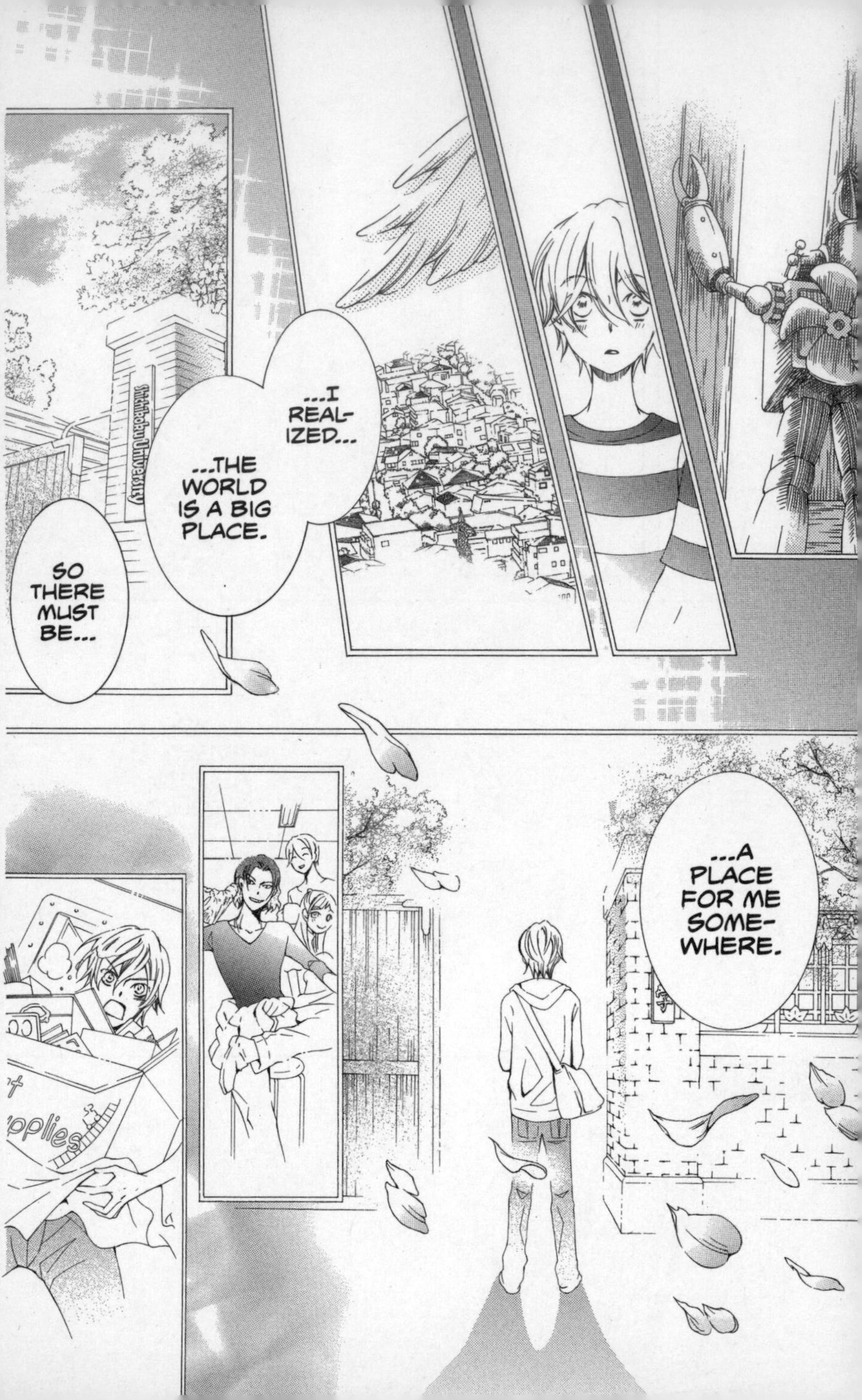
...I REALIZED...
...THE WORLD IS A BIG PLACE.
Shichikoku University
SO THERE MUST BE...
...A PLACE FOR ME SOMEWHERE.

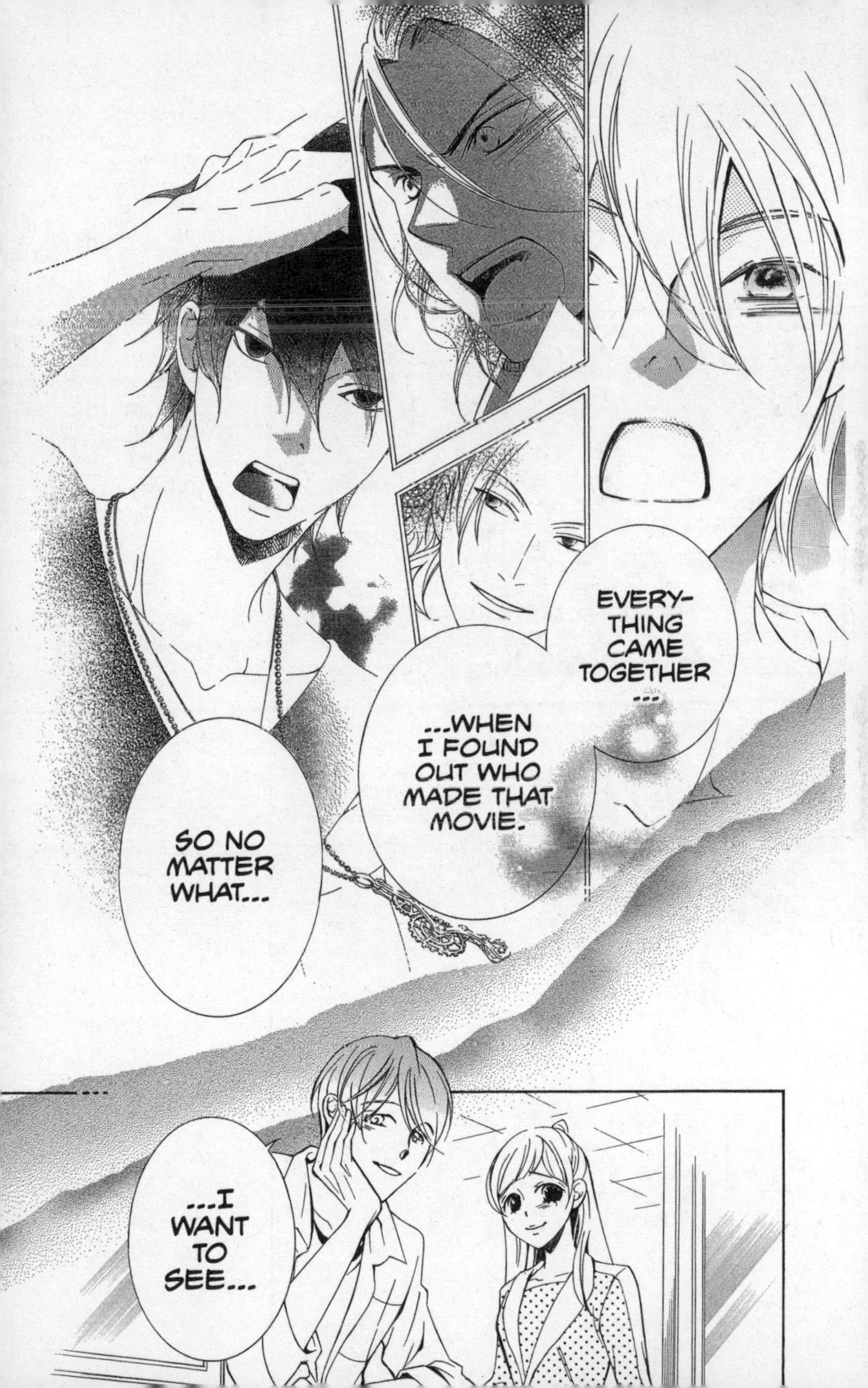
EVERY-THING CAME TOGETHER...
...WHEN I FOUND OUT WHO MADE THAT MOVIE.
SO NO MATTER WHAT...
...I WANT TO SEE...

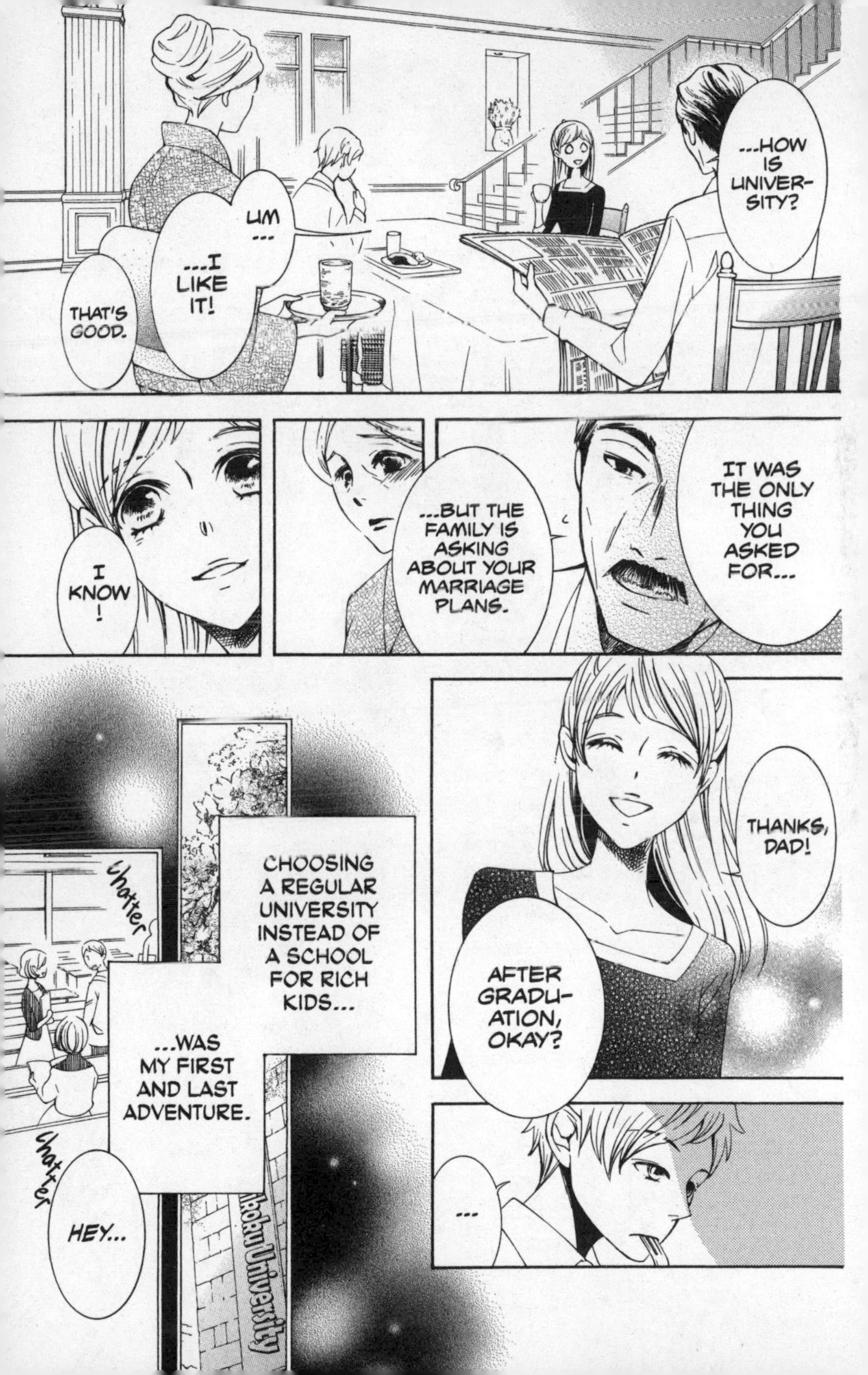

...HOW IS UNIVER-SITY?
UM ...
...I LIKE IT!
THAT'S GOOD.
IT WAS THE ONLY THING YOU ASKED FOR...
...BUT THE FAMILY IS ASKING ABOUT YOUR MARRIAGE PLANS.
I KNOW!
THANKS, DAD!
AFTER GRADU-ATION, OKAY?
...
CHOOSING A REGULAR UNIVERSITY INSTEAD OF A SCHOOL FOR RICH KIDS...
...WAS MY FIRST AND LAST ADVENTURE.
chatter
chatter
HEY...

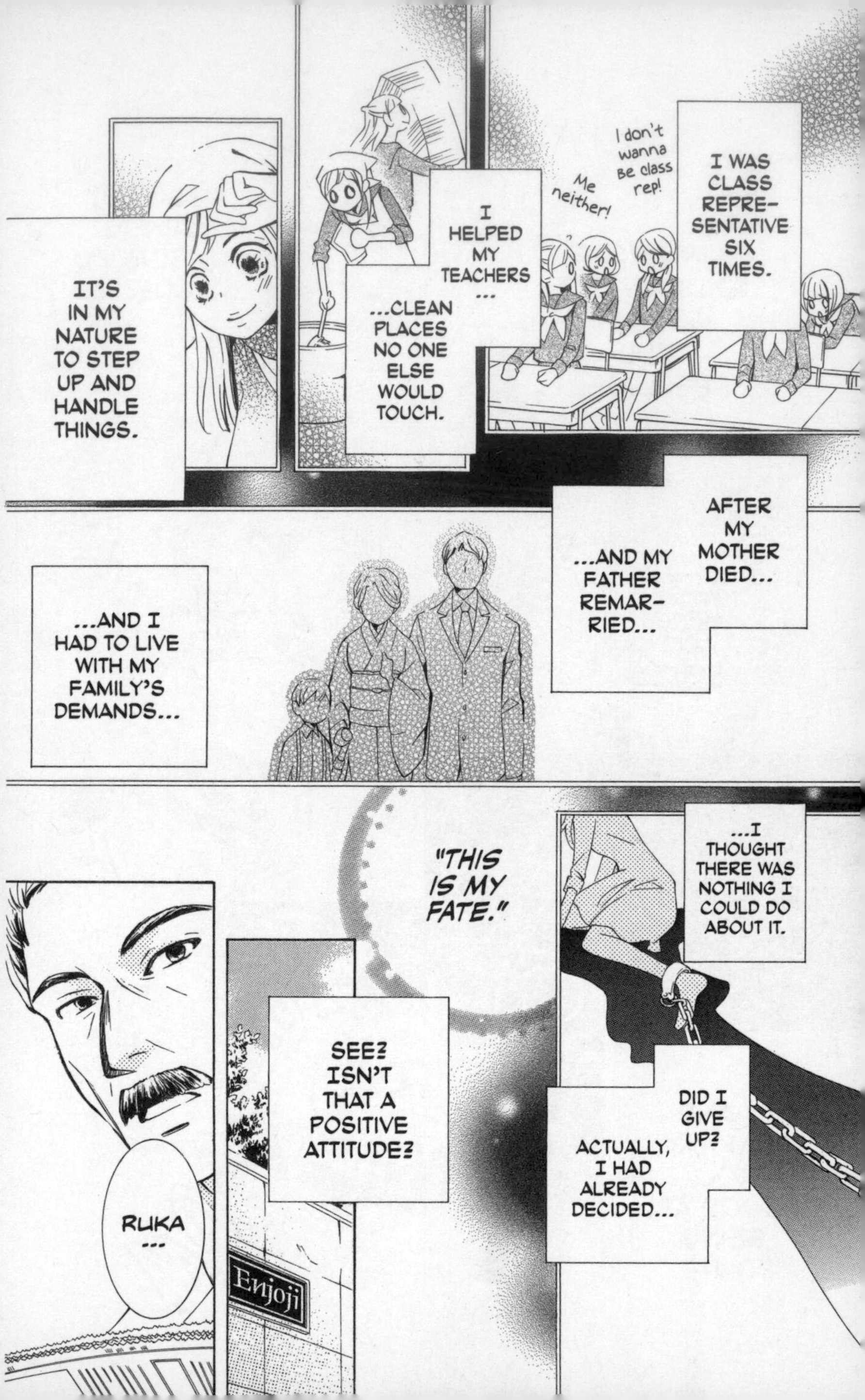
I WAS CLASS REPRE-SENTATIVE SIX TIMES.
I don't wanna be class rep!
Me neither!
I HELPED MY TEACHERS...
...CLEAN PLACES NO ONE ELSE WOULD TOUCH.
IT'S IN MY NATURE TO STEP UP AND HANDLE THINGS.
AFTER MY MOTHER DIED...
...AND MY FATHER REMAR-RIED...
...AND I HAD TO LIVE WITH MY FAMILY'S DEMANDS...
...I THOUGHT THERE WAS NOTHING I COULD DO ABOUT IT.
DID I GIVE UP?
ACTUALLY, I HAD ALREADY DECIDED...
"THIS IS MY FATE."
SEE? ISN'T THAT A POSITIVE ATTITUDE?
Enjoji
RUKA...

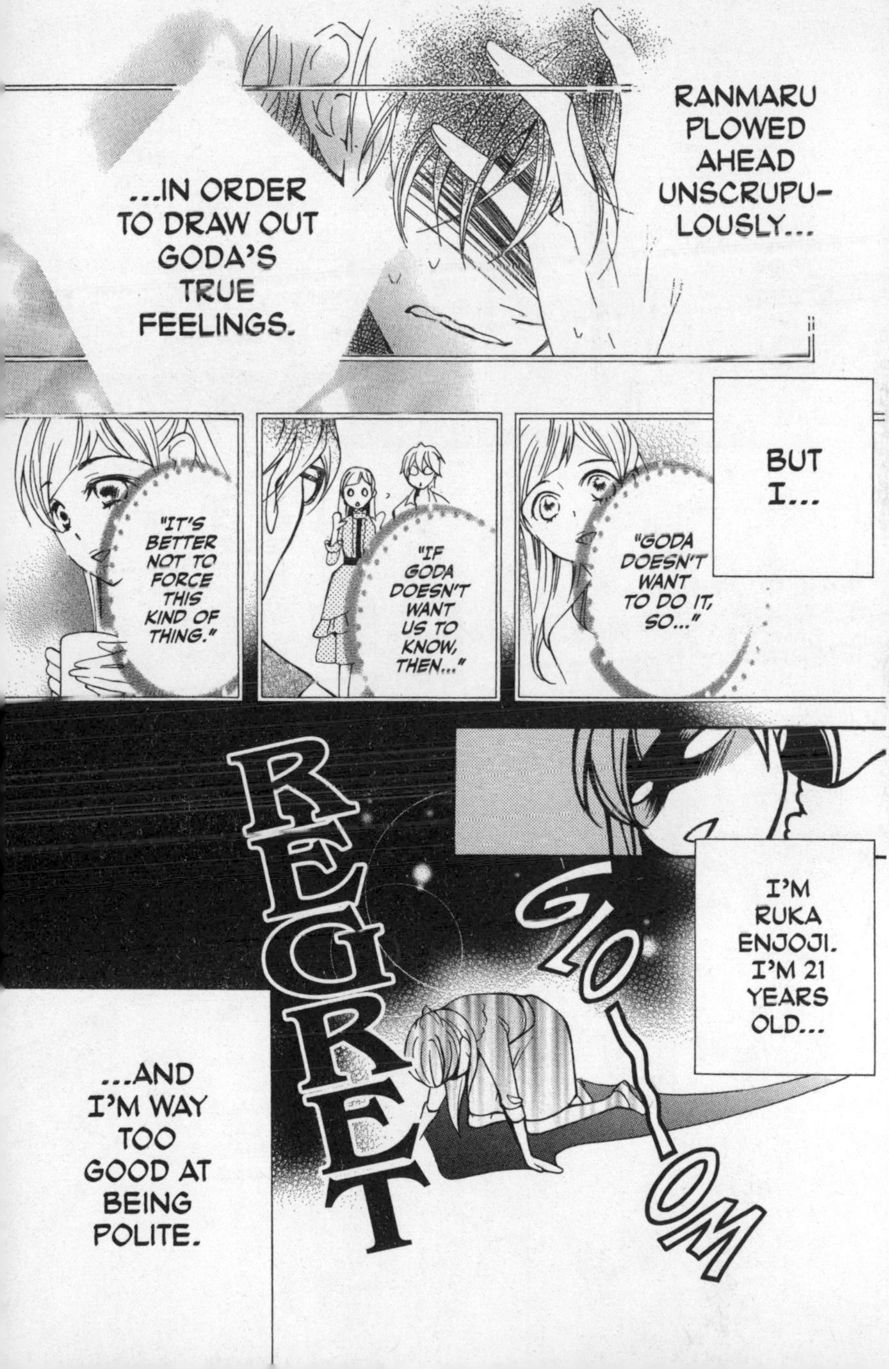
RANMARU PLOWED AHEAD UNSCRUPU-LOUSLY...
...IN ORDER TO DRAW OUT GODA'S TRUE FEELINGS.
BUT I...
"GODA DOESN'T WANT TO DO IT, SO..."
"IF GODA DOESN'T WANT US TO KNOW, THEN..."
"IT'S BETTER NOT TO FORCE THIS KIND OF THING."
I'M RUKA ENJOJI. I'M 21 YEARS OLD...
GLO-OM
REGRET
...AND I'M WAY TOO GOOD AT BEING POLITE.

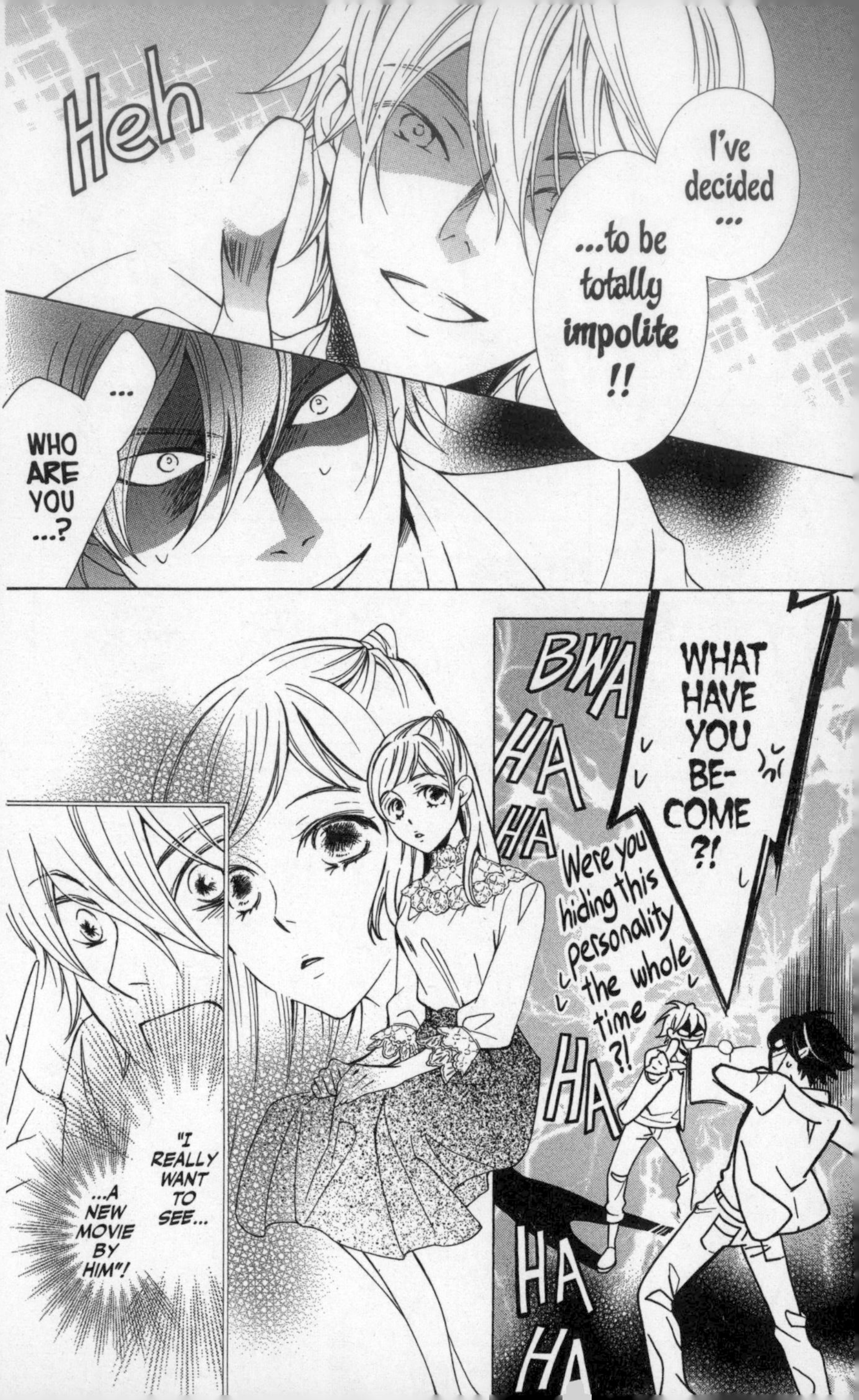
I've decided...
...to be totally impolite!!
Heh
...
WHO ARE YOU...?
BWAHAHA
WHAT HAVE YOU BECOME?!
Were you hiding this personality the whole time?!
HAHA
HAHA
"I REALLY WANT TO SEE...
...A NEW MOVIE BY HIM"!

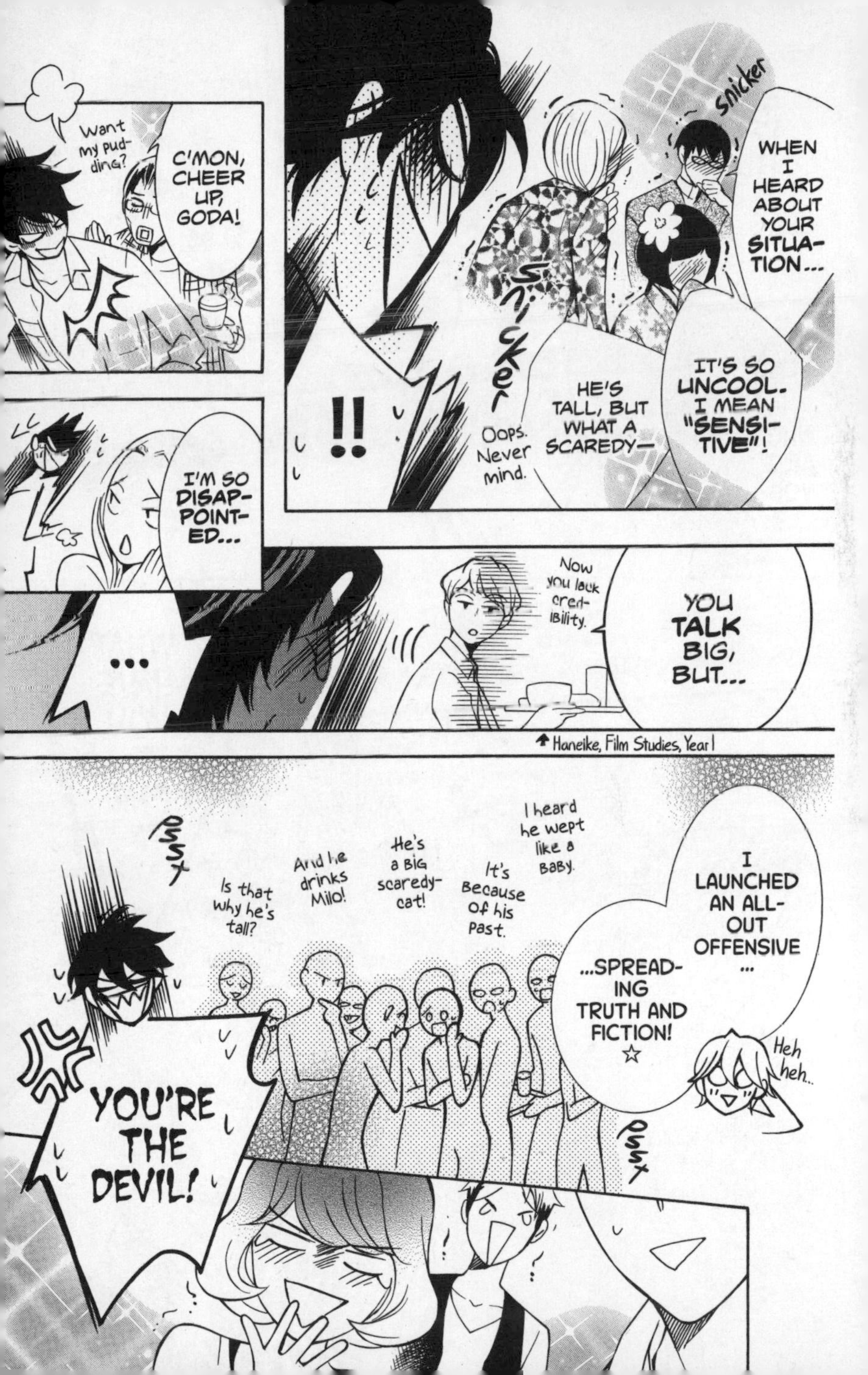
Snicker
WHEN I HEARD ABOUT YOUR SITUATION...
IT'S SO UNCOOL. I MEAN "SENSITIVE"!
HE'S TALL, BUT WHAT A SCAREDY—
Oops. Never mind.
Snicker
!!
C'MON, CHEER UP, GODA!
Want my pudding?
I'M SO DISAPPOINTED...
YOU TALK BIG, BUT...
Now you lack credibility.
...
Haneike, Film Studies, Year 1
I LAUNCHED AN ALL-OUT OFFENSIVE...
...SPREADING TRUTH AND FICTION! ☆
Heh heh..
I heard he wept like a baby.
It's because of his past.
He's a BIG scaredy-cat!
And he drinks Milo!
Is that why he's tall?
Psst
Psst
YOU'RE THE DEVIL!

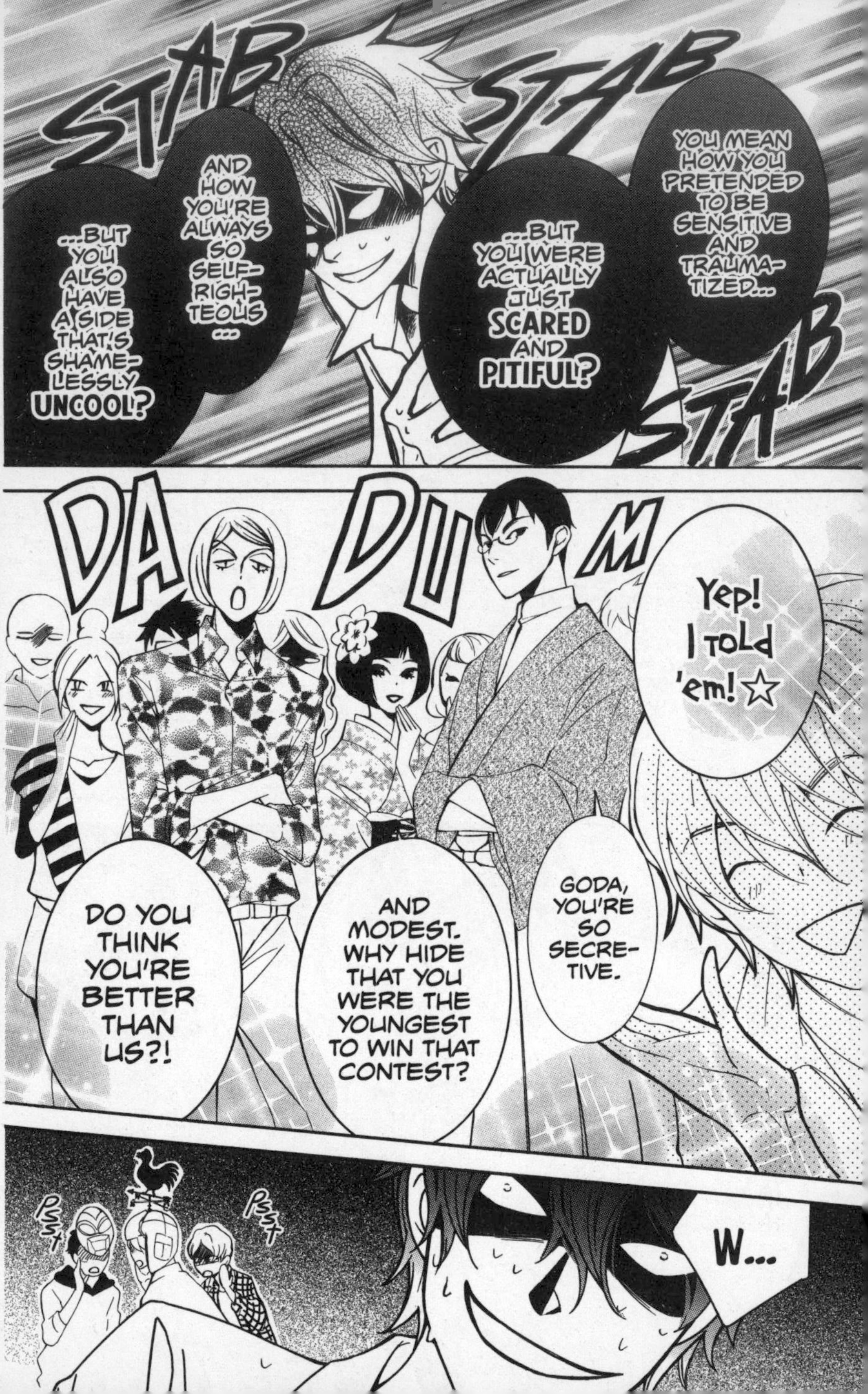
STAB
YOU MEAN HOW YOU PRETENDED TO BE SENSITIVE AND TRAUMA-TIZED...
...BUT YOU WERE ACTUALLY JUST SCARED AND PITIFUL?
STAB
AND HOW YOU'RE ALWAYS SO SELF-RIGH-TEOUS...
...BUT YOU ALSO HAVE A SIDE THAT'S SHAME-LESSLY UNCOOL?
STAB
Yep! I told 'em! ☆
DA DUM
GODA, YOU'RE SO SECRE-TIVE.
AND MODEST. WHY HIDE THAT YOU WERE THE YOUNGEST TO WIN THAT CONTEST?
DO YOU THINK YOU'RE BETTER THAN US?!
W...
Psst
Psst

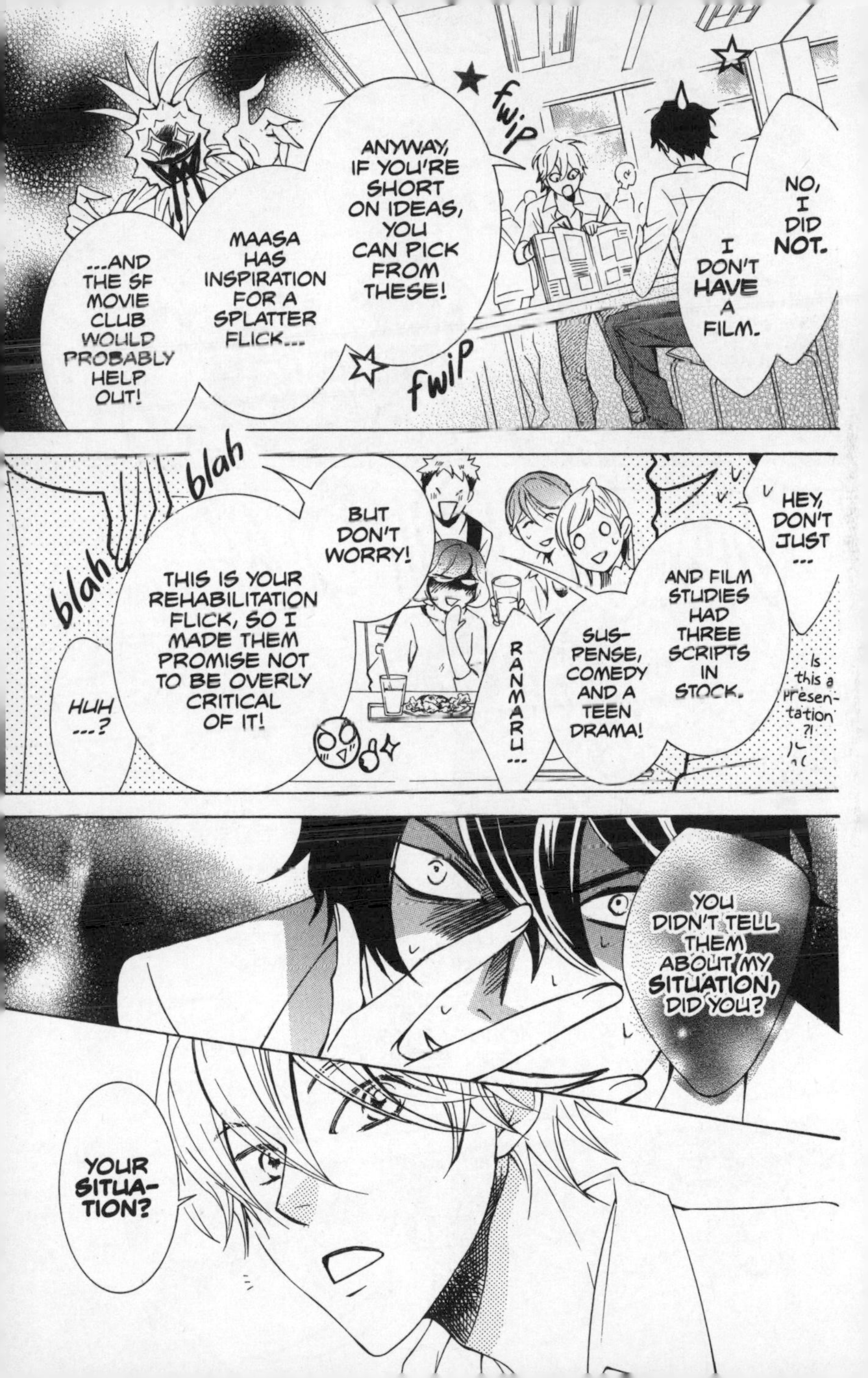
NO, I DID NOT.
I DON'T HAVE A FILM.
fwip
ANYWAY, IF YOU'RE SHORT ON IDEAS, YOU CAN PICK FROM THESE!
fwip
MAASA HAS INSPIRATION FOR A SPLATTER FLICK...
...AND THE SF MOVIE CLUB WOULD PROBABLY HELP OUT!
HEY, DON'T JUST ...
Is this a presentation?!
AND FILM STUDIES HAD THREE SCRIPTS IN STOCK.
SUS-PENSE, COMEDY AND A TEEN DRAMA!
RANMARU...
BUT DON'T WORRY!
THIS IS YOUR REHABILITATION FLICK, SO I MADE THEM PROMISE NOT TO BE OVERLY CRITICAL OF IT!
blah
blah
HUH...?
YOU DIDN'T TELL THEM ABOUT MY SITUATION, DID YOU?
YOUR SITUA-TION?

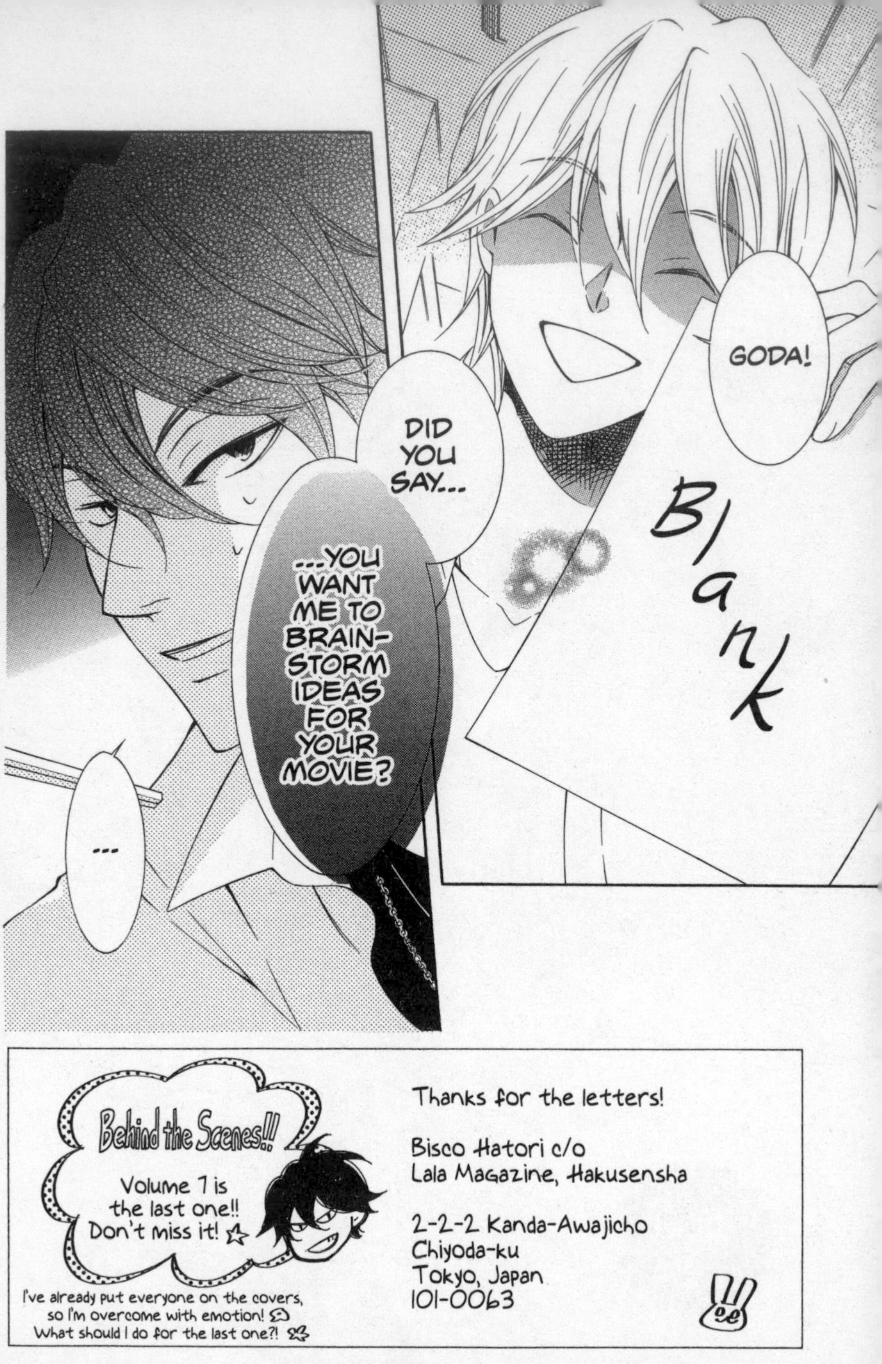
GODA!
Blank
DID YOU SAY...
...YOU WANT ME TO BRAIN-STORM IDEAS FOR YOUR MOVIE?
...

Behind the Scenes!!

Volume 7 is the last one!! Don't miss it! ☆

I've already put everyone on the covers, so I'm overcome with emotion! What should I do for the last one?!

Thanks for the letters!

Bisco Hatori c/o
Lala Magazine, Hakusensha

2-2-2 Kanda-Awajicho
Chiyoda-ku
Tokyo, Japan
101-0063

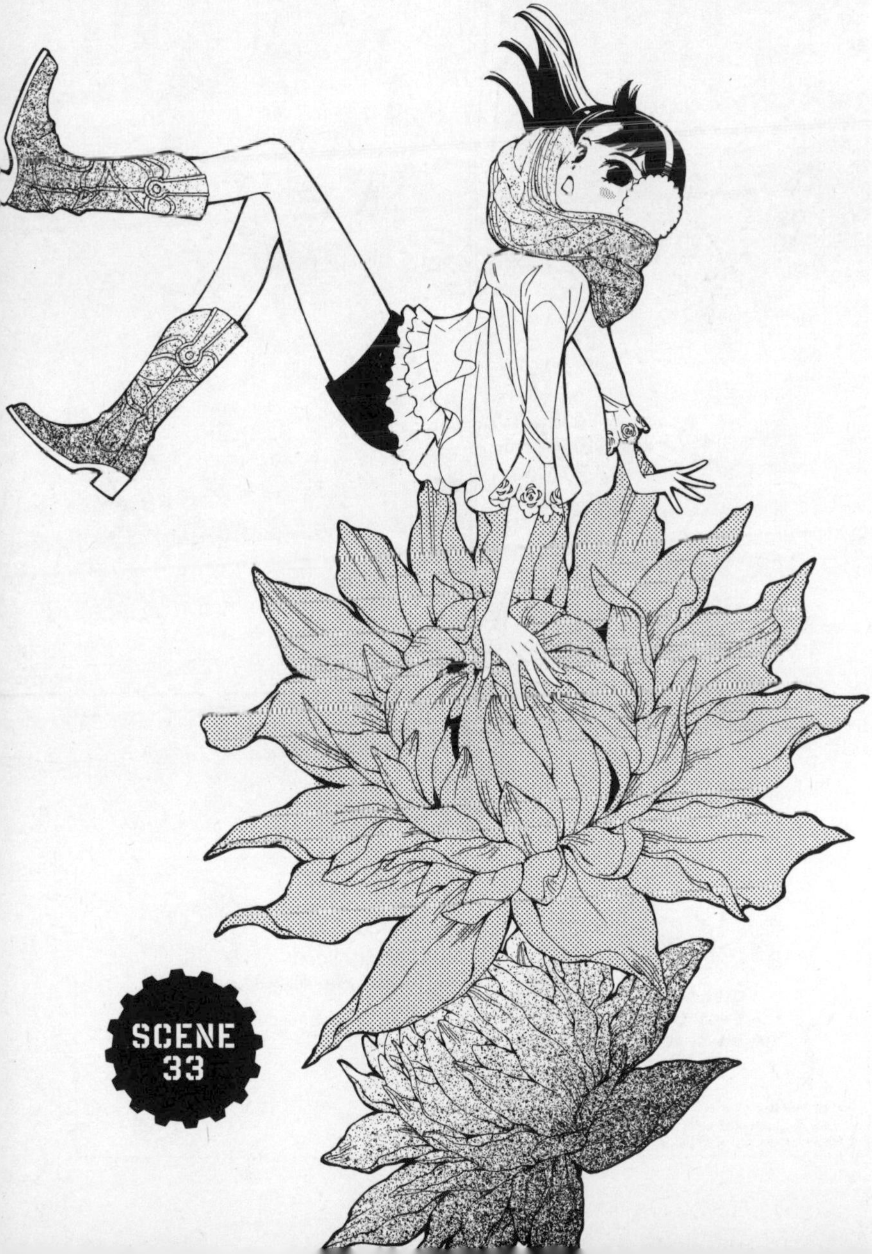
SCENE
33

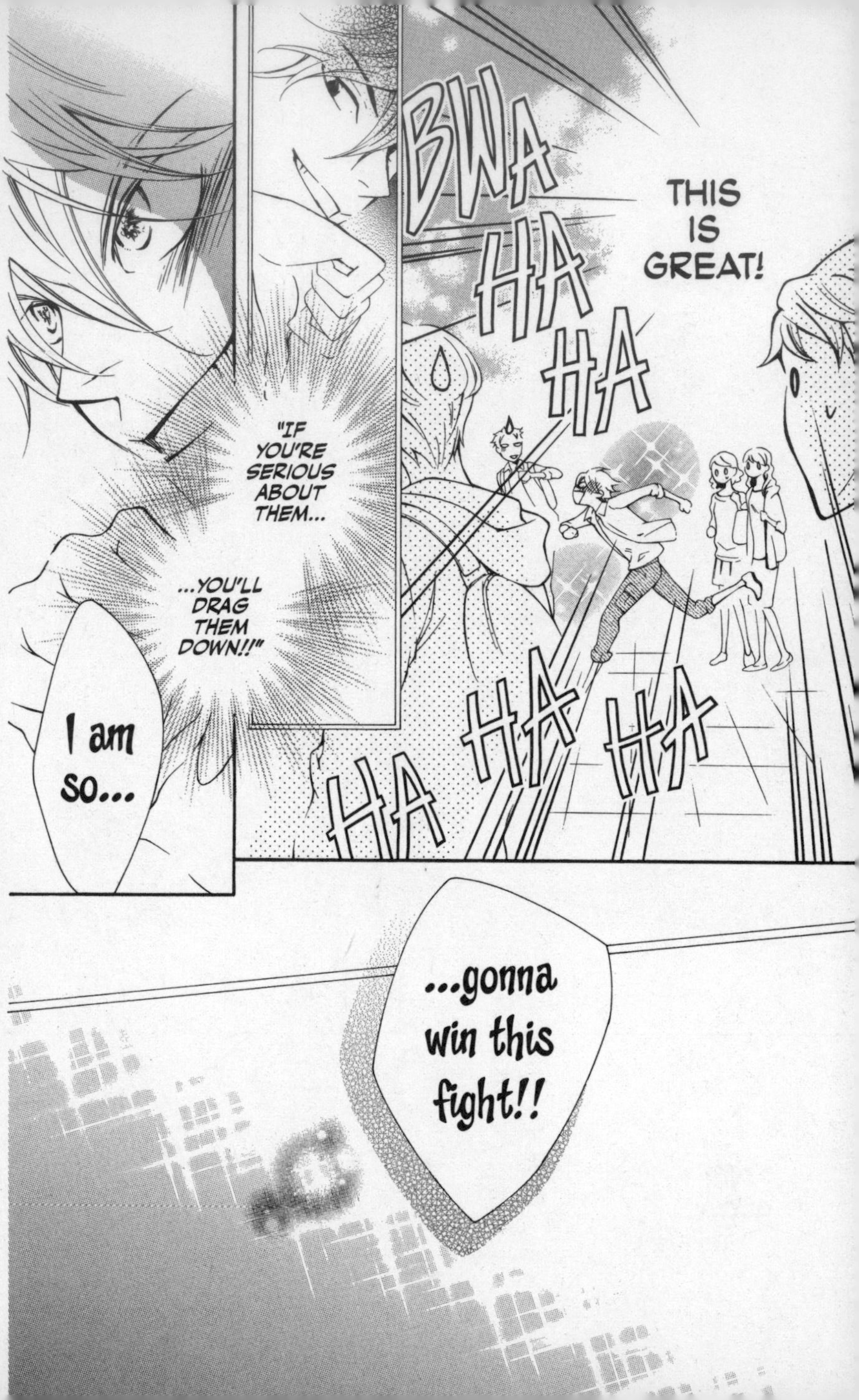
THIS IS GREAT!
BWA HA HA
HA HA HA
"IF YOU'RE SERIOUS ABOUT THEM...
...YOU'LL DRAG THEM DOWN!!"
I am so...
...gonna win this fight!!

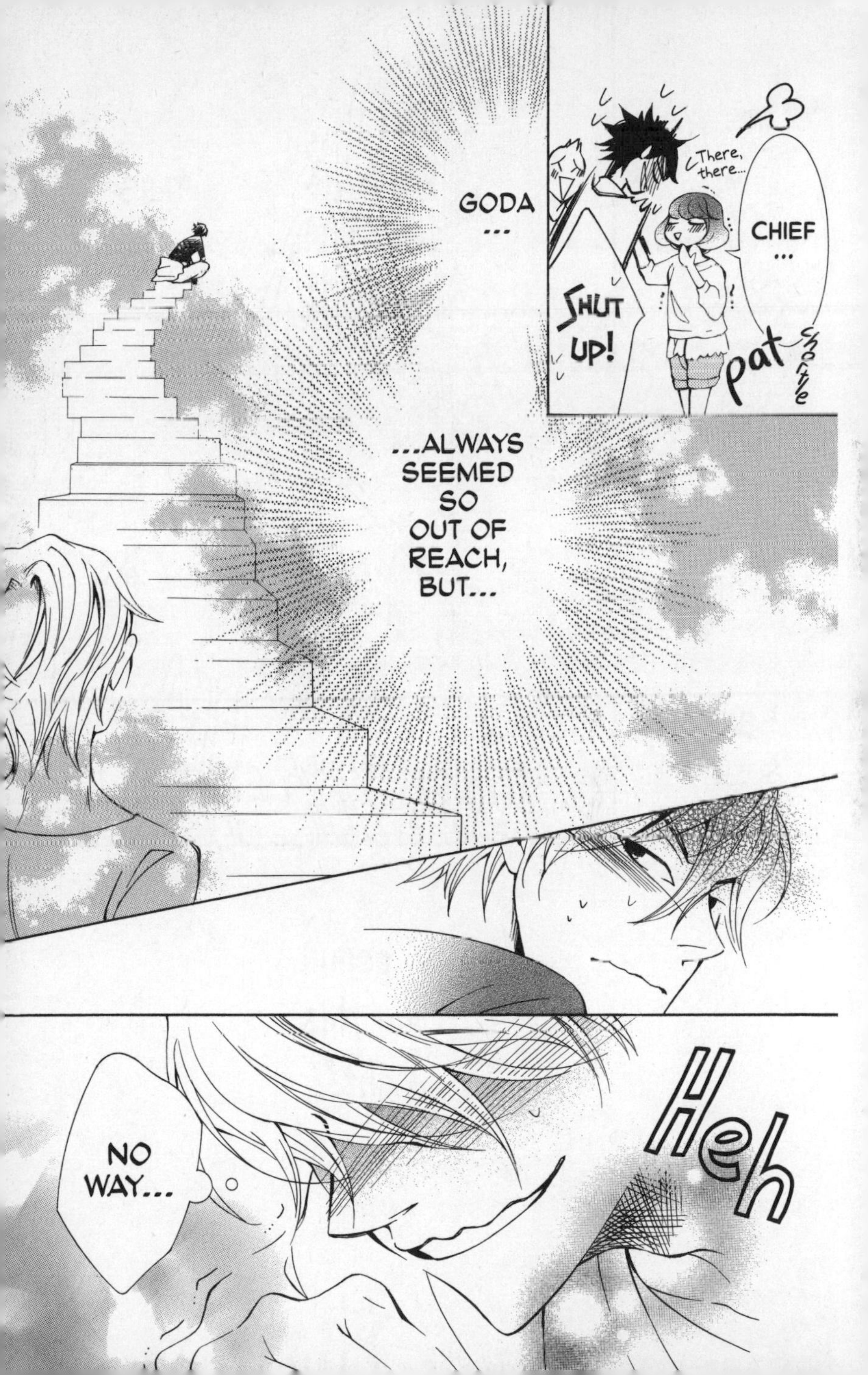
CHIEF ...
There, there...
pat
chortle
SHUT UP!
GODA ...
...ALWAYS SEEMED SO OUT OF REACH, BUT...
Heh
NO WAY...

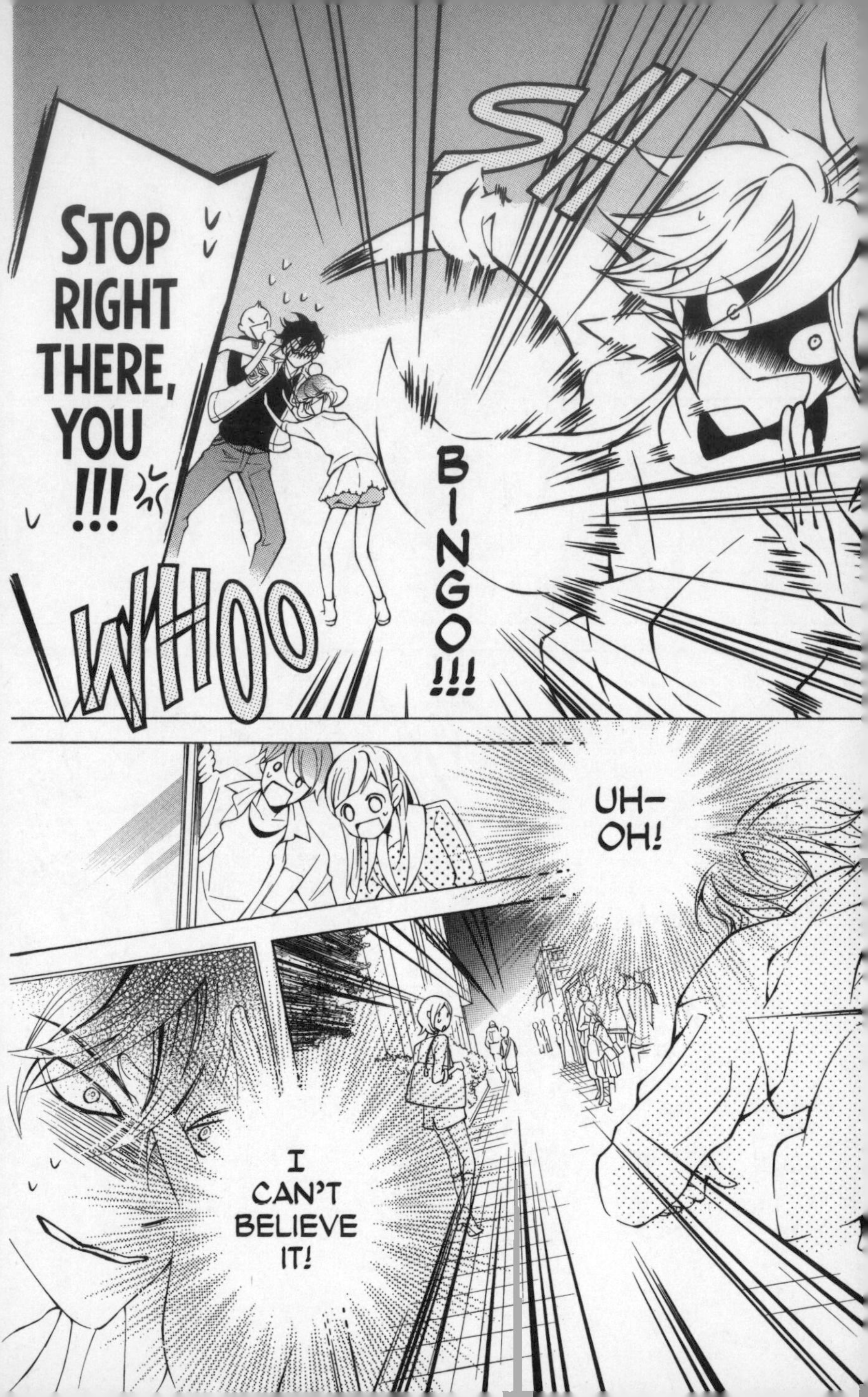
BINGO!!!
STOP RIGHT THERE, YOU!!!
WHOO
UH-OH!
I CAN'T BELIEVE IT!

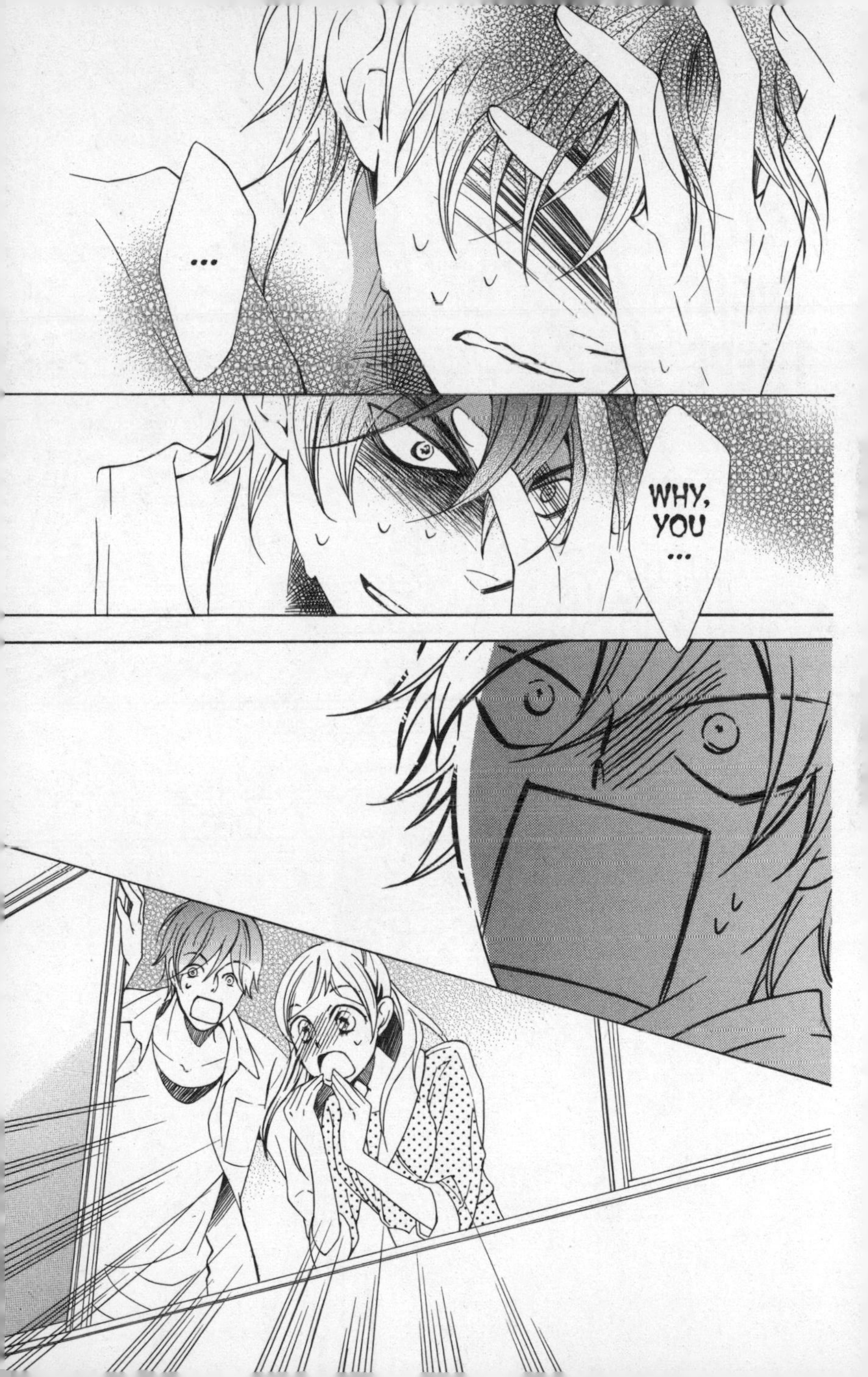
...
WHY, YOU ...

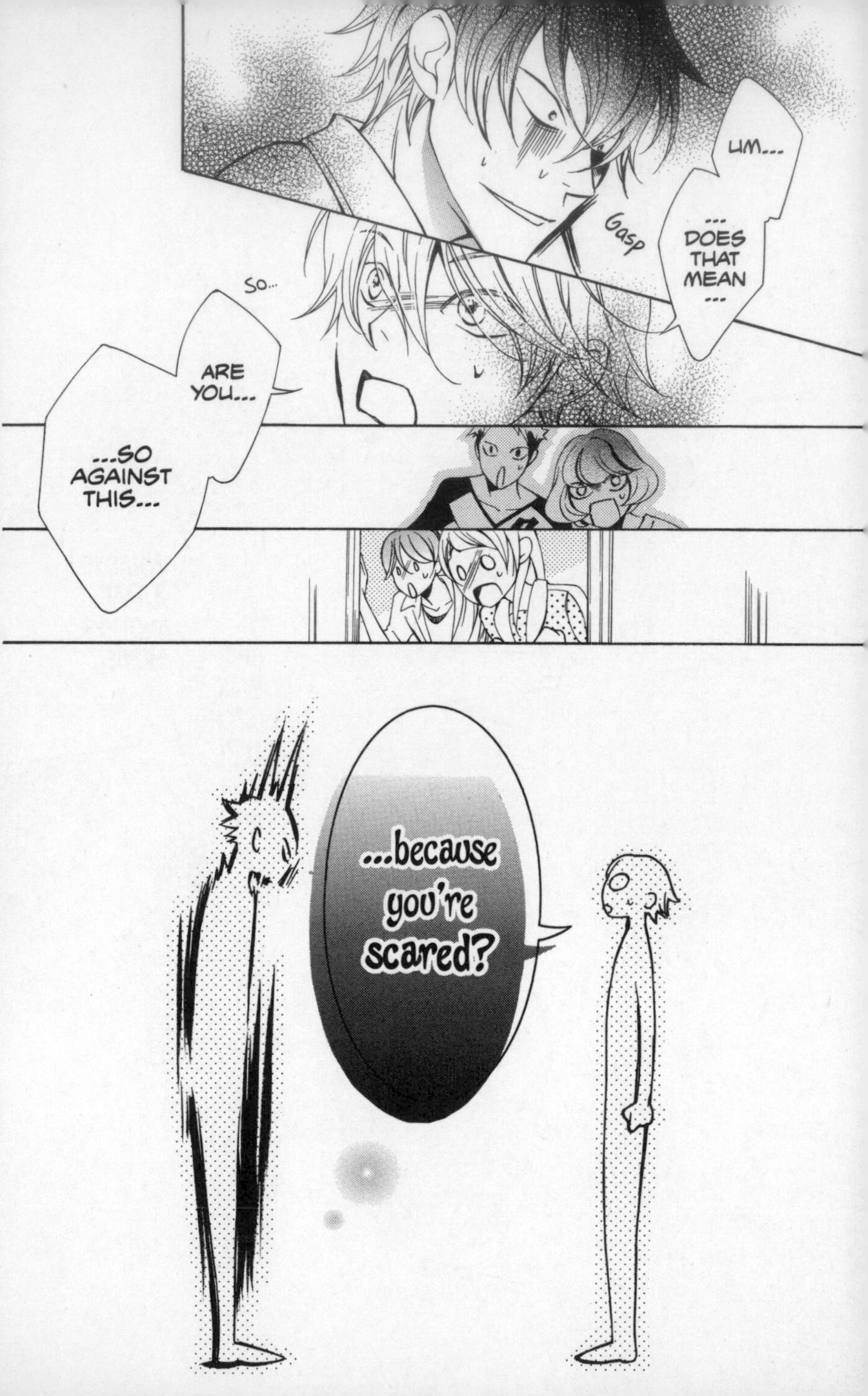
Um...
Gasp
...Does that mean...
So...
Are you...
...so against this...
...because you're scared?

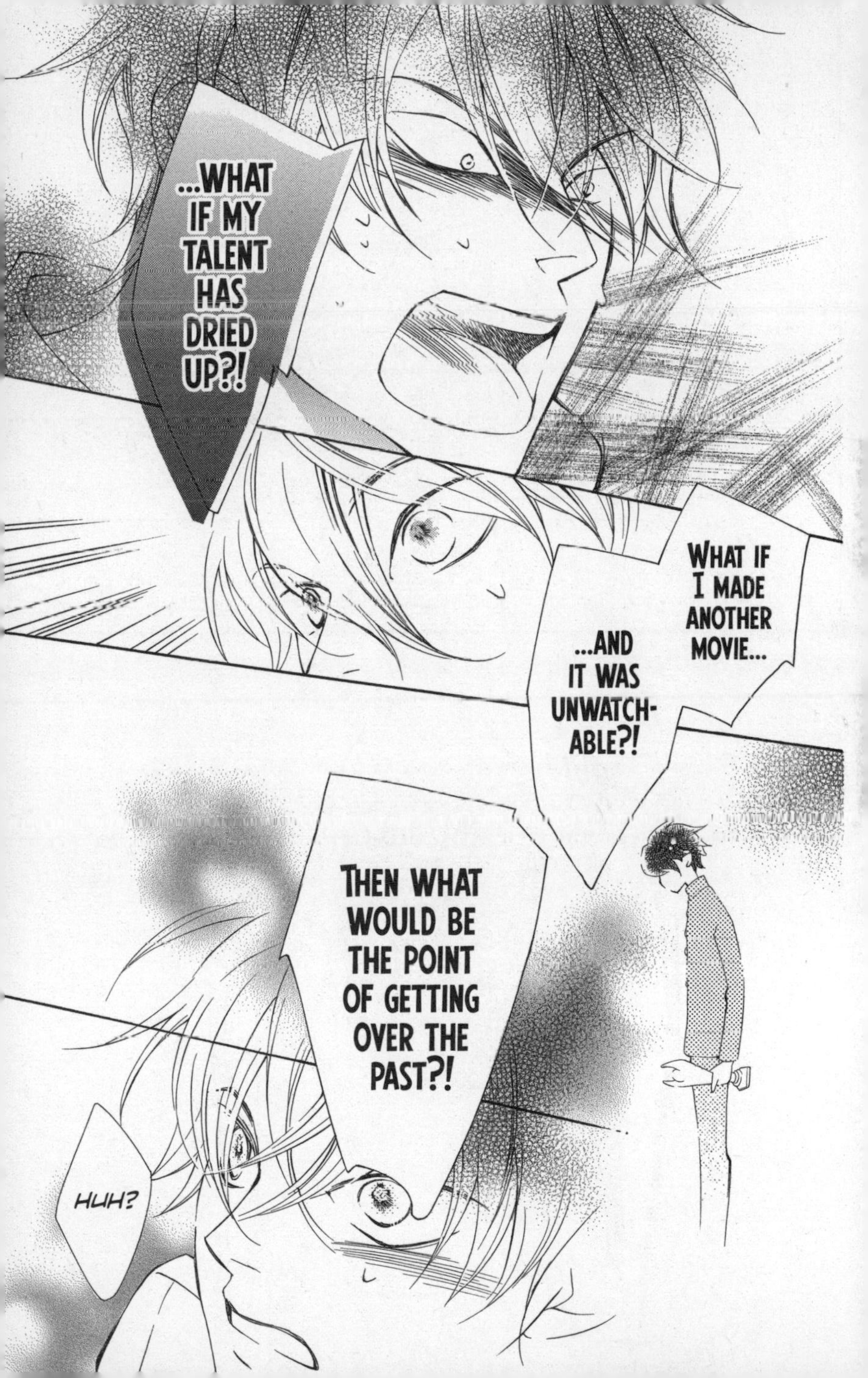
...WHAT IF MY TALENT HAS DRIED UP?!
WHAT IF I MADE ANOTHER MOVIE...
...AND IT WAS UNWATCHABLE?!
THEN WHAT WOULD BE THE POINT OF GETTING OVER THE PAST?!
HUH?

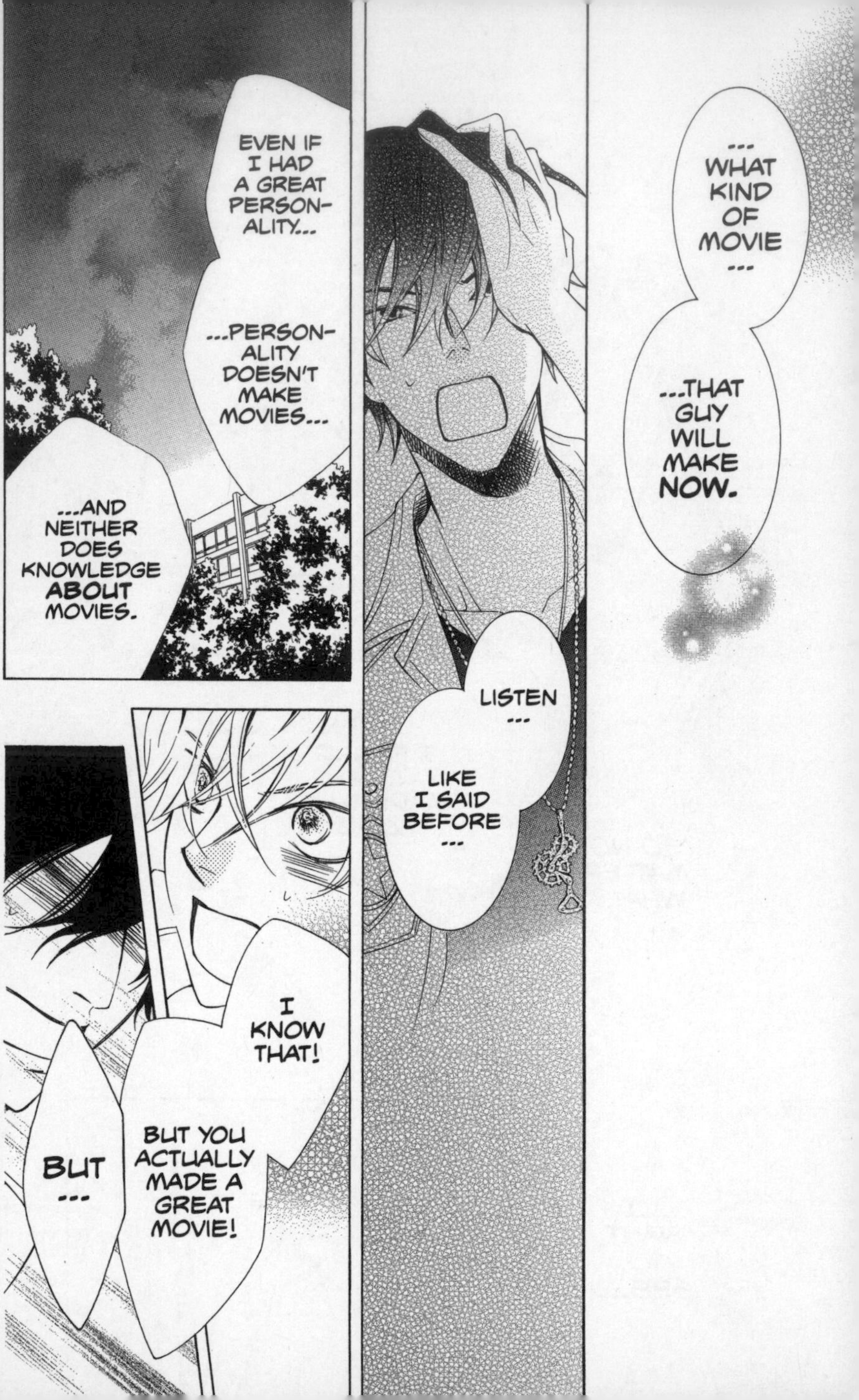
...WHAT KIND OF MOVIE...
...THAT GUY WILL MAKE NOW.
LISTEN...
LIKE I SAID BEFORE...
EVEN IF I HAD A GREAT PERSON-ALITY...
...PERSON-ALITY DOESN'T MAKE MOVIES...
...AND NEITHER DOES KNOWLEDGE ABOUT MOVIES.
I KNOW THAT!
BUT...
BUT YOU ACTUALLY MADE A GREAT MOVIE!

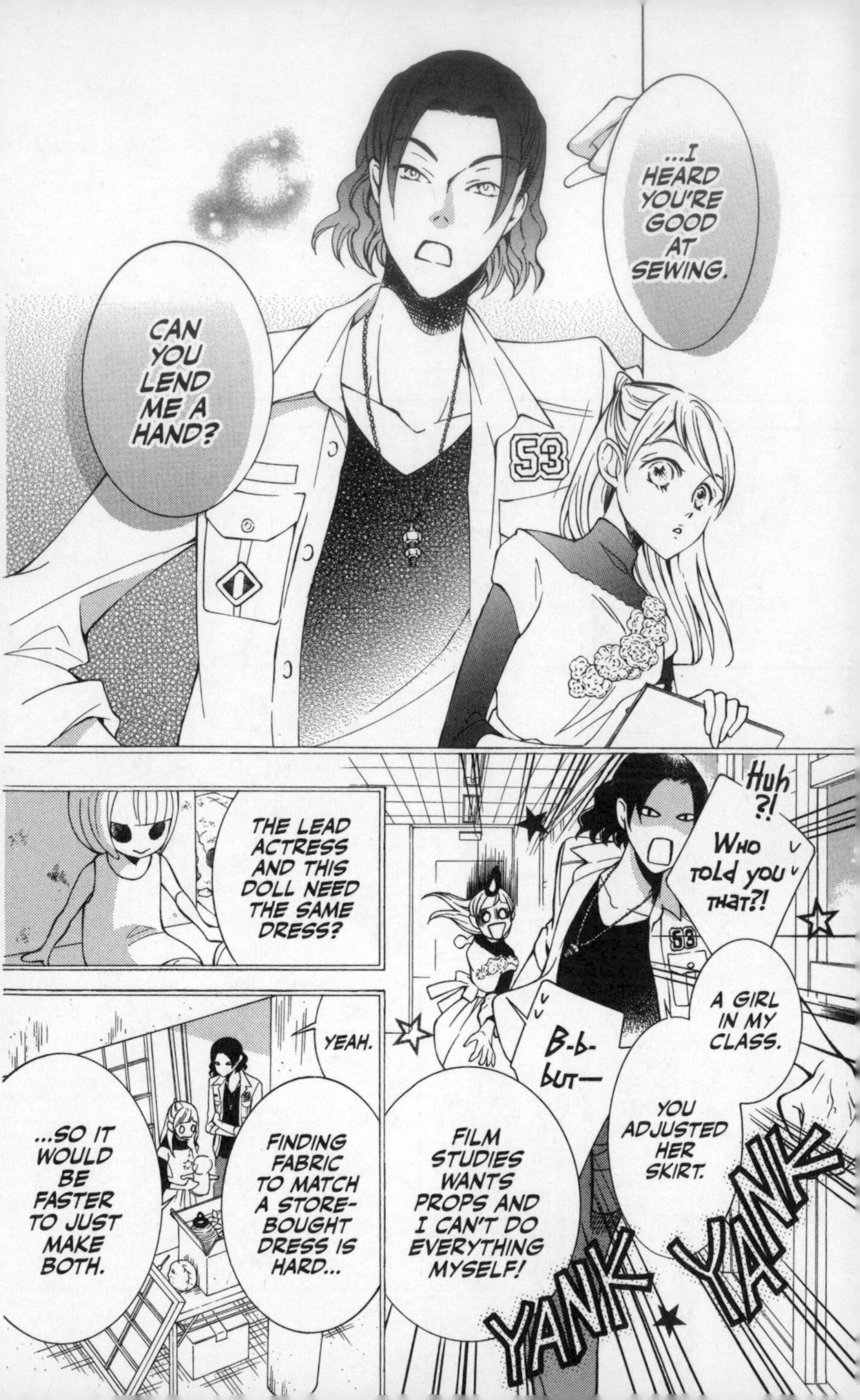
...I HEARD YOU'RE GOOD AT SEWING.
CAN YOU LEND ME A HAND?
Huh?!
Who told you that?!
A GIRL IN MY CLASS.
YOU ADJUSTED HER SKIRT.
B-b-but—
FILM STUDIES WANTS PROPS AND I CAN'T DO EVERYTHING MYSELF!
YANK YANK
THE LEAD ACTRESS AND THIS DOLL NEED THE SAME DRESS?
YEAH.
FINDING FABRIC TO MATCH A STORE-BOUGHT DRESS IS HARD...
...SO IT WOULD BE FASTER TO JUST MAKE BOTH.
53

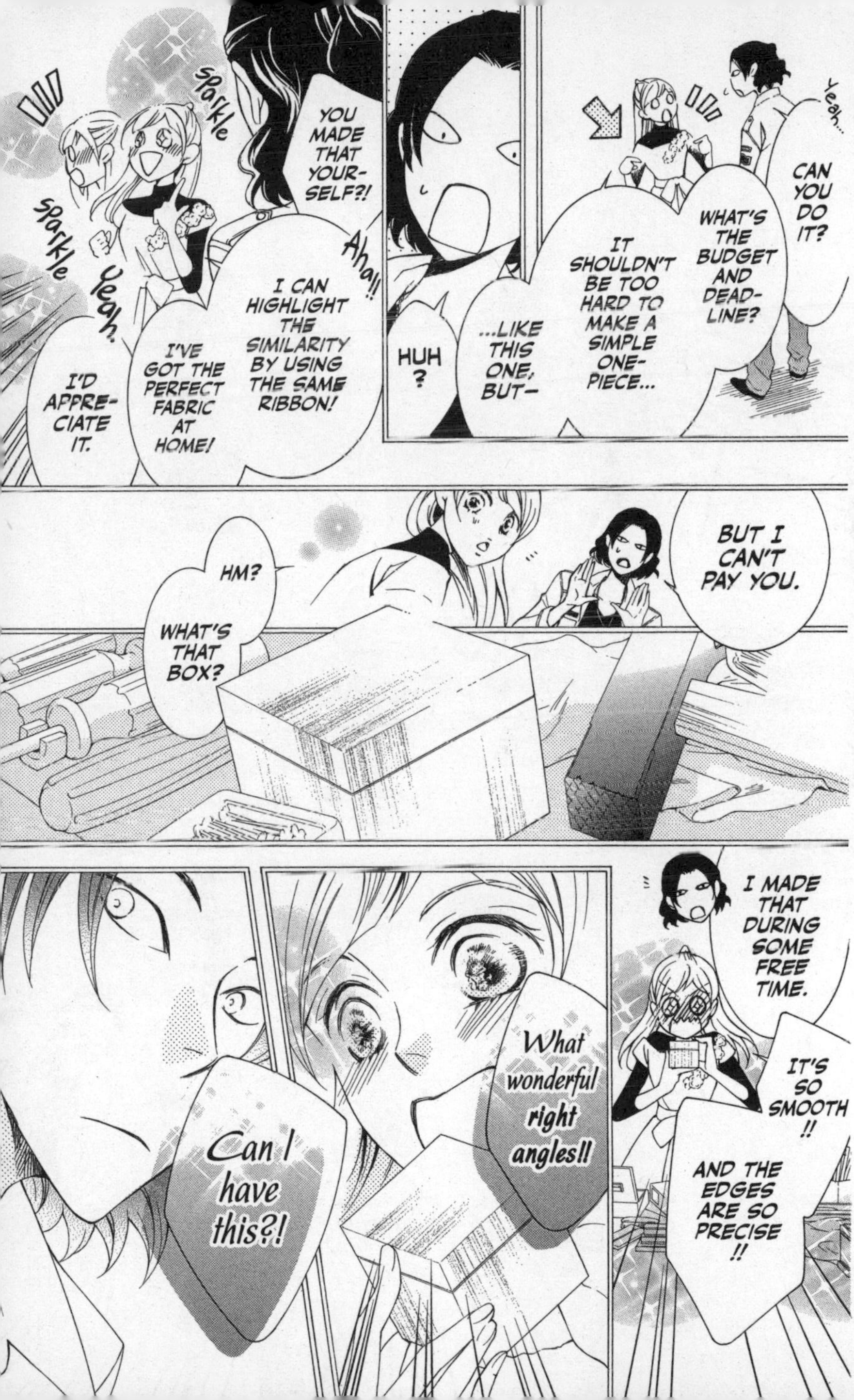
Yeah...
CAN YOU DO IT?
WHAT'S THE BUDGET AND DEADLINE?
IT SHOULDN'T BE TOO HARD TO MAKE A SIMPLE ONE-PIECE...
...LIKE THIS ONE, BUT—
HUH?
YOU MADE THAT YOURSELF?!
Aha!!
Sparkle
I CAN HIGHLIGHT THE SIMILARITY BY USING THE SAME RIBBON!
I'VE GOT THE PERFECT FABRIC AT HOME!
Sparkle
Yeah.
I'D APPRECIATE IT.
BUT I CAN'T PAY YOU.
HM?
WHAT'S THAT BOX?
I MADE THAT DURING SOME FREE TIME.
IT'S SO SMOOTH!!
AND THE EDGES ARE SO PRECISE!!
What wonderful right angles!!
Can I have this?!

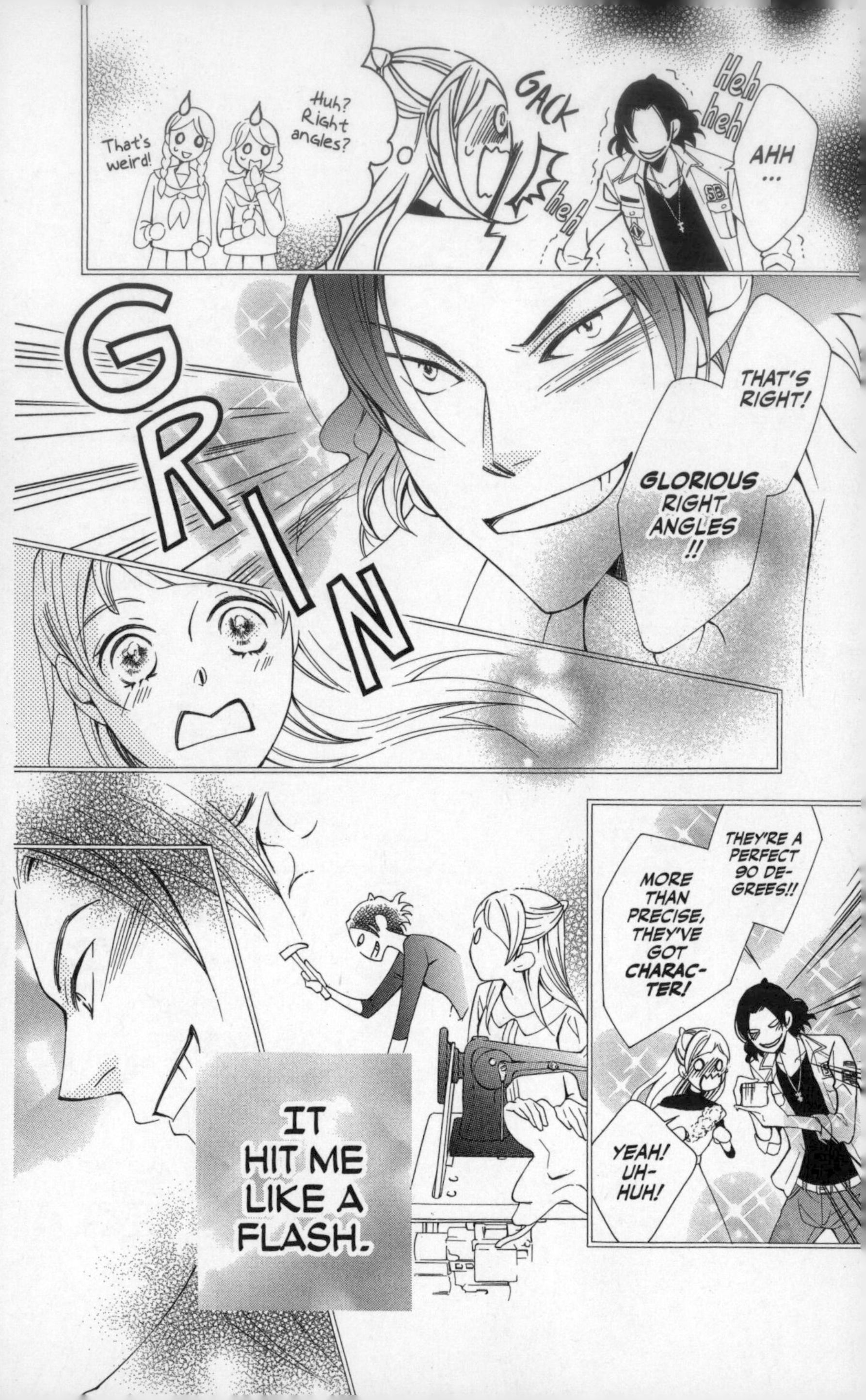
AHH ...
Heh heh heh
GACK
Huh? Right angles?
That's weird!
THAT'S RIGHT!
GLORIOUS RIGHT ANGLES !!
GRIN
THEY'RE A PERFECT 90 DEGREES!!
MORE THAN PRECISE, THEY'VE GOT CHARACTER!
YEAH! UH-HUH!
IT HIT ME LIKE A FLASH.

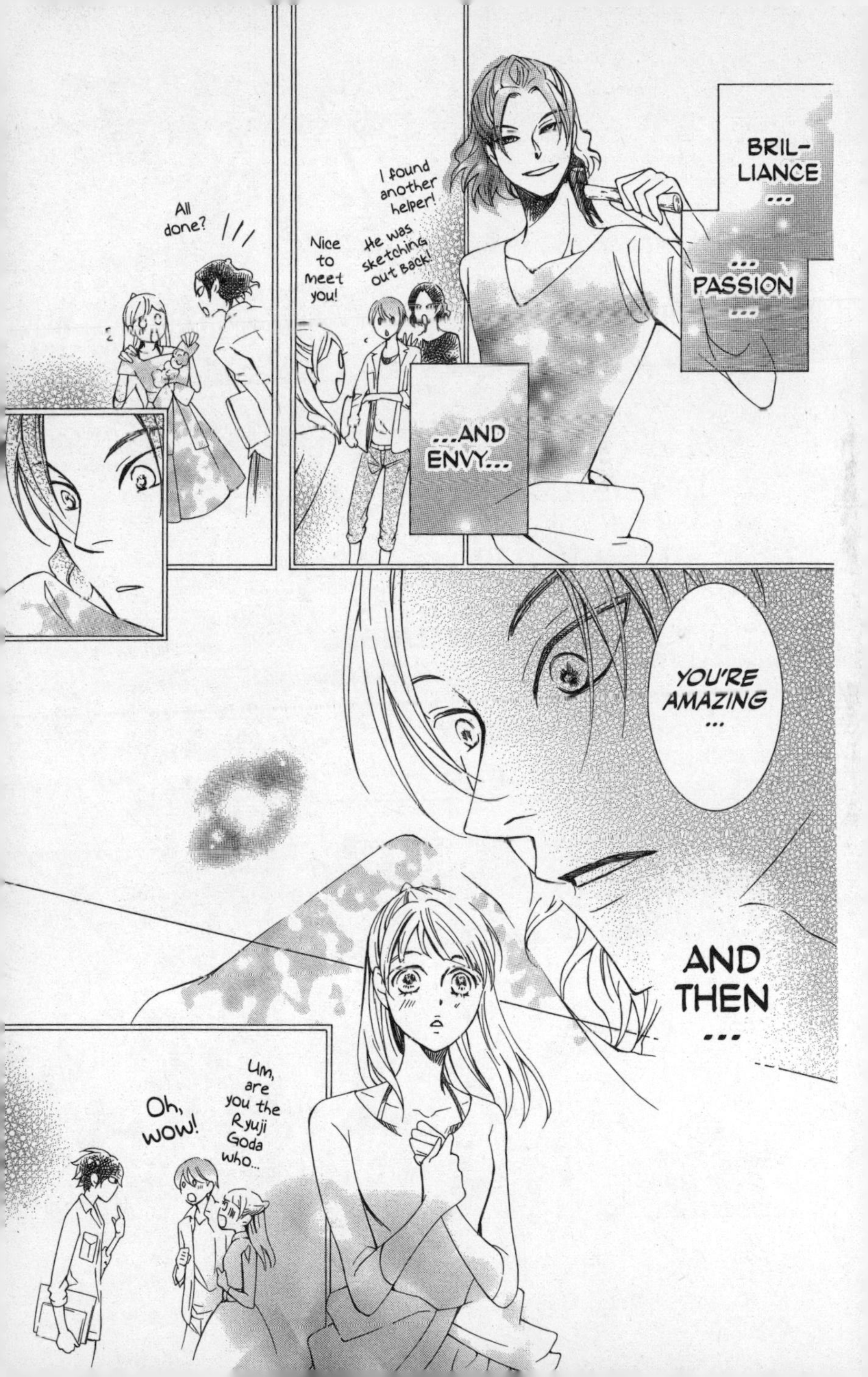
BRIL-LIANCE...
...PASSION...
...AND ENVY...
I found another helper!
He was sketching out back!
Nice to meet you!
All done?
YOU'RE AMAZING...
AND THEN...
Um, are you the Ryuji Goda who...
Oh, wow!

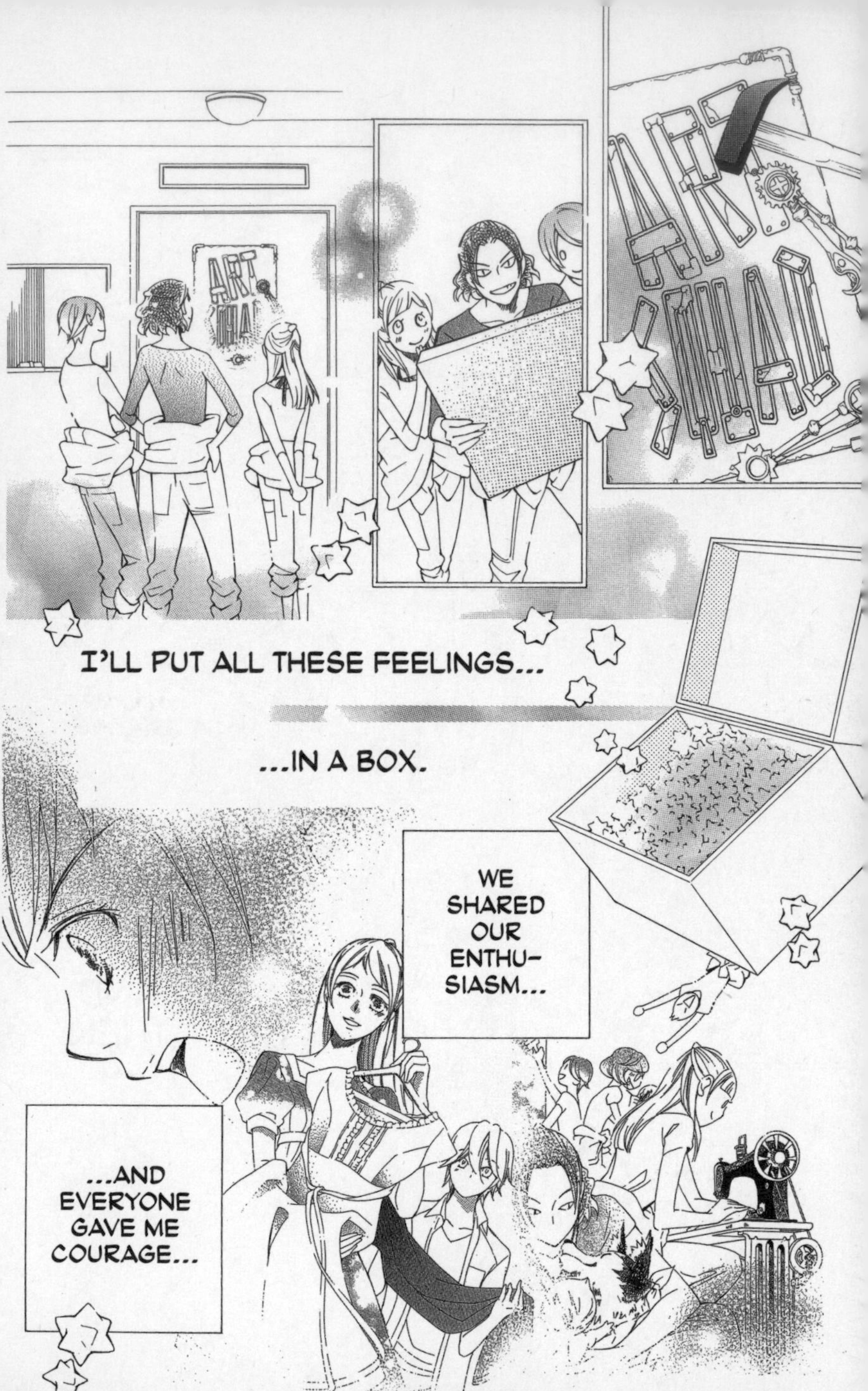
I'LL PUT ALL THESE FEELINGS...
...IN A BOX.
WE SHARED OUR ENTHUSIASM...
...AND EVERYONE GAVE ME COURAGE...

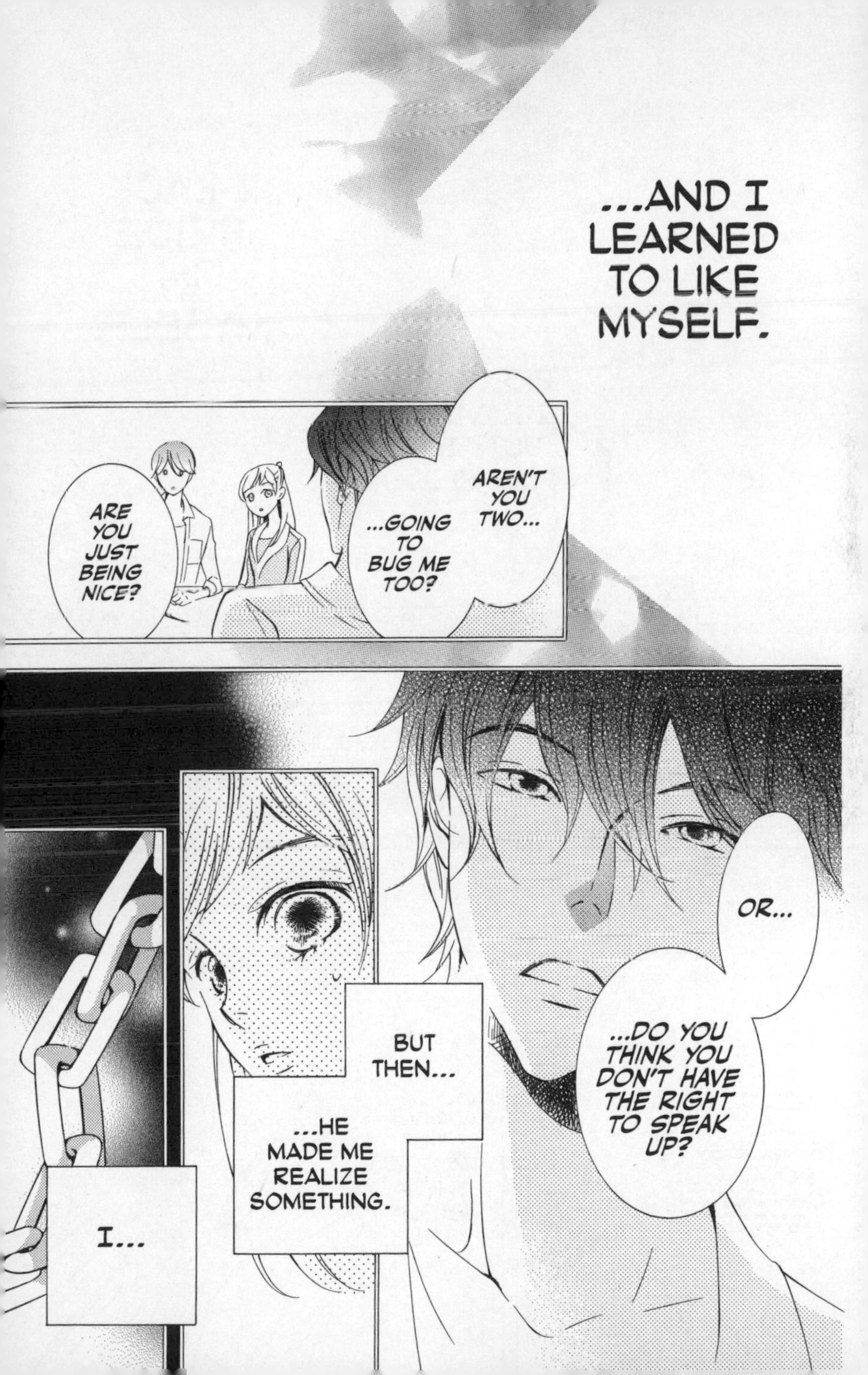
...AND I LEARNED TO LIKE MYSELF.
AREN'T YOU TWO...
...GOING TO BUG ME TOO?
ARE YOU JUST BEING NICE?
OR...
...DO YOU THINK YOU DON'T HAVE THE RIGHT TO SPEAK UP?
BUT THEN...
...HE MADE ME REALIZE SOMETHING.
I...

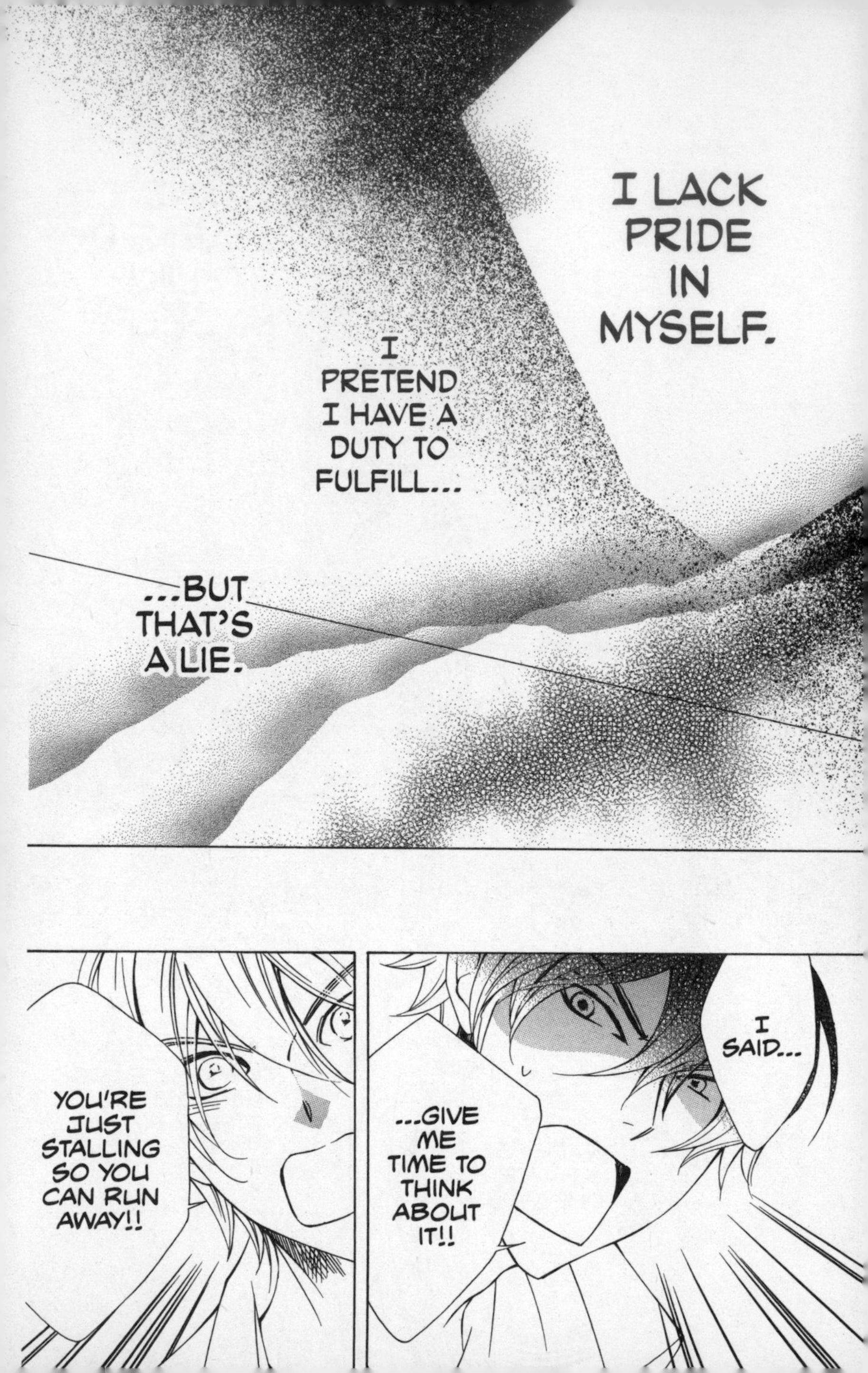
I LACK PRIDE IN MYSELF.
I PRETEND I HAVE A DUTY TO FULFILL...
...BUT THAT'S A LIE.
I SAID...
...GIVE ME TIME TO THINK ABOUT IT!!
YOU'RE JUST STALLING SO YOU CAN RUN AWAY!!

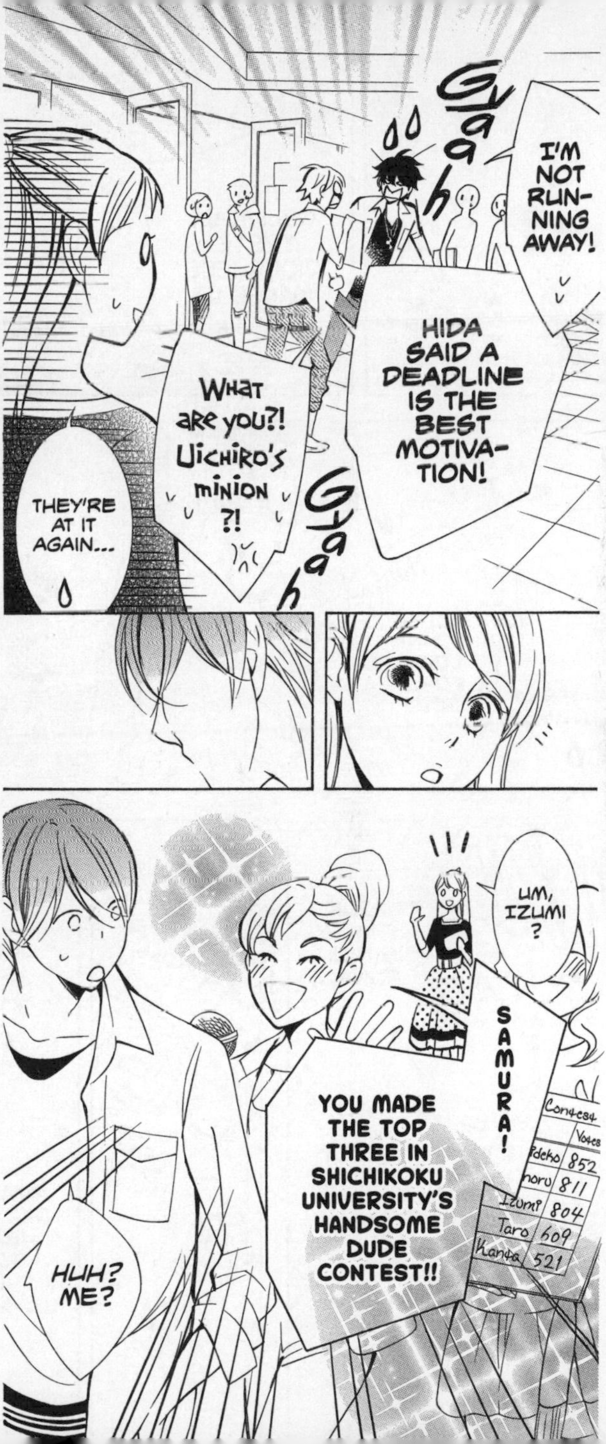
I'M NOT RUNNING AWAY!
Gyaah
HIDA SAID A DEADLINE IS THE BEST MOTIVATION!
Gyaah
WHAT are you?! Uichiro's minion?!
THEY'RE AT IT AGAIN...
UM, IZUMI?
SAMURA!
YOU MADE THE TOP THREE IN SHICHIKOKU UNIVERSITY'S HANDSOME DUDE CONTEST!!
Votes
852
811
Izumi 804
Taro 609
Kanta 521
HUH? ME?

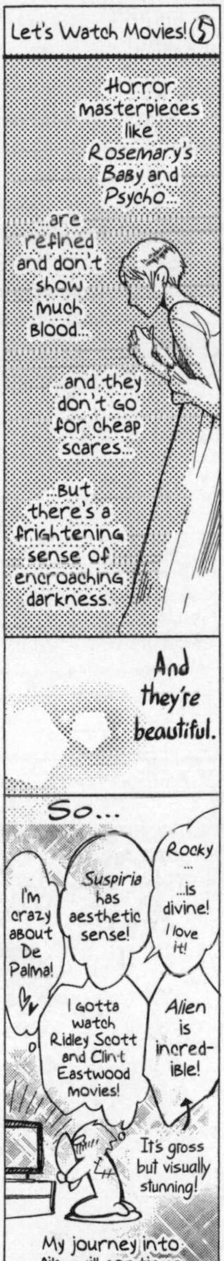
Let's Watch Movies! 5
Horror masterpieces like Rosemary's Baby and Psycho...
...are refined and don't show much blood...
...and they don't go for cheap scares...
...but there's a frightening sense of encroaching darkness.
And they're beautiful.
So...
I'm crazy about De Palma!
Suspiria has aesthetic sense!
Rocky... ...is divine! I love it!
I gotta watch Ridley Scott and Clint Eastwood movies!
Alien is incredible!
It's gross but visually stunning!
My journey into film will continue for some time.

I also wanted to talk about Japanese films, but...

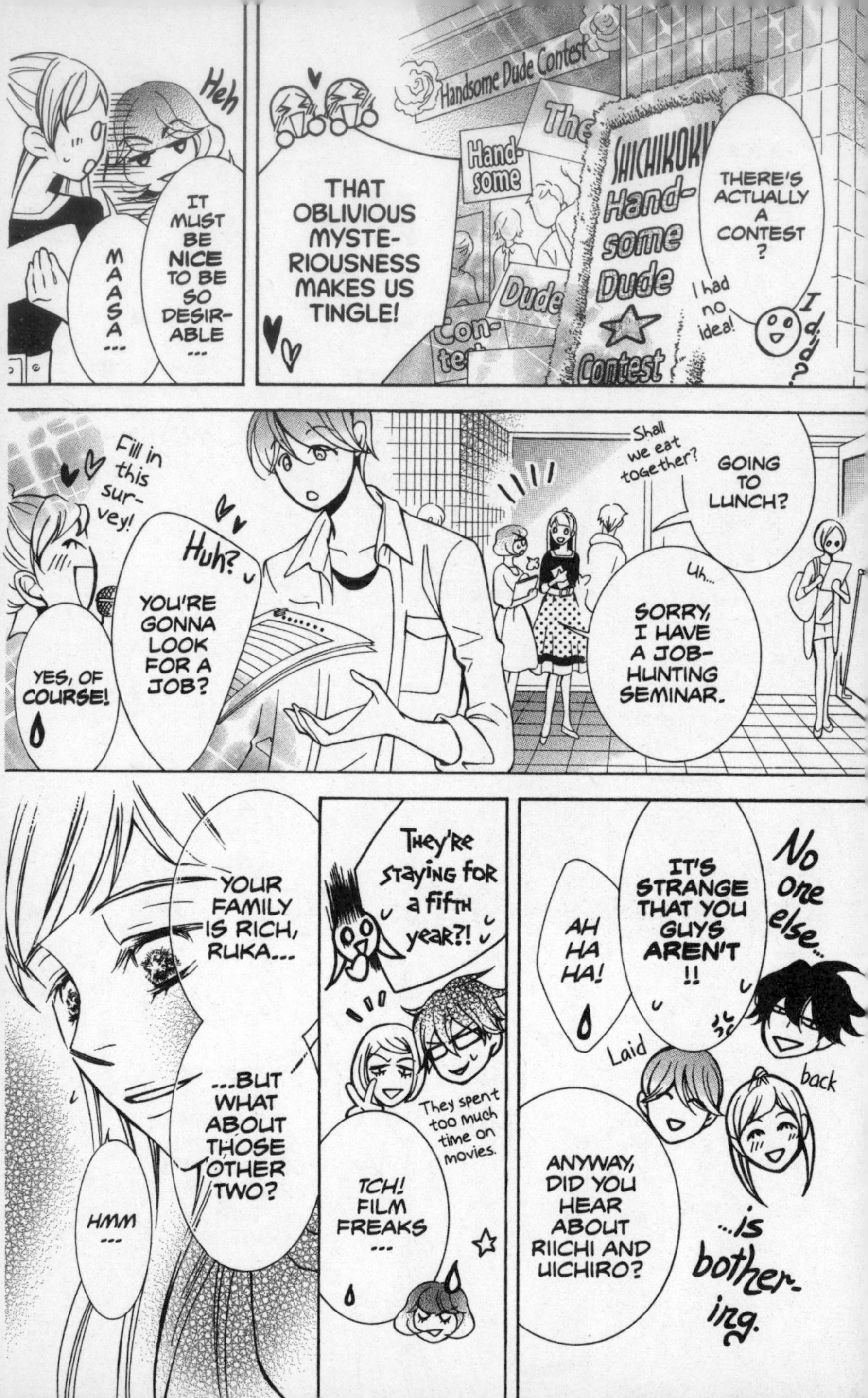
Handsome Dude Contest
SHICHIKOKU Handsome Dude ☆ Contest
The Handsome Dude Contest
THERE'S ACTUALLY A CONTEST?
I had no idea!
I did?
THAT OBLIVIOUS MYSTERIOUSNESS MAKES US TINGLE!
Heh
IT MUST BE NICE TO BE SO DESIRABLE...
MAASA...
GOING TO LUNCH?
Shall we eat together?
Uh...
SORRY, I HAVE A JOB-HUNTING SEMINAR.
Fill in this survey!
Huh?
YOU'RE GONNA LOOK FOR A JOB?
YES, OF COURSE!
No one else...
IT'S STRANGE THAT YOU GUYS AREN'T!!
AH HA HA!
Laid back
ANYWAY, DID YOU HEAR ABOUT RIICHI AND UICHIRO?
...is bothering.
They're staying for a fifth year?!
They spent too much time on movies.
TCH! FILM FREAKS...
YOUR FAMILY IS RICH, RUKA...
...BUT WHAT ABOUT THOSE OTHER TWO?
HMM...

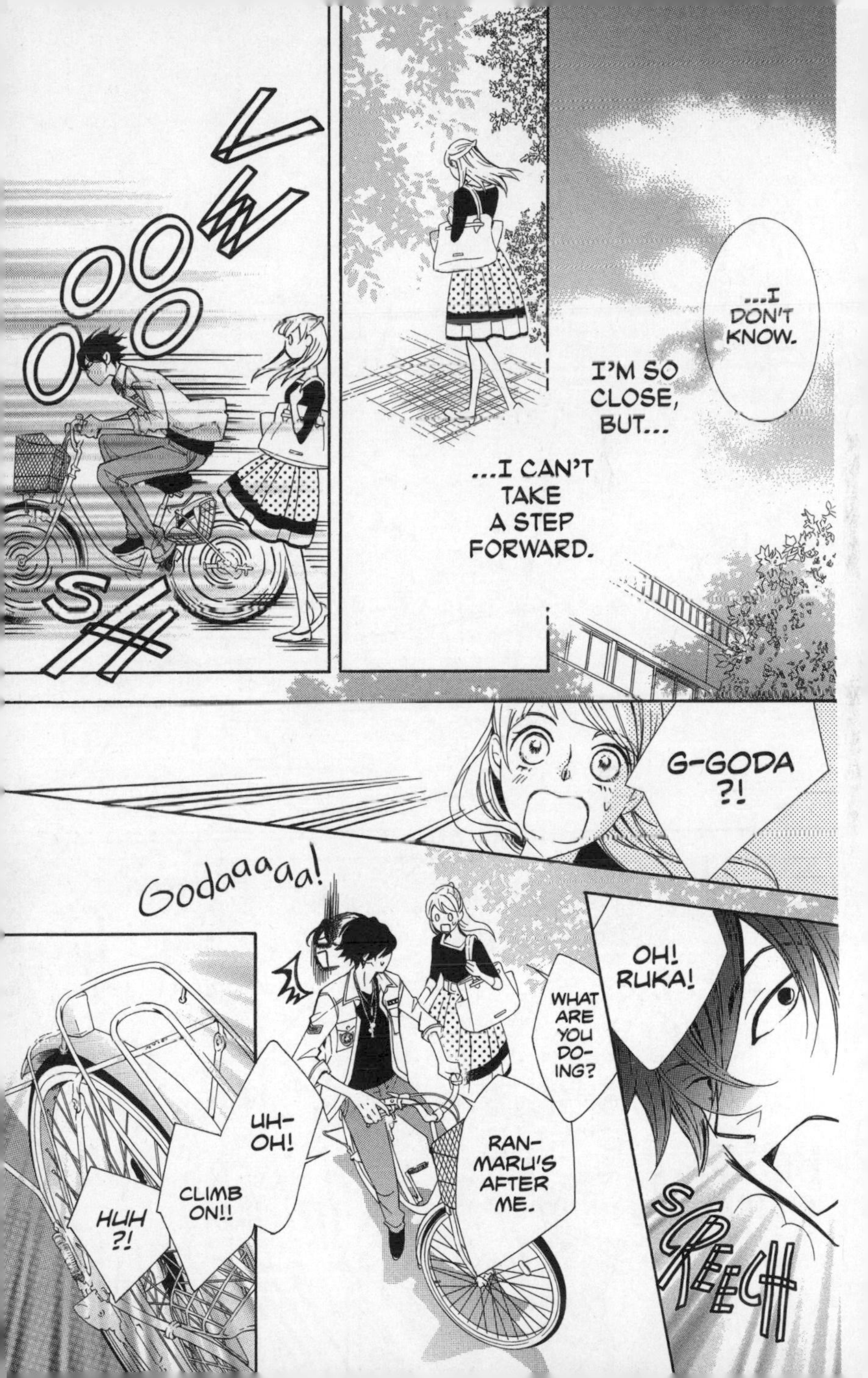
...I DON'T KNOW.
I'M SO CLOSE, BUT...
...I CAN'T TAKE A STEP FORWARD.
VWOOOOO
SH
G-GODA ?!
OH! RUKA!
SCREECH
Godaaaaaa!
WHAT ARE YOU DO-ING?
RAN-MARU'S AFTER ME.
UH-OH!
CLIMB ON!!
HUH ?!

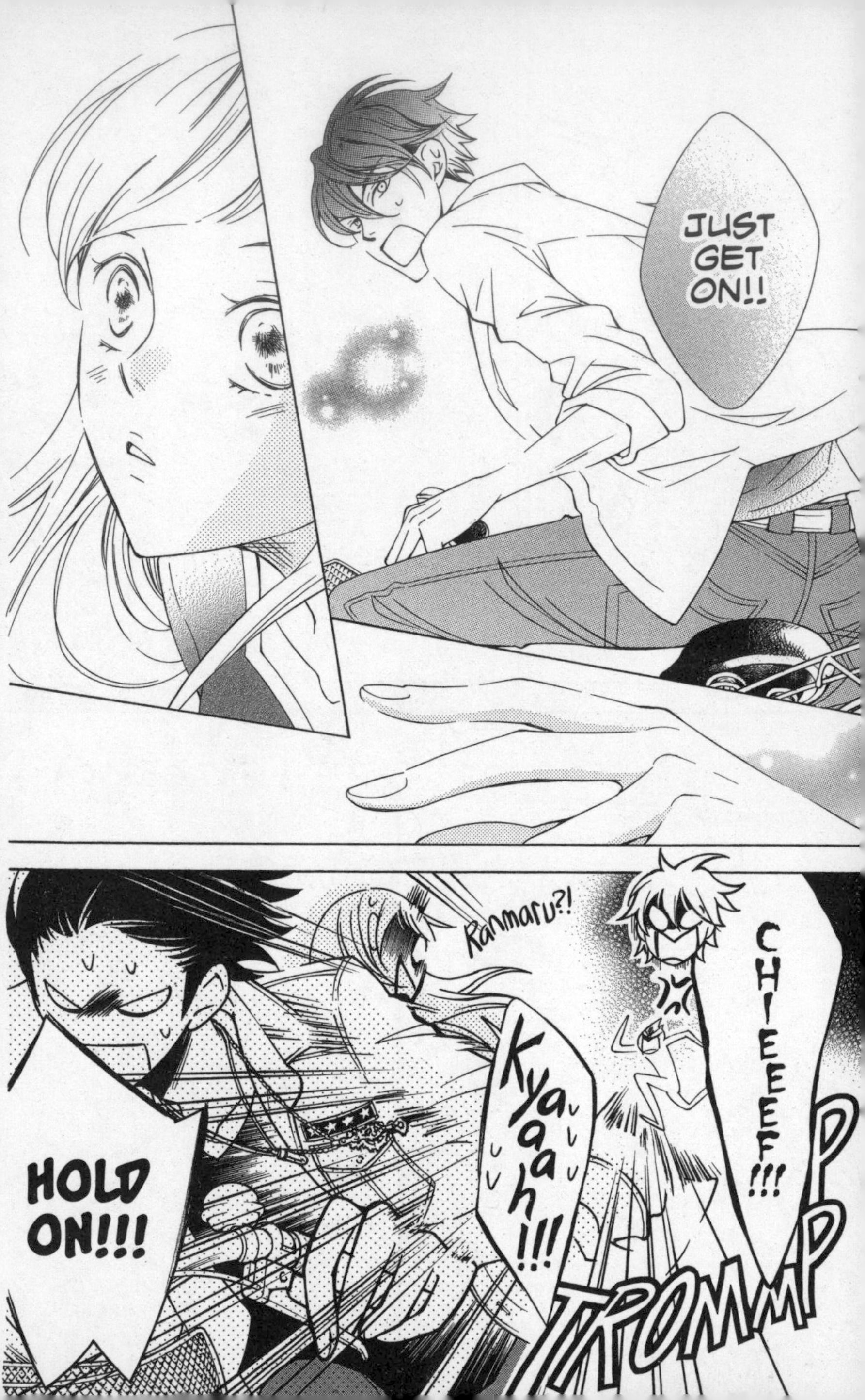
JUST GET ON!!
CHIEEEF!!!
Ranmaru?!
Kyaaaah!!!
HOLD ON!!!
TROMMP

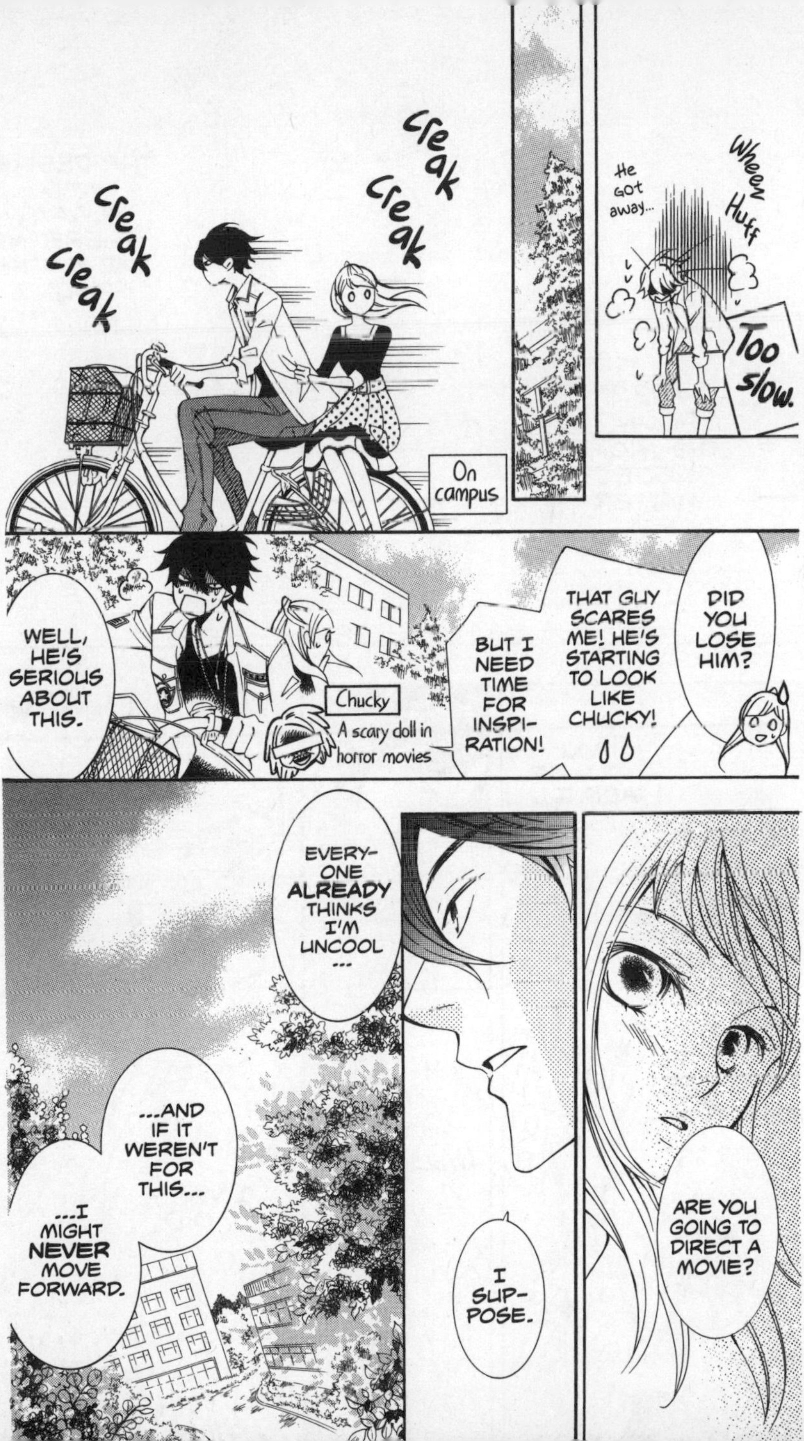
Wheeen Huff
He got away...
Too slow.
creak creak
creak creak
On campus
DID YOU LOSE HIM?
THAT GUY SCARES ME! HE'S STARTING TO LOOK LIKE CHUCKY!
BUT I NEED TIME FOR INSPIRATION!
Chucky
A scary doll in horror movies
WELL, HE'S SERIOUS ABOUT THIS.
ARE YOU GOING TO DIRECT A MOVIE?
I SUPPOSE.
EVERYONE ALREADY THINKS I'M UNCOOL...
...AND IF IT WEREN'T FOR THIS...
...I MIGHT NEVER MOVE FORWARD.

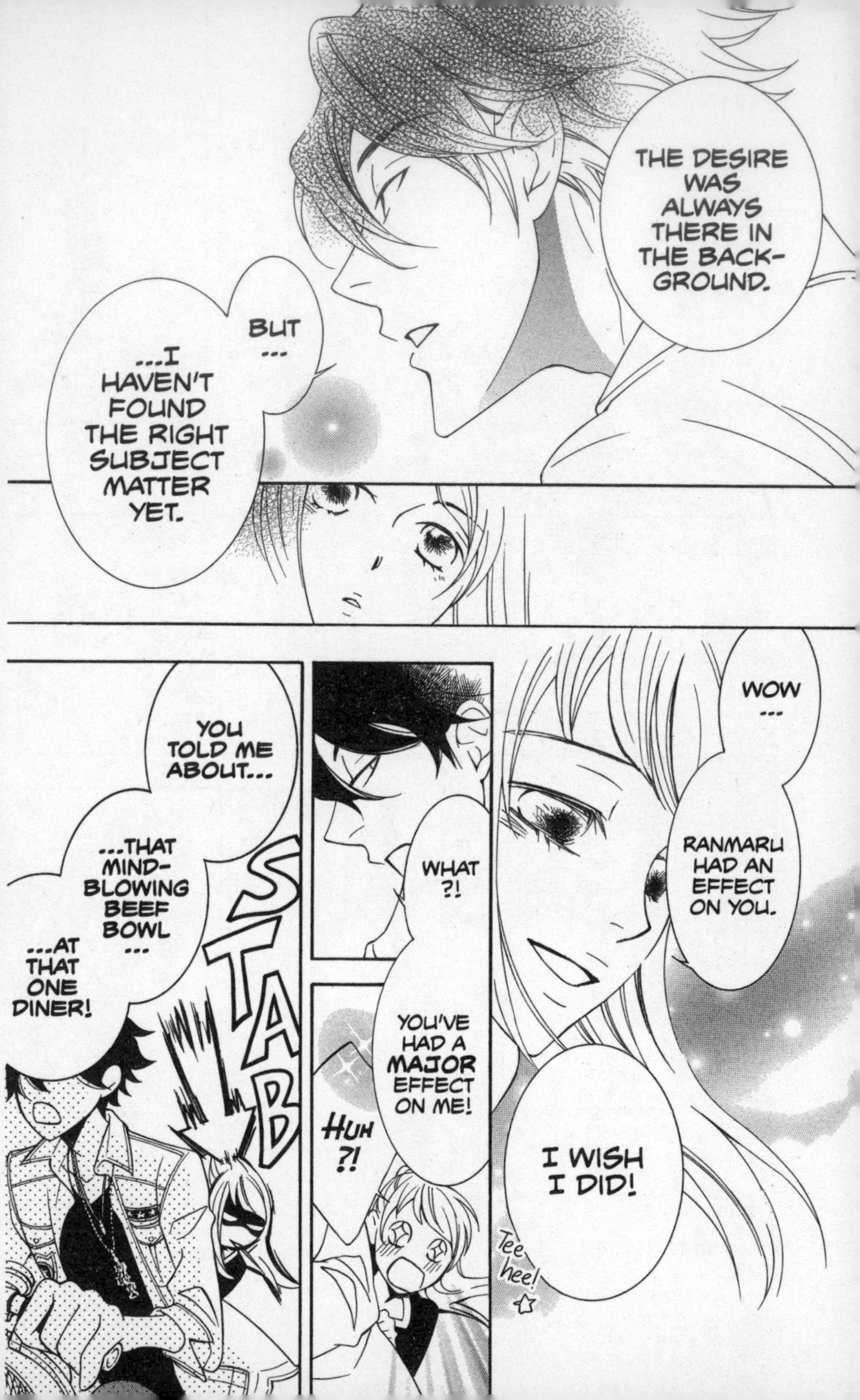
THE DESIRE WAS ALWAYS THERE IN THE BACK-GROUND.
BUT ...
...I HAVEN'T FOUND THE RIGHT SUBJECT MATTER YET.
WOW ...
RANMARU HAD AN EFFECT ON YOU.
I WISH I DID!
Tee hee!
WHAT ?!
YOU'VE HAD A MAJOR EFFECT ON ME!
HUH ?!
YOU TOLD ME ABOUT...
...THAT MIND-BLOWING BEEF BOWL ...
...AT THAT ONE DINER!
STAB

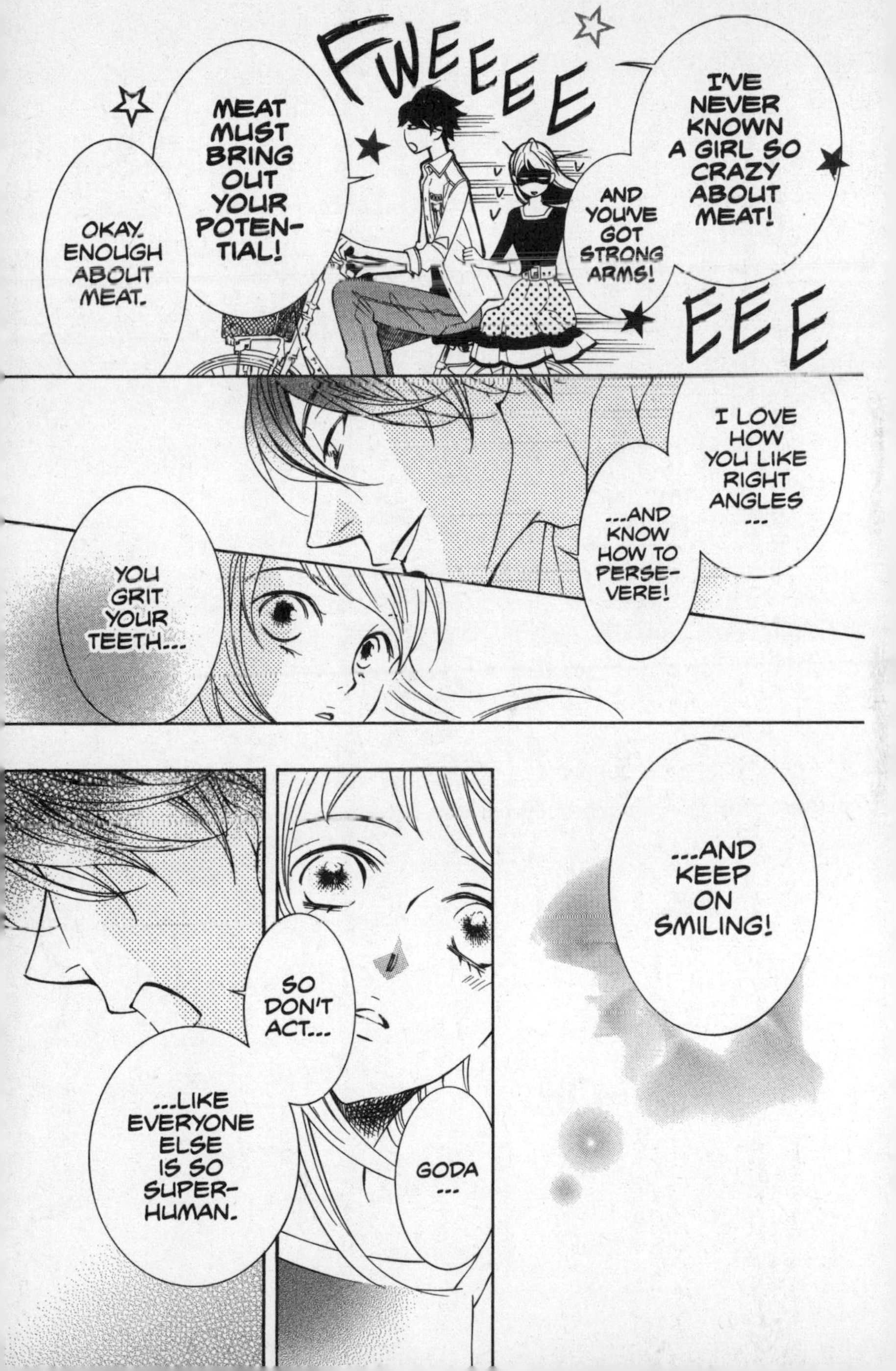
FWEEEEE
I'VE NEVER KNOWN A GIRL SO CRAZY ABOUT MEAT!
AND YOU'VE GOT STRONG ARMS!
EEE
MEAT MUST BRING OUT YOUR POTEN-TIAL!
OKAY. ENOUGH ABOUT MEAT.
I LOVE HOW YOU LIKE RIGHT ANGLES...
...AND KNOW HOW TO PERSE-VERE!
YOU GRIT YOUR TEETH...
...AND KEEP ON SMILING!
SO DON'T ACT...
...LIKE EVERYONE ELSE IS SO SUPER-HUMAN.
GODA...

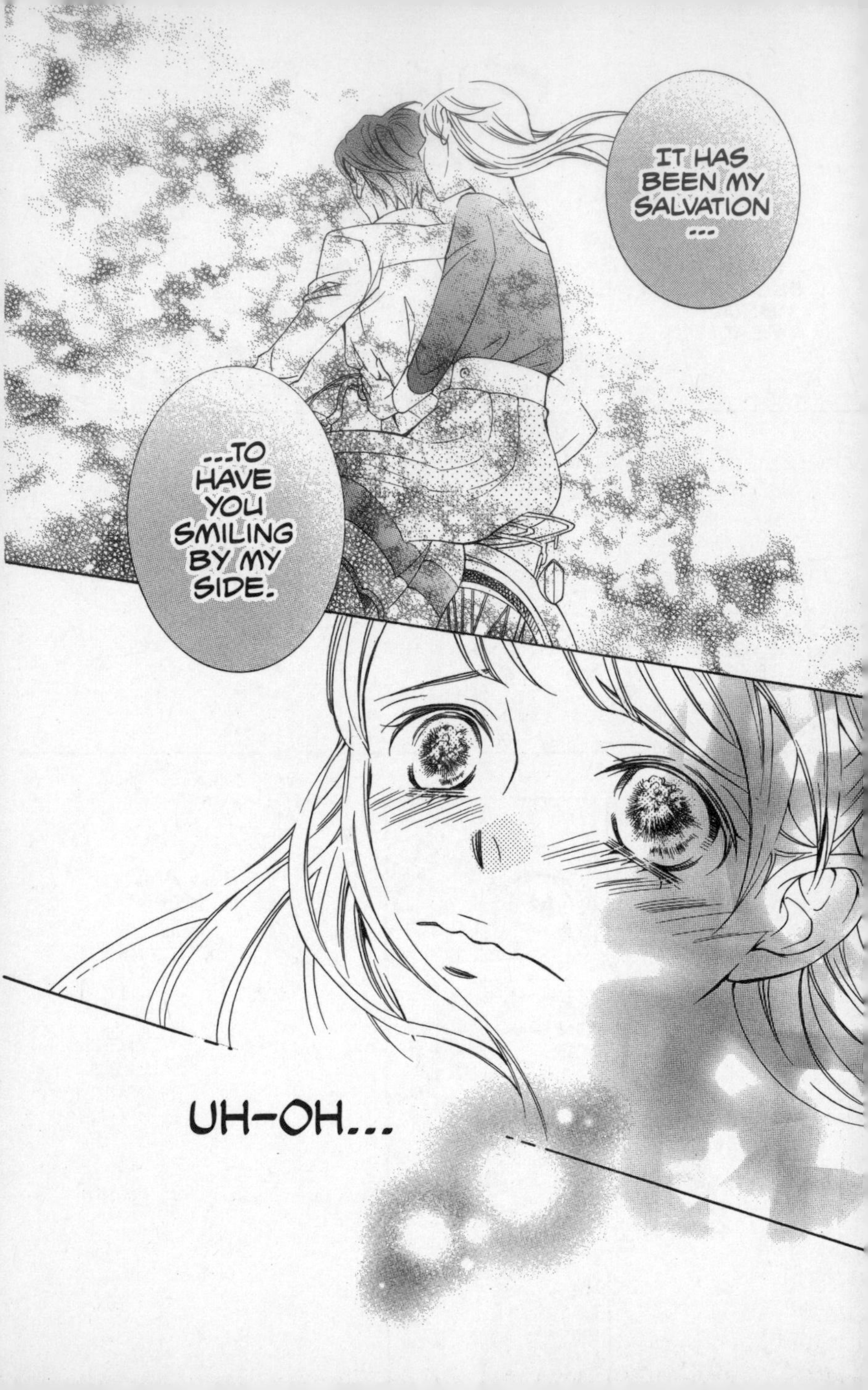
IT HAS BEEN MY SALVATION ...
...TO HAVE YOU SMILING BY MY SIDE.
UH-OH...

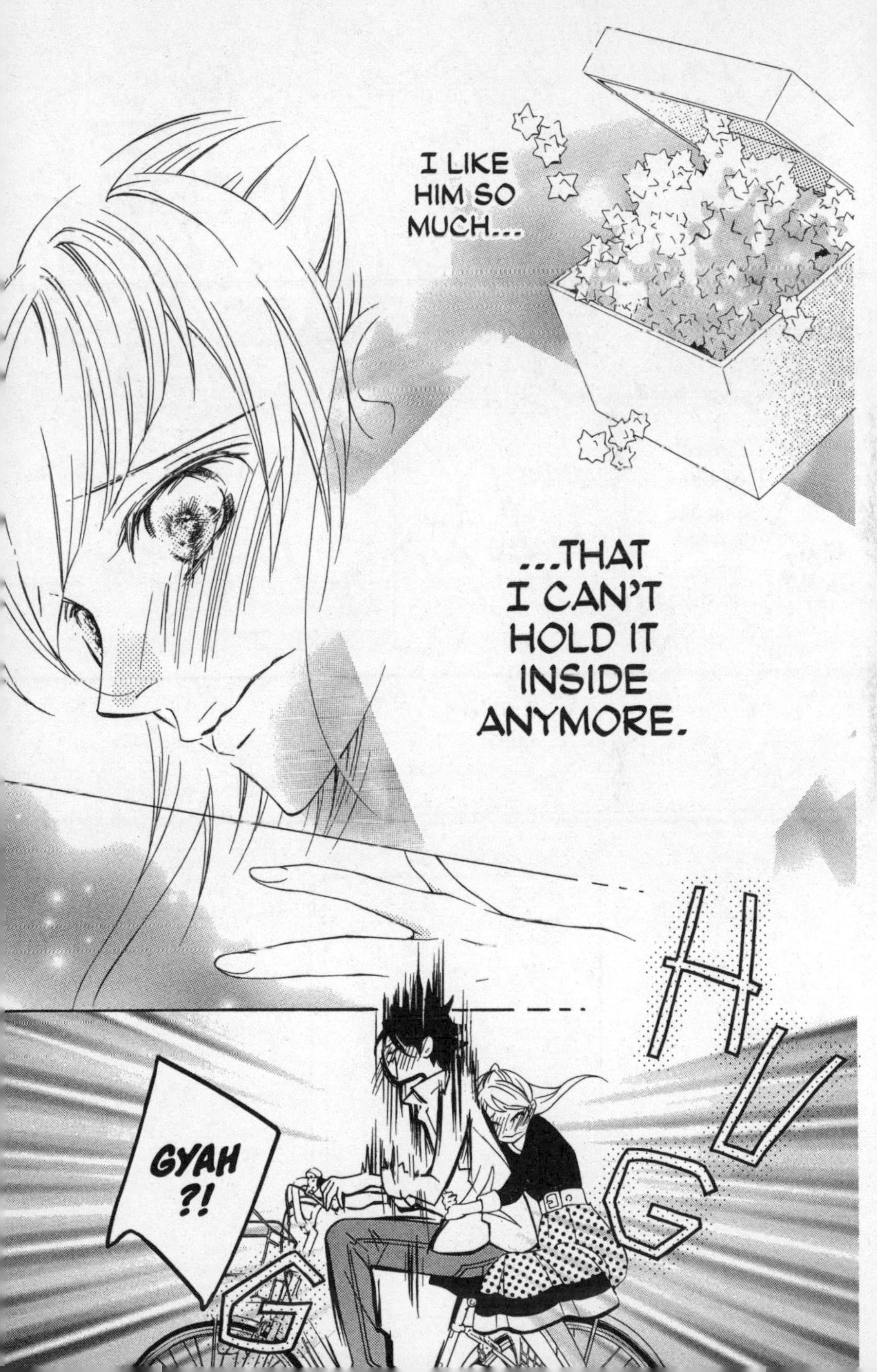
I LIKE HIM SO MUCH...
...THAT I CAN'T HOLD IT INSIDE ANYMORE.
HUGG
GYAH ?!

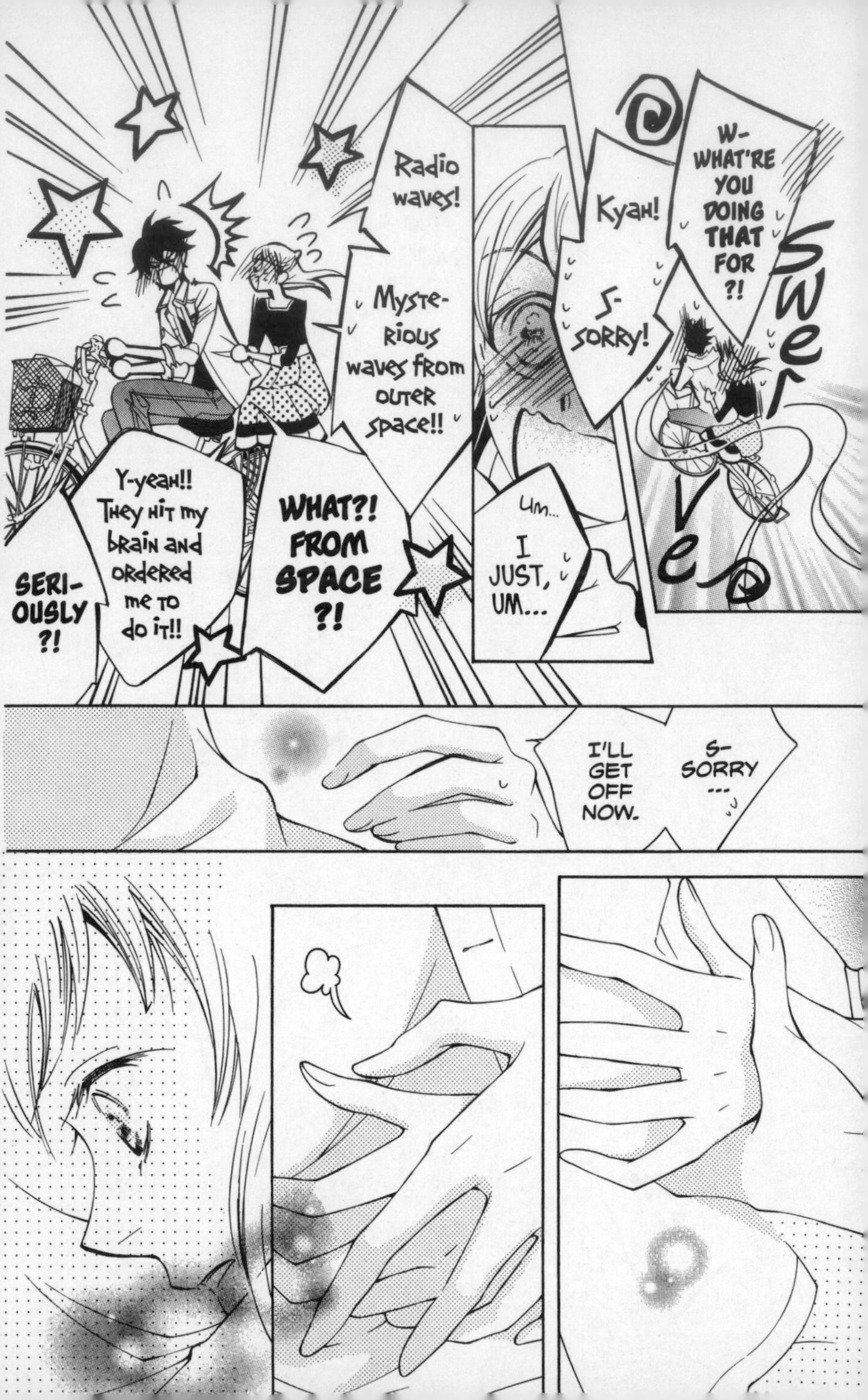

W-WHAT'RE YOU DOING THAT FOR?!
SWERVE
Kyah!
S-SORRY!
Um... I JUST, UM...
Radio waves!
Mysterious waves from outer space!!
WHAT?! FROM SPACE?!
Y-yeah!! They hit my brain and ordered me to do it!!
SERIOUSLY?!
S-SORRY...
I'LL GET OFF NOW.

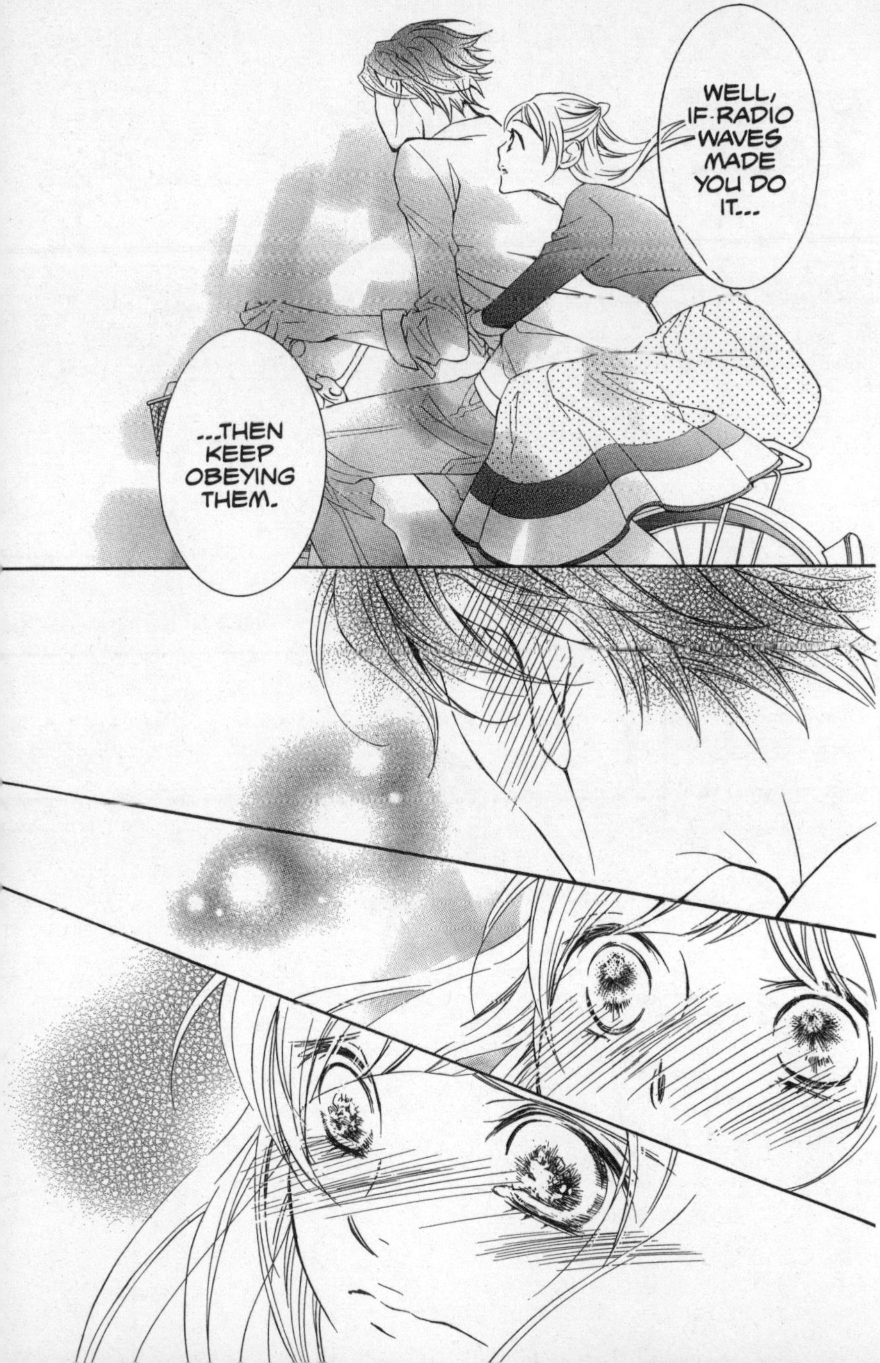
WELL, IF-RADIO WAVES MADE YOU DO IT...
...THEN KEEP OBEYING THEM.

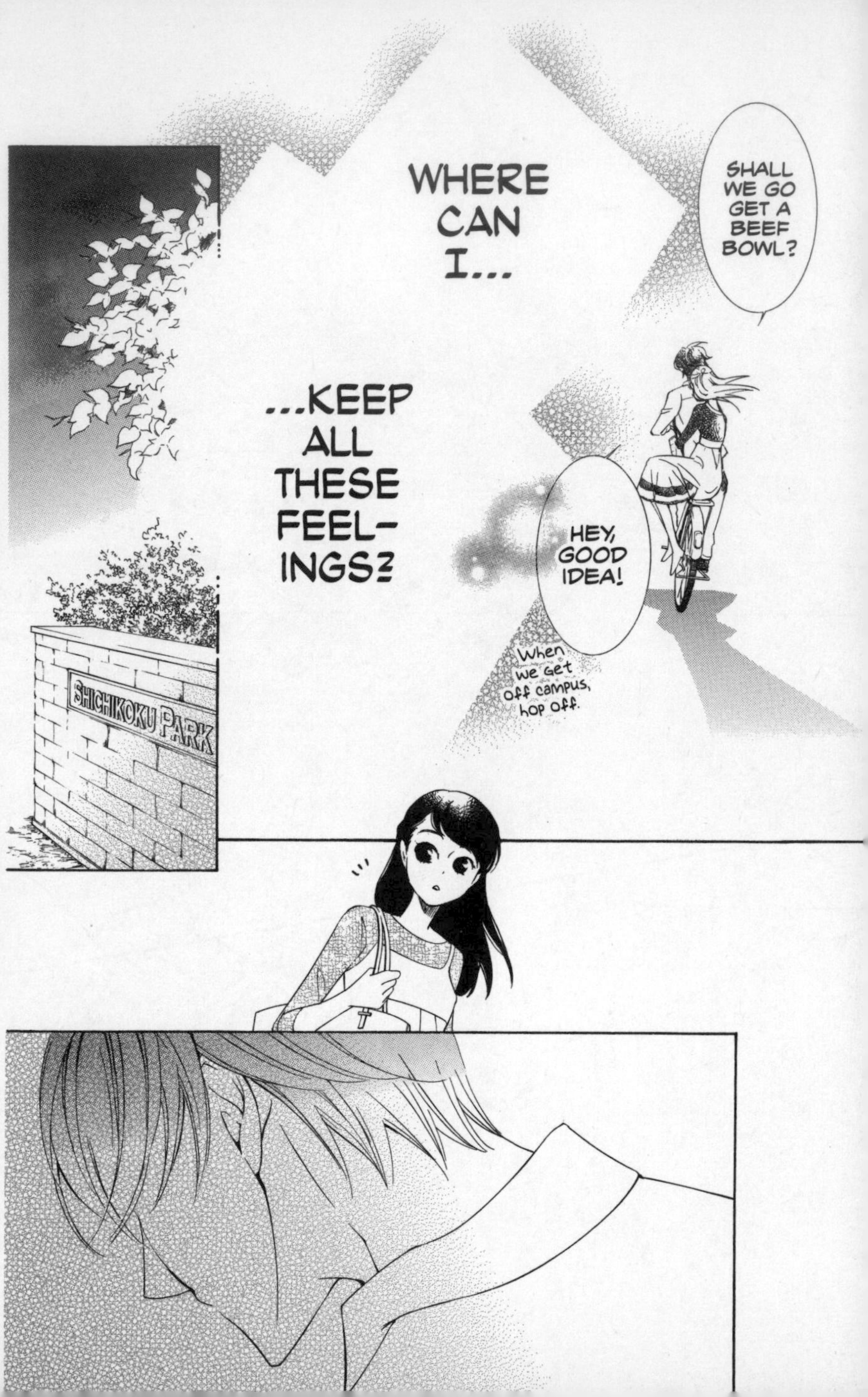
SHALL WE GO GET A BEEF BOWL?
HEY, GOOD IDEA!
When we get off campus, hop off.
WHERE CAN I...
...KEEP ALL THESE FEEL-INGS?
SHICHIKOKU PARK

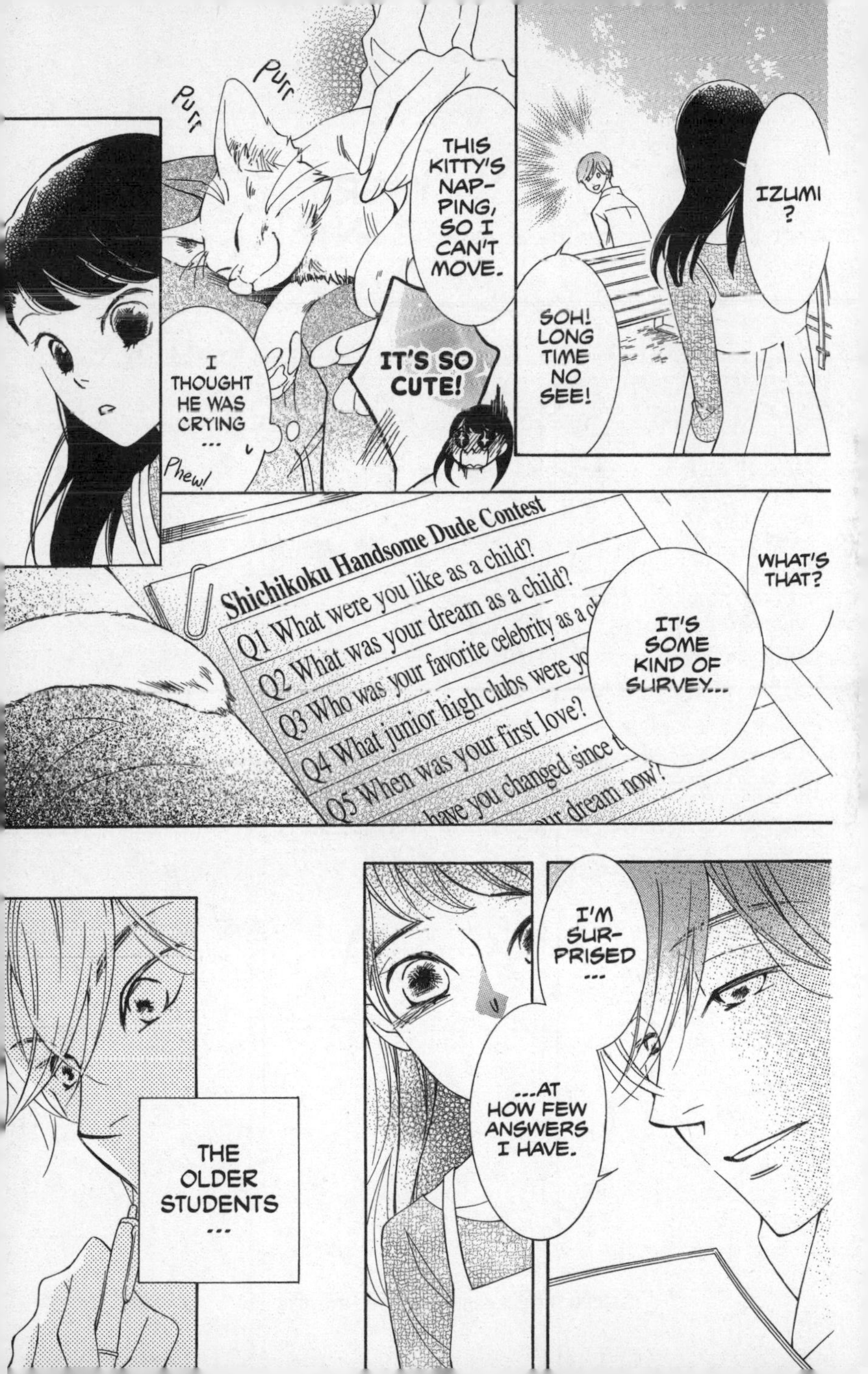
IZUMI?
SOH! LONG TIME NO SEE!
Purr
Purr
THIS KITTY'S NAP-PING, SO I CAN'T MOVE.
IT'S SO CUTE!
I THOUGHT HE WAS CRYING...
Phew!
WHAT'S THAT?
IT'S SOME KIND OF SURVEY...
Shichikoku Handsome Dude Contest
Q1 What were you like as a child?
Q2 What was your dream as a child?
Q3 Who was your favorite celebrity as a
Q4 What junior high clubs were
Q5 When was your first love?
have you changed since
your dream now?
I'M SUR-PRISED...
...AT HOW FEW ANSWERS I HAVE.
THE OLDER STUDENTS...

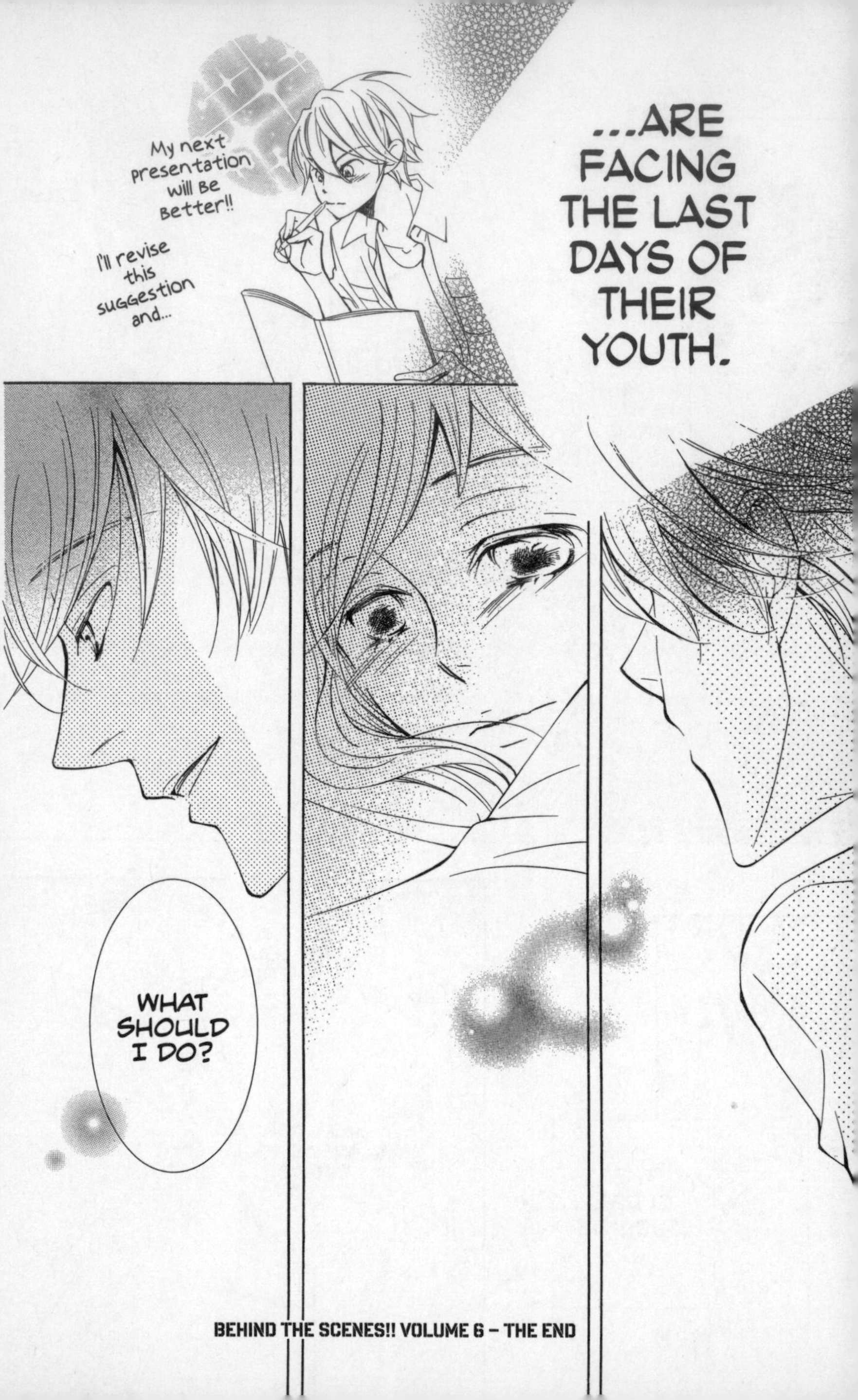
...ARE FACING THE LAST DAYS OF THEIR YOUTH.
My next presentation will be better!!
I'll revise this suggestion and...
WHAT SHOULD I DO?
BEHIND THE SCENES!! VOLUME 6 – THE END

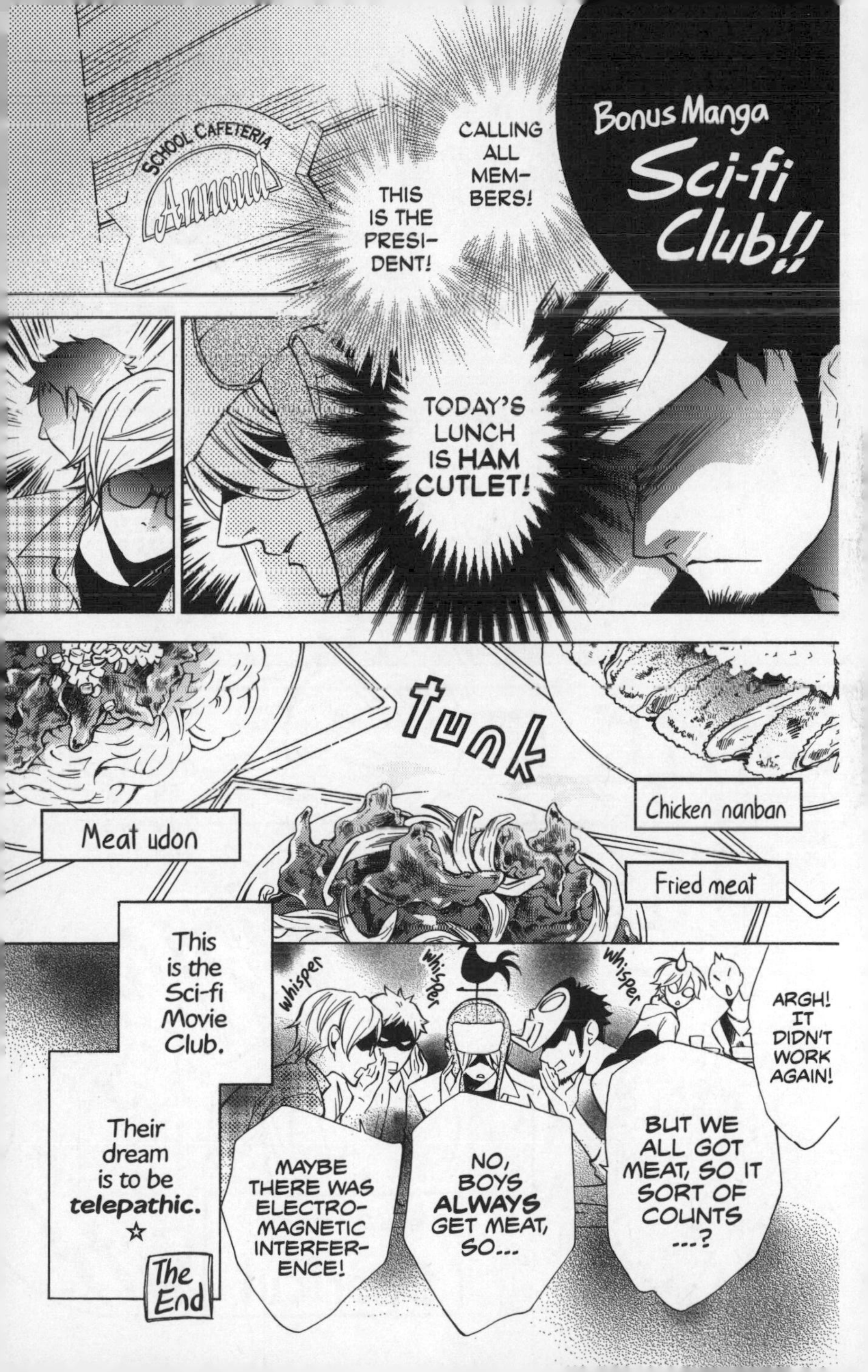
Bonus Manga
Sci-fi Club!!
CALLING ALL MEMBERS!
THIS IS THE PRESIDENT!
SCHOOL CAFETERIA
Annaud
TODAY'S LUNCH IS HAM CUTLET!
tunk
Chicken nanban
Fried meat
Meat udon
ARGH! IT DIDN'T WORK AGAIN!
whisper
whisper
whisper
BUT WE ALL GOT MEAT, SO IT SORT OF COUNTS ...?
NO, BOYS ALWAYS GET MEAT, SO...
MAYBE THERE WAS ELECTRO-MAGNETIC INTERFER-ENCE!
This is the Sci-fi Movie Club.
Their dream is to be telepathic. ☆
The End

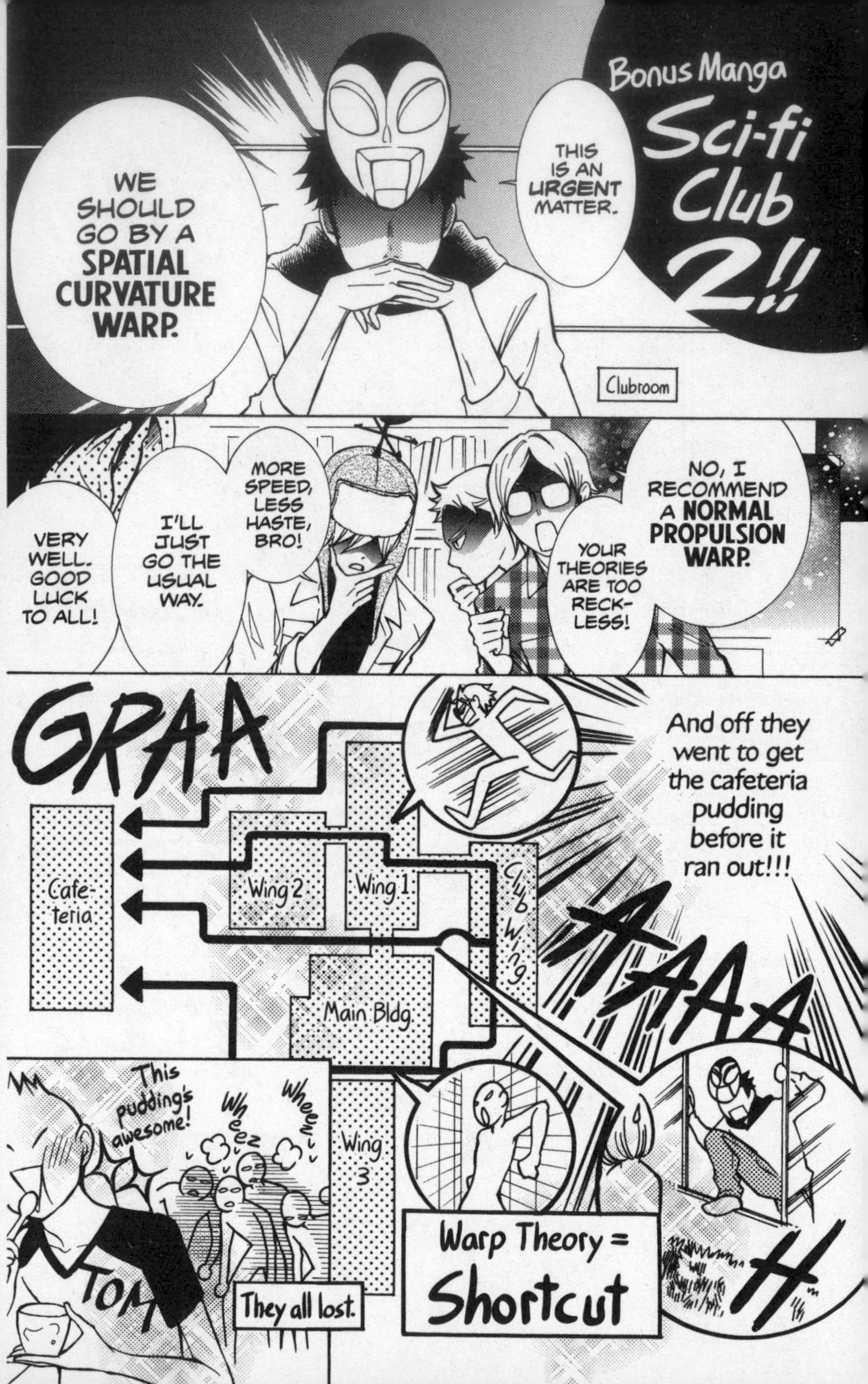
Bonus Manga
Sci-fi Club 2!!
THIS IS AN URGENT MATTER.
Clubroom
WE SHOULD GO BY A SPATIAL CURVATURE WARP.
NO, I RECOMMEND A NORMAL PROPULSION WARP.
YOUR THEORIES ARE TOO RECKLESS!
MORE SPEED, LESS HASTE, BRO!
I'LL JUST GO THE USUAL WAY.
VERY WELL. GOOD LUCK TO ALL!
And off they went to get the cafeteria pudding before it ran out!!!
GRAAAAAAH
Club Wing
Wing 1
Wing 2
Cafe-teria
Main Bldg
Wing 3
Warp Theory = Shortcut
Wheez
Wheez
This pudding's awesome!
TOM
They all lost.

Special Thanks!

★Nakajima-sama
★Okazaki-sama
★Everyone on the editorial staff
★Everyone involved in publishing
this book

★Jewelry Forêt
Jho-sama / Michiko-sama

★Takashi Iwabuchi-sama

★Yajima-sama

★Staff.
Yui Natsuki / Aya Aomura /
Shizuru Onda / Umeko / Keiko /
Miki Namiki / Shii Tsunokawa

Meiji-sama
Haruka Chino-sama

And everyone who reads this book!!

Bisco H.
2018. mar.

GLOSSARY

Page 50, panel 2: Koshien
A stadium in Japan, and the usual site of a prestigious high school baseball tournament.

Page 110, panel 6: Haitorei Edict
An 1876 act by the Meiji government that prohibited all but former daimyo lords, the military and law enforcement from carrying swords in public.

Page 159, panel 5: Milo
A powdered chocolate malt drink for kids popular in the southern hemisphere and Japan.

Pieces by Forêt-sama have appeared in the manga. This time, I made the simple ring above.

-Bisco Hatori

Bisco Hatori made her manga debut with *Isshun kan no Romance* (A Moment of Romance) in *LaLa DX* magazine. The comedy *Ouran High School Host Club* was her breakout hit and was published in English by VIZ Media. Her other works include *Detarame Mousouryoku Opera* (Sloppy Vaporous Opera), *Petite Pêche!* and the vampire romance *Millennium Snow*, which was also published in English by VIZ Media.

Behind the Scenes!!

VOLUME 6

Shojo Beat Edition

STORY AND ART BY Bisco Hatori

English Translation & Adaptation/John Werry
Touch-Up Art & Lettering/Sabrina Heep
Design/J. Shikuma
Editor/Pancha Diaz

Urakata!! by Bisco Hatori
© Bisco Hatori 2018
All rights reserved.
First published in Japan in 2018 by HAKUSENSHA, Inc., Tokyo.
English language translation rights arranged with HAKUSENSHA, Inc.,
Tokyo.

The stories, characters and incidents mentioned in
this publication are entirely fictional.

Printed in the U.S.A.

Published by VIZ Media, LLC
P.O. Box 77010
San Francisco, CA 94107

10 9 8 7 6 5 4 3 2 1
First printing, March 2019

www.viz.com

www.shojobeat.com

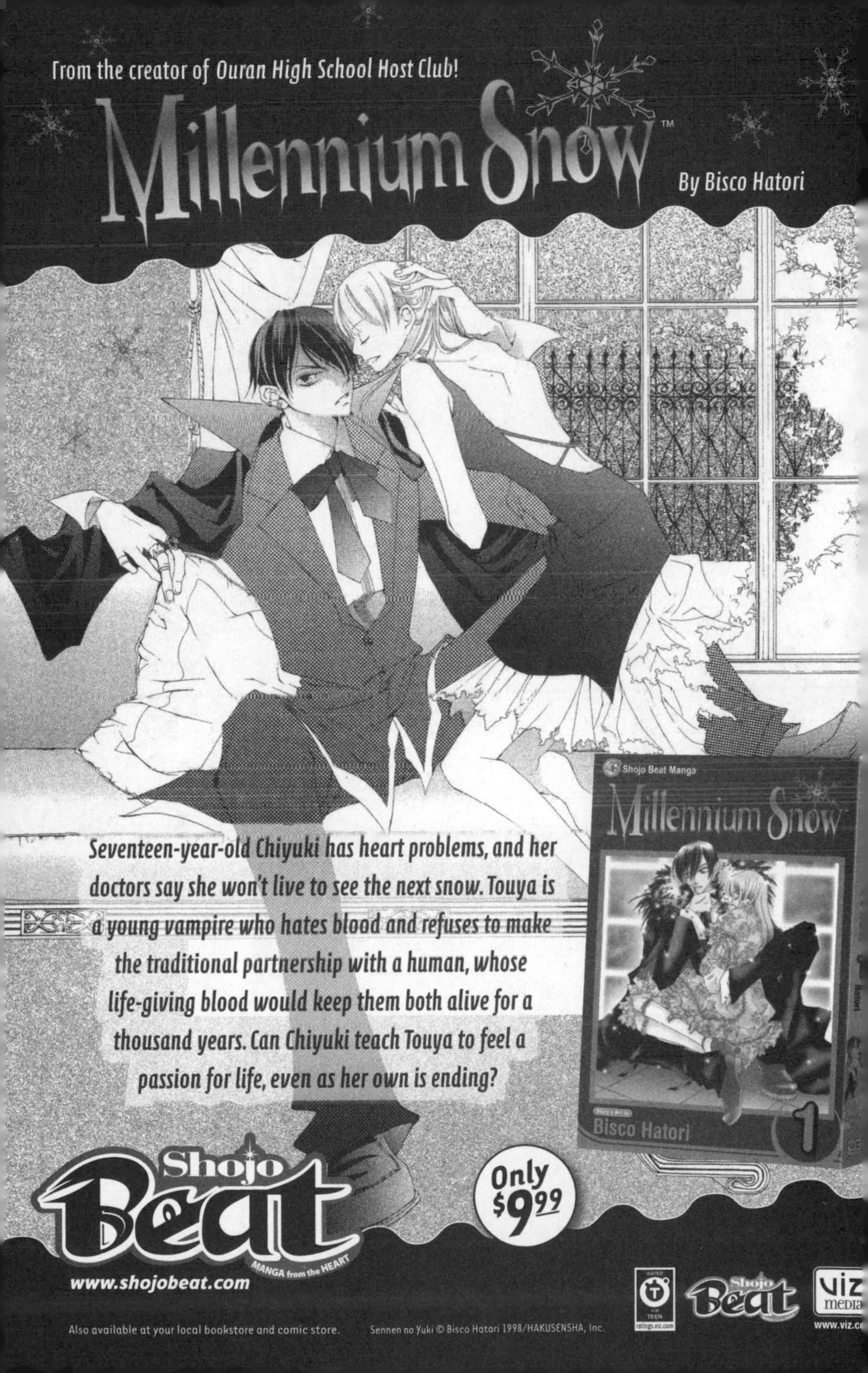
From the creator of Ouran High School Host Club!
Millennium Snow™
By Bisco Hatori
Seventeen-year-old Chiyuki has heart problems, and her doctors say she won't live to see the next snow. Touya is a young vampire who hates blood and refuses to make the traditional partnership with a human, whose life-giving blood would keep them both alive for a thousand years. Can Chiyuki teach Touya to feel a passion for life, even as her own is ending?
Shojo Beat Manga
Millennium Snow
Bisco Hatori
1
Shojo Beat
MANGA from the HEART
Only $9.99
www.shojobeat.com
Also available at your local bookstore and comic store.
Sennen no Yuki © Bisco Hatori 1998/HAKUSENSHA, Inc.
ratings.viz.com
viz media

YOU MAY BE READING THE WRONG WAY!

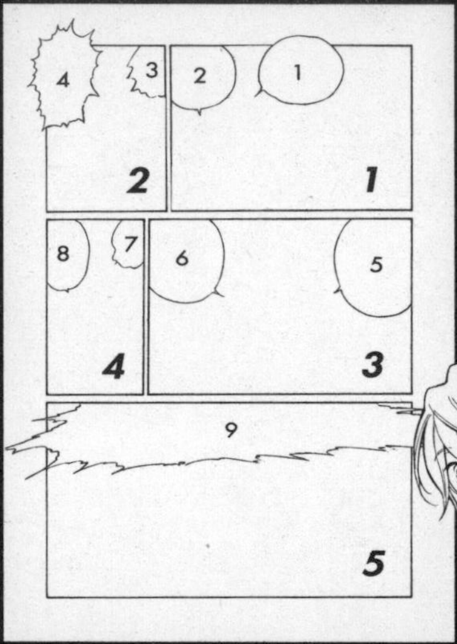
1
2
3
4
5
6
7
8
9
1
2
3
4
5

This book reads from right to left to maintain the original presentation and art of the Japanese edition, so action, sound effects and word balloons are reversed. This diagram shows how to follow the panels.
Turn to the other side of the book to begin.

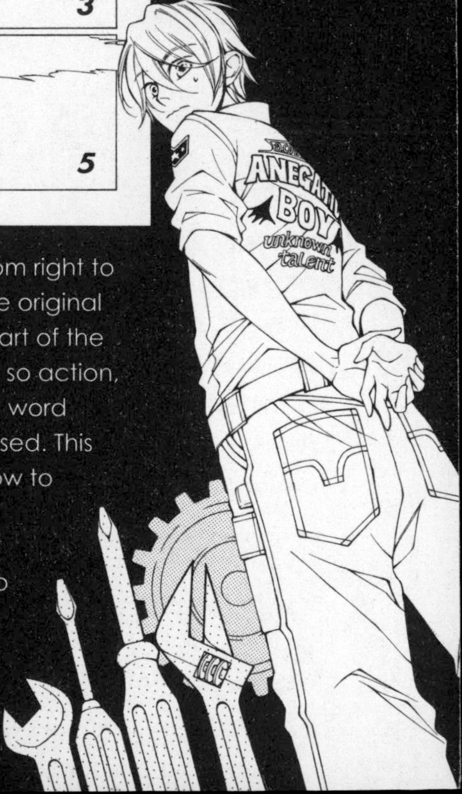
BOY
unknown
talent